Gale Library of Daily Life

Slavery in America

Gale Library of Daily Life

Slavery in America

VOLUME 1

Orville Vernon Burton

EDITOR

GALE
CENGAGE Learning

Detroit • New York • San Francisco • New Haven, Conn • Waterville, Maine • London

Gale Library of Daily Life
Slavery in America

Orville Vernon Burton, Editor

Project Editor
Brad Morgan

Editorial
Mark Drouillard, Andrea Fritsch, Carly S. Kaloustian, Angela Doolin

Permissions
Margaret Abendroth, Dean Dauphinais, Aja Perales, Tim Sisler

Imaging
Lezlie Light

Product Design
Pamela A. Galbreath

Composition
Evi Seoud

Manufacturing
Drew Kalasky

For product information and technology assistance, contact us at Gale Customer Support, 1-800-877-4253.

For permission to use material from this text or product, submit all requests online at www.cengage.com/permissions.

Further permissions questions can be emailed to permissionrequest@cengage.com.

Since this page cannot legibly accommodate all copyright notices, the credits constitute an extension of the copyright notice.

While every effort has been made to ensure the reliability of the information presented in this publication, Gale does not guarantee the accuracy of the data contained herein. Gale accepts no payment for listing; and inclusion in the publication of any organization, agency, institution, publication, service, or individual does not imply endorsement of the editors or publisher. Errors brought to the attention of the publisher and verified to the satisfaction of the publisher will be corrected in future editions.

Cover image credits:
"Slaves Using First Cotton Gin," © Bettman/ CORBIS
"Advertisement for a Slave Sale," © CORBIS
"Abyssinian Slaves" © Hulton-Deutsch Collection/ CORBIS

LIBRARY OF CONGRESS CATALOGING-IN-PUBLICATION DATA

Slavery in America / Orville Vernon Burton, editor.
    v. cm. -- (Gale library of daily life)
    Includes bibliographical references and index.
    ISBN-13: 978-1-4144-3013-3 (set : hardcover)
    ISBN-10: 1-4144-3013-2 (set : hardcover)
    ISBN-13: 978-1-4144-3014-0 (v. 1 : hardcover)
    ISBN-10: 1-4144-3014-0 (v. 1 : hardcover)
    [etc.]
    1. Slavery--United States--History. 2. Slavery--United States--History--Sources.
3. Slaves--United States--Social conditions. 4. Plantation life--United States--History.
5. African Americans--History--To 1863. 6. United States--Social conditions--To 1865.
I. Burton, Orville Vernon.
    E443.S58 2008
    973.7'1--dc22
                                            2007038576

ISBN-13	ISBN-10
978-1-4144-3013-3 (set)	1-4144-3013-2 (set)
978-1-4144-3014-0 (vol. 1)	1-4144-3014-0 (vol. 1)
978-1-4144-3015-7 (vol. 2)	1-4144-3015-9 (vol. 2)

Printed in the United States of America
10 9 8 7 6 5 4 3 2 1

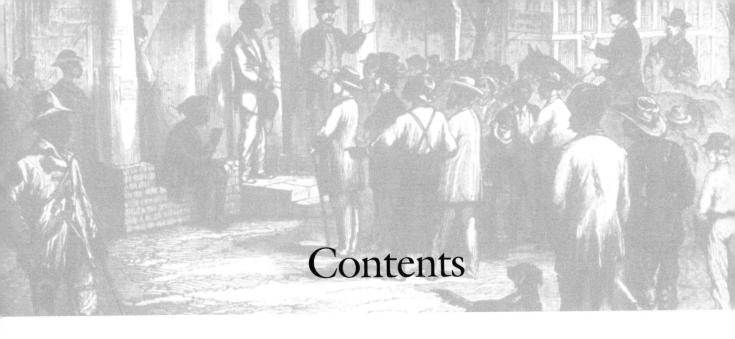

Contents

Culture and Leisure

VOLUME 2

Health, Medicine, and Nutrition

Regulating Slavery

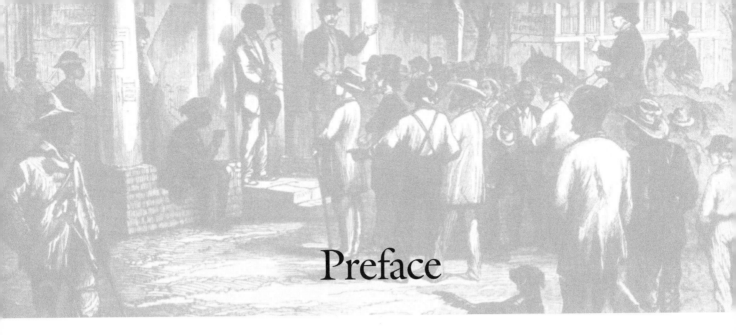

Preface

In writing several books on slavery and American history, most recently, *The Age of Lincoln*, I realized that in the thousands of reference works covering slavery, I could not find one that emphasized the effect slavery had on the daily lives of everyone who lived in America from 1619 through the end of the Civil War. For example, tens of thousands of pages have been written about the Emancipation Proclamation, but I could find precious few that covered how that landmark document influenced the day-to-day lives of the enslaved, slave-owners, and non-slave-owning whites. *Daily Life: Slavery in America* lives up to its name by doing exactly that, for the Emancipation Proclamation and other important slavery-related topics.

To bring together the essays in this volume, I consulted with the editors at Gale, a number of faculty experts, and graduate students working in this field, especially my own students at the University of Illinois. This volume examines the effects of slavery in such areas as work, family, community, culture and leisure, health and medicine, and religion. Topics are organized around these areas as well as business and regulation of slavery, the plantation way of life, and slave resistance and rebellion. The book also examines regional differences, and how slavery and freedom operated in the North. These larger organizational themes became the table of contents for *Daily Life: Slavery in America*.

The compilers of this collection have endeavored to be as thorough and representative as possible. The collection includes material on slaveholders as well as the enslaved, and on poor whites, Native Americans, and free blacks who owned slaves themselves. In addition, many contemporary written arguments for and against slavery, and legal pronouncements on the subject by both the United States and the Confederacy, have been included. This collection also covers certain significant works of literature. Some, like *Uncle Tom's Cabin*, are of an abolitionist bent, whereas other works, such as the novels of Thomas Dixon, are decidedly in favor of the Old South's "peculiar institution." Here, too, researchers will find William Wells Brown's *Clotel* (1853), a novel about slavery written by an escaped slave. In short, this collection provides sufficient documentation for a comprehensive survey of slavery in the United States.

The authors of these essays are well respected in U.S. History. In combining primary documents with the latest scholarly research, these writers have produced a unique contribution to our understanding of slavery, race, and America, often in the words of contemporaries. In seeking the latest interpretations of slavery by historians, the writers for this volume wanted useful primary documents and information on daily life in a slave society. To this effect, they were given access to a unique resource, Gale's *Sources in U.S. History Online: Slavery in America*. They researched their essays through slave narratives, first-person accounts, newspaper articles, pamphlets, broadsides, and other primary source documents available online as well as in special collections housed at academic libraries at numerous colleges and universities. The culmination of their work is extraordinary in scope and detail.

I am particularly grateful to all those who authored the essays in this book. In addition, three of my Ph.D. graduate students were especially helpful to me and labored hard to help shape this book: Troy Smith, Lawrence T. McDonnell, and Simon Appleford. I appreciate Nathalie Duval's assistance; she and I are working on a different electronic project for Gale, and she has been generous and supportive of my efforts on these reference books. I have been fortunate to have two wonderful and knowledgeable editors to assist me in putting these books together. Both Mark Drouillard, with whom I began the project and with whom I worked through the organizational and contents issues; and Brad Morgan, who has guided me through the process of gathering, evaluating, and editing the more than 240 essays, have been wonderful. Working with the two of them rendered this project a joy, and I have learned much from each of them.

This book is dedicated with love to my grandchildren, Katie Carrillo, Toby Gouliard, Piper Gouliard, Alex Gouliard, Aurora Johnston, and Charlotte Harleston.

That you are reading these essays, and using this educational tool, shows that you have realized the importance of slavery. Use them well, and do not be afraid of the voices from the past that may haunt you—as long as you can hear them, their existence is validated and yours is enriched. You are looking at the biggest questions of national identity and of humanity here, with the largest implications for our common future as a nation.

Orville Vernon Burton

Contributors

Christina Adkins
Doctoral Candidate, Program in the History of American Civilization
Harvard University
Fatherhood
Sexual Exploitation and Miscegenation
Sexuality and Reproduction

Simon J. Appleford
Project Manager, Illinois Center for Computing in Humanities, Arts, and Social Science
University of Illinois at Urbana-Champaign
Amistad and Slave Ship Rebellions
Gabriel's Rebellion
Harpers Ferry
The Middle Passage and Africa Overview
Nat Turner's Rebellion
Rebellion
Resistance and Rebellion Overview
Vesey Conspiracy
White Fears of Rebellion

Steven Barleen
Doctoral Candidate, Department of History
Northern Illinois University
Family Structure

Regina N. Barnett
Graduate Student, Department of African
American and African Diaspora Studies
Indiana University at Bloomington
Coded Messages

Dorothy Bauhoff
Curriculum Consultant
American Folk Art Museum
Artwork
Basket Weaving
Crafts and Slave Handicrafts
Craftsmen
Pottery
Sewing
Skilled Labor
Woodcraft

M. K. Beauchamp
Doctoral Candidate, Department of History
Texas A&M University
Rice Plantations
Slavery in the Lower South (AL, FL, GA, LA, MS, SC, TX)
Sugar Plantations

Jackie R. Booker
Associate Professor, Department of History
Claflin University
Family Separation and Reunion
Slave Renting
Systems of Work

Carol Brennan
Freelance Writer

Clotel; Or, The President's Daughter, William Wells Brown
Lydia Maria Child's *Liberty Bell* Series for Children
"Le Mulatrê," Victor Sejour
The Planter's Northern Bride, Caroline Lee Hentz
Society in America, Harriet Martineau
The Sword and the Distaff, William Gilmore Simms

Deliah Brown
Professor, Department of History
Texas Southern University
Relationships among Slaves

William H. Brown
Editor, Section of Historical Publications
North Carolina Office of Archives and History
Manumission

Todd Steven Burroughs
Freelance Researcher
Journalism
The Provincial Freeman
The North Star

Beatrice Burton
Graduate Student, Department of History
University of Georgia at Athens
Decisions Leading to Emancipation

Emancipation and the
Emancipation Proclamation
Preserving the Institution of
Slavery

Orville Vernon Burton
Professor, Department of History
Director of the Center for
Computing in Humanities,
Arts, and Social Science
University of Illinois at
Urbana-Champaign
Family and Community
Overview

John Sean Condon
Assistant Professor, Department
of History
Merrimack College
Tobacco Plantations

Amy Crowson
Instructor, Department of
History
Miles College
Overseers and Drivers

Jocelyn M. Cuffee
Professor, Department of Legal
Research and Writing
Western New England College
Free Blacks
Monetary Value of Slaves
Regulating Slavery Overview
Slave Codes
Slavery in the Border States
(DE, Dist. of Columbia, KY,
MD, MO)

James F. Dator
Graduate Student, Department
of History
University of Michigan
Agricultural Work
Cotton Plantations
Seasonal Rhythms of Life

Anna M. Dempsey
Assistant Professor, Department
of Art History
University of Massachusetts at
Dartmouth
Festivals

Kwasi Densu
Instructor, Department of
Political Science

Clark Atlanta University
Apprenticeship
House Slaves
Literacy and Anti-Literacy
Laws
Task System

Alejandra Dubcovsky
Graduate Student, Department
of History
University of California,
Berkeley
Slave Narratives

Charles H. Ford
Professor, Department of
History
Norfolk State University
Industrial Work

Jeff Forret
Assistant Professor, Department
of History
Lamar University
Alcohol
Conflict between Slaves
Poor Whites

John French
Doctoral Candidate,
Department of History
Marquette University
Slavery in the Upper South
(AR, NC, TN, VA)

Nicholas Gaffney
Doctoral Candidate,
Department of History
University of Illinois at
Urbana-Champaign
Socials
West African Influences

Marguerite P. Garvey
Assistant Professor, Department
of Social Sciences
South Carolina State
University
Animal Husbandry
Shuckings

Carol J. Gibson
Independent Scholar
Slave Entrepreneurs

James Gigantino II
Doctoral Candidate,
Department of History

University of Georgia
Interstate Slave Trade
Slavery in the Middle States
(NJ, NY, PA)
The Thirteenth Amendment

Rodney D. Green
Professor, Department of
Economics
Howard University
The Business of Slavery
Overview

Gwendolyn N. Hale
Assistant Professor, Department
of English
Fisk University
Rites of Passage

Josh J. Hem Lee
Graduate Student, Department
of Languages, Literatures,
and Cultures
University of South Carolina
Customs and Practices

David F. Herr
Associate Professor, Department
of History
St. Andrews Presbyterian College
Attitudes toward Religion
Baptism
The Bible
Christianity
Church Attitudes toward
Slavery
The Great Awakening
Identification with Biblical
Israel and the Exodus Story
Negro Churches
Preachers
Religion Overview
Religious Instruction
Sermons
Slaveholder Controlled
Practice of Religion
Slaveholder Opposition to
Practice of Religion

Kathleen Hilliard
Assistant Professor, Department
of History
University of Idaho
Exchange Relations
Hiring Time for Wages
Internal Economy

Property Accumulation
Slave Gardens
Slave Money

Kwame A. Holmes
Doctoral Candidate,
Department of History
University of Illinois at
Urbana-Champaign
Abolitionist Newspapers
Constitutional Arguments
Moral and Racial Arguments
Political and Economic
Arguments
Proslavery Arguments
Religious Arguments

Marilyn K. Howard
Associate Professor,
Departments of Social and
Behavioral Sciences and
Humanities
Columbus State Community
College
The Northwest Ordinance
Slave Quarters

Leonne M. Hudson
Associate Professor, Department
of History
Kent State University
Field Slaves

Brian M. Ingrassia
Doctoral Candidate,
Department of History
University of Illinois at
Urbana-Champaign
Culture and Leisure Overview

Sandra Johnston
Lecturer, Department of English
and Modern Languages
University of Maryland,
Eastern Shore
The Geography of Slavery
Overview

Christopher Jones
Doctoral Candidate,
Department of History
Brown University
Slavery and the Economy

Mark S. Joy
Professor, Department of
History

Jamestown College
Auctions and Markets
Construction and Clearing
Land
Hunting, Trapping, and
Fishing
Slavery in the Far West (CA,
CO, NM, NV, OR, UT, WA)

Kamau Kemayo
Chair, Department of African
American Studies
University of Illinois at
Springfield
Work Overview

Raymond James Krohn
Doctoral Candidate,
Department of History
Purdue University
Rights of Slave Owners

Ondra Krouse Dismukes
Doctoral Candidate,
Department of English
University of Georgia
African American Literature

Lauren E. LaFauci
Doctoral Candidate,
Department of English
University of Michigan
A South-Side View of Slavery,
Nehemiah Adams

Anthony A. Lee
Visiting Professor, Department
of History
University of California, Los
Angeles
Games

Talitha L. LeFlouria
Doctoral Candidate,
Department of History
Howard University
Infanticide

Jeanne M. Lesinski
Freelance Writer
A Narrative of the Life of
Frederick Douglass, an
American Slave
Democracy in America, Alexis
de Tocqueville
The Economic Impact of
Slavery in the South

Fugitive Slave Laws
Poems on Various Subjects,
Phillis Wheatley
Quilting
Uncle Tom's Cabin

Johnnie M. Maberry-Gilbert
Chair, Department of Fine
Arts
Tougaloo College
Elder and Old Age
The Master
The Master's Family
Mealtimes

Lawrence T. McDonnell
Assistant Professor, Department
of History and Government
Erskine College
Branding Slaves
Confinement
Fire-Eaters
Journal of a Residence on a
Georgian Plantation in
1838–1839, Fanny Kemble
Relationships between Masters
and Slaves
Slave Bodies

Aileen E. McTiernan
Juris Doctor Candidate, School
of Law
Rutgers University
Suicide and Self-Mutilation

Tanya M. Mears
Professor, Department of History
Norfolk State University
Hygiene
Kinship
Names and Naming
Pamphlets

Claus K. Meyer
Independent Researcher
Gang System

Khadijah O. Miller
Chair, Department of
Interdisciplinary Studies
Norfolk State University
Reactions to Slavery Overview

Matthew Mitchell
Graduate Student, Department
of History
Tulane University

Escape
Exclusion Laws
Harvest Time

Damian Nemirovsky
Graduate Student, Department
of History
University of Connecticut
Gender Roles

Caryn E. Neumann
Visiting Assistant Professor,
Department of History
Miami University of Ohio
Slavery in New England (CT,
ME, MA, NH, RI, VT)

Euthena M. Newman
Associate Professor, F. D.
Bluford Library
North Carolina Agricultural
& Technical State University
Diet and Nutrition

Yusuf Nuruddin
Visiting Assistant Professor,
Africana Studies Program
University of Toledo
Islam

James Onderdonk
Associate Director, Illinois
Center for Computing in
Humanities, Arts and Social
Science
University of Illinois at
Urbana-Champaign
The Confessions of Nat Turner
Walker's Appeal

Kerry L. Pimblott
Doctoral Candidate,
Department of History
University of Illinois at
Champaign-Urbana
American Anti-Slavery Society
American Colonization Society
Childhood and Adolescence
Freedom's Journal
Rumors and Communication
Networks
Underground Railroad

Kelly M. Ray
Graduate Student, Department
of History
University of Houston

Life Expectancy and Mortality
Rates

John Reilly
Professor, Department of
Communications and Modern
Languages
Cheyney University
Missouri Compromise
State Laws

Nelson Rhodes
Freelance Writer
Breeding
Childbirth and Midwifery
Courtship and Marriage
Death and Funeral Customs
Holiday and Celebration
Incidents in the Life of a Slave
Girl
The Mistress
Motherhood
Nurses and Mammies
Personal Servants
Skin Color
Slavery in the Middle West
(ND, SD, IL, IA, KS, MI,
MN, NE, OH, WI)

T. E. Robinson
Assistant Professor, Department
of History
University of Nevada, Las
Vegas
Day-to-Day Resistance
Discipline and Punishment
Runaway and Fugitive Slaves
Sabotage
Whipping

Donald Roe
Assistant Professor, Department
of History
Howard University
Tobacco and Smoking
Tools and Technology

Katherine E. Rohrer
Freelance Writer
The Big House
Child Rearing and Education
Language and Dialects

Daniel Sauerwein
Graduate Student, Department
of History
University of North Dakota

Balance Between Free and
Slave States
Slavery and the Constitution

Jodi M. Savage
Equal Employment
Opportunity Officer, Coney
Island Hospital
New York Health and
Hospitals Corporation
Buying Freedom
Health, Medicine, and
Nutrition Overview
Property Tax on Slaves
Suing for Freedom

Tiwanna M. Simpson
Assistant Professor, Department
of History
Louisiana State University
1808 Congressional Ban on
Importing Slaves

Yvonne Sims
Assistant Professor, Department
of American and Ethnic Studies
Pennsylvania State University-
Harrisburg
Elder Care

Troy D. Smith
Doctoral Candidate,
Department of History
University of Illinois at
Urbana-Champaign
African Heritage
American Revolution
Antislavery Songs
Bounty Hunters and
Kidnapping
Civil War
Disease and Treatment
Dreams
Folk Religion
Folk Remedies
Folklore and Folk Tales
Maroon Communities
Medicine and Medical Care
Mental Illness
Musical Instruments
Native Americans and Slavery
The Ring Shout
Root Doctors
The Sick House
Slave Reactions to the Civil
War

Slavery in the Caribbean
Slavery in Haiti
Song and Dance
Spirituals
Superstition
Trickster Tales
Vodou and Obeah
War Overview
Work Songs

George Sochan
Assistant Professor, Department of History and Government
Bowie State University
Impact of Slavery on the Northern Economy
Moral Debates on Slavery
Slavery and the Rise of Capitalism

Carmen P. Thompson
Doctoral Candidate, Department of History
University of Illinois at Urbana-Champaign
Capture

Life in Africa
Middle Passage

Philip Troutman
Assistant Professor, University Writing Program
The George Washington University
Broadsides
Outsiders' Views of Slavery

Micki Waldrop
Education Program Specialist
University of Georgia
Food

Tamara Walker
Teaching Fellow, Department of History
University of Michigan
Gift Exchange

Jamie Warren
Doctoral Candidate, Department of History
Indiana University
Health

John J. Wickre
Graduate Student, Department of History
University of North Dakota
The Slave Trade

A. B. Wilkinson
Doctoral Candidate, Department of History
University of California at Berkeley
Antislavery Arguments
Antislavery Literature

Thomas Wiloch
Freelance Writer
Proslavery Literature: "Anti-Tom Novels"
Uncle Remus

Fay A. Yarbrough
Assistant Professor, Department of History
University of Oklahoma
Black Slave Owners

A Chronology of Slavery in North America

1581 At the order of King Phillip II of Spain five hundred slaves, the first documented Africans in North America, were sent to St. Augustine in Spanish Florida.

1619 A Dutch man-of-war arrived in Jamestown, Virginia, where, in exchange for supplies, it set ashore twenty captive "Negars," the first Africans brought to the British colonies. Six years later, the Jamestown census counted ten slaves. Tobacco farming produced a consistent labor shortage for which slavery was seen as the remedy.

1626 Eleven male African slaves were imported to New Netherlands by the Dutch West India Company, formed in 1621, to serve on farms in the Hudson Valley. Dutch law specified that the children of freed slaves were to remain enslaved.

1636 The colonies entered the slave trade as the first American-built slave ship was launched in Massachusetts.

1638 The first public slave auction in British America was held in Jamestown square, where twenty-three individuals were sold.

1640 Records show that there were three hundred African slaves in Virginia. When a runaway black servant, John Punch, was captured with two runaway European servants, he alone was punished with servitude "for the time of his natural Life."

Massachusetts became the first of the English colonies to legalize slavery.

A new Dutch colonial law forbade giving assistance to runaway slaves.

In Virginia the corporal punishment of slaves, including whipping and branding, was adopted from the Spanish, whose treatment of slaves reflected practices handed down from the Roman Empire.

1641 In New Amsterdam the first marriage between Africans in North America was recorded.

1643 The New England Confederation (which included Plymouth, Massachusetts, Connecticut, and New Haven) adopted a fugitive slave law that made the return of runaway slaves to their owners a legal obligation.

1650 Connecticut legalized slavery.

1652 Rhode Island limited enslavement to ten years.

1654 A Virginia court granted African Americans the right to own slaves.

1657 Virginia required by law the arrest and return of fugitive slaves.

1661 Virginia established the legality of slavery.

1662 A Virginia law introduced hereditary enslavement, whereby the offspring of enslaved mothers inherited the status of slaves for life.

Massachusetts, Connecticut, New Hampshire, and New York prohibited slaves from bearing arms.

1663 Maryland legalized slavery.

The first slave rebellion documented in the colonies occurred in Gloucester County, Virginia.

1664 Slavery became legal in New York and New Jersey.

Maryland became the first colony to prohibit and punish marriages between white women and black men.

Enslavement for life was mandated for all African American slaves in Maryland, New York, New Jersey, the Carolinas, and Virginia.

1666 Maryland passed a fugitive slave law.

1667 Virginia declared that Christian baptism does not alter the condition of a slave; nonetheless, owners were encouraged to "Christianize" their slaves.

1668 New Jersey passed a fugitive slave law.

1670 Virginia prohibited free blacks and Native Americans from keeping "Christian" (i.e., white) servants.

1672 England chartered the Royal African Company, which soon began delivering shiploads of slaves to the trading centers of Jamestown, Hampton, and Yorktown.

1674 New York declared that blacks who converted to Christianity after their enslavement would not be freed.

1676 In Virginia, black slaves joined white indentured servants in Bacon's Rebellion, an uprising against the colonial government.

1680 Virginia prohibited free blacks and slaves from bearing arms, assembling together, attempting to escape, or committing violence against "Christians" (whites).

1682 Virginia declared that all imported black servants must serve as slaves for life.

1684 New York prohibited slaves from practicing commerce.

1688 In Pennsylvania, Quakers presented the first resolution formally denouncing slavery.

1691 Virginia forbade marriages between whites and Native Americans or African Americans. Virginia ordered any freed slaves out of the colony.

In South Carolina, where the introduction of rice-growing increased the demand for labor, the first extensive slave codes became law.

1700 Pennsylvania legalized slavery.

1702 New York's Act for Regulating Slaves banned gatherings of more than three slaves, and disallowed slaves from testifying in court.

1705 The Virginia Slave Code classified slaves as real estate; thus, masters could not be charged with murdering their human property.

1712 The first major slave revolt in New York City occurred when twenty-five slaves rose up together and killed nine whites; eighteen were later executed.

New York prohibited Negroes, Native Americans, and slaves from murdering others of the same "class," and barred them from owning real estate.

In Charleston, South Carolina, slaves were prohibited from hiring themselves out.

1715 Rhode Island legalized slavery.

Maryland proclaimed that all slaves and their descendants were slaves for life.

Twenty-four percent of Virginia's population was enslaved.

1717 The New York Assembly passed a fugitive slave law.

1723 Virginia outlawed the manumission of slaves.

1724 French Louisiana forbade slaves from marrying without their owners' permission.

1732 Slaves mutinied aboard the *Don Carlos*, killing the British captain and briefly seizing the vessel. Twenty-seven of the slaves were executed.

1733 Elihu Coleman published the first Quaker tract opposing slavery.

1735 Georgia, which had prohibited the importation or ownership of black slaves, petitioned Britain for the legalization of slavery.

French law specified that when an enslaved woman gave birth to the child of a free man, mother and child became entitled to freedom.

1738 In England, the trustees for Georgia assented to the residents' petition demanding permission for the importation of slaves and the legalization of slavery.

To attract runaway slaves, Spanish Florida promised slaves freedom and land.

1739 Eighty slaves in Stono, South Carolina, seized and burned an armory and killed twenty-one whites while trying to flee to Spanish Florida. The militia put down the rebellion and killed forty-four blacks.

1740 South Carolina passed the "Negro Act," forbidding slaves to emigrate, assemble, cultivate their own crops, earn money, or learn to read. Owners were explicitly entitled to kill rebellious slaves.

Georgia and Carolina attempted to invade Florida because of the encouragement it was offering runaway slaves.

1741 In New York City, thirty-one slaves and five whites were hanged and burned at the stake when rumors of a "Negro conspiracy" instigated by Catholic priests produced a public hysteria.

1749 Georgia ended its prohibition against the importation of slaves. [See entry at 1738.]

1750 The slave population of the English colonies was estimated at 236,400—20 percent of the total population—of which just 30,000 lived north of Pennsylvania.

1758 The earliest black church in Virginia was established in Lunenburg County.

Pennsylvania Quakers forbade members to own or trade slaves.

1760 New Jersey prohibited slaves from enlisting in the militia without their owner's permission.

1767 To protest new British laws increasing taxation and forcing compliance, Virginia and three other states boycotted the British slave trade.

The first separate black church in America was founded in South Carolina.

1773 Slaves in Massachusetts unsuccessfully petitioned the government for their freedom.

1774 The First Continental Congress banned trade with Britain and vowed to discontinue the slave trade after the 1st of December. Connecticut, Rhode Island, and Georgia prohibited the importation of slaves.

1775 The slave population in the colonies reached almost 500,000. In South Carolina, two-thirds of the inhabitants were slaves.

On April 19th, the War of Independence began with the battles of Lexington and Concord, Massachusetts—together dubbed "the shot heard round the world." The colonists' militia included black Minutemen.

The Pennsylvania Society for the Abolition of Slavery, sponsored by Quakers, became the first organization of its kind on the continent.

Under General George Washington, the Continental Army accepted the service of free blacks.

1776 The Continental Congress signed the Declaration of Independence.

Following the lead of the Pennsylvania Quakers [see entry at 1758], Quakers elsewhere forbade the ownership of slaves.

Delaware prohibited the importation of African slaves.

1777 Vermont became the first state to abolish slavery and to entitle all adult males to vote.

New York allowed all free men who owned property to vote.

1778 Rhode Island prohibited the exportation of slaves from the state; Virginia prohibited their importation.

1780 The Pennsylvania Gradual Abolition Act was the first statute in the United States to support emancipation.

The Massachusetts constitution was interpreted as prohibiting slavery; two slaves successfully sued for their freedom.

1783 Virginia emancipated slaves who had fought against Britain, providing their owners concurred.

1784 Rhode Island and Connecticut endorsed gradual emancipation.

Jefferson failed to restrict the expansion of slavery in the West.

1785 New York passed a gradual emancipation law and outlawed the importation of slaves.

In Virginia, "Negroes" were defined as persons with *any* African blood, including all mulattos.

1787 The Northwest Ordinance outlawed slavery, except as criminal punishment, in the Northwest Territory (which would become the states of Ohio, Indiana, Illinois, Michigan, and Wisconsin); citizens, however, were required to return fugitive slaves.

The U.S. Constitution, drafted in Philadelphia, avoided any mention of the word "slave"; however, it included a distinction between "free Persons" and "others," whereby only three-fifths of a vote was given to each slave (this vote, furthermore, was to be cast by the slave owner). It also included a fugitive slave law, and guaranteed that the importation of slaves would not be terminated for at least twenty years.

In Philadelphia the Free African Society was founded by a freedman, Richard Allen, who also established the African Methodist Episcopal Church.

South Carolina outlawed both the domestic and international slave trade.

1788 New Hampshire became the ninth state to ratify the U.S. Constitution, thereby making certain its adoption into the Union.

A New York law established that all current slaves were slaves for life.

Connecticut and Massachusetts outlawed the slave trade.

1789 The Maryland Society for Promoting the Abolition of Slavery was founded.

1790 The first Census of the United States, prescribed by the Constitution, recorded 757,000 blacks in the United States, almost 20 percent of the total population of four million.

Congress forbade citizenship to all but free whites and gave its support for the expansion of slavery in the Southwest.

1792 Congress excluded blacks from military service.

In West Africa, Freetown was founded by a thousand slaves freed by the British after the War of Independence.

Eli Whitney's cotton gin increased cotton production dramatically, from 140,000 pounds in 1791 to 35 million pounds in 1800, and generated a boom in Northern cotton mills, as well as the slave trade.

1793 The federal Fugitive Slave Law was passed, giving slave owners the right to cross state lines in the pursuit of runaways and prohibiting aid to fugitives.

1794 Congress outlawed the slave trade between the United States and foreign countries.

1798 Georgia outlawed international slave trade.

1800 Gabriel Prosser organized the most ambitious documented slave revolt, aimed at seizing the city of Richmond, Virginia, and its arsenal. A thousand armed slaves gathered near the town, but a rainstorm washed out a crucial bridge. Before their delayed plans could be carried out, they were betrayed to white authorities. Governor James Madison called out the militia, who captured the leaders of "Gabriel's

Insurrection." Prosser and some thirty-five conspirators were executed.

Congress prohibited the export of slaves.

1801 Congress ordered the District of Columbia to adopt the slave laws of adjoining Virginia and Maryland, thereby obliquely establishing a federal slave code.

1803 The purchase of the Louisiana Territory from France roughly doubled the size of the United States.

Ohio was admitted to the Union as a free state.

1804 The Underground Railroad had its beginning in Columbia, Pennsylvania, when General Thomas Boudes refused to surrender a runaway slave to authorities.

New Jersey introduced gradual emancipation.

1816 Andrew Jackson led U.S. troops fighting the Seminoles into Spanish-held Florida, where large numbers of fugitive slaves had taken sanctuary.

1817 During the First Seminole War, some three hundred fugitive slaves seized Fort Blount on Apalachicola Bay for several days before being defeated by U.S. troops.

The American Colonization Society, aimed at helping free blacks resettle in Africa, was founded.

Georgia officially banned the slave trade.

1819 Federal law instituted the death penalty for trading in slaves.

Canada denied the American government the right to pursue runaway slaves within its borders.

Virginia and North Carolina removed legal restraints on interstate slave trade.

Virginia outlawed teaching blacks to read and write, and forbade blacks and mulattos from gathering for schooling.

1820 The Missouri Compromise maintained parity in the U.S. Senate: By its terms, Maine was admitted as the twelfth free state and Missouri as the twelfth slave state; thereafter, all territories north of 36°30' were to remain free.

South Carolina outlawed the importation of abolitionist writings into the state.

In Charleston, South Carolina, slaves were ordered to wear distinctive identification tags, which were soon required for free blacks as well.

1822 In Africa, Liberia was established as a colony for blacks fleeing America.

Denmark Vesey, a freedman in South Carolina, planned a massive slave uprising that was betrayed before it began. Almost forty slaves, including Vesey, were executed, and others were sold out of state.

1823 At Middlebury College, Vermont, Alexander Lucius Twilight became the first black student to graduate college in the United States.

1826 Pennsylvania passed an anti-kidnapping law in an effort to protect free blacks.

1827 The slave trade was formally outlawed in Tennessee.

In the Texas Territory, the sale of slaves between individuals was authorized.

1829 Mexico abolished slavery, and soon became a refuge for runaway slaves from across the Southern states.

1830 The slave population in the United States reached two million; the white population was nine million.

1831 The First Annual Convention of People of Color was held in Philadelphia.

The first edition of *The Liberator*, William Lloyd Garrison's abolitionist newspaper, was published in Boston, and the New England Anti-Slavery Society was founded.

Nat Turner, an enslaved Baptist preacher who believed he was divinely inspired, led a bloody rebellion by some sixty slaves in Southampton, Virginia, that killed fifty-five whites; the rebellion was put down by the militia, and Turner was captured and hanged. Slave codes throughout the South became much harsher as a result.

1833 The first Convention of the American Anti-Slavery Society was held in Philadelphia.

1834 Slavery was abolished throughout the British colonies.

1836 The Republic of Texas declared its independence from Mexico; slavery was legalized, and free blacks were barred.

The U.S. House of Representatives passed a gag rule that tabled any and all abolitionist arguments.

1837 The first convention of the National Anti-Slavery Society was held in New York.

1839 Slaves from Africa mutinied aboard the *Amistad*, a Spanish ship, under the leadership of Cinque, from Sierra Leone. The slaves petitioned a Connecticut court for emancipation.

1840 South Carolina passed new Black Codes that forbade slaves the right to assemble, to produce food, to earn money, to become literate, or to own any but the cheapest clothing.

1841 The mutinous Africans aboard the *Amistad*, represented by former President John Quincy Adams, brought their case before the U.S. Supreme Court, where they were adjudged free men.

1842 The U.S. Supreme Court upheld the constitutionality of the 1793 Fugitive Slave Law.

The Georgia legislature refused to recognize the citizenship of free blacks.

1844 Slavery was prohibited in the Oregon Territory.

1845 Texas was admitted into the Union as a slave state.

1846 Missouri legalized the slave trade between states.

1847 After dissolving his ties with William Lloyd Garrison, Frederick Douglass established *The North Star*, the first black abolitionist newspaper.

1848 The Free Soil Party—forerunner of the Republican Party—was established by various anti-slavery organizations to combat the expansion of slavery to the West, with Martin van Buren as its presidential candidate.

The first Women's Rights Convention at Seneca Falls, New York, asserted its opposition to slavery.

Connecticut prohibited every aspect of slavery.

1849 Harriet Tubman escaped to the North from enslavement in Maryland and became a "conductor" on the Underground Railway. Joseph Jenkins Roberts, a black Virginian, became the first president of Liberia.

Kentucky prohibited interstate slave trade.

1850 The Compromise of 1850 established that California would be admitted to the Union as a free state, that Utah and New Mexico would decide by popular vote whether to become slave or free states (thus violating the 36°30' clause of the Missouri Compromise), and that the slave trade (but not slavery) was banned in the District of Columbia.

The new Federal Fugitive Slave Law reinforced slave owners' rights.

Virginia ordered the emigration of freed slaves, and forbade the further emancipation of any slaves.

1851   Sojourner Truth became a national figure in the abolitionist movement after speaking at the Women's Rights Convention in Akron, Ohio.

1852   Harriet Beecher Stowe's *Uncle Tom's Cabin*, a novel about the plight of a Kentucky slave family, was published and quickly became the most influential piece of anti-slavery literature.

1854   The Kansas-Nebraska Act established the borders of the Kansas and Nebraska Territories, with their status as slave or free to be decided by popular vote, thus nullifying the anti-slavery clause of the Missouri Compromise.

John Mercer Langston became the first black person to serve in the U.S. government when he was elected the town clerk of Brownhelm Township, Ohio.

1856   The Free Soil Party was absorbed into the newly formed Republican Party.

The "Bleeding Kansas" hostilities erupted when the "free-soil" town of Lawrence was attacked by proslavery posses; John Brown, a radical white abolitionist, led his men on retaliatory raids.

1857   U.S. Supreme Court Chief Justice Roger Taney, from Maryland, wrote the verdict in *Dred Scott v. Sanford*, which ruled that neither Scott (a slave who was transported to Minnesota) nor any other black could ever become a U.S. citizen wherever he resided, thus striking down the Missouri Compromise of 1820 as unconstitutional, and dismissing the right of Congress to outlaw slavery in the territories.

1858   Vermont decreed that citizenship would not be denied on the basis of African descent.

Kansas was admitted to the Union as a free state.

1859   The first novel by an African American, *Our Nig*, by Harriet E. Wilson, was published in Boston.

In New Mexico, a slave code was introduced.

The last ship to import African slaves, the *Clothilde*, arrived in Mobile, Alabama. The radical abolitionist John Brown led an attack on Harper's Ferry, Virginia, and, together with twenty-one whites and blacks, seized the U.S. Armory before being captured and hanged.

1860   According to the eighth national Census, the total U.S. population reached 34,400,000, including four million slaves.

In Arizona, the Expulsion Act went into effect, banishing free blacks and bestowing slave status on any who remained.

Abraham Lincoln was elected president, precipitating the secession of South Carolina and six more states in the Deep South before his inauguration four months later.

1861   South Carolina seceded from the Union, followed by Mississippi, Florida, Alabama, Georgia, Louisiana, and Texas. Later in the year, Virginia, Arkansas, Tennessee, and North Carolina also seceded.

The Union of Confederate States elected Jefferson Davis as its president. The Civil War began when the Federal Arsenal at Fort Sumter, near Charleston, South Carolina, was fired on by Confederate troops. It would continue until the surrender of the Confederacy in 1865.

Incidents in the Life of a Slave Girl, an autobiography by Harriet Jacobs, was published in Boston.

Runaway slaves who joined Northern troops were declared "contraband of war." According to the Union's Confiscation Act, slaves who served to support the rebellion were subject to imprisonment.

1862   Congress abolished slavery in Washington, DC, as well as in the territories.

Lincoln urged the border states to adopt gradual emancipation, with compensation for former owners. He also advocated the colonization of freed blacks.

According to the Homestead Act, signed by Lincoln, land in the public domain was given to qualified private citizens, including black families.

The Militia Act authorized Lincoln to employ all persons, including blacks, in military service; it also guaranteed freedom to slaves who served in Union forces, effectively annulling the Fugitive Slave Law.

The first part of the Emancipation Proclamation was published. It provided for the emancipation of all slaves in states at war with the Union and unrepresented in Congress—but did not emancipate slaves in the border states.

1863   The Emancipation Proclamation theoretically freed slaves in Arkansas, Texas, Mississippi, Alabama, Florida, Georgia, South Carolina, North Carolina, and Virginia, as well as parts of Louisiana. Slaves in the border states were not affected until their state governments each outlawed slavery.

1864   The Maryland State Constitution was amended to forbid slavery.

1865   The Thirteenth Amendment was passed by Congress and signed by President Lincoln; it declared that "Neither slavery nor involuntary servitude, except as a punishment for crime whereof the party shall have been duly convicted, shall exist within the United States, or any place subject to their jurisdiction."

Introduction

Slavery and racism, intricately related, are the ugliest stains on the national character of a country "birthed in liberty." Because slavery is difficult to look at, many Americans have chosen to ignore this part of their history, considering the country to have moved past it. Why should we try to understand this dark period in American history—is it not better to forget the past and move on?

Any attempt to study United States history has to include an examination of slavery because it is part and parcel of what liberty was and is. We have to comprehend it because it was the chassis around which America was built. Slavery provided the labor for the foundation of the U.S. economic system. Human bondage made possible the Industrial Revolution, and with it the great wealth that developed in the emerging capitalist democracy that became the United States. If we forget the past, we will never move beyond it. Ignored wounds are festering wounds. We need to shine the light on them if they are ever to be healed.

Perceptions of slavery—both public and historical—have shifted over time. Memory is malleable, and "truth" has often depended on who was looking at what "facts," from which sources, at what time, and for what reason. Users of this collection of essays are challenged to sift through these documents and interpret the sources. Historians seeking to understand why Americans embraced the institution of slavery have offered wildly varying interpretations. The vehemence with which they made their arguments indicates how high they saw the social, moral, and spiritual stakes of coming to terms with slavery. By tracing the debate on slavery as it unfolded among scholars, and by examining the different types of sources and evidence historians introduced and the problems each new interpretation raised, researchers can see how historians actually create history. Grappling with historical interpretation is necessary to approach any understanding of the past.

Many early white scholars saw slavery as economically backward but socially progressive, as "education" for blacks by mostly kind masters. Ulrich B. Phillips, for example, relied largely on planters' records when he published pioneering research in *American Negro Slavery* (1918), in which he argued that slavery was more of a social tool than an economic one. Phillips regarded slavery as a "school for civilizing savages." He felt that Africans needed guidance, and slavery was the ideal vehicle for delivering it. This argument—hard to read today for more culturally sensitive readers—dominated the writing on slavery during the first half of the twentieth century. This view is also reflected in popular culture in such influential American films as D. W. Griffith's *Birth of a Nation* (1915) and Victor Fleming's *Gone with the Wind* (1939).

Further research led historian Kenneth Stampp to refute Phillips's point by point in *The Peculiar Institution: Slavery in the Ante-bellum South* (1956). Examining plantation records, newspaper ads for runaway slaves, abolitionist documents, and the autobiographies of former slaves (which introduced African American voices), Stampp argued that, in fact, white masters drove slaves harshly. In a famously controversial phrase in which he referred to African Americans as "white men with black skins," Stampp proclaimed that blacks were equal, not intrinsically inferior, to white Americans and that slavery functioned as a profitable, albeit exploitative, commercial enterprise. Stampp opened up another debate with his opinion that American society provided neither the space nor the cultural difference for the formation of a separate slave community.

An analysis by subsequent scholars of travelers' accounts, government reports and documents, and legal records introduced a sociological perspective to the study of slavery. In *Slavery: A Problem in American Institutional and Intellectual Life* (1959), Stanley Elkins jumbled the debate on the harshness and cruelty of slavery by introducing a psychological argument that led some scholars to depict slaves as either hapless victims or dependent beneficiaries. Some historians responded to Elkins by further examining African American testimony, especially the personal histories that resulted from the Works Progress Administration (WPA) slave narratives project of the 1930s. These scholars studied the people who were enslaved as they described their modes of resistance and the formation of a unique culture. John Blassingame, Nathan Irvin Huggins, George Rawick, and Herbert Gutman explored the cultural resiliency, separate spheres, and strong families of America's slaves. They proved that Africans and their descendants in America, despite severe difficulties, managed to create a community that provided some protection from the worst abuses of slavery. Once members of widely disparate African ethnic groups that represented a variety of languages and social backgrounds, each enslaved group mingled elements of its own traditions with European languages, religions, and cultures—and with some Native American ingredients as well—to lay the foundations for the vibrant African American community that would see its members through the vicissitudes of American history. Slaves found ways to offer resistance—both active and passive—with the aim of building family lives, spirituality, and community. They did not just persevere, they lived, in the harshest of circumstances. Historian Sterling Stuckey has argued, for example, that slaves Africanized American Christianity rather than the other way around. Although slave owners used Christianity to control slaves, sometimes religion helped to ameliorate the worst aspects of the system.

Economic historians Robert Fogel and Stanley Engerman reintroduced economic data to the study of slavery. In their quantitative study, *Time on the Cross: The Economics of American Negro Slavery* (1974), they attacked the stereotype that enslaved African Americans were not hard workers. Fogel and Engerman clarified that the slave economy was vibrant and the profits that whites made were substantial. The African American workers were industrious and also profit-minded, budding capitalists who were unfairly restrained by slavery. For Fogel and Engerman, true freedom really is the freedom to participate in the market. The debate on slavery became even more intense as historians discussed the implications of the argument that slavery was profitable.

Adding Marxist theory to a wide range of sources, especially the WPA slave narratives, historian Eugene Genovese focused on the centrality of questions of power. Genovese's argument in *The Political Economy of Slavery* (1965) that slavery was a precapitalist institution that inhibited economic growth provoked a renewed debate about the economics of slavery. In a series of works, especially *Roll, Jordan, Roll: The World the Slaves Made* (1974), Genovese explored how slave owners and slaves struggled over the boundaries of slavery and freedom. Responding to Genovese, later historians teetered between concepts of victimization and the cost of slavery to enslaved people and to American society (Peter Kolchin), and the resilience and accomplishments of enslaved peoples (Ira Berlin).

Despite this research, much about slavery remains unknown or unclear. The work of most scholars who study slavery reflects two broad themes: slavery as a business and slavery as a way of life. The consensus among those studying slavery as a business is that slavery was a commercial enterprise; whether or not it can be called "capitalist," it was qualitatively different from merchant or industrial capitalism. An analysis of slavery as a way of life includes much more than an examination of a labor system; slavery included vast investments of social, intellectual, and political resources. Scholars who study slavery as a way of life agree for the most part that, despite the power of the master class, many slaves were able to find space for themselves and create a culture and community rooted in African memories, religion, and family life. Historian Ira Berlin writes that "the slaves' history—like all human history—was made not only by what was done to them but also by what they did for themselves." While not ignoring slavery's harshness, nor contending that the cultural achievement of the slaves was easy, this group of scholars found that enslaved men and women, despite their lack of freedom, created areas of control outside of white supervision, and with heroic determination tried to support their families.

By the mid-nineteenth century, half of all American slaveholders held no more than five slaves; at the same time, most enslaved men and women belonged to holders of twenty or more slaves. The isolation of these large plantations was an important factor in keeping the enslaved cut off from the outside world. At the same time, the living quarters generally provided a buffer away from white supervision. On plantations large enough to include slave quarters—the minority of plantations, but holding the majority of enslaved workers—most slaves worked from sunup to sundown in the fields and lived from sundown to sunup in the quarters. The residents of slave quarters shared religious traditions, songs, and stories, and they told trickster tales that outlined tactics and attributes necessary to cope with a world where the good and the right did not generally prevail. Nowhere, of course, was safety guaranteed. Slaves were never free from the threat of harsh treatment, humiliation, degrading punishment, or the insecurity that sale might break up the family. In spite of that, slave communities created barriers behind which African American culture might grow and thrive.

Historians still debate whether slavery produced racism or racism produced slavery. In *White Over Black: American Attitudes Toward the Negro, 1550–1812* (1968), Winthrop Jordan offered a disturbing answer to this question. Jordan argued that from first contact whites held deep fears and hatred toward people from Africa, whom they perceived as different. Similar to claims made earlier by black novelist and playwright James Baldwin, Jordon believed a dominating racism filled a collective psychological need of white people. If slavery was the consequence of racism, as Jordan suggested, then the outlook for America's future was deeply troubling. If slavery caused racism, however, then change was possible and racism could be eradicated. Historian Edmund Morgan argued in *American Slavery, American Freedom: The Ordeal of Colonial Virginia* (1975) that racism had come to early America as an ideological rationalization for slavery. Moreover, racism was carefully cultivated by America's ruling class to prevent blacks and poor whites from uniting. Jordan and Morgan traced their arguments on slavery back to colonial, mostly white, sources. Clearly more was at stake than a need for labor, for slavery produced additional cultural and social benefits for enslavers. Planters ended up at the top of the hierarchy, but the white middle and lower classes were invested in slavery as well, for the entire institution was bolstered by a broad base of "inferior" slaves. This was the "way of life" that white southerners were anxious to defend when the Civil War began in 1861—a way of life that would not have been possible without slavery as an underpinning.

In the end, whether one is a professional historian or not, it is the words and documents of history's actors that must be investigated.

Orville Vernon Burton

The Middle Passage and Africa

The Middle Passage and Africa Overview

The year 1619 was a momentous one for the struggling young colony of Virginia, which was just beginning to achieve some viability. In the same year that the House of Burgess was established, the fledgling colony's future was assured by the arrival of its first boatload of women— or, as the colonists described them, "many virgins." Also in 1619, a Dutch privateer arrived in Jamestown transporting twenty "Negars," men who were taken from a slaver on the high seas by the Dutch and brought to Virginia to be sold to the colonial government, which in turn sold them to individual planters at a profit. Although these men were officially referred to as indentured servants, who would be freed after several years of service, this actually marked the beginning of the North American British colonies' participation in the worldwide slave trade.

Ulrich Phillips's *American Negro Slavery* (1918) remained the standard work on the subject of the slave trade until the 1950s. In that book and in his later work *Life and Labor in the Old South* (1929), Phillips's view of Africa was overwhelmingly negative. "No people is without its philosophy and religion," he admitted, but "of all regions of extensive habitation equatorial Africa is the worst" (1918, pp. 3 and 5). As for the Africans, "the climate in fact not only discourages but prohibits mental effort of severe or sustained character, and the negroes have submitted to that prohibition as to many others, through countless generations, with excellent grace" (p. 4). In his view, men and women of African descent were nothing more than naturally inferior "savages" who benefited from the "civilizing" influence of slavery. In starkly contrasting interpretation, Kenneth Stampp's 1956 synthesis *The Peculiar Institution* described the institution of slavery as an oppressive means of economic exploitation. Stampp depicted the slaves as captives violently uprooted from an organic position in a viable African society and placed between two cultures in a

New World. Subsequent scholars have built on Stampp's work to provide a nuanced portrait of life in the sub-Saharan Africa, revealing a diverse society with sophisticated social, economic, and political structures.

These studies have also provided important insights into the way in which the slave trade operated on the African continent. Whereas some early writers had assumed that the trade was an almost exclusively European enterprise, David Eltis has shown in *The Rise of African Slavery in the Americas* (2000) that Africans were in many ways fully complicit in the Atlantic slave trade. European buyers rarely ventured beyond the coastline themselves, so they depended almost exclusively on the extended networks and contacts of African merchants. As such, Africans exerted significant control over the dynamics of the slave market and conducted the trade on their own terms. For example, African sellers influenced who was sold into captivity—usually prisoners of war, those convicted of crimes, and those already in servitude rather than victims of kidnapping—and controlled the rate at which traders were able to fill their ships. Traders also were forced to deal with local tribal governments, which levied taxes that the Europeans had to pay and, in some areas, even insisted that slaves were purchased at a standard price that they set.

Although many people think of the slave trade as consisting solely of the so-called Middle Passage, in fact the voyage across the Atlantic was but one part of the ordeal faced by potential slaves, many of whom died long before they saw the interior of a ship. After being captured, slaves were forced to march for distances of up to 500 miles or more from the African interior to trading posts along the coast, where they were incarcerated in pens for up to a year before finally being boarded onto specially converted ships bound for the New World. Conditions aboard these slave ships were literally sickening. With profit the sole motive, humanitarian considerations were rarely, if ever, a consideration for the crew. Instead, the object of a voyage was to arrive in the Americas with as many live slaves as possible at a minimum cost. Slave ships were consequently loaded as efficiently as possible. Slaves were chained together, stripped naked, and crowded into spaces so small that they allowed no individual movement and often forced them to live and breathe in each other's waste and blood. Those who showed any sign of disease generally were thrown overboard for fear that they would infect the rest of the ship. And because suicides and uprisings were common among the cargo on these ships, punishments were harsh, and any sign of defiance was brutally put down to dissuade others from doing the same. Notwithstanding the fact that slave mortality rates onboard ship declined throughout the nineteenth century, death rates averaged as high as 20 percent.

Historians have long argued about exactly how many Africans were torn from their homeland and delivered under appalling conditions and with astounding loss of life into slavery in the New World. The most recent estimates, based on a thorough analysis of voyage-by-voyage shipping data, reveals that over the course of three centuries as many as 11 million men, women, and children were transported out of Africa as part of the transatlantic slave trade (Eltis 2001, p. 29).

BIBLIOGRAPHY

Curtin, Philip D. *The Atlantic Slave Trade: A Census.* Madison: University of Wisconsin Press, 1969.

Eltis, David. *The Rise of African Slavery in the Americas.* Cambridge, UK: Cambridge University Press, 2000.

Eltis, David. "The Volume and Structure of the Transatlantic Slave Trade: A Reassessment." *William and Mary Quarterly* 58, no. 1 (2001): 17–46.

Klein, Herbert Sanford. *The Atlantic Slave Trade.* Cambridge, UK: Cambridge University Press, 1999.

Phillips, Ulrich Bonnell. *American Negro Slavery: A Survey of the Supply, Employment, and Control of Negro Labor as Determined by the Plantation Régime.* New York: D. Appleton, 1918.

Phillips, Ulrich Bonnell. *Life and Labor in the Old South.* Boston: Little, Brown, 1929.

Stampp, Kenneth M. *The Peculiar Institution: Slavery in the Antebellum South*, 1st ed. New York: Knopf, 1956.

Simon J. Appleford

■ Life in Africa

Life in Africa can best be understood historically by understanding Africa from two dichotomous periods: the pre-Atlantic slave trade period, prior to the seventeenth century, and the post-Atlantic slave trade period, after the seventeenth century. The Atlantic slave trade is a useful marker for conceptualizing African life because it registers an important time in Africa that has all too often been neglected in popular narratives about the continent—the most important of which was that the regions and states within Africa all had longstanding and well-organized social systems that integrated with the lives of its citizens prior to European contact.

Their systems were in many ways differently organized than many western societies, but nonetheless, African social systems were alive and operating wonderfully long before white men landed upon their shores. This point needs to be strenuously emphasized because unfortunately many depictions of African peoples and their institutions have been, and to some extent still are, portrayed as being backward and inferior to the societies of the west and the east. Part of this difference can be explained by the Atlantic slave trade, and yet the Atlantic slave trade should by no means wholly encompass one's understanding of Africa and African peoples. On the contrary, the saliency of the Atlantic slave trade as a historical marker lies in the remarkable dexterity that it has for contextualizing the striking shifts in African life as a direct result of its influence. Therefore the notion of a pre- and post-slave trade Africa helps to illuminate the stability and strength of African societies prior to and after the trade, without over-determining its importance in African life. That said, in order to get at the uniqueness of African life, a grounding in the important social systems that influenced the lived experiences of African people prior to the disruption that occurred from the Atlantic slave trade helps us to conceptualize the beauty and complexity of African cultures. From this vantage point the wholeness of African life is given primacy over the slave trade, and thereby allowing for a more sophisticated critique of African life apart from this extremely complex social and political phenomenon.

In the ancient and medieval era African states operated as autonomous regions from each other. In fact, before the middle of the fifteenth century the primary contact between African regions were along the coastal waterways along East Africa, across the Red Sea, and the Sahara Desert (Lovejoy 2000, p. 12). The trade of natural resources was primary impetus for contact between coastal and inland regions during this period and beyond. Valuable natural resources such as gold, copper, and salt, as well as plant items such as the kola nut, was what facilitated movement between inland and coastal states in Africa. It was around the growth and the trade of plants and minerals that regional development ensued and where the isolation that previously marked the inland and coastal regions began to dissipate.

Social systems based on ethnicity and kinship developed as a result of the forage of regional contacts around the trading of plants and minerals across inland and coastal states. As such, much of African kinship systems were either matrilineal, group power and inheritance that was derived from one's mother's side, or patrilineal, group power and inheritance that was derived from one's father's side. Moreover, within this kinship form, lineage was a vital component that determined a variety of privileges, or not, within a society. For example, one's lineal relation within a group

Daily life in an African village in the Congo Basin.   The regions and states within African all had longstanding and well organized social systems prior to European contact.   *© North Wind Picture Archives.*

determined one's rank within the group. Consequently one was marginalized or exalted based on one's lineage lines to group leaders. As such, how one would come into the group, via marriage or birth for example, and to whom one married or had children with, had an important impact on one's lived conditions socially, politically, and materially within a clan group. And whereas freedom via individual autonomy and independence was acknowledged as the highest form of socialization in the West, in the lineage based social systems of Africa, it was conceptualized through notions of belonging and acceptance into a kinship network (Miers and Kopytoff 1977, p. 7). Thus it is through belonging to a group where one would derive his or her identity as a citizen and person, not by their individuality. As such, group membership could entail protection against maltreatment by other groups; it could determine one's marital partner or prospects, and even predict one's religious affiliation. In essence, many of a person's needs were met from within the group.

These examples of lineage group networks are of course more complex than what has been described here. Within lineal societies there were strict and complex rules that governed African societies. For example, women were key members of African societies organized around lineage. The fertility of a woman was vital to clan groups. Her reproductive capacities would mean increased power

to a group because of the increase in population that her fecundity engendered. As such, fertility was a highly prized, praised, and sought-after asset because a clan's sustainability in many precolonial African societies hinged on a women's reproductive capacity. Because of this, male leaders within a clan sought to have multiple wives who possessed the gift of fertility. Likewise, women during this era recognized the value of this asset and would on occasion use it to move up in rank within a clan or sometimes even change clans to improve their living conditions.

Besides her reproductive labor, a woman's productive labor was important to African societies. Within lineal-based societies women were the primary agricultural workers and therefore their skill and acumen at planting, growing, and harvesting a variety of vegetation was crucial to the day-to-day survival of African peoples. A woman's skill for crop cultivation and management cannot be overestimated here as Africa's climate and landscape ranges from dry and drought conditions to moist and flooding conditions. Thus tremendous skill and dexterity to cope with a variety of landscape and climate conditions was required to coax the bounty of the land, and women were essential to this process.

Another aspect of African life that grew out of its reliance on lineage and kinship-based societies was the concept of dependent relations. These were relations that were

WOMEN AND RICE

In her book *Black Rice: The African Origins of Rice Cultivation in the Americas* (2001), Judith Carney indicated that throughout the West African rice region, which included the Upper Guinea coast, women played a vital role in African rice production. According to Carney, in Senegambia women held the important job of pounding rice: "In Africa the standard device for preparing all cereals is the mortar, formed from a hollowed-out tree trunk. Grain is placed into the cavity of the mortar, where the hulls are removed by striking them with a wood pestle" (p. 27). The removal of rice hulls and the underlying bran was a skilled operation that women performed prior to the Atlantic slave trade.

SOURCE: Carney, Judith. *Black Rice: The African Origins of Rice Cultivation in the Americas*. Cambridge, MA: Harvard University Press, 2001.

necessitated within kinship societies for those who were detached or estranged from their natal clan for any number of reasons, and in order to survive these, men and women were forced into a low-ranking status within a clan. Again, unlike in the West where a person in this situation would simply strike out on his or her own and make it the best way they could, in a kinship-based society such as those in Africa, this simply was unimaginable. As was mentioned earlier, one's economic, social, and political survival, as well as one's identity was often bound up within a connection to and acceptance within a clan group. As such, when persons became detached from a clan they were in a very vulnerable position within African society. During these times, they often would look to incorporate themselves into a clan group in order to decrease their vulnerability to harm or exploitation. Protection against undue harm was mitigated by the successful integration into a new social group. Still, during the process of integration, group members could experience vulnerability and various levels of unfreedom based on the circumstances that predicated their entrance into the group. For example, women in certain precolonial African societies could be treated differently if they came to the group as a wife, as a concubine, or as a servant. Moreover, their degree of acceptance by group leaders often hinged on their perceived usefulness or the benefit that their presence added to the overall stability and substance of the group. Additionally, their treatment, as was mentioned earlier, in some cases could be assuaged depending in the woman's fecundity or the extent to which some women had male family members (fathers, brothers, or uncles) inside or even outside the group to rely on for protection against unreasonable treatment.

This type of complex social organization that included various levels of kinship statuses worked well to order most African societies until the Atlantic slave trade changed the dynamics of belonging and incorporation within the kinship system. During the years between 1600 and 1800, the trans-

atlantic slave trade altered the coherence of Africa's social organization that privileged kinship and lineage rights as the terms for belonging. As such, those newly incorporated into a lineal line or those detached from familial ties were the most vulnerable for sale to European slave traders. It is important here to underscore that the sale of some African peoples to Europeans for enslavement be viewed cautiously before jumping to conclusions that they were equally as culpable as European slave traders to the forced enslavement of blacks. The situation was much more nuanced and complex than simply inferring that comparable blame be bestowed onto Africans as to Europeans. This shortsightedness often happens through the conflation of the continent of Africa as a monolithic locale and identity. And although most of Africa's indigenous citizens had black skin and similar cultural traditions and social organizations, the many states in Africa still held many different religious orders, languages, and ways of knowing. That said, one can no more paint Africa with a monolithic brush as they can any other continent. Thus, the complexities surrounding the sale of an African person by other African persons remains even in the early twenty-first century a subject of much debate within the scholarly field for those who specialize in the subject. Therefore, one must undertake a more in-depth and detailed study of these debates before weighing in on this important topic.

After the transatlantic slave trade was abolished, the ravages of the slave trade made it difficult to readapt the old African cultural and productive qualities to a changing and ever-increasing industrialized world. Population losses, the underdevelopment of its natural resources, an atmosphere of war, and intense factional divisions among clan groups were but a sampling of the problems that engulfed Africa in the wake of the transatlantic slave trade and its abolition. Equally, colonialism proved to be no panacea for stabilizing Africa. In fact, it has shown to do more harm than good for African countries as they sought to move toward economic independence and social and political stability. Yet, to understand Africa fully one must consider African life at two poignant intervals, prior to and after the transatlantic slave trade.

BIBLIOGRAPHY

Lovejoy, Paul E. *Transformations in Slavery: A History of Slavery in Africa*. 2nd ed. Cambridge, U.K. and New York: Cambridge University Press, 2000.
Miers, Suzanne, and Igor Kopytoff, eds. *Slavery in Africa: Historical and Anthropological Perspectives*. Madison: University of Wisconsin Press, 1977.

Carmen P. Thompson

■ Capture

The Atlantic slave trade brought upward of 15 million Africans to the New World. According to historian Michael Gomez (2005), nearly 85 percent of those who survived the middle passage to the Americas came

An undated woodcut showing captured Africans who will be sold as slaves. Once captured, African men and women were chained together and marched to the sea. The trek could last for months and it was not uncommon for captured Africans to die while en route. © *North Wind Picture Archives.*

from one of four regions: West Central Africa (36.5%); the Bight of Benin (20%); the Bight of Biafra (16.6%); and the Gold Coast (11%). Africans were captured for the purpose of enslavement in a variety of ways. Slaves were captured by warring factions in Africa and sold to European slave traders for guns, munitions, money, alcohol, and other products. It is important that the sale of Africans captured in war to Europeans for enslavement not be conflated with the slave trade in the Americas. This is because the capture and sale of Africans by African nations in no way contemplated the destructive and derisive consequences of the chattel slave system that would come to be associated with the Americas. The two systems were dissimilar in many respects. Namely, those captured in Africa and held or sold as slaves were usually from different regions in West Africa. For example, coastal warriors would often capture inland peoples as prisoners of war for use as domestic servants; or, perhaps, those captured would be sold as slaves to other African clans or to Europeans. Thus from this context, Africans were not selling or enslaving their comrades but, rather, they were selling their enemies (Lovejoy 2000).

Besides the regional differences in the capture and sale of Africans as slaves, these potential slaves usually spoke a different language than that of their captors. Moreover, they often had different religions and social customs. As such, this whole enterprise was extremely complex and deserves substantial research and study before leaping to a one-on-one correlation with the chattel slave system in the Americas. That said, the sale of Africans by Africans out of the spoils of war was one means that contributed to the transatlantic slave trade.

Once captured by African warriors, African men and women were chained to one another and would walk in these coffles to the sea where they were held and prepared for a trip of no return. This trek could last for months and could become quite debilitating for those in the coffle. It was not uncommon for captured Africans to die while en route to the coastal shores or to perish in the slave pens while waiting for slave ships to reach port. While in slave coffles that often reached 100 strong, the men and women were often ill-fed and harshly treated. As a result, the loss of life during this process could be staggering. One report estimates the loss of life to have averaged 10 to 15 percent. Others estimate it as high as 40 percent in certain instances (Gomez 2005, p. 73).

African women who were captured in war were less likely than men to be sold as slaves to rival clans or to European slavers. This was because women were important to maintaining African clan societies. The labor of female captives was seen as valuable to clan life. This was because women in African societies were the primary

PSYCHOLOGICAL PREPARATIONS

In trying to understand the process that went into preparing enslaved men and women for the Middle Passage, it is important to consider the psychological nature of the process that included attacking the dignity and cultural conventions of the captives. For example, men and women were stowed separately during the arduous voyage, with men being shacked in irons and kept in the cargo holds and women kept on the quarter deck without shackles. This separation offended enslaved African mens' cultural sensibilities that were embedded in the belief that men were the protectors of women and children. Other processes of preparation for embarking on the "trip of no return" can be understood through the following passage by a slave ship captain who articulates the twisted "science" involved in the process:

> On the appointed day, the *barracoon* or slave pen is made joyous by the abundant 'feed' which signalizes the negro's last hours in his native country. The feast over, they are taken alongside the vessel in canoes; and as they touch the deck, they are entirely stripped, so that women as well as men go out of Africa as they came into it—*naked*. This precaution, it will be understood, is indispensable; for perfect nudity, during the whole voyage, is the only means of securing cleanliness and health. (Mayer 1854, p. 102)

SOURCE: Mayer, Brantz. *Captain Canot, or, Twenty Years of an African Slaver.* New York: Appleton, 1854.

agricultural workers and, as such, their skill in this area was extremely valuable to the sustenance of many African societies. Moreover, women were valued for their fertility. Consequently, their ability to bear children added to the perceived power of a clan culture where the largeness of ones kin group was seen as evidence of the strength of the group. And finally, women were valued in African culture for their socializing function. Because women captives were less likely to flee, and because of their physical vulnerability, they were often easier to acculturate into a new clan group. As such, women were often the teachers of those who were unfamiliar with the ways and customs of the clan. This was a vital and important process in the cultural cohesion of clan life. In many ways, women were more instrumental than men to maintaining clan stability.

Another way that Africans were captured was through trickery. Although the presence of Europeans on the African continent was underway decades before the beginnings of the Atlantic slave trade, they would often capture Africans by appealing to this familiarity. Before the slave trade Europeans came quite frequently to Africa with the hopes of establishing trade relations. As a continent, Africa was rich with minerals such as gold and copper, and vegetation, such as yams and plantains,

as well as kola nuts and palm oil. Europeans would trade such commodities as guns and alcohol to African leaders for these goods. Out of this trade relationship a modicum of mutual trust and respect had developed. As such, when the institution of slavery was in its developmental stages, Europeans saw Africans as holding great potential as slave prospects to reinforce the pool of indentured servants of European descent. As the demand for slaves in the Americas rapidly grew, European slave traders would use all sorts of trickery to get slaves to voluntarily board slave ships. For example, once aboard, slavers would ply unsuspecting Africans with alcohol and food and then refuse to let them off the ship.

Once purchased by European slave traders the slaves were branded, stripped naked and taken aboard the ship. It could take up to one year from the time of capture, to boarding a ship, for a group of African slaves to arrive in the Americas. This time frame, however, was never certain given the precariousness of having human beings as cargo. Thus, there were many things that could go wrong during this period, particularly because the shipping business in general during this time was in its infancy. Therefore, calculus for a voyage had to consider the appropriate amount of provisions for the captives (which was minimal) and crew. Moreover, slavers were oftentimes paid by the number of slaves they could ferry from Africa to the Americas for sale on auction blocks. Complicated calculations such as these had to be considered before embarking on a transatlantic voyage.

BIBLIOGRAPHY

Gomez, Michael A. *Reversing Sail: A History of the African Diaspora.* New York: Cambridge University Press, 2005.

Lovejoy, Paul E. *Transformations in Slavery: A History of Slavery in Africa*, 2nd ed. Cambridge, UK: Cambridge University Press, 2000.

Carmen P. Thompson

■ Middle Passage

The Middle Passage was a journey millions of African people made aboard European slave ships during the 300-year span of the Atlantic slave trade between 1600 and 1900. The Middle Passage should be viewed as a transformational midpoint in the history of African peoples that began in Africa and crossed the Atlantic Ocean into Europe and the Americas. By conceptualizing the Middle Passage in the middle of a historical chronology of enslavement, Africa and African life becomes the central interpretative milieu for understanding the complexities of this international system of human exploitation.

There is much that is still not known about the Middle Passage. For example, the exact numbers of Africans who successfully survived the Middle Passage is still a subject of immense debate. Scholars estimate the number of survivors to be anywhere from a low of 9 million to a high of 15 million people. Of even greater debate is the number of Africans who perished in the 3,700 mile journey from the west coasts of Africa to the Americas, a journey that could take up to four months to complete. Sadly, it is just not known, nor will there likely ever be an accurate accounting of the living and the dead as a result of the Middle Passage. However, the scholarly record on the causes of death for African people during this period is widely known.

There were many reasons why many Africans perished during these periods. The primary one was because of disease as a result of poor sanitation. In the holds of slave ships, African men and women were packed tightly and shackled at the wrists and ankles onto large multilevel vessels in spaces no bigger than a grave, and oftentimes they were stacked in spoon-like fashion on top of each other. In these cramped spaces these men and women were left to wallow in each other's excrement and mucous. The lack of adequate sanitation and ventilation in these tight quarters led to the outbreak of numerous diseases such as smallpox and dysentery.

Insurrection was another cause for the high death rate among African men and women. On the few occasions that they were released from their chains and shackles for exercise or to entertain their captors, many men and women would attempt to overpower the crew. Most of these attempts were unsuccessful and the African men and women who participated in these acts were severely beaten, whipped, and even killed for their subversiveness.

Suicide was also a prevalent cause of death to African men and women during the Middle Passage. Taking one's life as a response to their enslaved condition was not viewed as morally abhorrent in African cultures as it was in many Western cultures. This was because in most African religious orders, deceased ancestors were prayed to, worshiped, or called upon for guidance in many areas of everyday life in Africa. As such, death, even by suicide, was in many ways seen as an inevitable reunion with one's ancestors.

Besides the untold death rates, rape and sexual abuse aboard slave vessels was equally difficult to enumerate, yet it was believed by most scholars to have frequently occurred over the many voyages and passages from Africa to the Americas. African women were vulnerable to sexual exploitation primarily because they were mostly separated from African men on the slave ships. Equally, once captured, the men in the crew held compete control over the lives of their captives. And as was mentioned earlier, the captors could beat, whip, and kill the African men and women with impunity. As such, sexual access to African women was unbridled and their sexual availability was in many ways seen as part of the spoils for maintaining human cargo over the long and arduous voyage.

The deck of a slave ship, *Wildfire*. This illustration, *The Slave Deck of the Bark* Wildfire, published in the June 2, 1860, issue of *Harper's Weekly*, shows the cramped conditions for Africans on a bark, or sailing vessel. Conditions on the *Wildfire*, which was captured by an American streamer for illegal importation of slaves, were better than most. On some slave ships, Africans were packed tightly, shacked at the wrists and ankles in spaces no bigger than a grave, and often were stacked in spoon-like fashion on top of one another. © *Bettman/Corbis.*

The Middle Passage has been called a "quintessential moment of transfiguration" for African people sent to the Americas (Gomez 2005, p. 71). For it was from this violent period of alienation and disorientation that Africans had to adapt to life in a new world. And the process by which Africans adapted to their new environment has been one of critical study for scholars of slavery. Of particular interest to scholars of this adaptive process was the extent to which generations of African-descended people have retained cultural traditions and folkways that were indigenous to African societies. In effect, many scholars of African history are interested in the tenacity of African traditions across time and space when exposed to violent social disruptions. As such, the Middle Passage can be viewed as a central period in the transformation of a people from Africans to African Americans. Consequently, the study of African culture prior to and after the Middle Passage, and the subsequent slave trade, is crucial for a complete understanding of slavery in the Americas and elsewhere.

BIBLIOGRAPHY

Gomez, Michael A. *Reversing Sail: A History of the African Diaspora*. New York: Cambridge University Press, 2005.

Lovejoy, Paul E. *Transformations in Slavery: A History of Slavery in Africa*, 2nd ed. Cambridge, U.K., and New York: Cambridge University Press, 2000.

Carmen P. Thompson

The Business of Slavery

■ The Business of Slavery Overview

As explorers and merchants from Europe spread around the globe from the fifteenth to the seventeenth century in search of treasure and trade, they discovered that trafficking in African slaves was a most profitable venture. Seeking labor for the plantations in the Americas beginning in the sixteenth century, European merchants, colonial plantation owners, and the crowned heads of Europe created the notorious Middle Passage in which at least 12 million Africans were taken from their native lands through the complicity of African chiefs, lashed like cords of wood in the hulls of the ships of European slavers, seasoned by whipping in the Caribbean islands, and then sold like cattle in auction blocks throughout the Americas. At least a million Africans perished during the Middle Passage from disease and harsh treatment, their bodies dumped unceremoniously in the oceans. Ironically, insurance policies often covered the market value of these losses for the slaver.

The impact of the slave trade on Africa went beyond these numbers, as millions more Africans died in European-inspired wars and under the subsequent direct colonial rule of the continent in the nineteenth century. The population of Africa shrank and the continent's economic development was thwarted by these centuries of slave trade and colonialism.

The Middle Passage was part of the triangular trade that enriched the upper classes of Europe and the Americas. European merchants exported goods such as muskets and various other manufactured items to Africa to exchange with African chiefs for slaves they had captured during their conflicts with other African ethnic groups (or for captives simply kidnapped by African slavers for sale to the Europeans). The merchants then sold their slaves in the Americas, buying American primary products (e.g., cotton, sugar, tobacco, molasses, and rum) to sell in Europe.

Put to work on sugarcane plantations in the Caribbean, Brazil, and Louisiana, in tobacco plantations in Virginia and North Carolina, in rice plantations in South Carolina and Georgia, and ultimately in the rigorous cotton plantations of the Deep South, African slaves labored and died under the lash of slave masters interested only in maximizing their financial return from plantation operations. Thus did world capitalism gain much of its early accumulations of wealth from the blood, sweat, and misery of African slaves.

The termination of the transatlantic slave trade in 1808 by the United States did not end slavery or the internal slave trade in the Americas. The *peculiar institution*, as slavery was sometimes delicately termed, developed pathologies beyond the simple injustice of one person owning another, pathologies fueled by the pursuit of profit in the complex market for human chattel. When soil exhaustion rendered slavery less profitable in the Virginia tobacco fields, slave breeding for the Old Southwest cotton plantations became another source of profit for the slave owners of Virginia. Upper South slave owners found another profitable outlet in the slave-hiring market, through which slave owners could lease their slaves via urban brokers to rich families needing domestics, to chewing tobacco factories in Richmond, Petersburg, and Lynchburg, to the salt mines of Kanawha (in today's West Virginia), and to railroad companies needing laborers to clear the way for the westward march of the iron rails of commerce.

Breaking apart slave families to sell slave offspring (or rebellious adult slaves) down the river to cotton plantations in Alabama, Mississippi, and Louisiana was commonplace, and yet slaves struggled mightily, and often successfully, to maintain connections with families separated by hundreds of miles of difficult terrain.

The accumulations of capital from the slave trade and plantation slavery spurred the growth of manufacturing in the northern United States and in Europe. The textile, metal, and food industries grew apace with the growth of primary commodities produced in

Estimated volume of the transatlantic slave trade by African region and half-century

African regions	Western Africa	West Central Africa	Southeast Africa	Total	West Central Africa %
1501–1600	126,999	149,294	0	276,293	54.0%
1601–1650	146,321	526,522	934	673,777	78.1%
1651–1700	771,932	408,618	29,876	1,210,426	39.7%
1701–1750	1,833,573	728,344	17,674	2,579,591	28.2%
1751–1800	2,496,420	1,417,562	61,773	3,979,755	35.6%
1801–1850	1,491,348	1,736,772	394,183	3,622,303	47.9%
1851–1867	46,870	84,077	89,447	220,394	38.1%
1501–1867	6,974,586	5,051,189	593,887	12,558,491	40.2%

*Data in columns for West Central Africa and Southeast Africa and the Total trade are summed from the source table; the data in the column for Western Africa are calculated from these sums. Percentage column is calculated from the bolded column for West Central Africa and the totals for each period. The original data include varying estimated components, and the numbers are not in fact known as precisely as their expression in the table. Confidence levels are generally in the 95% range, or above.

SOURCE: Calculated* from "Introduction," in Eltis, David, and David Richardson, eds. "Introduction." *Extending the Frontiers: Essays on the New Transatlantic Slave Trade Database*. New Haven: Yale University Press, 2007.

Table showing the estimated volume of the transatlantic slave trade. During the Middle Passage at least a million Africans died from disease and harsh treatment. *Illustration by GGS. Gale.*

the Americas. State and local governments also thrived on slavery, as slave owners paid substantial property taxes on their slaves. The enslavement of Africans was the economic engine for the growth of the American economies.

Justifying slavery in the midst of a democratic revolution in the American colonies required vast intellectual dishonesty. Quoting selected passages from the Bible, asserting African inferiority, and even claiming that Africans were a different, lower species from Europeans, Southern planters and their political and intellectual allies created a thoroughgoing racist ideology that still tragically resonates today. The pro-slavery argument intensified in the 1830s after rebellions and resistance among slaves and assaults from abolitionists challenged, in practice, the specious reasoning of the pro-slavery apologists. Pro-slavery apologists no longer claimed that slavery was merely a necessary evil, but was instead a positive good, needed to Christianize the savages and control their supposedly animalistic behavior. But underneath this rhetoric lay the bald truth: slavery was profitable for the Southern planter oligarchy, for the world capitalist system, and for the individual plantation owner. Some have argued that the lack of incentives for slaves to work hard rendered slavery unprofitable, and that only the gentleman farmer culture kept planters in the slave-owning business. Nothing could be further from the truth. While controlling slaves was complicated, the low cost of slave maintenance and the brutal coercion of slave labor kept planters rich, yeoman farmers poor, and slaves in misery.

The profitability of slavery is no longer in dispute; it was fundamental to the rise of wealth in the Americas.

Slavery encountered serious obstacles, however, when adapted to the urban environment and used in manufacturing activities, for slaves brought together in such settings saw greater opportunities for individual and collective resistance. Factories mysteriously burned, overseers were killed, and slaves escaped by ship and by foot, often assisted by emerging urban black institutions such as the First African Baptist Church of Richmond, as well as national black and white abolitionist groups. The problem of social control engendered by the modest presence of slaves and free blacks in urban industrial centers reduced the ability of the Southern U.S. colonies to develop a balanced economy of industry and agriculture.

Even in the plantation setting, however, slave owners faced the threat of rebellion. The memory of Nat Turner's rebellion in 1831 remained vivid throughout the South. Ultimately, slave resistance doomed the Southern armies defending slavery because masses of slaves defected from plantation labor after the Emancipation Proclamation of 1863. Their refusal to fuel the South's economy meant that the economic base for the Southern armies quickly withered. Slavery was, of course, ultimately defeated and abolished. Yet, its legacy remains throughout the world in the form of inequality, racial discrimination, underdevelopment, and poverty.

BIBLIOGRAPHY

Aitken, Hugh G. J., ed. *Did Slavery Pay? Readings in the Economics of Black Slavery in the United States.* Boston: Houghton Mifflin, 1971.

Franklin, John Hope, and Alfred A. Moss Jr. *From Slavery to Freedom: A History of African Americans*, 8th ed. New York: Alfred A. Knopf, 2000.

Genovese, Eugene D. *The Political Economy of Slavery: Studies in the Economy and Society of the Slave South*, 2nd ed. Middletown, CT: Wesleyan University Press, 1989.

Green, Rodney D. "Black Tobacco Factory Workers and Social Conflict in Antebellum Richmond: Were Slavery and Urban Industry Really Compatible?" *Slavery and Abolition* 8 (September 1987): 183–203.

O'Brien, John T., Jr. "Factory, Church, and Community: Blacks in Antebellum Richmond." *Journal of Southern History* 44, no. 4 (1978): 509–536.

Wade, Richard C. *Slavery in the Cities: The South, 1820–1860*. New York: Oxford University Press, 1967.

Rodney D. Green

■ The Slave Trade

THE SLAVE TRADE: AN OVERVIEW
John J. Wickre

AUCTIONS AND MARKETS
Mark S. Joy

SLAVE RENTING
Jackie R. Booker

INTERSTATE SLAVE TRADE
James J. Gigantino II

MONETARY VALUE OF SLAVES
Jocelyn M. Cuffee

BREEDING
Nelson Rhodes

BUYING FREEDOM
Jodi M. Savage

THE SLAVE TRADE: AN OVERVIEW

The desire to introduce slavery into the New World began shortly after the arrival of the first Europeans. The situation faced by these new settlers was an abundance of land and too few laborers. In order to make the land profitable the settlers introduced slavery as a means to cultivate the land. Originally Native Americans were sought to perform this task. However, their special vulnerability to European diseases and fear of antagonizing conflict among local Native Americans made enslaving Africans more desirable.

Prior to the Enlightenment, slavery was a widely accepted economic system, the legitimacy of which was unchallenged. With the Enlightenment, moral questions began to emerge that challenged the system's legitimacy. In his work *Two Treatises on Government* (1690), the English philosopher John Locke wrote, "the natural liberty of man is to be free from any superior power on earth" (1980, p. 17). Yet within the Enlightenment framework, Locke justified slavery in certain circumstances. If a person committed a crime worthy of execution or was captured in a just war, then, according to Locke, it would be an act of benevolence to "delay" death by submitting the prisoner into a condition of slavery. Later advocates of the slave trade used this reasoning to justify the practice. In *A Defence of the Planters in the West Indies* (1792), the author contended slaves taken from Africa were "prisoners taken in war—criminals—such negroes as the mode of African government had judged to be sacrificed to their laws" (Foot 1792, p. 47). While the author is mostly correct in his assertion that the enslaved were made so by local African authorities, most were not enslaved by the Lockean conception of criminality or "just war," but rather kidnapped by force.

While the ghastly cruelties of the slave trade concerned many, John Newton, a former slave trader turned abolitionist, explained that while "the Slave Trade was always unjustifiable . . . inattention and [self] interest prevented . . . the evil from being perceived" by many (Newton 1788, p. 7). Further, those involved in the trade became so familiar "with the suffering of the slaves" they could "become callous, and insensible to the pleadings of humanity" (p. 16). This callousness became so entrenched that Newton described incidences where as many as 100 slaves were thrown overboard due to low levels of provisions. In another case, a slave trader snatched an infant child from the arms of his mother to be thrown overboard when his cries overly annoyed the crewmember.

The slave trade became so notoriously cruel that statesman Thomas Jefferson sought to include the practice within his original draft of the Declaration of Independence. Here he condemned the king of England who had "waged cruel war against human nature itself, violating it's [*sic*] most sacred rights of life & liberty" by "captivating & carrying [humans] into slavery in another hemisphere . . . where men should be bought and sold" (1950, p. 426). Despite being considered an odious institution by many, it was nevertheless struck out of the final draft. Northern shippers who engaged in the Atlantic slave trade certainly took offense. Also, representatives from Georgia and South Carolina, while not yet in a position to argue slavery as a moral good, felt slavery was necessary for labor in their regions. They believed the Atlantic slave trade was essential for the time being, as large swaths of empty land required labor, which was scarce at the time. Yet, aside from pro-slavery sentiments was also a sense of the propriety condemning the king in such a manner. For delegates who felt slavery was an embarrassment for the nation, it seemed hypocritical to blame King George III for a trade in which members within the colonies participated. Rather than highlight such an egregious contradiction, many felt it was better to ignore it.

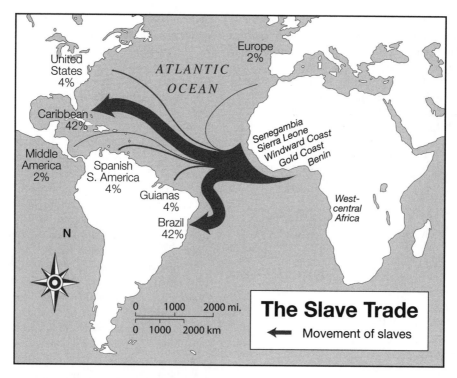

Map showing the Atlantic slave trade routes. A map showing the movement of slaves from Africa to the Western Hemisphere. The slave trade became so notoriously cruel that Thomas Jefferson sought to include the practice in his original draft of the Declaration of Independence. *Map by XNR Productions. Reproduced by permission of Gale.*

During the Constitutional Convention questions over the future of the slave trade caused some controversy. Originally a proposal was introduced that would allow Congress to outlaw the slave trade by 1800. However, Charles Pinckney of South Carolina introduced a plan to extend this provision until 1808. James Madison, generally a moderate on the issue, immediately objected to this plan stating, "twenty years will produce all the mischief that can be apprehended from the liberty to import slaves." Madison continued, "so long a term will be more dishonorable to the national character than to say nothing about it in the Constitution" (Farrand 1966, p. 415). Ultimately the convention settled on 1808 as the first year the trade could be outlawed. Between the ratification of the Constitutional Convention in 1887 and the closing of the slave trade in 1808, unprecedented influxes of slaves were transported to the United States. The unintended consequence of this window of time was to fuel the slaveholders' desire to obtain all the slaves they could before law prohibited the trade.

By 1806 Congress started making legislative preparations to outlaw the practice. The debate centered not on whether to outlaw the practice—but how. The original bill allowed for Africans seized by illegal slave trading to be sold as "goods" by the government. Congressman John Smilie of Pennsylvania immediately objected, stating such a policy would "take upon ourselves the odium of becoming slave traders." (*Annals of Congress*, 9th Congress, 2nd Session (1806, p. 170) Efforts were made to set the seized "cargo" free, setting off a sectional debate in Congress. Finally a compromise was reached where state authorities would settle the fate of the illegally traded slaves. Ultimately the slave trade was outlawed with a House vote of 113 to 5. Two of the dissenting votes came from Northern antislavery representatives upset with how the ban would be implemented. Opposition to the Atlantic slave trade by this time in America had achieved near universal consensus. While, to be sure, opposition had a strong moral base, for some wealthy planters, closure of the slave trade ensured the value of their slaves remained high by closing the supply.

By 1820 the Atlantic slave trade had become so detested that Congress almost unanimously passed a provision making illegal slave trading the equivalent of piracy with the punishment of death. During this congressional move, Virginian Charles Mercer issued the following committee report:

> Your committee cannot perceive wherein the offence of kidnapping an unoffending inhabitant of a foreign country; of chaining him down for a series of days, weeks, and months, amidst the

dying and the dead, to the pestilential hold of a slaveship; of consigning him, if he chance to live out the voyage, to perpetual slavery in a remote and unknown land, differs in malignity from piracy, or why milder punishment should follow then on the other crime (U.S. Congress, *Annals of Congress* [1820], p. 2209).

Yet with the close of the Atlantic slave trade came the rise of the interstate slave trade. Though Deep South regions of the United States (abundant in land and short on laborers) could no longer import the enslaved from Africa, there were plenty to be brought in from the northern regions of the United States. At the close of the eighteenth century and early nineteenth century Northern states moved to gradually abolish slavery. In the process they set time limits and age thresholds for persons to be freed. However, such rules only went into effect for the enslaved if they remained in the North. Owners not wishing to take a financial loss sold their slaves South in what became known as the interstate slave trade.

The enslaved across the North and the upper regions of the South were "sold down the river" and sent into the Deeper South regions of South Carolina, Georgia, Alabama, and Mississippi where slavery and the lash were applied with greater force. In addition to being sent into a harsher world of slavery, among the enslaved the trade displaced marriages and separated children from their parents. As the former slave and famed lecturer Frederick Douglass once observed referring to the often bar room deals, "many a child has been snatched from the arms of its mother by bargains arranged in a state of total drunkenness" (Douglass 1945, p. 46).

During a visit into the South, William H. Seward, the antislavery politician from New York and eventual secretary of state in the Lincoln administration, and his wife came across an old blind enslaved woman turning the wheel of a machine. She was unaware if she had a husband since he had long been sold away. When asked if she had any children she replied, "I don't know mistress; I had children, but they were sold" and had "never herd from any of them since" (Seward 1916, p. 15).

While the interstate slave trade flourished, most slaveholders recognized the cruelties of the trade. As Abraham Lincoln observed speaking to the South, "you have amongst you, a sneaking individual, of the class of native tyrants known as the 'SLAVE-DEALER.'" If these slaveholders "cannot help it, you sell to him; but if you can help it, you drive him from your door. You despise him utterly. You do not recognize him as a friend, or even as an honest man" (Lincoln 2001, p. 302). Lincoln used this observation to demonstrate to Southerners that they recognized the humanity of the enslaved, and understood them to be more than mere property.

THE CONVERSION OF A BRITISH SLAVE TRADER

Amazing grace! (how sweet the sound)
That saved a wretch like me!
I once was lost, but now am found,
Was blind, but now I see.
Born in 1725, John Newton spent the early part of his life on the sea with his father. His life on the sea eventually led to his own enslavement in Africa. After his release, Newton became involved in the slave trade and worked his way up to shipmaster of several slave ships. During his time on the sea, Newton both witnessed and participated in the most brutal and inhumane aspects of slavery. It was also during this time that he began his own religious awakening. Newton eventually quit the slave trading business and by 1764 became an Anglican priest.

During his years as a priest Newton grew in repentance for his life as a slave trader. Soon he joined forces with William Wilberforce and other abolitionists in Great Britain to put an end to the slave trade. In 1779 Newton wrote and published his famous hymn *Amazing Grace*, cataloging his conversion from a life of sin to devotion for God and love. The song quickly gained international renown as the anthem for the antislavery movement.

SOURCE: Turner, Steve. *Amazing Grace: The Story of America's Most Beloved Song*. New York: Harper Perennial, 2003.

Yet as antislavery sentiment seemed poised to make Americans reach the logical conclusion that opposition to the slave trade meant an inherent opposition to slavery itself, proponents of the institution disagreed. They instead sought to not only strengthen the interstate slave trade, but also to reopen the Atlantic slave trade. While politicians on both sides of the Mason-Dixon near unanimously opposed reopening the Atlantic slave trade from its close in 1808 until the early 1850s, a younger generation of proslavery zealots took up the cause to reopen. In 1853, Leonidas Spratt, a young newspaper editor of the *Charleston Standard*, became one of the first important figures to argue in favor of reopening the Atlantic slave trade. By 1856 the governor of South Carolina, James Adams, expressed his backing for reopening the trade as support for the issue grew. However, opposition resoundingly remained strong. In reaction to its growing popularity, the United States House of Representatives voted 183 to 8 on a resolution declaring the Atlantic slave trade to be "inexpedient, unwise, and contrary to settled policy of the United States." An earlier resolution passed by the same body calling the Atlantic slave trade "shocking to the moral sentiment" passed by a vote of 152 to 57 (Fehrenbacher 2001, p. 181).

The closest reopening of the Atlantic slave trade came to being policy, occurred in Louisiana in 1858. Through use of a clever loophole to get around federal law, a bill was introduced which would allow "voluntary" African "apprentices" to be imported into the state. These persons would labor in their condition for fifteen years, after which they "might" return to Africa. In reality the bill was a ruse to import slaves. The bill quickly passed the Louisiana House and tentatively passed the Louisiana Senate by one vote. However, one state senator, upon reflection, switched his vote causing the bill to go down in defeat.

Though reopening of the Atlantic slave trade grew in popularity during the turbulent political crisis over slavery, support for reintroducing the practice remained small. At the outbreak of secession and Civil War in 1861, even the Confederate government, whose "cornerstone" was said to have rested on the institution of slavery, outlawed the Atlantic slave trade within its own constitution. During the Civil War, under an antislavery Republican Congress for the first time, the United States federal government and Lincoln administration established a treaty with Great Britain to strengthen the suppression of the Atlantic slave trade. Further, during the Lincoln administration, Nathaniel Gordon became the first American slave trader to be convicted and hanged by the federal government for engaging in the notorious trade.

Yet, as the enforcement mechanisms against the illegal Atlantic slave trade began to tighten, the institution of slavery in the United States began to unravel. With Abraham Lincoln's Emancipation Proclamation in 1863 and the Thirteenth Amendment in 1865 forever outlawing slavery in the United States, the prospects of reopening the slave trade in America were forever put to rest.

BIBLIOGRAPHY

Douglass, Frederick. *Frederick Douglass: Selections from Writings,* ed. Philip S. Foner. New York: International Publishers, 1945.

Farrand, Max, ed. *The Records of the Federal Convention of 1787,* vol. 2. New Haven, CT: Yale University Press, 1966.

Fehrenbacher, Don E. *The Slaveholding Republic: An Account of the United States Government's Relations to Slavery.* Ed. Ward M. McAfee. New York: Oxford University Press, 2001.

Foot, Jesse. *A Defence of the Planters in the West Indies.* London, 1792.

Jefferson, Thomas. *The Papers of Thomas Jefferson,* ed. Julian Boyd. Princeton, NJ: Princeton University Press, 1950.

Lincoln, Abraham. *Abraham Lincoln: His Speeches and Writings,* ed. Roy Basler. Cleveland: DeCapo Press, 2001.

Locke, John. *Two Treatises on Government,* ed. C. B. Macpherson. Indianapolis: Hackett Publishing, 1980.

Newton, John. *Thoughts upon the African Slave Trade.* London: 1788.

Seward, Frederick. *Reminiscences of a War-Time Statesman and Diplomat.* New York: Nickerbocker Press, 1916.

U.S. Congress. *Annals of Congress.* 9th Cong., 2nd sess., 1806.

U.S. Congress. *Annals of Congress.* 16th Congress, 1st sess., 1820.

John J. Wickre

AUCTIONS AND MARKETS

The average slave could expect to be sold at least once in his or her lifetime, and many experienced the wrenching dislocation caused by a sale several times over. In the early days of the importation of slaves from Africa, slaves were sold in numerous ways. Even before the slaves disembarked the ship, they might be sold by the "scramble." Buyers would agree to a set price for different categories of slaves—young males, adult women, children, for example. Then the buyers would be allowed to scramble onboard the ship and collect as many slaves of each category as they wished to purchase. On a smaller scale, a few slaves at a time might be sold in auctions in taverns or other public buildings. Sometimes they were sold "by inch of candle," meaning that bids would be accepted while a candle burned one inch. Dealers in slaves, often called soul drivers, bought slaves in the port towns and took them into the interior to sell to landowners who could not visit the ports regularly.

As slavery expanded in the colonial and early national period, a large-scale internal slave trade developed as slaves were sold from place to place within the country. Congress ended the importation of slaves from overseas in 1807. Slave owners generally did not oppose this strenuously, because it meant that the value of slaves already in the United States would increase. By the early nineteenth century, tobacco cultivation had exhausted the soil in many places in the Upper South, and slavery was becoming economically less viable in these regions. Slave owners in this region often moved to new lands in Alabama, Mississippi, Louisiana, or Texas. If they did not move themselves, they often sold their slaves to dealers who resold them in these newer regions. Historian Peter Kolchin estimates that between 1790 and 1860, approximately one million slaves were relocated through this internal migration (2003, p. 96). Historian Michael Tadman estimates that sales made up 60 percent to 70 percent of the internal migration of slaves, with the balance going West or South with their masters. Tadman suggests that a slave child living in the upper South in 1820 had about a 30 percent chance of being sold South by 1860 (1989, p. 45).

A slave auction. An 1861 engraving of a slave auction. Nearly every major southern city had numerous brokers and auction houses where slaves were sold. The facilities for these businesses were simple and would include a storefront building to house a showroom or large hall where the slaves could be exhibited for sale, and a smaller office where the payments could be made and the paperwork could be handled. *Archive Photos, Inc./Getty Images.*

It is clear that slave owners recognized the profit potential in marketing slaves to newly developing areas where strong demand would bring good prices. Did masters in the Upper South slave states actually breed slaves for the market? While it appears that this was not as common as once believed, there is clearly evidence that it did happen. Even if they were not approaching slave breeding as a business operation, sellers and buyers both paid keen attention to the potential of young slave women to bear children. Historian Frederic Bancroft noted, "A girl of seventeen years that had borne two children was called a 'rattlin' good breeder' and commanded an extraordinary price" (1959, p. 82). Young women with children also sold well. If one or more of the children appeared to be part white, however, this depressed the price—there was a reluctance to deal in slaves that appeared to be part white. The exception to this was the trade in what were often called *fancy girls*— attractive young women that a master might desire for his own sexual use, or who might earn great profits as a prostitute. Light-skinned women brought a high price in this market, and there was brisk trade in such women throughout the South.

Individual slaves or small lots of slaves might be sold privately, either to traveling dealers or through the agency of a broker who matched buyers' needs with available slaves for sale. Nearly every major southern city had numerous brokers and auction houses where slaves were sold. The facilities for these businesses were simple and would include a storefront building to house a showroom or large hall where the slaves could be exhibited for sale, and a smaller office where the payments could be made and the paperwork could be handled. Behind this building would be the yards and pens where the slaves were held while awaiting sale. These were often called slave jails. Because the slaves normally would not inhabit these jails for long, the conditions were often bleak. Some southern cities had ordinances requiring that these jails be kept out of public view.

In the room where the auctions were conducted, there were rough benches for the slaves waiting to be sold, chairs at the opposite end of the room for the buyers, a platform or podium for the auctioneer, and the auction block where an individual slave or a small lot of slaves might stand while the bidding was conducted. Slaves might be told to move about, to demonstrate

INTERVIEWING SLAVES AT THE AUCTION

It might seem that it would not be necessary to interview people that were going to be forced to work. But masters wanted to avoid potential problems whenever possible. Talking to a slave before making a purchase allowed the master to gauge the slave's intelligence and perhaps to assess how difficult it might be to get this person to cooperate. In addition, a buyer might be looking for a slave to perform a certain task and asking about skills and experience might be important. For a domestic servant such as a cook or nanny, who would be around the master's family almost continuously, it was important to find someone with an acceptable personality and demeanor. Slaves tried to direct these interviews toward the outcome they felt was best for them—to avoid a feared master or to promise cooperation with a person who seemed to be a potentially good owner.

SOURCE: Johnson, Walter. *Soul by Soul: Life Inside the Antebellum Slave Market.* Cambridge: Harvard University Press, 1999.

their agility and health; sometimes they were forced to dance.

Whether at auctions or at private sales, buyers were given the opportunity to make a thorough inspection of the slaves. The sellers would try to have the slaves in the most presentable condition, they were often clad in new clothing so they would look good for the sale. Skin might be oiled to give the slave a more healthful appearance. Gray hairs might be plucked from the heads of older slaves, or hair dyed—although this was illegal in many localities. Most states had strict regulations that were designed to protect the buyer, to make sure that the age or health of the slaves were not misrepresented by the dealers.

Physical examination included looking for obvious signs of disease or infirmity, and looking for signs of punishment, such as welts from whipping. This might signal a slave that was hard to control and who should not be purchased. For slaves that were expected to be put to strenuous labor, muscles were examined. Buyers also checked the slave's teeth, because good teeth were thought to be indicative of overall health.

Neither buyer nor seller shied away from intimate inspection of female slaves. A woman's breasts and pelvic area were often examined in an attempt to determine her child-bearing potential. A separate room or screened-off area was often provided for these inspections.

After the early colonial period, most slaves knew at least some English, and buyers would often spend some time talking to potential purchases. They might ask about particular skills or the ability to work hard, but they were also looking for any sign that the slave might be troublesome and hard to control. Slaves responded to these interrogations as they deemed best. If a potential buyer

was thought to be a cruel master, or would be taking the slave far from home, the slave might attempt to derail the sale. Historian Leslie Owens refers to a traveler who heard a slave tell a potential buyer, "You may buy me, but I will never work for you" (1976, p. 188). Conversely, if the potential master seemed acceptable, the slave might try to ingratiate himself or herself to the customer.

Although slavery could hardly have existed without them, slave dealers or traders were often seen as disreputable by other southern whites, even by slaveholders. Although the slave trade could be highly lucrative, traders were seen as uncouth, low-class people. Slave owners often expressed concern about having to sell slaves, especially when it might entail separating families or sending away a loyal slave who had served the master's family for a long time. In personal letters and diaries, masters often tried to shift the blame, claiming that they had no choice, that circumstances beyond their control demanded the sale.

The sale of slaves had a fearsome impact on slave families and individuals. The fear of being sold away from their families and the only world they knew haunted many slaves. Masters knew this and would use the threat of sale to try to elicit cooperation from their slaves. Many slaves ran away when they believed they were about to be sold. There were isolated cases of slaves committing suicide and parents killing their own children to avoid enduring the separation that a sale might entail. Besides the impact on family ties, being "sold South" or "sold down the river" meant going from a situation in the Upper South to a place in the Deep South or Southwest where the climate and labor conditions might be much less favorable. Slaves already in these areas where labor was in great demand faced less chance of being sold, as did elderly slaves who were difficult to market. Understandably, the memories of separations from loved ones lingered long after freedom came. Nearly seventy-five years after being freed, Anna Harris told interviewers that she had never let a white person enter her home, explaining "Dey sole my sister Kate. I saw it wid these here eyes. Sole her in 1860 and I ain't seed nor heard of her since. Folks say white folks is all right dese days. Maybe dey is. But I can't stand to see 'em. Not on my place" (Kolchin 2003, p. 127).

BIBLIOGRAPHY

Bancroft, Frederic. *Slave Trading in the Old South* [1931]. New York: Ungar, 1959.

Baptist, Edward E. "'Cuffy,' 'Fancy Maids,' and 'One-Eyed Men': Rape, Commodification, and the Domestic Slave Trade in the United States." *American Historical Review* 106, no. 5 (December 2001): 1619–1650.

Fogel, Robert W., and Stanley L. Engerman. *Time on the Cross: The Economics of American Negro Slavery*, 2 vols. Boston: Little, Brown, 1974.

Gudmestad, Robert H. *A Troublesome Commerce: The Transformation of the Interstate Slave Trade.* Baton Rouge: Louisiana State University Press, 2003.

Johnson, Walter. *Soul by Soul: Life Inside the Antebellum Slave Market.* Cambridge, MA: Harvard University Press, 1999.

Kolchin, Peter. *American Slavery, 1619–1877.* Rev. ed. New York: Hill and Wang, 2003.

Owens, Leslie Howard. *This Species of Property: Slave Life and Culture in the Old South.* New York: Oxford University Press, 1976.

Tadman, Michael. *Speculators and Slaves: Masters, Traders, and Slaves in the Old South.* Madison: University of Wisconsin Press, 1989.

Mark S. Joy

SLAVE RENTING

Slave trading produced an ancillary institution called *slave renting*, or *slave hiring*. As slave traders transported slaves and distributed them throughout the South, some whites developed a need for short-term slave labor, but did not wish to own slaves, in some cases because they wanted to avoid the stigma of slave ownership. Other whites who could not afford to own slaves did the next best thing—they rented slaves, especially during the harvest season to clear land for cultivation. Some slave owners rented out or hired out their slaves when the cycle of crop production did not demand their intensive labor. Thus, while slave owners and slave renters had various reasons for engaging in the practice, most either wanted to maximize their ownership of slaves or needed slaves on a temporary basis.

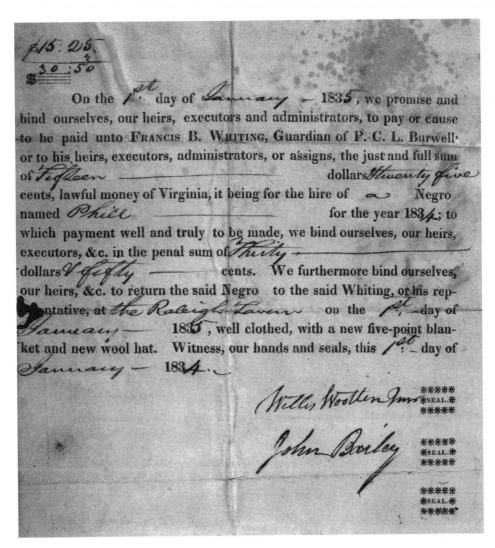

Receipt for the hire of a slave. A receipt for the hire of a Virginia slave named Phill in 1834. Phill was hired out for $15.25. Prices might go up to $600 for a year-long rental of a slave. *Michael Graham-Stewart/ Bridgeman Art Library.*

The process of slave hiring or slave renting began during the early 1700s as an informal practice based on verbal agreements between slave owners and renters. Later, the practice expanded and became more formal, and written agreements became necessary. Owners and renters signed contracts obligating a single slave or group of slaves to perform work for a specific time period—from a few months to a year—and for an agreed-upon amount of money. Some owners advertised in newspapers the availability of slaves for rent or hire, with prices ranging from $100 per year for an agricultural worker, to as much as $600 per year for a skilled slave. Slaves who were blacksmiths, carpenters, and brick masons typically demanded the highest prices.

By 1800 the business of slave hiring had become even more specialized, with agents drawing up contracts between parties. Moreover, newspapers carried even more advertisements, and there was less of a stigma attached to renting a slave. Owners generally profited from this practice, and renters had the labor of unskilled or skilled slaves without the costs of permanent ownership; the expense of slave ownership and prices for slaves rose between 1820 and 1850 in most regions.

Charleston, South Carolina, more than any other city, became the capital for slave hiring or renting. By 1800 Charleston was home to nearly 10,000 slaves, and about 20 percent were hired out during that year. Most were skilled slaves, including tailors, barbers, cooks, brick masons, butlers, maids, carpenters, and blacksmiths. The city's newspaper printed notices offering the services of skilled slaves for hire by the month or the year. The practice of slave hiring became so common that some whites were fearful of the freedom so many slaves had to walk about the city, and in 1845 the South Carolina General Assembly passed a law making it illegal to rent or hire slaves. Few masters or renters adhered to the legislation, and renting and hiring continued unabated in and around Charleston. In some instances, masters allowed slaves to hire themselves out; this practice permitted some slaves to save enough money to purchase their freedom. Slave-hiring in Charleston became so complex that many slaves wore a badge around their necks with a number indicating their particular skill or craft. The Charleston city council taxed those badges, masters still received money for renting out their slaves, renters had laborers or skilled slaves for extended periods of time, and some slaves earned money in this elaborate process.

In the decade before the Civil War there were an estimated 400,000 urban slaves in the United States. Most were in the cities of Charleston, Richmond, Washington, DC, Baltimore, and New Orleans. About 5 percent were hired or rented. In addition to the skilled slaves hired out in urban areas, slave masters rented out their agricultural slaves after harvests and before the next planting seasons. As the cotton belt extended across the Mississippi River after 1800, many whites in need of additional laborers hired more slaves to clear the land in preparation for planting cotton.

For masters, hiring or renting out their slaves brought additional income; for slaves with skills, especially those who rented themselves out, the process could lead to freedom. Even when masters took a good portion of their money, good carpenters, brick masons, and blacksmiths could, over a period of time, earn enough to buy their freedom. In one such example, William Ellison, born into slavery near Sumter, South Carolina, became a master cotton-gin maker. After working on Sundays for several years, he acquired enough money to purchase his freedom, and then, over the course of more than twenty years (1822–1845), the freedom of his wife and his children. On the eve of the Civil War, Ellison owned more slaves than most white slave holders in South Carolina. His success as a master craftsman led to both social freedom and economic success.

Slave hiring was a complex business within the system of slavery. It was driven by the demand for slaves and relieved renters of the stigma attached to slave ownership. It also helped people who could not afford the outright ownership of slaves. Skilled and resourceful slaves could use slave renting as a means of acquiring freedom. What began as a practice for a few had become a lucrative business for many by the eve of the Civil War.

BIBLIOGRAPHY

Davis, David Brion. *Inhuman Bondage: The Rise and Fall of Slavery in the New World.* Oxford, U.K.: Oxford University Press, 2006.

Franklin, John, and Alfred Moss. *From Slavery to Freedom: A History of African Americans.* 8th ed. New York: McGraw-Hill, 2000.

Greene, Harlan; Harry S. Hutchins, Jr.; and Brian E. Hutchins. *Slave Badges and the Slave-Hire System in Charleston, South Carolina, 1783–1865.* Jefferson, NC: McFarland, 2004.

Johnson, Michael P., and James L. Roark. *Black Masters: A Free Family of Color in the Old South.* New York: W. W. Norton, 1984.

Jackie R. Booker

INTERSTATE SLAVE TRADE

Trading slaves across state (or colony) lines had been common in the United States since the earliest slaves appeared in the American colonies. However, the closing of the transatlantic slave trade in the later years of the eighteenth century limited the possibilities of slave supply; therefore, southerners renewed their interest in slave trading within the United States. A slave trading system developed in the early nineteenth century to feed the demand for slaves due to westward

Gang of Slaves journeying to be Sold in a Southern Market.

A gang of slaves traveling to be sold in a Southern market. An 1842 engraving from Buckingham's *Slave States of America* showing slaves crossing a river as they journey to a Southern market. Men riding horses corral the slaves with whips. Smaller traders who could not afford ships would march slaves hundreds of miles to the south. The traders would sell slaves along the way. © *Corbis.*

expansion. White settlers moving west into Kentucky, Tennessee, Alabama, and Mississippi demanded new slaves to tame this new frontier territory they found themselves in. Slaves could clear fields, build roads, and help transform the landscape to a more hospitable and productive enterprise.

Slave demand by white settlers in the western United States coupled with the excess supply of slaves in the Upper South in the late eighteenth and early nineteenth centuries led to a very profitable slave-trading system. Among the Upper South states, Virginia especially transformed itself from a slave-dominated tobacco plantation society into a more diverse agricultural state, growing not only tobacco but food crops as well. The transformation of the Virginia economy led to a surplus of slave labor, because the new agricultural commodities did not need the same attention from labor as tobacco did. Many white Virginians saw this growing surplus of

slaves as dangerous to Virginia society because a surplus of slaves always held the possibility of revolt. Therefore Virginians saw the interstate slave trade as a way to eliminate this burdensome element from their society. At the same time, Virginians recognized the interstate slave trade could be a vehicle for economic gain. Selling slaves farther south could bring Virginians massive profits. As Charles Pinckney of South Carolina correctly identified, Virginia "will gain by stopping the importations (the transatlantic slave trade). Her slaves will rise in value and she has more than she wants" (Farrand 1911, p. 369).

Although the interstate slave trade became more common after the closing of the transatlantic trade, Eli Whitney's cotton gin and the cotton revolution in the South remained the real impetus for propelling the interstate trade in slaves. Whereas western demand had been significant in beginning the interstate trade in slaves the

SLAVE BREEDING IN THE UPPER SOUTH: A MYTH?

During the nineteenth century, abolitionists claimed that Virginians engaged in slave breeding to provide slaves to sell to the Lower South. Edmund Ruffin, the prominent pro-slave farmer and future supporter of the Confederacy, argued, "It is an old calumny, often repeated in these older Southern States for sale, and that the surplus individuals were annually selected for market, precisely in the same manner as a grazier selects his beasts for sale" (p. 655).

Ruffin claimed the abolitionists' criticisms were false and indeed most historians agree that systematic slave breeding operations most likely did not occur in the Upper South. However, the idea of slave breeding in Virginia permeated abolitionist critiques and popular nineteenth-century literature as an example of the evils of slavery. Although slave breeding probably did not take place, the power of a female slave's reproduction continued to attract slaveholders because of the opportunity to sell slave children into the interstate trade.

SOURCE: Ruffin, Edmund. "The Effects of the High Prices of Slaves." *Debow's Review* (1859).

late eighteenth century, the cotton revolution in the Old Southwest (Alabama, Mississippi, and Louisiana) caused demand for new slaves to skyrocket. The need for new labor sources to grow cotton and feed the ever-growing market revolution that enthralled the entire United States made the interstate slave trade a part of everyday slave life in the South. The cotton boom in the South linked the price of cotton with the price of slaves and tied the two together for the next fifty years.

Although Virginia was the largest supplier of slaves in the interstate slave trade, Maryland, Delaware, and Kentucky also supplied many slaves who traveled farther south in the trade. In these states, the edges of the southern slave society, slavery gradually became less economically important (due to the lack of cotton), and it became more profitable to sell a slave to Mississippi than to keep him in Virginia. After the cotton boom, a slave in the Upper South had approximately a one in three chance of being sold into the interstate slave trade. Most of those sold were male slaves between the ages of fifteen and twenty-five. The trade also broke up about 20 percent of marriages in the Upper South, leading to women taking an ever-increasing role in family leadership in the aftermath. The effect on marriage and the family led Frederick Douglass to exclaim that the domestic trade "was the most cruel feature of the system" of slavery and the foremost example of the "revolting barbarity and shameless hypocrisy" that Americans allowed to exist (Douglass 1845; 1852).

The interstate slave trade broke up entire communities as well as individual families. The slave community stood as an important feature in slave life because in order

to ameliorate their condition of servitude, slaves formed communities with each other that helped them survive the toughest and harshest punishments, as well as organize hope for freedom. Religion joined slaves together with a message of hope and frequently helped them organize resistance activities against the institution. The community offered slaves an alternative vision of life, one not polluted by death, degradation, and hopelessness. The interstate slave trade broke community apart and forced slaves across the country into new social settings unfamiliar to them. While slaves eventually did join new communities in the Lower South, breaking up and reforming community structure represented a major change in slaves' lives.

Slaves traveled south by two methods: land or sea. Larger slave-trading companies owned ships that, like those that carried slaves from Africa, transported slaves from ports in the Upper South to the Lower South on the Atlantic and on inland rivers. So important was the use of water to slave transport that in 1830 a newspaper in New Orleans claimed that the Mississippi was becoming a common highway for the traffic of slaves (Deyle 2005). Smaller traders opted for the less expensive option of moving slaves overland. Marching slaves the hundreds of miles from Richmond, one of the major supply centers, to the Lower South enabled traders to sell slaves the entire length of the journey to points along the trail to their final destination. As railroads became more widespread in the South, traders also transported their slaves via railcar to the Lower South. Whether by ship or by land, slave traders made New Orleans and Natchez, Mississippi, the two end points of the interstate slave trade.

Once at their final destinations, slaves were sold by one of two means: public auction or private sale. Public auctions were more visible in southern society and indeed more memorable for their sinister connotations. Abolitionists particularly targeted the slave auction as representative of the evils of slavery in the South. William Lloyd Garrison noted, "We know that their bodies and spirits are daily sold under the hammer of the auctioneer as household works or working cattle; we need no nice adjustment of abstractions, no metaphysical reasoning, to convince us that such scenes are dreadful and such practices impious" (Garrison 1852, p. 322).

Although auctions remained common in the South, the majority of slaves transported in the interstate trade were sold by private sale. Slave traders ran holding pens where they could store slaves and where potential buyers could examine them. Traders separated slaves by gender and physical characteristics, highlighting their favorable qualities for buyers while attempting to hide those that would lower their price. Essentially, the buying process illustrated that slaves were a commodity to be merchandized as well as to be bought and sold.

The interstate slave trade benefited both the Upper South, which reaped large profits from the sale of its slaves, and the Lower South, which gained profits from the use of those slaves on its cotton plantations. However, while economically profitable, the interstate slave trade attacked southern justifications of slavery. After northern abolition groups reenergized themselves after 1830, the South defended slavery as "a positive good," showing the country that slavery's paternalistic elements actually helped African Americans instead of hurting them. At the heart of the paternalism of slavery rested the idea that a slave belonged to the master's family and that a master would take care of them for their entire lives, guiding them as a father would guide his children. Reducing the slave to an economic commodity as the interstate slave trade did attacked the foundation of the paternalistic system and challenged southerners to rethink how to defend slavery and the interstate slave trade. Southern slaveholders divorced themselves from the interstate slave trade by creating the image of the villainous slave trader, who was fundamentally different than themselves. By reviling the trader, they washed their hands of any responsibility for the non-paternalistic attributes of the trade.

The interstate slave trade allowed the Lower South an almost unlimited supply of slaves in order to expand their economic operations, especially the cultivation of cotton. The trade funneled so much southern money into slavery that slaves became the key indicator of wealth and power in southern society. With so much of their capital invested in slavery, the South had little choice but to secede from the Union and fight the Civil War in order to defend the system that dominated their lives.

BIBLIOGRAPHY

Deyle, Steven. *Carry Me Back: The Domestic Slave Trade in American Life*. New York: Oxford University Press, 2005.

Douglass, Frederick. "I Am Here to Spread Light on American Slavery." Address delivered in Cork, Ireland, October 14, 1845. *The Frederick Douglass Speeches, 1841–1846*. Available from http://www.yale.edu/glc/archive/1014.htm.

Douglass, Frederick. "The Hypocrisy of American Slavery." Speech given in Rochester, New York, July 4, 1852.

Farrand, Max, ed. *The Records of the Federal Convention of 1787*. New Haven, CT: Yale University Press, 1911.

Garrison, William Lloyd. *Selections from the Writings and Speeches of William Lloyd Garrison*. Boston: R.F. Wallcut, 1852.

Johnson, Walter. *Soul By Soul: Life Inside the Antebellum Slave Market*. Cambridge, MA: Harvard University Press, 1999.

Tadman, Michael. *Speculators and Slaves: Masters, Traders, and Slaves in the Old South*. Madison: University of Wisconsin Press, 1989.

James J. Gigantino II

MONETARY VALUE OF SLAVES

The entire Southern economy before the Civil War was based on the labor and value of enslaved people of African descent. People of African descent were treated like chattel, property that could be bought and sold like livestock and other commodities that slave owners valued. However, some American jurisdictions such as Virginia classified slaves as real estate instead of chattel. According to a 1705 Virginia statute, "[a]ll Negro, mulatto, and Indian slaves within this dominion shall be held as real estate and not chattel and shall descend unto heirs and widows according to the custom of land

A FORMER SLAVE'S ACCOUNT OF A SLAVE AUCTION IN VIRGINIA

James Martin was a former slave who was born in Virginia in 1847. In an interview from 1937, Martin recounted a Virginia slave auction:

> The slaves are put in stalls like the pens they use for cattle—a man and his wife with a child on each arm. And there's a curtain, sometimes just a sheet over the front of the stall, so the bidders can't see the "stock" too soon ... Then, they pulls up the curtain, and the bidders is crowdin' around. Them in back can't see, so the overseer drives the slaves out to the platform, and he tells the ages of the slaves and what they can do ... and one of the bidders takes a pair of gloves and rubs his fingers over a man's teeth, and he says to the overseer, "You call this buck twenty years old? Why there's cut worms in his teeth. He's forty years old, if he's a day." So they knock this buck down for a thousand dollars. They calls the men "bucks" and the women "wenches"... At these slave auctions, the overseer yells, "Say, you bucks and wenches, get in your hole. Come out here." Then, he makes 'em hop, he makes 'em trot, he makes 'em jump. "How much," he yells, "for this buck? A thousand? Eleven hundred? Twelve hundred dollars?" Then the bidders makes offers accordin' to size and build. (Rawick 1972–1979, vol. 5, pp. 62–65)

SOURCE: Rawick, George P., ed. *The American Slave: A Composite Autobiography*, 19 vols. Westport, CT: Greenwood Press, 1972–1979.

RECEIPT.

RECEIVED of *Geo N Sims* of *Jefferson* county, one slave named *Thomas*, aged *22*, color *Black*, height *5 ft 5"* Weight *150* appraised at *forty five hundred* dollars, impressed this *9* day of *February*, A. D. 186*5*, under the act of Congress, approved February 17, 1864, "To increase the efficiency of the army by the enrollment of Free Negroes and Slaves in certain capacities," and to be employed for the purposes therein specified, and who is to be returned at the expiration of twelve months from the date of impressment at *Monticello*

J. P. Sanderson Impressing Agent.

CERTIFICATE OF APPRAISEMENT.

WE, the undersigned, chosen by *J. P. Sanderson* agent on the one part, and by *D. G. Huge agt* on the other part, first being duly sworn, do this *9* day of *February*, 186*5*, appraise and value the slave described in the foregoing receipt at *forty five hundred* dollars. *& Clothing $20*

Total $ 4520

Witness our hands and seals.

The above appraisement is ⎫

appd ⎬
P. Sanderson ⎭
Imp Agt

Geo W Taylor [L. S.]
E A Willie [L. S.]

_____ Umpire.

SURGEONS' CERTIFICATE.

The Board of Surgeons for the examination of Conscripts for the *Second* Congressional District do hereby certify that we have carefully examined the slave named in the foregoing receipt and find him sound, able-bodied and fit for the required service.

February 9 186*5*

Elihu Foland ⎫
⎬ Surgeons.
⎭

A receipt for a slave during the civil war. A receipt and appraisal certificate from 1865 for a 22-year-old male slave named Thomas. The value of slaves varied, depending on sex, age, skills and physical characteristics. Adult males such as Thomas were the most valuable because they could perform the greatest amount of hard labor. Thomas sold for $4500, plus $20 in clothing costs. © *Bettman/Corbis* inheritance" (Higginbotham, Jr. 1980, p. 52). However, the children of slaves were categorized as chattel and were "considered no otherwise than Horses and Cattle" (p. 53).

According to a former slave, J. W. C. Pennington, "[t]he being of slavery, its soul and its body, lives and moves in the chattel principle, the property principle, the bill of sale principle: the cart-whip, starvation, and nakedness are its inevitable consequences" (Johnson 1999, p. 218). African slaves endured this harsh treatment from the inception of the slave trade in the American colonies in 1619 until the total abolition of slavery in the United States in 1865. Slave owners treated their black slaves like animals, buying and selling these human beings as though they were horses or cows. Fountain Hughes, who was a 101-year-old ex-slave from Charlottesville, Virginia, when he was interviewed in 1949, recalled how the slave owners treated their slaves like livestock. "It was what they call, we were slaves. We belonged to people. They'd sell us like they sell horses an' cows an' hogs an' all like that. Have an auction bench, an' they'd put on, up on the bench an' bid on you jus' same as you bidding on cattle you know." Hughes also stated that "[t]he'd have a regular, have a sale every month, you know, at the court house. An' they they'd sell you, an' get two hundred dollar, hundred dollar, five hundred dollar." (Bailey 1991, pp. 29-37)

During the 250-year period when slavery was legal in the American colonies and the United States, slaves were very valuable to the slave traders and slave owners who bought and sold them as a source of labor. The value of individual slaves varied depending on the sex, age, skills, and physical characteristics of individual slaves. Adult males were the most valuable slaves because they could do the greatest amount of hard labor under the most intense conditions. Adult females were almost as valuable as adult males. Because infants and small children could not work like full-grown, healthy male and female slaves, they did not have much monetary value and were often sold away from their families. For example, when an Arkansan slaveholder, James Milton, first arrived in that state in 1842, he owned only one slave between the ages of eight and sixty, the ages for which the state of Arkansas taxed slave owners for their human property. In 1850 Milton owned nine working slaves valued at $3,200 for taxation purposes and three slave children who were under the age of eight and were not old enough to work (Gillmer 2007, pp. 508–509).

Just as their farm animals were characterized by color and appearance, slaveholders classified their slaves of African descent by skin color from jet black to almost white. Slave traders and slave owners invented terms like mulatto, quadroon, and octoroon to describe the percentage of white parentage of a particular slave. Slaves with the greatest percentage of white blood tended to have a greater monetary value than slaves with a greater percentage of African ancestry, but other factors were important in determining the monetary value of a particular slave. The price of each slave was largely dependent upon the actual market at the time that a slaveholder sold a slave and whether the owner had to sell a slave when money was needed for the slave owner's family or business because of financial difficulties of settlement of a descedent's estate.

The value of each slave increased after the U.S. Congress banned the importation of slaves to the United States in 1807. Because of the laws of supply and demand, as the demand for African slaves as sources of labor increased with the expansion of United States the importation ban severely reduced the supply of new slaves from Africa. Black slaves were important to the expansion of the United States westward because they were the primary labor source of landowners. The market value of able-bodied slaves who were already in the United States and its territories increased because importation of slaves was illegal and the only other way for a slaveholder to obtain more slaves was to buy them from another slave owner or to actively breed new slaves. For slaveholders who actively bred their slaves, it was very profitable. One Virginia slave owner claimed that his slave women were "uncommonly good breeders" and gave birth very quickly—"every one of them ... was worth two hundred dollars ... the moment it drew breath," and were very valuable to the slaveholders (Franklin 2004, p. 132).

Slave owners bought, sold, and raised slaves of African descent like farm animals, considering them to be instruments of profit and labor. These slaveholders placed a specific value on them as human property, until the abolition of slavery in the United States at the end of the Civil War.

BIBLIOGRAPHY

Bailey, Guy; Natalie Maynor; and Patricia Cukor-Avila; eds. *The Emergence of Black English: Text and Commentary* (Creole Language Library, vol. 8). Philadelphia: John Benjamins Publishing, 1991, 29-37.

Born in Slavery: Slave Narratives from the Federal Writers' Project, 1936–1938. Online collection of the Manuscript and Prints and Photographs Divisions of the Library of Congress. Available from http://memory.loc.gov/ammem/snhtml/snhome.html.

Franklin, John Hope; and Alfred A. Moss, Jr. *From Slavery to Freedom: A History of African Americans.* 2 vols. New York: Random House, 2004.

Gillmer, Jason A. "Poor Whites, Benevolent Masters, and the Ideologies of Slavery: The Local Trial of a Slave Accused of Rape." *North Carolina Law Review* 489 (January 2007): 508–509.

Higginbotham, Jr., A. Leon. *In the Matter of Color, Race and the American Legal Process: The Colonial Period.* New York: Oxford University Press, 1980.

Johnson, Walter. *Soul by Soul: Life Inside the Antebellum Slave Market.* Cambridge, MA: Harvard University Press, 1999.

Jocelyn M. Cuffee

BREEDING

Reproduction for slaves was not a practice marked by love or marriage but rather a function of their status as property. Their reproductive rights belonged to their owners, many of whom viewed breeding as a profitable business venture. Animal imagery abounded: the strongest males were referred to as "bucks" or "thoroughbreds" and put out "to stud." Females were judged in much the same manner, their worth determined by either their skills as a cook and personal servant or their breeding potential. The hardier the stock, the higher the price for the breeding males and females, as well as for their offspring on the auction block. Healthy males sold for from $900 to $2000 each, with females of reproductive age (with thirteen to twenty being prime years) selling for as much as two thousand dollars.

Many slaveholders "mated" their robust males with as many females as possible to create a stable of sturdy slave labor. Physically powerful male slaves were feared and admired by white men and women, and their prowess and virility sometimes took on mythic proportions. These males were not allowed to marry or settle down and could be loaned out like a horse for stud duties. The Federal Writers' Project interviewer of the slave Charlotte Martin recounts what she told him about her owner: "Wilkerson found it very profitable to raise and sell slaves. He selected the strongest and best male and female slaves and mated them exclusively for breeding" (*Born in Slavery*, vol. 3, p. 167).

Newborn slave boys were inspected for their future usefulness, as J. W. Whitfield, a slave born in New Bern, North Carolina, explained: "When a boy-child was born . . . they would reserve him for breeding purposes if he was healthy and robust. But if he was puny and sickly they were not bothered about him" (*Born in Slavery*, vol. 2, p. 139). Charlotte Martin's interviewer confirms this observation: "The huskiest babies were given the best of attention in order that they might grow into sturdy youths, for it was those who brought the highest prices at the slave markets" (*Born in Slavery*, vol. 3, p. 167).

For slave women, reproduction could be harsher still—they could be forced to breed with one or more males or raped by slaveholders. Attractive bondwomen faced the worst circumstances. If they were pretty or shapely, they were desired by men of all races and ages and often hated by the white women of the homestead, who suspected their own fathers, husbands, and brothers would chase after them. It was always perceived to be the female slave's fault, however, if she was raped—she either seduced her attacker or was unable rise above her base, animalistic nature.

According to Alice Wright, an Alabama-born slave, breeding was of utmost importance at the plantation where she lived and worked. "My father said they put medicine in the water (cisterns) to make the young slaves have more children. . . . If his old master had a good breeding woman he wouldn't sell her. He would keep her for himself" (*Born in Slavery*, vol. 2, part 7, p. 246). Indeed, slaveholders frequently kept female slaves for themselves, not only for breeding purposes but as mistresses. It was an open secret that slave owners slept with female slaves; their mixed-race children lived side by side with their white offspring—unless a slave child bore too close a resemblance to the slave owner, in which case he or she was quickly sold. However, in some cases, as Charlotte Martin explained to her interviewer, slaveholders overtly proffered their mixed-race children, believing their biological input made these children more intelligent and useful than black slaves. The interviewer reports: "Sometimes the master himself had sexual relations with his female slaves, for the products of miscegenation were very remunerative. These offspring were in demand as house servants" (*Born in Slavery*, vol. 3, p. 167).

Observers of slavery from both within the United States and beyond its borders weighed in on the issue of the breeding of slaves. George Fitzhugh, a Virginian who championed slavery, quoted approvingly an editorial from the *Edinburgh Review* extolling the excellent treatment of black slaves in the United States as opposed to poor whites in England: "No man in the South, we are sure, ever bred slaves for sale. They are always sold reluctantly, and generally from necessity, or as a punishment for misconduct" (Fitzhugh 1857, p. 236). Josiah Conder, a Briton who opposed slavery in the British West Indies, found slavery objectionable not on humanistic grounds but because of the "fecundity of the negro race." As he wrote in his antislavery tract, blacks were an unruly race incapable of controlling themselves reproductively: "Nature herself is the constant enemy of the slave-owner, threatening him continually with an inundation of his living capital, that shall destroy his profits, and ruin him with his own wealth" (Conder 1833, p. 24). In truth, slaveholders sold their property whenever they pleased, and if there ever were too many mouths to feed, a trip to the auction took care of the problem. For slave owners, the inhuman practice of breeding was in fact a profit-making venture.

BIBLIOGRAPHY

Born in Slavery: Narratives from the Federal Writers' Project, 1936–1938. Manuscript Division, Library of Congress. Arkansas Narratives, vol. 2, part 7. Available from http://memory.loc.gov/ammem/ snhtml/snhome.html.

*Born in Slavery: Narratives from the Federal Writers'
   Project, 1936–1938.* Manuscript and Prints and
   Photographs Division, Library of Congress. Florida
   Narratives, vol. 3, part 7. Available from http://
   memory.loc.gov/ammem/snhtml/snhome.html.

Conder, Josiah. *Wages or the Whip: An Essay on the
   Comparative Cost and Productiveness of Free and
   Slave Labour.* London: Hatchard, 1833.

Fitzhugh, George. *Cannibals All! or, Slaves without
   Masters.* Richmond, VA: V. Morris, 1857. (Repr.,
   ed. C. Vann Woodward, Cambridge, MA: Belknap
   Press, 1960.)

Nelson Rhodes

BUYING FREEDOM

As stated by the New England Anti-Slavery Society in
1833:

> Multitudes of [our free colored brethren] have
> risen spontaneously from the lowest depths of
> slavery, have bought their freedom by years of toil,
> have risen amidst unmeasurable reproach and
> obloquy to an eminence that has extorted the
> admiration of their oppressors." (*The Abolitionist*
> 1833, p. 124)

Slaves were often allowed to work for people other
than their owners, which allowed them to earn income,
save money, and purchase their freedom several years later.
A North Carolina slave and "fine blacksmith" named Tom
was allowed to hire his time out. He eventually bought his
freedom circa 1820 "at a price far below his worth; he was
a very valuable man" (Wilson 1912, p. 491).

Slaves not only used money earned from hiring
themselves out to purchase their own freedom, but they
often purchased the freedom of loved ones. A Washington, DC, slave named Sophia Browning, for instance,
used the proceeds of her market garden to purchase her
husband's freedom for $400. Mrs. Browning's husband
subsequently purchased her freedom. In 1818, Alethia
Tanner purchased her own freedom for $1,400. Ms.
Tanner then bought the freedom of her sister Laurena
Cook and five children in 1826.

Even when slave owners demanded prices slaves
deemed exorbitant, no price was too high for the right
of freedom. In one such case, a slave owner demanded
$500 from a slave who wished to purchase his freedom.
The slave thought the price too high, "considering he
was an elderly man." However:

> Shortly afterwards …, he came to his employer
> again, and said that although he thought his
> owner was mean to set so high a price upon him,
> he had been thinking that if he was to be an old
> man he would rather be his own master, and if he
> did not live long, his money would not be of any
> use to him at any rate, and so he had concluded he
> would make the purchase. (Olmstead 1861–1862,
> pp. 148–149)

Slaves were also purchased by friends, relatives, sympathizers and abolitionists. Harriet Jacobs, who was
ambivalent about the prospect of having her freedom
purchased, was one such slave. In her autobiography,
Jacobs said:

> I received letters from the City of Iniquity,
> addressed to me under an assumed name. In a
> few days one came from Mrs. Bruce, informing
> me that my new master was still searching for me,
> and that she intended to put an end to this persecution by buying my freedom. I felt grateful for
> the kindness that prompted this offer, but the
> idea was not so pleasant to me as might have
> been expected. The more my mind had become
> enlightened, the more difficult it was for me to
> consider myself an article of property; and to pay
> money to those who had so grievously oppressed
> me seemed like taking from my sufferings the
> glory of triumph. I wrote to Mrs. Bruce, thanking
> her, but saying that being sold from one owner to
> another seemed too much like slavery; that such a
> great obligation could not easily be cancelled; and
> that I preferred to go to my brother in California.
> (1861, p. 300)

After her freedom was purchased, Jacobs said of the
bill of sale given in exchange for payment of her:

> I well know the value of that bit of paper; but
> much as I love freedom, I do not like to look upon
> it. I am deeply grateful to the generous friend who
> procured it, but I despise the miscreant who
> demanded payment for what never rightfully
> belonged to him or his. (1861, p. 301)

Jacobs' resentment at being reduced to chattel—
even for benevolent purposes—weighed little in comparison to the relief and confidence her new-found freedom
had imbued in her. Ms. Jacobs wrote:

> I had objected to having my freedom bought, yet
> I must confess that when it was done I felt as if a
> heavy load had been lifted from my heavy shoulders. When I rode home in the cars I was no longer
> afraid to unveil my face and look at people as they
> passed. (1861, p. 301)

Many former slaves moved to other states after their
freedom was purchased, including Moses Grandy who
wrote: "I have lived in Boston ever since I bought my
freedom, except during the last year, which I have spent
at Portland, in the state of Maine" (1844, p. 32). Slaves
also moved to the African country of Liberia.

Former slaves who bought their freedom often
became quite successful. As Edward Needles stated, for
those who

> … bought their freedom with the hard-earned
> fruits of their own industry, the love of liberty
> often imparts a desire for improvement and a
> consciousness of their own worth as men, that
> invigorate all their powers and give energy and
> dignity to their character as freemen. (1849,
> pp. 7–8)

After buying his freedom, the North Carolina slave named Tom became so successful that he bought two or three slaves. Paul Cuffee was another successful former slave.

> Paul Cuffee was the youngest son of an honest and enterprising African, who was stolen from his home and sold into slavery, near New Bedford, Massachusetts. He purchased his freedom, bought a farm of one hundred acres, and married an Indian woman. Paul was really talented; and having chosen the mercantile profession, he pressed on through innumerable difficulties until he became possessed of competence, and thus able, in some degree, to indulge his benevolent affections. Some idea may be formed of his great mental capability, by the fact that he attained such a knowledge of navigation in two weeks as enabled him to command a vessel in several voyages, which he afterwards made to a number of different ports in the United States, Africa, England, Russia, and the West Indies." (Green 1858, p. 319)

According to an 1869 article in the *Cleveland Daily Herald*, another slave bought his freedom in 1851 and "working hard, early and late, soon was able to buy his wife. He has been prospering since, and he now owns the finest livery stable and back-stand in the State, and is said to be worth fifty thousand dollars" (July 8, 1869, p. 4) This slave later provided medical care and a home for his former owners when they returned to Richmond after the Civil War. Upon his former master's death, the former slave paid for his funeral, burial and tombstone, and gave his former mistress a home.

Martha Pettiford, another former slave, asked a Mr. Jeptha Dudley to purchase her from her owner and to give her permission to work and pay for herself. Dudley did buy Pettiford and gave her a passport to go where and as she pleased. Pettiford

> .... Hired herself to captains of large steamers [traveling] between Louisville and New Orleans, and served in the capacity as chambermaid on a number of those steamers for several years, always reserving a certain proportion of her wages for her owner. In due time, and long before the war, she was a free woman (*St. Louis Globe-Democrat* February 11, 1881, p. 9)

After she purchased her freedom, Pettiford worked as a wet nurse. Pettiford later married and paid $600 for a home. Pettiford lived the rest of her days in that home, and was "liberal in her donations to her children and grandchildren, laid by a certain sum for the dreaded rainy day and won the good opinion of both the white and black people of the community by her exemplary conduct." It was said of Mrs. Pettiford that "[w]hen she dies her race may refer to her history with some pride, and emulating her honesty, industry, economy and regularity of habit, say of her, 'She did not live in vain.'"

The same is equally true of the many other slaves who toiled and saved for many years to purchase what should have been free—their freedom.

BIBLIOGRAPHY

The Abolitionist, or, Record of the New-England Anti-Slavery Society. Boston: New England Anti-Slavery Society, 1833.

The Daily Cleveland Herald, July 8, 1869; pg. 4; Issue 162; col F.

Grandy, Moses. *Narrative of the Life of Moses Grandy: Formerly a Slave in the United States of America.* Boston, 1844.

Green, Frances Harriet. *Shahmah in Pursuit of Freedom, or, The Branded Hand.* New York, 1858.

Jacobs, Harriet Ann. *Incidents in the Life of a Slave Girl.* Boston, 1861.

Needles, Edward. *Ten Years Progress or, A Comparison of the State and Condition of the Colored People in the City and County of Philadelphia from 1837 to 1847.* Philadelphia, 1849.

Olmsted, Frederick Law. *The Cotton Kingdom: A Traveller's Observations On Cotton and Slavery in the American Slave States: Based Upon Three Former Volumes of Journeys and Investigations by the Same Author,* vol. 1. New York, 1861–1862.

St. Louis Globe-Democrat, "Aunt Martha" Incidents in the Life of One Who Bought Her Freedom and Piloted a Judge Through the Milky Way. February 11, 1881. pg. 9, Issue 256, col G.

Wilson, Calvin Dill. *Negroes Who Owned Slaves.* New York, 1912

Jodi M. Savage

■ Slavery and the Economy

SLAVERY AND THE ECONOMY: AN OVERVIEW

Forced labor was an essential component of the Southern economy from the time Europeans first settled the

American South in significant numbers. Seventeenth-century planters required field hands to cultivate and harvest cash crops, but had a tiny wage labor force from which to draw. Enslaving Indians to meet their labor needs proved to be an unsuccessful experiment. Indentured servants provided a temporary solution and comprised the majority of forced laborers until the 1680s, but a combination of factors led to a sea change in the labor market after that point. On both the supply side and the demand side, the market for indentured servants began to dry up. Economic conditions in England improved, and as a result fewer English laborers were willing to indenture themselves to get to America. In 1676 Bacon's Rebellion, an uprising in Virginia involving mostly indentured servants, instilled a fear of class revolt in the colonial landed gentry. Planters started looking elsewhere to meet their labor needs.

At the same time, African slaves in the American colonies experienced a dramatic rise in their fertility rate and a simultaneous drop in their mortality rate. Slave traders had brought the first African slaves to Jamestown in 1619, but for the better part of the century most planters considered slaves a risky investment. By 1700, however, African slaves were living long enough and reproducing sufficiently to attract the interest of planters, especially those wealthy enough to afford the initial cost of purchase. With indentured servants in short supply and falling out of favor, racial slavery inexorably became the dominant form of labor in the South and the defining feature of Southern economic development.

Slavery in the eighteenth century existed throughout the British colonies, but the systems of commercial agriculture that took hold in the South utilized and exploited slave labor more effectively than did the North. Three economies developed in the South, each revolving around different commodities, but sharing the plantation form as the ideal method of production. Planters in the upper South in the Chesapeake Bay area used slave labor to produce tobacco. In coastal South Carolina and Georgia, slaves worked rice plantations. By the late eighteenth century, Louisiana planters used slaves on sugar plantations. In the North, where colonial economies did not rely on the production of cash crops, slaves served most often as domestic servants. After the American Revolution, Northern states began to abolish slavery, a strong indication that slaves were superfluous to the functioning of the Northern economies.

Even in the South, the slave economy began to lose its luster after the Revolution as the price of tobacco fell and agricultural profits in the upper South declined. At the same time, some members of the founding generation, including slaveholders like Thomas Jefferson, expressed their doubts about the viability and wisdom of slavery. But in 1794 Eli Whitney reinvigorated the slave labor economy with his patented cotton gin, an invention that would make cotton the most important and lucrative agricultural commodity in America for the next sixty years.

Cotton cultivation before the cotton gin existed only in the low country of coastal South Carolina, where a handful of planters produced long-staple cotton. Outside that region, long-staple cotton would not grow. Its close relative, short-staple cotton, flourished outside the low country, but removing its many seeds from the cotton fiber by hand was simply too difficult and time-intensive to be profitable. The cotton gin, however, could do this job mechanically and produce as much as fifty pounds of cotton per day. All that was required were slaves to work the plantation.

A short-staple cotton crop could only reach maturity after 200 days without frost. Consequently, cotton was bound by climate to the Deep South. There, cotton grew exceptionally well, especially in the Black Belt, a region of dark, fertile soil stretching from central Alabama into northeast Mississippi. In 1790 about 3,000 bales of cotton were produced annually in America. By 1810, planters were producing more than 175,000 bales. The meteoric rise in cotton production fueled the nascent industrialization taking place in Britain and the Northern American states. Textile mills multiplied. Even as these regions gravitated toward abolishing slavery—Britain would emancipate its slaves in 1833—the development of their market economies relied on a product harvested by slave labor.

Within the South, the impact of slavery and "King Cotton" was profound and indelible. Cotton production continued to soar; by 1860, the South exported more than 4 million bales of cotton. Such growth depended on securing more acreage for cotton crops and a constant supply of slaves to harvest them. The imperative to find more land was compounded by the very nature of cotton, because the cotton plant quickly denudes the soil of its nutrients. Taking their slaves with them if they could, planters seeking new land migrated westward, where the climate remained conducive to cotton cultivation. Planters who remained in the upper South still grew tobacco, but their revenues were marginal compared with those of cotton planters.

The great demand for slaves in the Deep South, coupled with the decline of the plantation economy in the Upper South, gave rise to a new, rapidly expanding economy of internal slave trading. Professional slave traders purchased slaves and marched them west where, as historian Michael Tadman showed in his book *Speculators and Slaves* (1996), they earned massive profits reselling them to cotton planters. According to Tadman's estimates, the number of slaves forced to migrate from the Upper South to the Lower South grew over the course of the antebellum period in tandem with cotton production. In the 1790s, between 40,000 and 50,000 slaves were "sold South;" in the 1820s, the number rose to 150,000 slaves; and in the 1830s and 1850s, the decades with the highest slave migrations, the number reached 250,000 slaves. The internal slave trade tore husbands and wives and slave families apart. Nearly 60 percent of slaves took part in the process of cotton production (Fogel and Engerman 1995, p. 95).

The tremendous emphasis on cotton within the antebellum South, though it reaped great profits, tended to retard development in other areas. Cities in the South, for example, could not match the rapid urbanization of the North in the antebellum period. With the exception of New Orleans, the Deep South remained almost entirely rural. Conventional wisdom in the South held that slaves did not do well in urban settings, where less contact with masters allowed slaves greater personal freedom and eroded their obedience. (The latitude afforded abolitionist Frederick Douglass when he was a slave in Baltimore contributed significantly to his escape.)

Historian Peter Kolchin noted that lagging urbanization was a symptom of a larger problem: a lack of modernization caused by the slave labor economy. In *American Slavery* (1993), Kolchin wrote, "the South badly trailed the North in railroad construction, literacy (even excluding blacks), and education" (p. 176). As the South grew to rely more and more on the architecture of capitalism in the North, the failure to modernize its own region took an economic toll. In spite of high cotton profits, per capita income in the South was $103 in 1860, far behind the North's per capita income at $141. This disparity becomes more pronounced when the South's smaller population is taken into account.

Whereas the market revolution ushered in the trappings of capitalism and an ethos of free labor in the North, Southerners remained defiantly faithful to the agrarian lifestyle and the political economy of slavery. By the 1830s they no longer considered slavery a necessary evil, but a responsible and benevolent economic system in which paternal masters cared for their childlike slaves. The owner of a plantation stood at the pinnacle of the South's hierarchical society. Slave ownership signaled more than a financial investment; it represented prestige and power. Most whites in the South did not own slaves, but local and state legislative bodies were overwhelmingly peopled with slaveholders, a reflection of their influence within Southern communities. By the 1840s the primary agenda for Southern politicians was to defend the slave economy by protecting the right to own slaves and ensuring slavery's expansion westward.

For a long time, a school of historians argued that economic indicators in the 1850s pointed to the natural demise of slavery. Noting a large increase in cotton production between 1858 and 1860, they postulated that the temptation for planters to overproduce would cause a steady decline in cotton prices, ultimately making slavery unprofitable. Economic historians Robert Fogel and Stanley Engerman comprehensively refuted this

argument in their book *Time on the Cross* (1995). Setting the economic data of the 1850s in the context of the global cotton market, Fogel and Engerman found that cotton production in the South still could not meet worldwide demand, and so prices would have remained high. In 1861 slavery was as profitable as ever. As the next four years would show, Southerners were prepared to spend their blood and treasure protecting the slave economy and the culture that had evolved around it.

BIBLIOGRAPHY

Fogel, Robert, and Stanley Engerman. *Time on the Cross: The Economics of American Negro Slavery.* New York: W. W. Norton, 1995.

Kolchin, Peter. *American Slavery, 1619–1877.* New York: Hill & Wang, 1993.

Oakes, James. *The Ruling Race: A History of American Slaveholders.* New York: W. W. Norton, 1998.

Tadman, Michael. *Speculators and Slaves: Masters, Traders, and Slaves in the Old South.* Madison: University of Wisconsin Press, 1996.

Williams, Eric. *Capitalism and Slavery.* Chapel Hill: University of North Carolina Press, 1994.

Christopher Jones

THE ECONOMIC IMPACT OF SLAVERY IN THE SOUTH

With its mild climate and fertile soil, the South became an agrarian society, where tobacco, rice, sugar, cotton, wheat, and hemp undergirded the economy. Because of a labor shortage, landowners bought African slaves to work their massive plantations, and even small-scale farmers often used slave labor as their means allowed. As the region developed, industries developed too, particularly those needed to process the local crops or extract natural resources. These industries often employed nonlandowning whites as well as slaves, either owned or leased. In urban areas, most slaves were employed in domestic service; yet, some worked in transportation, manufacturing, and food processing.

Whereas farmers in Virginia, Kentucky, and Missouri focused on growing tobacco and hemp, wheat was a staple in Maryland and Virginia. In South Carolina and Georgia, farmers grew rice, and Louisiana was the primary sugar-growing state. Above all, cotton was the primary crop throughout the South, with the growing cotton region stretching from the Carolinas to Texas. In addition to large plantations that spanned hundreds of acres, smaller farms dotted the countryside.

The owners of plantations and large farms grew crops for the market, as well as for home use. From the earliest days of the nation until the 1850s, cotton was the most important of all the market crops, not just from the South but from the entire nation. By the time the Civil War (1861–1865) erupted, 4.9 million bales of

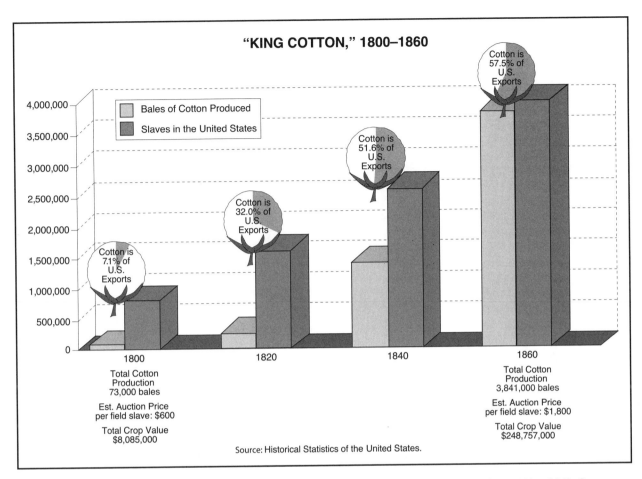

"KING COTTON," 1800–1860

Cotton is 57.5% of U.S. Exports

Cotton is 51.6% of U.S. Exports

Cotton is 32.0% of U.S. Exports

Cotton is 7.1% of U.S. Exports

Bales of Cotton Produced

Slaves in the United States

4,000,000
3,500,000
3,000,000
2,500,000
2,000,000
1,500,000
1,000,000
500,000
0

1800

Total Cotton Production 73,000 bales

Est. Auction Price per field slave: $600

Total Crop Value $8,085,000

1820

1840

1860

Total Cotton Production 3,841,000 bales

Est. Auction Price per field slave: $1,800

Total Crop Value $248,757,000

Source: Historical Statistics of the United States.

King Cotton graph. A graph showing the production of cotton as it correlates with the number of slaves from 1800 to 1860. Cotton was the most important of all the market crops, not just for the south, but for the entire nation. *Illustration by Smith & Santori. Gale.*

cotton were being harvested annually, and most of it was exported through Northern ports (Starobin 1970, p. 4). Yet cotton sapped the soil of its nutrients. Because there was not enough manure to fertilize fields on plantations with 500 to 600 acres under cultivation and because the new commercial fertilizers were prohibitively costly, crop yields gradually decreased (Genovese 1965, p. 95).

From the earliest days of the American colonies, African slaves played an important role in the South because there was a shortage of workers throughout the fledgling nation. Yet as the use of slaves diminished in the North over time, it increased in the Southern states. This was because it was advantageous for the landowners to use slaves instead of hiring white free laborers who might cost more, strike, or quit. Their plantations depended on increased production of export crops on increasingly tired soil.

Thus, the long-held view that slaves were poor workers due to such reasons as a lack of desire, poor-quality tools, and an insufficient diet has been challenged by a number of historians, including Roger Ransom, who maintains:

Contrary to views espoused by critics of the system at the time, slave labor was productive. Slaveholders in the South extracted sufficient labor from their slaves to produce a considerable surplus each year. They did this with a combination of coercion and incentives that implies a very close control of labor by the master. Even the smallest task was organized and supervised by the master or his "driver," and little regard was given to the desires of the slave for leisure time (1989, p. 45).

Considered under law to be both person and property, the slaves had no control over their lives as laborers. In 1860 approximately 400,000 white families owned 4 million slaves, which amounted to 12 percent of the white population controlling more than half of the slaves and creating a "power elite" (Starobin 1970, p. 5).

Purchasing records demonstrate how plantations varied in the extent to which they were self-sufficient. In addition to those slaves who were trained to accomplish household chores, such as spinning, weaving, and sewing, other slaves learned blacksmithing, barrel making, and tanning. Each slave received an allotment of clothing annually. If the fabric was not woven at the plantation, it

SLAVES AND SLAVEHOLDERS, 1860

States	Holders with 1-9 Slaves	Holders with 10-20 Slaves	Holders with 20-50 Slaves	Holders with 50-100 Slaves	Holders with 100-500 Slaves	Holders with 500-1000 Slaves	Holders with Over 1000 Slaves	Total Slave-Holders	Total Slaves
Alabama	21,793	5,906	4,344	1,341	346			33,730	435,080
Arkansas	941	142	56	10				1,149	111,115
Delaware	562	25						587	1,798
Florida	3,368	976	603	158	47			5,152	61,745
Georgia	27,191	7,530	5,049	1,102	211	1		41,084	462,198
Kentucky	31,819	5,271	1,485	63	7			38,645	225,483
Louisiana	14,886	3,222	2,349	1,029	543	4		22,033	331,726
Maryland	11,203	1,718	747	99	16			13,783	87,189
Mississippi	19,559	5,489	4,220	1,359	315	1		30,943	436,631
Missouri	21,380	2,400	502	34	4			24,320	114,931
North Carolina	24,520	6,073	3,321	611	133			34,658	331,059
South Carolina	16,199	5,210	3,646	1,197	441	7	1	26,701	402,406
Tennessee	28,389	5,523	2,550	335	47			36,844	275,719
Texas	16,292	3,423	1,827	282	54			21,878	182,566
Virginia	37,577	8,774	4,917	746	114			52,128	490,865
Total	275,679	61,682	35,616	8,366	2,278	13	1	383,635	3,950,511

Source: United States Census, Agriculture of the United States in 1860, p. 247.

Slaves and slaveholders. A chart showing the number of slaves and slaveholders. In 1860, 12 percent of the white population controlled more than half the slaves, creating a powerful elite. *Illustration by Smith & Santori. Gale.*

had to be purchased, usually from the North. The same held true for shoes and other necessities. Slaves augmented their food rations with gardens, and made herbal remedies. In certain cases a doctor might be called to tend to a valued slave. Despite the cost of maintaining slaves, particularly during the off-season, if gauged over the slave's lifetime, a slave owner would accrue a profit. In addition, female and child slaves, as well as adult males, were often leased to industrial employers during idle times. If profits lagged because of unforeseen developments, surplus slaves might be sold, because from 1805 to 1860 there was "a well-established market for slaves, which meant that the slave was a highly 'liquid' asset that could easily be converted to cash if the owners wished to sell the slave for any reason" (Ransom 1989, p. 46). Owning female slaves of childbearing age also meant an increase in the number of slaves, as all children of slaves belonged to the slaves' owners.

Although on even footing with Northern progress prior to 1815, industrialization in the South lagged behind that of the North afterward, with only 20 percent of the nation's manufacturers being located in the Southern states. Not coincidentally, wages were lower in the South as well, with per capita income in 1860 measured at $103 in the South, compared with $141 in the North (Kolchin 1993, p. 175). Southern industry did not develop as rapidly as that of the North for a number of reasons, including a lack of investment capital, well-trained managers, and up-to-date technology, and the absence of reliable transportation. Most entrepreneurial start-ups were funded by plantation owner's funds, not the conglomerates of shareholders found in the North. In addition, plantation owners often had difficulty hiring expert managers, who were in short supply nationally, and were frequently deterred by the South's withering climate; thus, they had to pay a premium to convince managers to come south. Furthermore, because of insufficient knowledge and capital, entrepreneurs were not necessarily able to use the most efficient methods that would allow them to create goods that could compete well in the North and abroad. Finally, the slow pace of railroad construction, which was not well funded by state and local governments, made for inefficient—thus costly—transportation routes. The businesses that had the most success in marketing their products in the North were located in the border states.

Most Southern businesses selling raw materials and products had to either sell locally or through the Northern middlemen who controlled shipping. Urban markets in the South were limited, because only 10 percent of the population lived in urban areas, with New Orleans and Baltimore being the largest cities. The 1860 census indicated that there were eight cities in the South with populations of more than 22,000 people: Louisville, St. Louis, New Orleans, Mobile, Savannah, Charleston, Richmond, and Baltimore (Starobin 1970, pp. 7–8). Even had there been larger population centers, earning power was low among poor whites and slaves, and plantations to some degree or another tried to be as self-sufficient as possible. Yet the products made in many of the manufacturing industries were tied to the needs of the plantations, so that other items still had to be purchased from the North. This need caused a trade imbalance, for Southern industries were largely not able to successfully market their products to the North and abroad.

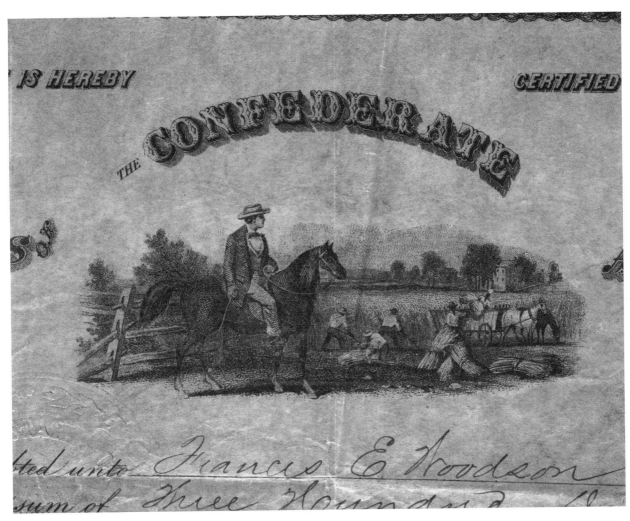

A $300 Confederate bond from Richmond, Virginia, 1863. Economic development did not occur as quickly in the South as it did in the North. *Michael Graham-Stewart/Bridgeman Art Library.*

Despite the difficulties inherent in doing business in the South, such industries as textiles, mining, lumbering, ironmongering, and gristmilling did develop because they served the needs of plantation owners. Furthermore, slave owners were sometimes required to supply slave laborers for public works projects, such as building railroads, repairing roads, and improving waterways (Starobin 1970, pp. 16–31). During the 1850s, from 160,000 to 200,000 bondmen and women of the approximately 4 million slaves in the United States worked in industry. Of these industrial slaves, 80 percent were owned by the business owner and 20 percent rented from their masters by the month or year (Starobin 1970, pp. 11–12).

As with the profitability of plantation slaves, the profitability of enslaved urban workers depended on a number of factors. One factor was the business owner's willingness to risk using slaves in anything other than fieldwork, as the prevailing notion was that the Africans could not learn to do complex tasks. Although some entrepreneurs did not believe slaves capable of doing industrial work, others, such as this visitor to a textile factory, noted, "The superintendent and overseers are white, and ... principally from the manufacturing districts of the North, and although strongly prejudiced on their first arrival at the establishment against African labor, from observation and more experience they testify to their equal efficiency, and great superiority in many respects" (*De Bow's Review* 1850, pp. 432–433). Yet many employers faced not only an overall labor shortage, but a pool of uneducated and undisciplined white workers who often resented working in industry because it lacked the status of being a landowner, or even a subsistence farmer. Thus entrepreneurs opted to risk using slaves, including women and children who cost less to purchase than prime male slaves. White managers often trained and oversaw the work of the slaves, but that was not all. They also trained slaves to become managers.

Business owners soon realized that even when rented from a planter, slaves cost significantly less than did their free counterparts. As historian Robert Starobin explains: "The cost of free labor ... totaled about $355 per annum, including supervision. The annual average maintenance cost per industrial slave was ... less than one-third the annual cost of wages and supervision of free common labors [*sic*]" (1970, p. 149). Some business owners ran enterprises using both free and enslaved laborers, whereas others, upon realizing that the bondmen and women were capable of accomplishing the same tasks as white workers, bought their slave workers outright and fired the white employees. Records show slaves acting as business agents, mill and locomotive engineers, and ferryboat operators—and all at a fraction of the cost of white skilled labor. It is not surprising, then, that nonlandholding whites may have felt resentful of slaves for having displaced them in the workplace.

It is estimated that 10,000 slaves were employed at ironworks, 5,000 at hemp (rope) factories, 20,000 in fishing and fish processing, and 30,000 at gristmills (for sugar, rice, corn, and flour processing). They also worked in coal, iron, lead, gold, and salt mines, and as lumberjacks, sawing trees and extracting turpentine. Tobacco factories used slave laborers (some 7,000) almost exclusively; they also used many women and children because, as in other light industries, they could be just as productive as the men and in some industries, where small and agile hands were needed, even more productive (Starobin 1970, pp. 11–28).

Profits varied from enterprise to enterprise. For example, "[t]he records of southern textile mills employing slave labor indicate that they usually earned annual profits on capital ranging from 10 to 65 percent and averaging about 16 percent." Commenting on the slave-owning enterprises for which records are still available, Starobin noted that the average annual rate of return on investment matched or exceeded 6 percent (1970, pp. 148–149). Moreover, the trend held true whether the slaves were owned or leased.

Planters took advantage of the opportunity for additional income from renting out slaves; yet, they wanted to keep the most able men to work in the fields. Most urban slaves worked as domestic servants (who were primarily women), though others worked as skilled craftsmen, dockworkers, washerwomen, factory workers, and day laborers. Planters also wanted to keep their slaves from the corrupting influence of the city, for as Frederick Douglass (1817–1895) wrote, "A city slave is almost a freeman, compared with a slave on the plantation" (1960, p. 50). A moderate amount of capitalism satisfied the Southern landholders: "The slave regime could tolerate and even embrace limited urbanization and industrialization, but it could never accept the ideals that underlay capitalist transformation, because central to those ideals was economic 'freedom,' including the freedom of laborers to contract for wages" (Kolchin 1993, p. 179).

BIBLIOGRAPHY

De Bow's Review 9 (1850): 432–433.

Douglass, Frederick. *Narrative of the Life of Frederick Douglass, an American Slave, Written by Himself* [1845]. Cambridge, MA: Belknap Press, 1960.

Genovese, Eugene D. *Political Economy of Slavery: Studies in the Economy & and Society of the Slave South.* New York: Pantheon, 1965.

Kolchin, Peter. *American Slavery, 1619–1877.* New York: Hill and Wang, 1993.

Ransom, Roger L. *Conflict and Compromise: The Political Economy of Slavery, Emancipation, and the American Civil War.* New York and Cambridge, U.K.: Cambridge University Press, 1989.

Shore, Laurence. *Southern Capitalists: The Ideological Leadership of an Elite, 1832–1885.* Chapel Hill: University of North Carolina Press, 1986.

Starobin, Robert S. *Industrial Slavery in the Old South.* New York: Oxford University Press, 1970.

Tocqueville, Alexis de. *Democracy in America*, trans. Arthur Goldhammer. New York: Penguin Putnam, 2004.

Jeanne M. Lesinski

IMPACT OF SLAVERY ON THE NORTHERN ECONOMY

One of the major themes in American history is sectionalism; some historians trace the origins of this development within the colonial regions. As John Garraty noted in *The American Nation* (1995, pp. 35–64), by the antebellum period the three colonial regional sections had coalesced, and there were now only two sections: the North and the South. Distinctive economies were the defining features of the two regions. Although the North was still predominantly agrarian, the industrial development in New England distinguished the North from the even more agrarian South. In the South, it was the plantation production of cotton, and not the pervasive subsistence agriculture practiced by poor whites, that was most distinctive. Although the two regions had very dissimilar economies, the North and the South did not develop independently of each other; in fact, they were intimately entwined around cotton. As Sen. James Henry Hammond noted in a speech to Congress just before the outbreak of the Civil War, "Cotton is King" (Dodge 1984, p. 2). During the first seventy years of the American Republic, cotton influenced the economic development of not only the South, but also the North.

At the end of the eighteenth century and the beginning of the nineteenth century the transatlantic economy underwent a transformation, first in Britain and later in

SCENE ON THE ALABAMA RIVER, LOADING COTTON.

Slaves loading cotton on the Alabama River. An 1857 illustration of slaves loading cotton onto a ship on the Alabama River. In 1860, the South produced 2.275 billion pounds of cotton, which accounted for 60 percent of the country's exports. © *Corbis.*

the United States. In Britain, inventors such as James Watt (1736–1819) and entrepreneurs such as Richard Arkwright (1732–1792) industrialized the textile business, transforming it from a cottage-based production held together by merchants into a factory operation run by businessmen. With the use of water-driven and steam-powered machinery tended by thousands of unskilled workers in factories, textile entrepreneurs prodigiously increased the amount of cotton cloth available. Unlike the British woolen industry, which was supplied domestically by English sheep, the textile industry needed to import its raw material. Through much of the eighteenth century the cottage textile industry had been adequately supplied by cotton imported from India, the Levant, and the colonies in the Western Hemisphere. But these sources could not supply the tremendous productive capacity of factories that had first appeared in England's Midlands; during the 1780s the consumption for cotton increased by 208 percent over the previous decade (Shapiro 1967, p. 183). Britain's voracious demand for cotton was met in the next decade by a tremendous increase in cotton production in the United States made possible by Eli Whitney's cotton gin. In 1793, the year before Whitney's gin went into operation, the South exported 487,000 pounds of cotton to Britain; with the use of the gin in 1794, that amount had

jumped to 1.6 million pounds (Yafa 2005, p. 86). During the first six decades of the nineteenth century, as the South's cotton economy continued to grow, some of that output was shipped north to the factories founded in the New England states.

U.S. industrial development began during the Napoleonic Wars, although attempts had been made earlier to start factory production in the United States. One successful effort occurred in 1790 at Pawtucket, Rhode Island, when Samuel Slater, "a former superintendent at one of Arkwright's partners' cotton mills," set up mass production of spinning yarn, but not woven cloth (Yafa 2005, p. 76). It was not until the next decade that some New Englanders sought to develop a textile industry that would make the United States independent of British manufactures.

The impetus for a fully developed U.S. textile industry came when the Embargo Act of 1807, the Non-Intercourse Act of 1809, and the War of 1812 disrupted trade with Britain. Just before the outbreak of war between the United States and Britain, Francis Cabot Lowell (1775–1817) had visited British factories in Manchester, where he learned the secrets of mass production of textiles. Lowell enlisted the financial support of other Boston Brahmins like himself, especially Nathan Appleton (1779–1861), and in 1814 the two men established a textile factory at Waltham on the Charles River, just northwest of Boston. Production began that same year with the importation of boatloads of cotton from the South, and in 1815 the quantity of imported southern cotton to Waltham and other factories in New England reached 27 million pounds (Yafa 2005, p. 107). To ensure that the Boston Manufacturing Company's production of cloth would dominate the market in the United States, Lowell and his associates argued that Congress should impose tariffs on certain types of imported British textiles. They pointed to the sudden decline in New England cloth production after peace between the two countries had enabled Britain to resume trade with the United States, flooding the U.S. markets with British goods. In 1815 the value of New England textiles had been $47,160, but in 1816 the value had dropped to $16,355 (Rosenbloom 2004, p. 381).

The historian Joshua Rosenbloom argues that during the antebellum period, federal tariffs protected New England textile manufacturing so that this "infant industry" could develop and expand within the U.S. domestic market (2004, pp. 390–391). By the middle of the nineteenth century the United States had become the world's second largest producer of textiles. During the course of the nineteenth century U.S. textile manufacturing could not compete with most varieties of Britain textiles on the world market, but tariff protection enabled U.S. companies to dominate the domestic market. At its inception, the rates of the Tariff Act of 1816 had received considerable southern support, notably from John C. Calhoun (1782–1850), but by the end of the next decade many southern planters had labeled the federal rates that protected northern industries the "abominable tariff." The dispute over the tariff rates, especially those on manufactures imported from Britain, led to the Nullification Crisis of 1831 to 1833, when South Carolinians seemed to threaten secession over the rates. Between 1816 and 1828 textile prices had decreased, due in part to a decline in cotton prices, but Congress had twice raised rates during the 1820s so that by 1830 the increase of costs on British imports reached 40 percent (Rosenbloom 2004, p. 388). For some southerners such as Calhoun, who wrote his *South Carolina Exposition and Protest* (1828) to justify state action against the federal tariff, it seemed that the economy and the consumption patterns of southerners was being used by northerners to protect their industrialization (Garraty 1995, pp. 257–259).

Indeed, by the early 1830s New England industries were consuming large quantities of southern-grown cotton as the mills propelled the United States into position as the second largest producer of textiles in the world. In 1831 a report authored by the Committee on Manufactures of the American Congress stated that New England industries consumed "seventy-eight million

pounds of cotton fiber per year." This figure indicated that the yearly consumption by U.S. industries, beginning in the 1830s and continuing through the 1840s and 1850s, equaled and eventually surpassed the whole export of U.S. cotton to Britain up to 1820. In 1807 there had been only fifteen mills in the nation; in 1831 there were 795. The committee's report stated that these 795 mills produced "nearly sixty-eight million pounds of spun yarn" and employed more than 57,000 workers (Dodge 1984, pp. 88–89). Clearly, in the take-off period of industrialization, the U.S. textile industry had grown tremendously. New England mills not only produced large quantities of inexpensive cloth—in 1834, the equivalent of 15,698 miles of cotton cloth—but also clothed the slaves in the cotton fields with a coarse fabric called "Negro cloth" (Yafa 2005, p. 112).

Lowell did not live to see the industrial development that he had started at Waltham in 1814—he died in 1817 at the relatively young age of forty-two. However, his manufacturing methods did survive him. Lowell's associates established the Merrimack Manufacturing Company, transplanting what Lowell had begun at Waltham on the Charles River to an even larger complex on the Merrimack River. This site became the city named in his honor, Lowell, Massachusetts. The industrial complex there was erected during the Age of Reform, a period of high ideals when some Americans, especially in the northern states, wanted to perfect society. Whereas reformers such as the transcendentalist George Ripley (1802–1880) sought to build a utopian community at Brook Farm, Massachusetts, the directors of the Merrimack Manufacturing Company attempted to construct an industrial utopia in Lowell. Appleton and the other associates who survived Lodge kept Britain's manufacturing processes while trying to avoid the slums that sprang up in British manufacturing towns. The investors, directors, and managers of the Merrimack Manufacturing Company adopted a paternalistic approach to the management of the factories and workers, who were primarily young unmarried women.

To evoke an academic atmosphere, Merrimack provided company-supervised boarding houses set on tree-lined streets and encouraged the young women to continue their self-education while employed; the mill women even began a journal, *Lowell Offering*. In the late twentieth century the historian Benita Eisler compiled many of the journal's essays written during the early 1840s into *The Lowell Offering: Writings of New England Mill Women*, presenting a picture of an industrial environment that was truly different, if not quite utopian (Dodge 1984, pp. 102–104, 100–112). During the halcyon years of the 1830s many visitors to Lowell, including some southerners such as President Andrew Jackson (1767–1845) and Davy Crockett (1786–1836), saw the place as a socioeconomic marvel based on the profitable economic integration of a southern cash crop with northern manufacturing. Apparently, a Jeffersonian economy in the South was mutually compatible with a Hamiltonian economy in the North (Nash and Graves 2005, p. 120), and this, especially the northern part, was the ideal of many in the Whig Party during the antebellum period.

Despite the initial acclaim bestowed upon Lowell, the Merrimack Manufacturing Company and other northern businesses soon became targets of strong censure. During the 1840s and 1850s there were two major subjects of criticism: work operations in the mills and the mills' economic connection with slave-produced cotton. Workers' complaints, especially regarding the long working hours and the ever-increasing pace of the machinery, are documented in a second, later worker publication, *Voice of Industry* (Yafa 2005, p. 116). The labor criticisms coincided with the abolitionists' condemnation of the mill owners' economic ties with southern planters. During the same period when the mills were established throughout the New England states, abolitionists founded the American Anti-Slavery Society and other antislavery organization, which were implacably opposed to slavery and anything connected to it, whether that meant buying slave-produced cotton or eating slave-produced sugar (Carson, Lapsansky-Werner, and Nash 2007, p. 188).

One of the reasons politicians such as Henry Clay (1777–1852) and Daniel Webster (1782–1852) had formed the Whig Party in 1833 was to promote economic development. This party followed the Federalists, and adopted much of Alexander Hamilton's economic agenda, which included an active role for the federal government in promoting commerce and industry. By the 1840s some of what Hamilton had envisioned for the United States had been achieved, even though the Federalists had disintegrated and the Whig Party only infrequently controlled the federal government during the early nineteenth century. Not surprisingly, the Whigs were strong in New England, where a commercial economy had long existed and where, during the first half of the nineteenth century, every state in the region had undergone at least partial industrialization. In fact, a wing of the Whigs, the Cotton Whigs, cooperated with southerners because they had a mutual economic interest in keeping the Union together. In a letter to one of the owners of the Merrimack Manufacturing Company, Abbott Lawrence (1792–1855), the South Carolina senator John C. Calhoun articulated that tie: "I am no opponent to manufactures or manufacturers, but quite the reverse. Cotton threads hold the union together: unites John C. Calhoun and Abbott Lawrence. Patriotism for holidays and summer evenings, but cotton thread is the Union" (Yafa 2005, pp. 122–123). Until the early 1850s, some Cotton Whigs actively maintained the tie with the agrarian South led by slave-owning planters and publicly denounced the abolitionists.

During the 1850s the U.S. economy grew rapidly, led by sales of public land, railroad building, gold mining, cotton production, and textile manufacturing. In 1860 the South produced 2.275 billion pounds of cotton. Moreover, cotton exports accounted for 60 percent of the country's exports, most of which were handled by New York City, the new emporium for the United States. The South supplied 80 percent of the cotton for textiles manufactured in Britain and all of the cotton for textiles manufactured in New England's mills. In that same year, 1860, those mills and the few established elsewhere in the North produced $115 million worth of textiles (Yafa 2005, pp. 129–130). These mills and the Yankee clipper ships delivered more cotton goods to East Africa than Britain and all of its empire combined (Coupland 1961, pp. 379–380). Nonetheless, political events trumped economics during the decade. The Whig Party disintegrated when popular sovereignty was introduced into the territories. Even the Cotton Whig Abbott Lawrence shied away from his ties with the South after a southern congressman, Preston Brooks (1819–1857), brutally assaulted the southern Whig senator Charles Sumner (1811–1874) on the Senate floor. Despite the mutual benefits of an economy integrated around cotton, the house of which Abraham Lincoln spoke was deeply divided.

BIBLIOGRAPHY

Carson, Clayborne, Emma J. Lapsansky-Werner, and Gary B. Nash. *The Struggle for Freedom: A History of African Americans*. New York: Pearson and Longman, 2007.

Coupland, Reginald. *East Africa and Its Invaders*. Oxford, UK: Oxford University Press, 1961.

Dodge, Bertha S. *Cotton: The Plant That Would Be King*. Austin: University of Texas Press, 1984.

Garraty, John A. *The American Nation: A History of the United States*, 8th ed. New York: Harper Collins, 1995.

Nash, Roderick, and Gregory Graves. *From These Beginnings: A Biographical Approach to American History*, Vol. 1, 7th ed. New York: Pearson and Longman, 2005.

Rosenbloom, Joshua L. "Path Dependence and the Origins of Cotton Textile Manufacturing in New England." In *The Fibre That Changed the World: The Cotton Industry in International Perspective, 1660–1990s*, ed. Douglas A. Farnie and David J. Jeremy. Oxford, UK: Oxford University Press, 2004.

Shapiro, Seymour. *Capital and the Cotton Industry in the Industrial Revolution*. Ithaca, NY: Cornell University Press, 1967.

Yafa, Stephen. *Big Cotton: How a Humble Fiber Created Fortunes, Wrecked Civilizations, and Put America on the Map.* New York: Viking, 2005.

                                                    George Sochan

SLAVERY AND THE RISE OF CAPITALISM

One of the structures that characterizes the modern Western world and separates it from medieval Europe is capitalism. A paramount and distinguishing feature of the eighteenth and nineteenth centuries is the capitalistic development that occurred within the transatlantic economy. Beginning in the late eighteenth century in Britain and then in other countries of the transatlantic world, industrialization became a major part of capitalistic enterprise in this economy. The first economic activity to be industrialized was the manufacture of textiles. This began in Britain during the 1780s and the 1790s, and that country's industrial expansion became strongly enmeshed within the transatlantic economy because the first textiles produced in British factories were made from a raw material—cotton—found within the transatlantic system but not in Britain. Similar economic transformations occurred in Belgium, France, and the northern part of the United States. From the early nineteenth century to the middle of the twentieth, cotton shaped the course of history. In the introduction to an edited work that presents the writings and findings of numerous historians and marshals an array of statistics, Douglas Farnie and David Jeremy further assert, "Cotton goods conquered a world market and created the prototype of a world economy in the form of an Anglo-American-Asian economic symbiosis, pivoting around Lancashire.... The cotton mill epitomized the new factory system and became the supreme symbol of the Industrial Revolution" (2004, p. 3). Because the overwhelming preponderance of cotton used in textiles was picked by labor in bondage, historians have had to consider the following question: To what extent did slavery contribute to the rise of capitalism?

Before that question can be answered, the term *capitalism* must be addressed. In his global study, *The World's History*, Howard Spodek references Adam Smith and then defines capitalism as "an economic system in which the means of production are privately owned and goods and services are exchanged according to levels of supply and demand in markets" (2006, p. 389). Using such a definition, De Lamar Jensen discerns the initial rise of capitalism in the towns of northern Italy during the fourteenth and fifteenth centuries, which he characterizes as presenting "a full-scale system of capitalism— that is, the private accumulation and employment of liquid wealth for the purpose of making further financial profits" (1992, pp. 91–95). Jensen is not untypical in finding the origin of capitalism in the Renaissance; many historians claim to have made the same discovery. It

should be noted that the Renaissance, a cultural period of the later Middle Ages, occurred centuries before Europeans became heavily involved in the slave trade and slavery. Historians, such as Jensen and Lewis Spitz (1987), identify the capitalism of that era as *merchant capitalism* or *financial capitalism*. During the early modern period, Europeans using a merchant capitalism developed the transatlantic economy, in which the slave trade and slavery had a significant role. According to the historian Seymour Drescher, "the plantations were set up as pure agricultural factories" and "labor approached the status of a pure commodity." Further, the world market, only minimally affected by human sentiments, determined the nature of social relations (1977, p. 3). Many historians now accept that out of the eighteenth-century transatlantic economy, based on sugar and slaves, evolved modern industrial capitalism, which during the early nineteenth century was based on textiles and cotton.

Since the first publication of Eric Williams's *Capitalism and Slavery* in 1944, a shift in the historiography of the transatlantic world has occurred, although by the end of the twentieth century Drescher and others had seriously challenged certain key parts of Williams's interpretation. One of Williams's arguments, which is germane to this article, asserts that through most of the eighteenth century Britain's mercantilist empire promoted economic development within the metropolitan country, including the industrialization of textiles. Central to Britain's economic development were slaves: first as the primary commodity in the Middle Passage and secondly as unpaid laborers in Britain's colonies. Employing considerable evidence, Williams (1961) develops his argument in the following key chapters: "British Commerce and the Triangular Trade" (pp. 51–84), "British Industry and the Triangular Trade" (pp. 98–107), and "The Development of British Capitalism, 1783–1833" (pp. 126–153). Within these chapters Williams takes great efforts to develop the case that, up until the end of the eighteenth century, the slave trade, which Britain dominated in that century, was very profitable for the metropole. During that same period, Britain's sugar colonies were profitable for the metropole because the government created a monopoly for the West Indies planters through the use of high tariffs; often these planters returned to England very wealthy and invested in other enterprises there, including textiles. Many businesses within the metropolitan country—such as the makers of iron chains, the builders of slave ships, and the handloom weavers who made the clothes sold on the West African coast—benefited by being the core of Britain's extensive mercantilist empire. Williams traces the rise of prominent cities such as Liverpool, which was tied to the slave trade, and Manchester, which arose because of the textile factories, and asserts that with the end of the slave trade and the decline of the

West Indies, Liverpool became the emporium to the world of textiles manufactured in Manchester (pp. 63 and 68). For Williams, this development epitomizes the emergence of Britain's new industrial capitalism from its earlier slave-centered economy.

Williams's hypothesis that during the eighteenth century "slavery had provided nothing less than the export demand and trade network for the British industrial revolution" (Drescher 1999, p. 364) ignited a significant scholarly controversy. According to Drescher (1999), the claim that slavery and the slave trade were the catalysts of British industrialization has the following problems: Profits from the slave trade were not inordinately large and, therefore, could not have been the major financial impetus for industrialization; economic historians have shown that Williams overstated the profits from the West Indies colonies; and historians of Britain's industrial revolution, such as Phyllis Deane and Eric Hobsbawn (b. 1917), consider other factors much more important causes of industrialization. In *The Cotton Industry in the Industrial Revolution*, Stanley Chapman (b. 1935) points out that Deane's use of eighteenth-century statistics have also been challenged. So, the consensus at the end of the twentieth century is that while Williams overestimated eighteenth-century profits, Deane and others at least slightly underestimated them. For Chapman and certain other historians, then, the key to the development of industrial capitalism is the "unique role of cotton" in the growth of Britain's economy, which was soon followed by comparable economic growth in other countries that developed a cotton-centered economy (1987, pp. 54–57). It follows, then, that if cotton had a unique role in the development of modern industrial capitalism, so too did slavery because, during the first half of the nineteenth century, the overwhelming majority of cotton used by Britain and other industrial capitalist countries was produced by slaves in the United States.

As Drescher (1999) notes in *From Slavery to Freedom: Comparative Studies in the Rise and Fall of Atlantic Slavery*, the two very different socioeconomic systems of industrial capitalism and plantation slavery, which still often relied on the slave trade, existed side by side during the nineteenth century. The analysis concerning the coexistence of these two socioeconomic systems can support an even stronger statement—that the two systems were mutually supportive of one another. Some statistics covering the decades from the end of the eighteenth century to the middle of the nineteenth century illustrate part of the relationship between the rise of industrial capitalism and slavery. From the period of 1781 to 1789, which is often considered the first decade of Britain's industrial takeoff, to the ten years between 1850 and 1859, which is the last decade of the antebellum period in U.S. history, British consumption of cotton increased by fifty-four times. Between 1781 and 1789 the annual mean amount consumed was 16.9 million pounds, whereas between 1850 and 1859 the annual mean amount was 927.9 million pounds. A table in *Capital and the Cotton Industry in the Industrial Revolution* shows that, through the first half of the nineteenth century, the increases through successive decades were regularly quite large (Shapiro 1967, p. 257). By the 1850s, moreover, 80 percent of the cotton imported into the country for use in British factories was from the United States (Yafa 2005, p. 130). It is ironic, then, that during the same period that Britain campaigned against the slave trade and emancipated slaves in its own empire, the British economy became heavily dependent on slave-produced cotton. A similar process occurred during the same period in the United States. In 1800 the value of the cotton crop was 1.83 percent of the gross domestic product (GDP), but by 1860 it accounted for 6.52 percent. As for cotton manufactures, in 1800 they accounted for only 0.037 percent of the GDP, but by 1860 that figure had increased to 3.01 percent (Farnie 2004, p. 572). Again, it should be noted that these tremendous increases in the part of the economy connected to cotton were tied either directly or indirectly to slavery; in the case of the cotton crop the connection was direct, while in the case of the manufactured textiles it was indirect.

As the demand for cotton, whether slaved-produced or not, steadily increased during the nineteenth century, so too did the number of workers in bondage in the southern regions of the United States. Whereas in 1790 the number of American slaves was less than 700,000, all of whom lived along the Atlantic Coast, by 1860 the number of slaves had increased to almost 4 million (Franklin and Moss Jr. 2000, p. 139). Moreover, this population was spread throughout fifteen southern states and was also expanding into the western territories. While the southern plantations were, to a considerable extent, self-sufficient, they did have certain economic needs, many of which were provided by industrial capitalist economies. Northern mills supplied the material, called Negro cloth, for the clothes that the slaves wore, in addition to household furnishings—including silks, linens, furniture, teacups, and bed sheets—for the planters' families, which were shipped into the South through New York City from the northern states or from Europe. New York City was also the port of export for most of the South's cotton and loans to planters came from northern or English banks (Yafa 2005, pp. 112, 133, and 135). Without the manufactured products of and financial credit from the capitalist industrial economies of the North or of Britain, the slave-labor economy of the South would not have been able to operate. So, while the South shipped the cotton to the capitalist industrial economies that the slaves had produced, it received much in return. As one southerner put it, "From the rattle . . . of the child born in the

South . . . to the shroud that covers the cold form of the dead, everything comes to us from the North" (Yafa 2005, p. 164).

In conclusion, then, slavery did play a significant role in the rise of modern capitalism. First, during the seventeenth and eighteenth centuries, key west European states, especially Britain, established mercantilist empires that laid the basis for the later development of industrial capitalism. Certain parts of these empires, such as the plantations in the Caribbean basin, were ruthlessly operated according to basic capitalistic principles; one of the results was the use of Africans as a labor commodity. The colonies in the Western Hemisphere and the African west coast were tied to metropolitan countries in Europe within a system of trade that promoted economic development and capital accumulation for the European country. For instance, the development of a large merchant fleet in Britain, both for direct trade with the West Indies and for the Middle Passage, provided the seamen and, on some occasions, the ships for Britain's navy. Britain's large navy first, during the eighteenth century, helped acquire new territories for an expanding empire, and then, during the nineteenth century, served to ensure the stable international relations that facilitated capitalistic enterprise, trade, and a global economy (Singleton 2004, pp. 59–69). Secondly, the industrial capitalism of the nineteenth century that replaced the mercantile capitalism of the eighteenth century was centered on cotton, and for more than half of the nineteenth century the cotton crop that fed the factories of Manchester, England, and Lowell, Massachusetts, was grown by slaves in the United States. For its part, Manchester developed during the nineteenth century into an economic zone comprised of many industries, providing employment for 4.75 million persons in a 500-square-mile area of Lancashire County. The many industries of Lancashire were all subsidiary to Manchester's textile industries, which employed 700,000 operatives (Farnie 2004, pp. 561–562). Finally, much of the cotton—up to 80 percent of which was imported during the mid-nineteenth century—was produced within the institution of slavery.

BIBLIOGRAPHY

Chapman, Stanley D. *The Cotton Industry in the Industrial Revolution.* 2nd ed. Houndmills, U.K.; Basingstoke, U.K.; Hampshire, U.K.: Macmillan, 1987.

Drescher, Seymour. *Econocide: British Slavery in the Era of Abolition.* Pittsburgh, PA: University of Pittsburgh Press, 1977.

Drescher, Seymour. *From Slavery to Freedom: Comparative Studies in the Rise and Fall of Atlantic Slavery.* New York: New York University Press, 1999.

Farnie, Douglas A., and David J. Jeremy, eds. *The Fiber That Changed the World: The Cotton Industry in International Perspective, 1600–1990s.* Oxford: Oxford University Press, 2004.

Franklin, John Hope, and Alfred A. Moss Jr. *From Slavery to Freedom: A History of African Americans.* Boston: McGraw-Hill, 2000.

Jensen, De Lamar. *Renaissance Europe: Age of Recovery and Reconciliation.* 2nd ed. Lexington, MA: D. C. Heath, 1992.

Shapiro, Seymour. *Capital and the Cotton Industry in the Industrial Revolution.* Ithaca, NY: Cornell University Press, 1967.

Singleton, John. "The Lancashire Cotton Industry, the Royal Navy, and the British Empire, c. 1700–1960." In *The Fiber That Changed the World: The Cotton Industry in International Perspective, 1600–1990s,* ed. Douglas A. Farney and David J. Jeremy. Oxford: Oxford University Press, 2004.

Spitz, Lewis W. *The Renaissance and Reformation Movements.* St. Louis, MO: Concordia, 1987.

Spodek, Howard. *The World's History.* 3rd ed. Upper Saddle River, NJ: Prentice Hall, 2006.

Williams, Eric. *Capitalism and Slavery.* New York: Russell & Russell, 1961.

Yafa, Stephen. *Big Cotton: How a Humble Fiber Created Fortunes, Wrecked Civilizations, and Put America on the Map.* New York: Viking, 2005.

George Sochan

PROPERTY TAXES ON SLAVES

The U.S. Constitution granted Congress the authority to tax slaves as property in Article I, Section 9, stating:

> The migration or importation of such persons as any of the States now existing shall think proper to admit, shall not be prohibited by the Congress prior to the year one thousand eight hundred and eight; but a tax or duty may be imposed on such importation, not exceeding ten dollars for each person. (Bowditch 121)

Despite the Framers' failure to use the word "slave," it was well-understood that the migration or importation of "persons" referred to slaves. As William I. Bowditch pointed out in his book *Slavery and the Constitution*:

> A person who is imported does not import himself, but is imported by some other person. He is passive. The importer is the free agent; the person imported is not a free agent . . . Whenever we hear an importation spoken of, we instantly infer an importer, an *owner*, and *property* imported . . . On our construction, Congress had power to lay a tax on persons imported as property or slaves, but had no right to tax free persons migrating. (p. 121)

Much controversy surrounded the drafting and adoption of Article I, Section 9. The final constitutional provision was the culmination of a compromise between the eastern states, which relied heavily upon sea trade, and the slave-holding southern states.

A constitutional delegate who served on the committee that considered the adoption of Article I, Section 9 summarized the "well-known history of the compromise involved in this clause:"

> *I found the Eastern States, notwithstanding their aversion to slavery, were very willing to indulge the Southern States, at least with a temporary liberty to prosecute the slave trade, provided the Southern States would in their turn gratify them, by laying no restriction on Navigation Acts;* and, after a very little time, the committee, by a great majority, agreed on a report, by which the general government was to be prohibited from preventing the importation of slaves for a limited time, and the restricted clause relative to the Navigation Acts was to be omitted. This report was adopted by a majority of the Convention, but not without considerable opposition (emphasis added). (Bowditch, p. 131)

Thus, the slave trade would be allowed to continue for at least twenty more years, to the advantage of the Southern states, and only a simple majority of Congress would be required to pass navigation and commerce laws, to the advantage of the Eastern states.

The adoption of Article I, Section 9 also represented a compromise between constitutional delegates who opposed slavery and those who advocated slavery. Several Framers opposed to the institution of slavery viewed Article I, Section 9 as a partial victory. In the Pennsylvania Constitutional Convention,

> Mr. Wilson said:
> Under the present confederation, the States may admit the importation of slaves as long as they please; but by this article, after the year 1808, the Congress will have the power to prohibit such importation, notwithstanding the disposition of any State to the contrary…" (Bowditch, p. 130).

Framer James Madison expressed similar sentiments in the Virginia Convention:

> I should conceive this clause to [be] impolitic, if it were one of those things which could be excluded without encountering greater evils… Under the articles of confederation, [the slave trade] might be continued for ever; but, by this clause, an end may be put to it after twenty years. There is, therefore, an amelioration of our circumstances. A tax may be laid in the meantime" (Bowditch, p. 131-32).

The taxation of slave property was also embraced by abolitionists at the American Anti-Slavery Society's Annual meeting in 1850 in New York:

> "The following resolutions were offered by George Doughty of Long Island:

> Resolved, That Congress be petitioned to tax slave property enough, at least, to pay the wages of the number of representatives that have their seats on Congress in consequence of their slave property; and,
> Resolved, That a pledge be circulated generally, pledging the signers not to vote for any man unless he is in favor of taxing slave property…" (*The Liberator*).

Many state constitutions provided for the "uniform and equal rate of taxation of all personal and real property," including Kansas (Greeley 154). A 1779 Virginia statute provided that a tax on property "shall not extend to any negro or mulatto servant or slaves" (Hurd 2:2-3). However, many states not only taxed slaves as property, but oftentimes taxed the slaves of non-residents at higher rates than the slaves of residents. During a legislative debate about whether non-resident slave owners should be compensated for slaves that are executed within Mississippi, the President of the Senate, Dabney Lipscomb, pointed out that Kentucky and two other states "had claimed the right to tax slave property of non-residents higher than that of the citizen" (*The Mississippian*). In addition, Mr. Lipscomb:

> believed that absenteeism is a grievous evil, and he was especially opposed to it in regard to the owners of large numbers of slaves. He was in favor of taxing them higher; much higher; than those of the citizen, and he believed the right of the state clear, and her duty to do so imperious (*The Mississippian*).

The District of Columbia also taxed the slaves of non-residents at a rate higher than slaves of residents:

> Sec. 36. From and after the tenth day of April, eighteen hundred and twenty-three, the following tax be, and the same is hereby, imposed on slaves of non-residents hired to persons residing within the city of Washington, to wit: On every male slave above the age of eighteen years, and under forty-five, twenty dollars per annum; on every male slave under eighteen and above twelve years of age, twelve dollars per annum; and on every female slave between fifteen and forty-five years of age, two dollars per annum. Act, 5th April, 1823 §1 (Washington [D.C.] 38).

The D.C. statute further provided for the payment of penalties by non-resident owners who failed to pay the annual taxes, and who attempted or were successful at evading payment of these taxes and penalties (Washington [D.C.] 38).

There was also a debate about whether slave property should be subject to direct taxes, *i.e.*, taxes based on the revenue they created, in the same manner in which all other property was taxed pursuant to Article I, Section 2 of the U.S. Constitution. Article I, Section 2 provided that:

Representatives and direct Taxes shall be apportioned among the several States which may be included within this Union, according to their respective Numbers, which shall be determined by adding to the whole Number of free Persons, including those bound to Service for a Term of Years, and excluding Indians not taxed, three fifths of all other Persons.

The writer of a July 23, 1860 article in the *Fayetteville Observer* framed the issues as such:

Shall the Constitution be so amended as to give the Legislature the same power to tax slave property, that it now has over all other kinds of property? Shall slave property pay its fair share of the public taxes? Mr. Pool and the Whigs are in favor of the change. Gov. Ellis and the Democrats are opposed to change.

In an editorial published on April 12, 1860, a proponent of the taxation of slaves "admonished the people of the State against all such men" who

say they are in favor of the proposition to so change the Constitution as to tax slave property as other property may be taxed, but nevertheless say they will vote for John W. Ellis for governor, notwithstanding he says this proposition is dangerous, impolitic and unjust.

Relief would not come for those in favor of the direct taxation of slave property until *after* the abolition of slavery. In the 1895 case of *Pollock v. Farmers' Loan & Trust Co.*, 157 U.S. 429, aff'd on reh'g, 158 U.S. 601 (1895), the United State Supreme Court ruled that taxes on income from property should be treated as direct taxes and thus subject to apportionment. After the ratification of the Sixteenth Amendment in 1913, no federal income taxes were required to be apportioned, regardless of whether they are direct taxes (taxes on income from property) or indirect taxes (all other income taxes).

BIBLIOGRAPHY

Bowditch, William Ingersoll. *Slavery and the Constitution*. Boston, 1849.

Fayetteville Observer, (Fayetteville, NC) Monday, July 23, 1860. Issue 2251, pg. 3, col C, "The Issue."

Greeley, Horace. *A History of The Struggle For Slavery Extension or Restriction In The United States: From The Declaration Of Independence To The Present Day*. New York, 1856.

Hurd, John C. *The Law of Freedom and Bondage In The United States*. Vol. 2. Boston, 1858–1862.

The Liberator, (Boston, MA) Friday, May 24, 1850. Issue 21, pg. 2, col C, "Annual Meeting at New York."

The Mississippian, Friday, March 03, 1848. Issue 10, pg. 1, col A, "Senate Proceedings."

The Slavery Code of the District of Columbia: Together With Notes and Judicial Decisions Explanatory of the Same. Washington [D.C.], 1862.

Jodi M. Savage

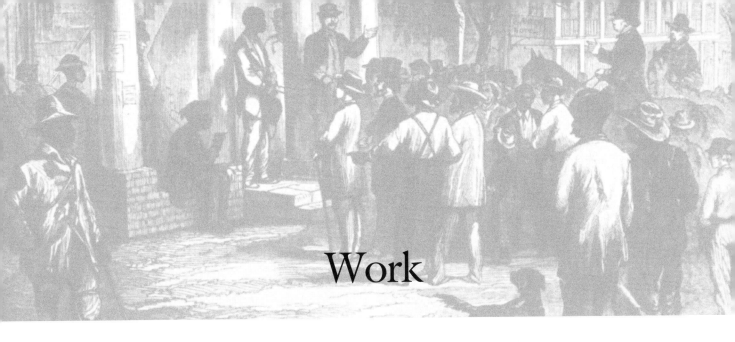

Work

■ Work Overview

Slave occupations were not as simple as the standard dichotomy between house slaves and field slaves suggests. These categories existed and are useful in understanding the social dynamics of master-slave relationships, especially on the plantations and farms. The work performed by house slaves in rural or city areas was limited to domestic activities—acting as personal servants, nurses, and mammies—and brought them into close proximity with whites, sometimes even extending to familiarity and intimacy with selected white individuals. Field slaves had fewer opportunities to develop relationships with whites. Their work was largely dependent on the seasonal rhythms associated with a specific major crop or product. Task or gang labor systems were the most popular and productive arrangements. In addition, some slaves worked as skilled laborers and artisans; they were in high demand and often rented out time. Hunting, trapping, and fishing were also lucrative vocations that allowed slaves to sell their catches and supplement their meager rations. This work combined with personal garden plots provided variety and substance to inadequate diets.

The article on agricultural work provides an overview of the cotton, rice, sugar, and tobacco industries that are further detailed in the separate entries on cotton plantations, tobacco plantations, rice plantations, and sugar plantations. Central to the plantation lifestyle were the master's house; nurses and mammies; slave entrepreneurs; hunting and trapping; seasonal rhythms; personal servants; and the gang system. Plantations were the locale for a cross-section of significant occupations of enslaved Africans in the New World. The following sections illuminate the broad range of blacks' participation in the economic world. For the majority of these Africans, their work contributed little to their personal well-being. It only sufficed to further the financial and life goals of their owners. The system of chattel slavery reduced the human equation to a single coefficient for enslaved Africans: The slave is property that works and

any other concerns are irrelevant. Yet the black population was more resilient and resistant than such a restrictive existence might imply. Cultural patterns developed around slave labor in the houses, on the plantations, and in the developing urban areas. A few occupations afforded the slaves opportunities to work toward freedom or personal development, although most only solidified their oppression.

Whether work is viewed from the perspective of the individual's need to express her or himself, or based on the value of the labor performed as a contribution to society, or the value of the labor to the capitalist owners, enslaved Africans played an invaluable and incalculable role in the United States and throughout the New World. The plantation and farm slave-owning classes could not do without slave labor in the fields preparing the land for cultivation, as planters, pickers, and harvesters. Similarly, unwilling African immigrants and their descendants—imported slave labor—worked in the master's house as personal servants, cooks, nurses, or mammies, or performed diverse skilled occupations necessary to a smoothly operating society. Separate entries in this chapter detail the specifics of rice, cotton, sugar, and tobacco production and cultivation. Other entries cover African Americans' economic participation in various aspects of slavery-era capitalism. The emphasis in this chapter is on the work provided for others, the slave owners, yet the context for this work is the tension between enslaved Africans providing forced labor for the benefit of others and the idea that this troublesome property also functioned as active agents for self-serving purposes. The process of loaning or hiring out time supplied additional income to owners while often granting the bondman or bondwoman opportunities to acquire the capital to purchase themselves or family members. Far from acting like acquiescent children, black men and women struggled in a variety of ways to provide a better life for themselves and their families, from making the inhumanly intolerable bearable to acquiring freedom by purchase or flight. Though not

Scenes of plantation slave life. An 1840 illustration of scenes from the lives of slaves in the South. Included are harvesting, cooking, compressing cotton and planting. A few occupations offered slaves a chance at work toward freedom or opportunity, but most only solidified their oppression. *Hulton Archive/Getty Images.*

detailed in this chapter, this impulse is the spirit of "Free Frank" McWhorter who first bought his wife Lucy out of slavery, then himself and their children. Free Frank moved from South Carolina to Kentucky where he oversaw his owner's plantation. Later, after purchasing his family's freedom, Free Frank moved his family to Illinois, eventually becoming the first black man in the United States to found a city, New Philadelphia.

Many enslaved Africans clearly performed their work with the pride of artisans and skilled craftspeople. A substantial number of free or enslaved blacks reaped economic and psychological rewards from jobs well done. Even when the labor was forced, blacks forged economic and personal relationships via their participation in cooperative economic endeavors and domestic necessities or plantation, farm, or urban lifestyles. The standard sunup-to-sundown workday did not allow for much of a social life, but the importance of social dynamics in the work environment cannot be ignored: the field or the big house, though more public than slave quarters, neverthe-

less provided opportunities for blacks to interact with each other, while developing and maintaining a cohesive culture of their own. Whereas most of the entries in this chapter focus on the specific dynamics of the work performed by enslaved Africans, some also illuminate the intricacies of how slaves made a world of their own, often in contradiction to their masters' wishes. Some of the entries note how various occupations enabled or encouraged resistance activities. The status of individual slaves was often determined by the nature of their work, but this could be a double-edged sword. Working in activities associated with the master's house or being closely affiliated with whites might ensure higher regard from some blacks and whites, but was more likely to provoke disdain, resentment, and distrust from other blacks, especially those who worked in the field and had less reason to interact with or trust the intentions of whites.

BIBLIOGRAPHY

Walker, Juliet E. K. *Free Frank: A Black Pioneer on the Antebellum Frontier.* Lexington: The University of Kentucky Press, 1983.

Kamau Kemayo

■ House Slaves

HOUSE SLAVES: AN OVERVIEW

House slave was a term used to refer to those enslaved Africans relegated to performing domestic work on American slave plantations. Typically slave labor on the plantation was divided into two broad categories: house servants and field hands. The process of turning a person into a house servant or field hand was called "seasoning." The goal of seasoning was to socialize the enslaved into disciplined, obedient workers. The practice itself was coercive and extremely violent. The central task was to remove the cultural memory of those enslaved to ensure that notions of African inferiority and white superiority could replace it within three years (Phillips 1914, p. 546). It is estimated that close to 20 percent of those who reached American shores perished during the seasoning process (Society of Friends 1842, p. 19). During the seasoning process people were divided into three categories: New Africans or saltwater Negroes; Old Africans; and Creoles. New Africans or saltwater Negroes represented those recently from Africa. They spoke indigenous languages, carried African names, and maintained a strong connection to the culture of their ancestors. They were often considered the most dangerous and prone to rebellion. Old Africans were those who were born in Africa but spent a considerable amount of time within the plantation system. Typically they were middle-aged and elderly persons. Creoles were persons of African descent who were born in the Americas. Their social experiences were limited to the culture of American slave plantations. For the most part Creoles and Old Africans were preferred as house servants.

The vast majority of those enslaved were field hands. Field hands were the backbone of the plantation economy. They performed the most difficult agricultural tasks on cotton, sugar, rice, and tobacco plantations, which included: the clearing of forests for new farmland; the digging of irrigation ditches and construction of dikes for rice production; picking by hand the thorny cotton bush; and the manual planting and harvesting of sugarcane with a machete. As part of the gang labor system, field hands were often divided into work groups based upon age, physical health, and skill level. During the height of the growing season, field hands typically worked eighteen-hour days, from sunup to sundown. The regimentation of work on the plantation was critical for its profitability. Violence was the principle method used by overseers, drivers, and plantation owners to discipline field hands. Although the lifestyle of field hands varied from plantation to plantation, generally speaking they often lived in deplorable housing conditions, consumed the worst food, and received little if any medical attention. For this reason the lifespan of field hands was relatively short. Men, women, and children of all ages served as field hands. Pregnant women would often work in the fields until they delivered. Elderly men and women worked until they were disabled. The lifestyle of the field hand was backbreaking for most.

In stark contrast to the field hand was the life of the house slave. House slaves primarily performed tasks associated with maintaining the domestic life and home of the plantation owner. Typically this would include the following: cooking; cleaning; the maintenance of kitchen gardens for house consumption; running errands; caring for domestic animals; sewing and repairing clothes worn by the master's family; performing common household chores; and caring for the master's young children. The house slaves, although free from the backbreaking work of the field slaves, worked long hours as well. They were required to organize their entire lives around the social needs of the master's family. This was particularly true if there were young children. African American women, who served as domestic slaves, often performed the work of wet nurse and surrogate mother to newborns. Men would play a variety of roles including playmate and personal servant to adolescents as well as drivers. Drivers

An African American man working in the kitchen. The house slave, though free from the hard labor of the field slave, worked long hours as well. They were required to organize their entire lives around the social needs of the master's family. © *North Wind Picture Archives.*

were essentially extensions of the overseer. They monitored the work of the field hands, disciplined the enslaved population through the use of violence, and participated in capturing runaways. Unlike field hands, house slaves were often given hand-me-downs from the master's family. In some cases instead of living in the slave quarters, they were given rooms in the master's home. Because they served as cooks they often consumed the leftovers from meals prepared for the master's family. Although learning how to read and write was illegal, many house servants learned from the wives and children of the plantation owner.

Differences between the work of house servants and field hands led to sharp social class distinctions within the plantation system. Socially speaking, house servants were considered a privileged class among the enslaved population. Because of their physical proximity to the home of the plantation owner, they often absorbed the culture and associated material benefits of the master (Ingraham 1860, pp. 34–36). The overseer, to control the behavior and work habits of the enslaved, used these divisions skillfully. Plantation owners who were disgruntled with their house servants would threaten to make these servants work out in the fields. Slave owners also made an attempt to ensure that house servants and field hands would remain socially isolated, both physically and psychologically, from one another even if they shared blood ties. House servants were threatened with flogging if they were caught interacting with field hands (Williams 1838, p. 48). In many ways, the notion of the happy house slave portrayed in movies such as *Gone with the Wind,* and the rebellious field slave are both mythic and simplistic. The lives and social consciousness of field hands and house servants were most often extremely complex.

The life of a house servant was often harsh and demeaning. Women house servants in particular were both desired and routinely raped by the plantation owner. Because they lived in close proximity to the master's family, the house servant was naturally absorbed into its many social conflicts. The master's desire for a slave mistress caused severe problems if he was married. In many cases the mistress of the house resented the presence of female house servants. Women house servants served as a constant reminder of marital infidelity. In response mistresses would often abuse their female house servants physically by slapping their faces, boxing their ears, and flogging. House servants were required to defer socially to the members of the master's family regardless of age differences. Elder men were required to refer to the teenage and adolescent children of the master as *sir* and *ma'am.* Elder women who often served as wet nurses for white infants were required to defer to them as adults (Jacobs 1861). In addition, house servants served as informants for the master and overseer, concerning the possibility of revolt by field hands. By the same token, house servants often performed the role of spy for field hands planning a rebellion. Being in close proximity to the master, they were privy to enormous amounts of information concerning the daily habits, hopes, fears, strengths, and weaknesses of the plantation system and its managers. This information would be vital to field hands who were planning an escape or a successful revolt. Although the nature of work performed by the house servant was much different from the work performed by the field hand, the overarching presence of the slave system and its coercive, violent, and humiliating methods of socialization invariably would define the lives of the enslaved regardless of their status within the plantation system.

BIBLIOGRAPHY

Friends, Society of. New England Yearly Meeting. *An Appeal to the Professors of Christianity in the Southern States and Elsewhere, on the Subject of Slavery.* Providence, RI: Knowles and Vose, 1842.

Ingraham, Joseph Holt. *The Sunny South, or, the Southerner at Home: Embracing Five Years' Experience of a Northern Governess in the Land of the Sugar and the Cotton.* Philadelphia: G.G. Evans, 1860.

Jacobs, Harriet. *Incidents in the Life of a Slave Girl.* Boston: Published for the Author, 1861.

Phillips, Ulrich Bonnell. "A Jamaica Slave Plantation" *The American Historical Review* vol. 19, no. 3 (April 1914): 543–558.

Williams, James. *Narrative of James Williams, an American Slave: Who was for Several Years a Driver on a Cotton Plantation in Alabama.* Boston, MA: Anti-Slavery Society, 1838.

Kwasi Densu

NURSES AND MAMMIES

The term "mammy," a variation on "mommy" or "mama," was used in the South to describe a black woman who cared for a slaveholder's children. There was often a strong bond between mammies and white children. The word was also used by slave children to refer to their own mothers or caretakers. Because many slave mothers were sold away from their young children, mammies often cared for all of a plantation's children regardless of bloodline.

The size of the homestead or the wealth of the slave owner determined the extent of a mammy's responsibilities. She might care solely for the white children or for all of the manor's children. On smaller plantations with fewer slaves, she might also serve as housekeeper, cook, seamstress, washerwoman, and caregiver with a full roster of chores to complete each day. Callie Williams, born and raised a slave in Alabama, recalled that "while mammy was tendin' de babies, she had to spin cotton and she was supposed to spin two 'cuts' a day. Four 'cuts' was a hard day's work" (*Born in Slavery,* Alabama Narratives, vol. 1, p. 426). On homesteads with an abundance of slaves, there could be two mammies—one to care for the slaveholder's children and another for slave children. These women were usually older and no longer useful in the fields, or barren, and had the help of slave boys and girls who were either too young to help with crops or were being trained as personal servants. The use of mammies allowed slaveholders to send new or young mothers back into the fields to work.

During the slavery era the term *nurse* or *nursemaid* referred to someone who helped out with the very young and the sick. These young people (both male and female) were trained either by their elders or white doctors to administer simple remedies for common ailments. Other "nurses" had no training whatsoever, as the term was synonymous with caregiver and could refer to slave girls and boys as young as five or six years old. George Womble, born in 1843, was taken in by his owner after both his parents were sold. At about the age of seven, his "job" was to wait tables, help with the house cleaning, and to act as nursemaid to three young children belonging to the master. George had a reputation as an "excellent house boy" and so was

Slave Nurses. A nurse holds her young mistress in this photo, circa 1850. In the slavery era, the terms "nurses" or "nursemaids" referred to slaves who cared for the very young or very sick. Some nurses could administer simple treatments, while others had no training at all and could be as young as five years old. *AP Images.*

North Carolina, recalled that her grandmother Sarah McDonald, who bore fifteen children of her own, served as wet nurse for the plantation of George McDonald. "She was called black mammy because she wet nursed so many white children. In slavery times she nursed all babies hatched on her master's plantation and kept it up after the war as long as she had children" (*Born in Slavery*, North Carolina Narratives, vol. 11, part 1, p. 54).

The story of Emiline Waddell, as told to and recited by an interviewer, is an example of the bond that black mammies and nurses often formed with their white masters' families. Emiline, born in 1826 in Georgia, "was a faithful old black mammy ... and refused her freedom at the close of the war as she wanted to stay and raise 'ol' Massa's chilluns' ... She was nursing her sixth generation in the Waddell family at the time of her death. Even to that generation there was a close tie between the Southern child and his or her black mammy" (*Born in Slavery*, Arkansas Narratives, vol. 2, part 7, p. 13).

BIBLIOGRAPHY

Born in Slavery: Slave Narratives from the Federal Writers' Project, 1936-1938. Manuscript Division, Library of Congress. Alabama Narratives, vol. 1; Arkansas narratives, vol. 2, part 7; Georgia Narratives, vol. 4, part 4; Indiana Narratives, vol. 5; North Carolina Narratives, vol. 11, part 1; Oklahoma Narratives, vol. 13. Available from http://memory.loc.gov/ammem/snhtml/ snhome.html.

Sydnor, Charles Sackett. *Slavery in Mississippi.* New York and London: Appleton-Century, 1933. (Repr., Gloucester, MA: P. Smith, 1965.)

Nelson Rhodes

"often hired out to the other white ladies of the community to take care of their children and to do their housework" (*Born in Slavery*, Georgia Narratives, vol. 4, part 4, p. 179).

Phyllis Petite, of Fort Gibson, Oklahoma, was also a nursemaid:

> I just played around until I was about six years old, I reckon, then they put me up at the Big House with my mammy to work. ... I done a whole lot of sweeping and minding the baby. The baby was only about six months old ... and I used to stand by the cradle and rock it all day. And when I quit I went to sleep right by the cradle sometimes before my mammy would come and get me. (*Born in Slavery*, Oklahoma Narratives, vol. 13, p. 237)

Wet nurses were different from nursemaids and mammies, though the terms were sometimes used interchangeably. Wet nurses were lactating slave women who nursed babies, both black and white, though the white children always came first. Sarah Louise Augustus, of Raleigh,

PERSONAL SERVANTS

Personal servants, in most cases, led better lives than other slaves, especially those who worked in the fields. The term *personal servant* differed from one plantation to another, as some applied the phrase broadly—encompassing all servants who worked within a household (as opposed to outside it)—while others considered personal servants only as butlers, houseboys, or personal maids assigned to one master for life. As related in *Born in Slavery: Slave Narratives from the Federal Writers' Project, 1936–1938*, "House servants were always considered superior to field hands" (Georgia Narratives, vol. 4, pt. 4, p. 314).

Personal slaves were often selected by skin color, as most slave owners believed the lighter the hue the more intelligent the slave. Many were the slaveholders' own progeny, their bloodline having secured them a position within the household and some privileges, though they were still slaves and required to work. That slaveholders were fathering children with their slaves was an open

A personal servant holding an umbrella over a woman in Baltimore, Maryland, 1861. Personal servants usually led better lives than other slaves. Many were the slaveholders' own progeny, though they were still slaves and required to work. *© North Wind Picture Archives.*

secret, as noted in *The Case of William L. Chaplin*: "The slaves of the District of Columbia are of a superior class; most of them house-servants, and not a few children of members of Congress, inheriting from their fathers not only a lighter complexion, but a higher degree, also, of intelligence and sensibility" (1851, p. 17).

Rebecca Hooks was a slave born in Jones County, Georgia to mulatto parents. Her mother was the daughter of William Lowe, the plantation owner, and because of her "blood mixture" Rebecca was far better off than other slaves on the homestead. "They were known as 'house niggers,' and lived on quarters located at the rear of the 'big house.' A 'house nigger' was a servant whose duties consisted of chores around the big house, such as butler, maid, cook, stableman, [gardener], and personal attendant to the man who owned them. These slaves were often held in high esteem by their masters and of course fared much better than the other slaves on the plantation" (*Born in Slavery*, Florida Narratives, vol. 3, p. 172).

Not all house servants fared well, however, for brutality was commonplace regardless of status. Joseph Henry, who wrote *A Statement of Facts Respecting the Condition & Treatment of Slaves*, was appalled by the

beatings and violence publicly inflicted upon slaves in Vicksburgh, Mississippi. "I have seen house servants kicked, cuffed, struck and beaten in the streets, and heard a great many stories of such treatments. They are matters of every day's occurrence in Vicksburgh; and are so perfectly common in that city, that nobody thinks of taking any special notice of them" (1839, p. 4).

Slaves living in the North were well aware of the harshness of life for their Southern brethren. Threats of selling slaves had long been used to keep them in line, but those living above the Mason-Dixon Line greatly feared the savagery of life upon Southern plantations. As related in *The Child's Anti-Slavery Book* (c. 1859), a wife commented upon her husband's strict rules regarding house servants: "He says if a slave is once allowed to retort, all discipline ceases, and he *must* be sold South."

Resentment: Inside the Homestead and Out

In rare cases, slaveholder offspring did not work at all and were companions to their stepsiblings and their place within the household was secure for life. While they were not treated as well as the white children, they were seldom assigned tasks and never forced into hard labor. If the slaveholder died, however, they could be sold or put out on the streets.

Such a life was definitely better than toiling from dawn to dusk in the fields, but the daily existence of personal servants—especially those who were the slaveholder's own children—ran to two extremes. Some were resented or hated by the house's mistress and their half-siblings because of the miscegenation they represented; others were treated exceedingly well and raised as if white. In the latter case, though they were still slaves, they were taught to speak proper English, dressed in good clothes, and ate the same fine foods as the rest of the family. Other slaves were given only rations, dressed in clothes they made themselves, and lived in shacks within the slave quarters.

"Aunt" Ellen Thomas of Georgia was not related by blood to her slaveholder, Judge P. G. Kimball, but led life as a well-regarded member of his household. As related in *Born in Slavery* editor Mary A. Poole wrote:

> … the story of 'Aunt' Ellen is unusual, in that having been raised as a house servant in a cultured Southern family, she absorbed or was trained in the use of correct speech and does not employ the dialect common to Negroes of the slavery era…. Thus brought up as a child among the Kimball children, and because of her duties as a house servant, she mingled little with field hands and learned none of their dialect. (Alabama Narratives, vol. 1, pp. 376–377)

House servants could also be resented by other slaves on a homestead, because they were seldom subjected to punishment or whippings. To field hands, personal servants often seemed more white than black and were not trusted. After the Civil War, slaves who had served as personal maids and house servants sometimes stayed with their former owners rather than leave, out of loyalty and kinship.

BIBLIOGRAPHY

Born in Slavery: Slave Narratives from the Federal Writers' Project, 1936–1938. Online collection of the Manuscript and Prints and Photographs Divisions of the Library of Congress. Available from http://memory.loc.gov/ammem/snhtml/snhome.html.

The Case of William L. Chaplin. Boston: Chaplin Committee, 1851.

The Child's Anti-Slavery Book. New York, 1859.

Henry, Joseph. *A Statement of Facts Respecting the Condition and Treatment of Slaves.* Medina, OH, 1839.

Lane, Lunsford. *The Narrative of Lunsford Lane.* Boston: Hewes and Watson, 1845.

Nelson Rhodes

THE BIG HOUSE

The house slave—one who was relegated to working in the *big house* (sometimes referred to as the *great house*), the master's and mistress's home—often enjoyed an easier and more comfortable existence when compared to their field hand counterpart. House slaves typically toiled as cooks, servers, butlers, carriage drivers, maids, laundresses, seamstresses, mammies, nurses, wet nurses, and even companions, who, in some cases, provided valued emotional support for the mistress and her children. In general, slaveholders provided for their house servants more substantial clothing, larger and more varied meals, better medical attention, more adequate housing, greater freedom and decision-making powers, and, not uncommonly, rudimentary educations, including Christian education, than they did for the slave population at large. And, not insignificantly, slaves in the big house could usually take comfort in the knowledge that they were less likely to be sold off the plantation and thus separated from their families. House servants were often valued employees whom the master and mistress did not want out of the big house.

Slaves who worked in the big house typically benefited from an elevated status within the slave community. House servants, according to Frederick Douglass, made up "a sort of black aristocracy" (1968 [1855], p. 9). Some of those bondmen not uncommonly became leaders within the slave community, some of them assumed high-profile roles as preachers, and all, by virtue of their positions, became conduits between their masters' white world and their own black world. In particular, house slaves relayed important information to the rest of the slave community, both useful instruction and salacious gossip. They, because of their proximity to white conversations in the big house, were able to warn fellow slaves about impending slave auctions and imminent slave punishments, as well as to transmit other salient information garnered from their exposure to white conversation. Slaves, by virtue of such transmission, were kept abreast of political activity, local and national, that affected them. Initial awareness of such political milestones as Nat Turner's Rebellion (1831), the Fugitive Slave Law of 1850, *Dred Scott v. Sandford* (1857), and others often came to the slave population via these conduits.

Despite some slaves respecting the social position of the big house servants, many others resented their elevated status and privileges, especially in instances where the black house staff had fully internalized the values of their masters and mistresses. Ellen Betts, one former field hand, recalled: "All the niggers have to stoop to Aunt Rachel [the cook in the big house] jes' lak dey curtsy to Missy" (Palmer 1998, p. 160). Lucy Thurston, another ex-field hand, reported that sometimes the house servants "get mighty upidy 'cause they served the Marster an' his family…" (Palmer 1998, p. 148). Finally, oft-cited ex-bondman Henry Bibb asserted that "the distinction among slaves is as marked as the classes of society are in any aristocratic community; some refusing to associate with others whom they deem beneath them in point of character, color, conditions, or the superior importance of the respective masters" (1968 [1849], p. 33).

Because they lived and worked in close proximity with one another, house servants and their owners tended to form more complex relationships than did field hands and owners. Several documented cases reveal that slaveholders often thought of house slaves as part of their own family, although they certainly did not remotely consider them their equals. For example, despite vehement and continual avowals that house servants were their inferiors, slaveholders celebrated the birth of their children and mourned the death of their favorite domestics who had served them in the big house. An even more extreme example, slaveholding families who had suffered the deaths of biological children brought carefully handpicked slave children to live in the big house as surrogates for their deceased sons and daughters. Still, in other instances, black house children and their white masters' offspring formed bonds with one another and even played together until puberty when it was considered inappropriate for young persons of different races to fraternize. Such interaction underscores at least some sense of humanity that some white slaveholders exhibited toward chattel whom they perceived as their racial inferiors. On one level, some plantation families came to know some of their enslaved domestics as persons—and not objects—and mutual bonds of affection did evolve among them. Nevertheless, status and racial differentials were never blurred, and each group always knew its place.

Although house slaves had more perks and privileges than field hands, one should not underestimate the

A plantation house slave announcing a visitor to his master, circa 1825.   In general, house servants received better clothing, house, meals, medical attention and greater freedom than other slaves. It was not uncommon for house slaves to receive a rudimentary educations.   *Three Lions/Hulton Archive/Getty Images.*

negatives of slave life in the big house. At first glance, house servant work appeared to be easier than that of the field hand; however, in some ways it was not. For example, slaves who habitually worked in the plantation house were constantly and often uncomfortably accessible to their masters and mistresses, and could thus be called upon for service at any time—day or night. Additionally, house servants—unlike the field hands—typically did not receive Sundays off and were usually obliged to perform their daily duties as well as to attend church services with the white family. Some house slaves, citing negatives of big house life, complained about their isolation from the rest of the slave community as a result of working in, and sometimes living at, the master's home. Another complaint often voiced by house servants was their lack of privacy; field hands, by virtue of geographical separation and very different types of social interaction, were afforded far more independent lives than their brothers and sisters who operated daily in the master's world.

Nevertheless, the dichotomy that is usually drawn between house slave and field slave is somewhat false because the occupational division of the two groups was not often all that clear-cut. Such was particularly the case on farms and smaller plantations.

Despite some evidence to the contrary, the majority of slaves in the Cotton Belt during the antebellum era did not enjoy much occupational mobility. In this region at that time, most bondmen and bondwomen performed the same jobs for the duration of their working lives, and children were more likely than not to inherit their parents' jobs. Ex-bondman Michael Johnson recalled that whether a slave would become a field hand, a house servant, or a skilled tradesman was more or less predictable at birth (Palmer 1998).

An undetermined number of house slaves—especially females—were the victims, both occasional and frequent, of white male-inflicted sexual abuse and violence. Such individuals had no power to resist those unwanted advances. Ex-slave Harriet Jacobs recounted:

Plantation slaves on Edisto Island, South Carolina. A photograph, circa the 1850s, shows the slaves of James Hopkins on his plantation on Edisto Island, South Carolina. House slaves—those who worked in the master and mistress's home, or "Big House"—often enjoyed an easier and more comfortable existence than field hands. *© Corbis.*

"My master met me at every turn, reminding me that I belonged to him, and swearing by heaven and earth that he would compel me to submit to him" (1861, p. 45). This difficult dynamic was further exacerbated by angry and jealous white plantation women whose male family members engaged in such behavior; they, in turn, punished—in both direct and indirect ways—those black victims of the white master population. Although there were some slaves who worked in the big house and enjoyed meaningful relationships with their white owners, many others—especially those who were the mistress's sexual competitors—experienced lives probably far more severe than those of the typical field hand.

BIBLIOGRAPHY

Bibb, Henry. *Narrative of the Life and Adventures of Henry Bibb, an American Slave* [1849]. New York: Negro Universities Press, 1968.

Blassingame, John W. *The Slave Community: Plantation Life in the Antebellum South.* New York: Oxford University Press, 1972.

Douglass, Frederick. *My Bondage and My Freedom* [1855]. New York: Arno Press, 1968.

Fox-Genovese, Elizabeth. *Within the Plantation Household: Black and White Women of the Old South.* Chapel Hill: University of North Carolina Press, 1988.

Jacobs, Harriet A. *Incidents in the Life of a Slave Girl, Written by Herself.* Boston: Published for the Author, 1861.

Palmer, Colin A. *Passageways: An Interpretive History of Black America*, vol. 1: 1619–1863. Fort Worth, TX: Harcourt Brace College Publishers, 1998.

Schwartz, Marie Jenkins. *Born in Bondage: Growing Up Enslaved in the Antebellum South.* Cambridge, MA: Harvard University Press, 2000.

Katherine E. Rohrer

■ Field Slaves

FIELD SLAVES: AN OVERVIEW

The disappearance of slavery in other parts of the country during the early national period did not inspire southerners to give up their peculiar institution. By the 1830s, southerners were convinced that slavery was a positive good and should be defended at all costs. The planter aristocracy enlisted the support of non-slave-holding whites to help them maintain their unique way of life. After all, masters wanted to maximize the return on their investment in human property. Slave labor was the lifeblood of farms and plantations across the South. The planters' economic system perpetuated the exploitation of black men and women during the antebellum years. Not surprisingly, the bulk of the slaves worked in the arena of cultivating crops. The evidence reveals that approximately three-quarters of the adult slaves worked as field laborers while one-quarter had other duties (Kolchin 1993, p. 105).

Field labor was as strenuous as it was varied. The seasons, regions of the South, and the size of the farms were significant factors in determining the treatment and performance expectations of field slaves. Doubtless, the summer months were the most arduous because of the long days and the increase in the quantity of work that had to be done. The harvesting of crops was an especially busy time on the plantations, which required workdays approaching fifteen hours. Sugar and cotton farmers of Louisiana had a reputation for working their laborers

hard. It should be mentioned that hard work and relentless pushing by slave owners were not limited to the states of the Deep South. Frederick Douglass (1817–1895), one of the most notable Americans of the nineteenth century, described his experience as an overworked field slave on a Maryland farm in his autobiography. He wrote: "We were worked in all weathers. It was never too hot or too cold; it could never rain, blow, hail, or snow, too hard for us to work in the field" (1960, p. 94).

Although it was the preference of planters to avoid night work, the practice was nonetheless widespread throughout the slave kingdom. According to one historian, "slaves rarely escaped it entirely" and working late into the night "was almost universal on sugar plantations during the grinding season, and on cotton plantations when the crop was being picked, ginned, and packed" (Stampp 1989, p. 80). Solomon Northup (b. 1808), a free Negro, who had the misfortune of being kidnapped and sold into slavery in Louisiana, remembered toiling at night on many occasions. He recorded for posterity his observations of field laborers. Northup noted that "The hands are required to be in the cotton fields as soon as it is light in the morning ... they are not permitted to be a moment idle until it is too dark to see, and when the moon is full, they often times labor till the middle of the night" (1968, p. 126).

Planters demanded that their bondmen do a full day's work whether in cotton, tobacco, rice, sugar, hemp, or building fences. Because of excessive expectations, field hands were routinely overworked. Although the slaves were bedeviled by difficult workdays, rest was essential for their survival. Louis Hughes (b. 1832) provided a vivid account of slave life on a cotton plantation in Virginia when he penned his autobiography. He reminisced that "The slaves never had any breakfast, but went to the field at daylight and after working till the sun was well up, all would stop for their morning bite" (1969, pp. 38–39). The main meal of the workday occurred at noon and coincided with a two-hour break for the slaves. It was standard practice for planters to give their slaves Sundays off for their personal use. Although cruelness and harshness were constant elements of the institution, the slaveholding class was not homogeneous. The recollection of Julia Brown, who was a slave on a plantation in Georgia, was that "[s]ome of the white folks was very kind to their slaves" (Yetman 2002, p. 22).

Slave owners frequently complained about the difficulty of managing their bondsmen. The management structure on large plantations often included an overseer and a driver. The overseer had to know when and how to prod the field hands under his control. Furthermore, he had the responsibility of maintaining discipline and administering punishment. The whipping of field slaves for the slightest transgression was a common occurrence in the South. It was clear that the expectation of the overseer was the production of a good crop by his workers. The black driver occupied a precarious position in

Field slaves working on the James Hopkins plantation in Edisto, South Carolina, 1862. Three-quarters of adult slaves worked as field slaves. Field slaves were routinely overworked and often worked all day and into the night. *Getty Images.*

the hierarchy of the plantation because his loyalties were divided between the master and the slaves. Planters devised various methods of managing their chattels, fully aware of the advantages and disadvantages of each scheme. The gang system and the task system were the most popular, and it was almost certain that a field hand would experience both during his time in bondage.

On many southern plantations, slave women toiled in the fields alongside the men. They picked cotton, plowed, hoed, and cleared new land. The performance threshold for women was usually lower than for men. Masters, however, required their female hands to work with alacrity and skill. The gender roles on the plantations were clearly defined. Historian Elizabeth Fox-Genovese concluded that the "overwhelming majority of adult slave women returned from their work in the fields to cook, wash, sew, knit, weave, or do other kinds of work" (1988, p. 177). Regardless of regional variations or diversity of tasks, slave women were unable to escape the brutal nature of plantation life.

The plantation was a complex enterprise consisting of many parts. Foremost among them were the field slaves. The work regimen of the slaves was commonly regulated by the size of the holdings and planter demands. Numerous masters believed that their workforce could only be productive by the imposition of strict supervision. No amount of control, however, could completely suppress the rebellious spirit of the slaves. Full-blown insurrections combined with individual acts of resistance served as constant reminders of the slaves' dissatisfaction with their condition of bondage. Looking through the telescope of retrospect, the field slaves appreciated their liberation at the hands of Union soldiers.

BIBLIOGRAPHY

Douglass, Frederick. *Narrative of the Life of Frederick Douglass: An American Slave*, [1845], ed. Benjamin Quarles. Cambridge, MA: Belknap Press of Harvard University Press, 1960.

Fox-Genovese, Elizabeth. *Within the Plantation Household: Black and White Women of the Old South.* Chapel Hill and London: University of North Carolina Press, 1988.

Hughes, Louis. *Thirty Years a Slave: From Bondage to Freedom; the Institution of Slavery as Seen on the Plantation and in the Home of the Planter; Autobiography of Louis Hughes* [1897]. Reprint, Miami: Mnemosyne, 1969.

Kolchin, Peter. *American Slavery, 1619–1877.* New York: Hill and Wang, 1993.

Northup, Solomon. *Twelve Years A Slave: A Slave Narrative of Solomon Northup* [1853]. Eds. Sue Eakin and Joseph Logsdon. Reprint, Baton Rouge: Louisiana State University Press, 1968.

Stampp, Kenneth M. *The Peculiar Institution: Slavery in the Antebellum South.* New York: Vintage, 1989.

Yetman, Norman R., ed. *When I Was a Slave: Memoirs from the Slave Narrative Collection.* Mineola, NY: Dover, 2002.

Leonne M. Hudson

AGRICULTURAL WORK

Africans and their children slaved in agricultural production since the earliest days of colonization in the Americas. The enslavement of Africans by Europeans antedates the emergence of the sugar plantation as the dominant context of slave labor in the New World, but it was the rapid expansion of the cane fields along the northern coast of South America that established black hereditary slavery as the singular model for agricultural production and export in the broader Caribbean. Black and brown people were enslaved to work on plantations controlled by Dutch, Danish, English, French, and Portuguese planters. The plantation generation did not appear in Virginia and South Carolina until the last quarter of the seventeenth century.

Slaves in the Northern colonies might work in a wide variety of crops—such as wheat, indigo, and corn—but in the eighteenth century most Africans and African Americans toiled on rice and tobacco plantations. Cotton did not become "king" in the South until the early nineteenth century, and the only place where sugarcane grew on the continent was Louisiana.

Numerous factors drove the rice and tobacco plantation revolutions in the South. Environment was certainly one of them. In the 1690s, planters from Barbados discovered that the marshy low country of South Carolina proved good soil for rice. Tobacco required rich soil and delicate care—floodwaters easily destroyed the luxury crop. Despite attempts to grow tobacco in the low country, the Chesapeake and Piedmont regions in Virginia proved conducive to the successful growth of the leaf. Tobacco was already commonly grown in Virginia before Bacon's Rebellion in 1676. After the gentry put down the rebellion, however, they ushered in a new era of tobacco production that focused increasingly on the enslavement of Africans.

As Philip Morgan noted, South Carolina and Virginia appeared very similar to visitors in the late seventeenth century—underpopulated and "signally unimpressive" (p. 27). By the middle of the eighteenth century, however, "two distinct plantation regimes emerged that framed the building of two contrasting slave societies and cultures" (p. 29). The crops slaves cultivated did not determine their experiences. Yet rice and tobacco required two very different systems of work. Thus, understanding how these two crops were raised and processed reveals much about daily life under slavery.

Virginia and Tobacco

Tobacco was a luxury crop that required careful attention during all phases of its production. Unlike rice production in South Carolina, it was common for masters to spend much of the day in the tobacco fields with their slaves watching over them while they worked. Planters arranged slave labor into small "gangs." Large gangs of eight or more, such as those that worked Landon Carter's plantation, might be divided into two or three groups according to their skill level. Masters expected every slave in the gang to work as fast as the quickest hand. Carter divided his slaves into "good, Middling, and indifferent hands" and calculated each laborer's output relative to the fastest worker. Drivers whipped slaves they did not think were working their hardest. Sometimes the best hands, weary of the conditions in the field, purposefully slowed down the pace to aid their tired or ill counterparts. Thus, as many of the large planters strove to develop a scientific regiment of tobacco production, slaves worked to thwart the constant supervision and intense expectations of their masters (p. 188).

Each African worked nearly two acres of the large plantations. Clearing the fields began in January or February, when slaves slashed and burned land in preparation for tilling and planting. Slaves tilled the cleared soil into small mounds arranged in rows, making sure to clear them of weeds and grubs so that the newly planted seed would not be leeched of nutrients. Morgan asserted that by the middle of the eighteenth century most planters expected a slave to till 350 mounds per day (p. 167).

After the tobacco plants sprouted in April, they were weeded and then transplanted into prepared soil. The plants were subsequently "primed," "topped," and "suckered" after they reached the size of twelve to sixteen leaves. The transplantation period was perhaps the most grueling part of the season. Slaves could only successfully transplant the crop into new soil after it rained in the late spring. Masters usually diverted their entire workforce to the transplantation process in April so that they could make sure the crop was cut and cured by August. According to Morgan, most slaves in Virginia ran away in April, the most grueling period of tobacco production (p. 167).

The tobacco harvest lasted from August through September. Slaves cut the plants and allowed them to dry in the field for a day before they were hauled to the

Returning from the cotton fields in South Carolina. Cotton did not become "king" in the South until the early nineteenth century. Before that, most slaves worked on tobacco or rice plantations. *Collection of the New-York Historical Society/Bridgeman Art Library.*

tobacco house. There, slaves drove pegs into the stalk of the plants and hoisted them to the rafters of the building so that they could dry and cure. After several weeks of drying, the plants were removed from the ceiling and the leaves were stripped away from the stalks. Slaves then rolled the leaves and packed them tightly into the hogsheads for shipping.

Slaves worked tirelessly throughout the harvesting period. Masters often justified the hard work of their slaves as something they enjoyed. One observer remarked on the labor of the slaves, noting, "It is astonishing and unaccountable to conceive what an amazing degree of fatigue these poor but happy wretches do undergo, and can support" (p. 168).

Tobacco cultivation was not restricted to slave labor, although most tobacco farmers owned slaves in Virginia. Tobacco farms and plantations along the Chesapeake exhibited higher ratios of American-born slaves to African-born when compared to South Carolina. By 1730, nearly 40 percent of the black people laboring near the Chesapeake were born in the region. Twenty years later, American-born blacks accounted for four-fifths of the slave population. At the onset of the American Revolution only 500 of the 5,000 slaves imported to Virginia came directly from Africa (Berlin 1998, p. 127). Many of the small tobacco farmers turned their interest toward cotton production in the early nineteenth century, and moved their slaves south into the Georgia hinterland in search of new profits.

South Carolina and Rice

In 1761, James Glen remarked on the low country, noting, "the only Commodity of Consequence produced in South Carolina is rice" (Morgan, p. 147). Whereas small farmers might profit from raising tobacco, rice required a large labor force and easy access to flowing water. Rice could not be grown on a whim; planters needed to have considerable access to credit if they wanted to take the risk. Rice was explicitly a plantation crop.

Longstanding connections with slave traders who plied the seas of the Lesser Antilles permitted planters in South Carolina to purchase Africans at resounding rates in the first half of the eighteenth century. Black and brown people rapidly became a majority in the colony. Between 1700 and 1740 the slave population increased from 2,400 to 39,000. Nearly 66 percent of the enslaved population was born in Africa on the eve of the 1739 Stono Rebellion. More than 75 percent of the Africans forced to work in the rice fields came from Angola and the Kingdom of Kongo during the boom years of the 1730s (Morgan, p. 61; Wood 1974).

By the 1750s, however, most Africans arriving in Charleston came from the British-controlled slave forts connected to the Gambia River. Regional differentiation aside, historians agree that rice was commonly grown along the Gambia River during the era of the Atlantic slave trade. Women were the primary cultivators of rice in Senegambia, but in South Carolina the British planters forced both men and women into the fields. The impact of African knowledge on rice cultivation in South

Carolina is difficult to gauge from the historical record. The heel-toe technique of planting rice, whereby the seed is planted with the feet instead of the hands, is believed to be a particularly African method of sowing the crop. Whether or not African knowledge about rice cultivation caught the attention of the planter class is unclear. The shift away from the Kongo River and toward the Senegambia slave trade remains an understudied element of the early cultural history of slavery in North America.

Slaves laboring in rice paddies were organized by task. Overseers assigned a specific quota of work to achieve. By the middle of the eighteenth century, most slaves were expected to weed and cultivate a quarter of an acre per day. In the tidewater region, cultivation required less hoeing, and slaves were expected to manage half-acre plots of rice each day. Masters in South Carolina did not loom over their slaves in the rice paddies the way their counterparts did in the Virginia tobacco fields. Task labor was not easy by any means, and conflicts between overseers and slaves about the amount of work assigned were not uncommon. Yet because individuals could speed up or slow down the rate of their work throughout the day by gauging the amount of work remaining, "slaves and their black drivers conspired to preserve a portion of the day for their own use while meeting the planters' minimum work requirements" (Berlin, p. 153).

The harvest season began in early September. The fields were drained, and slaves followed suit with sickles, cutting swaths of the rice stalks and stacking them to dry. Rice was processed without machinery for most of the eighteenth century. Slaves threshed the grain with a flail and removed the husk with a mortar and pestle. After winnowing the chaff from the grain of rice, the kernels were screened of the "rice flour" and broken pieces before being placed in barrels for shipment (Phillips, p. 90).

Rice remained a key staple in South Carolina into the nineteenth century. By the 1790s, however, planters along the coast began to use the task method in raising the long-staple variety of cotton. Cotton became the most important crop raised in the interior of South Carolina by the middle of the nineteenth century as it rapidly outpaced the production of rice. Originally, much of the rice produced by slaves in South Carolina was sent abroad, often to feed slaves who labored in the sugarcane fields of the Caribbean. By the nineteenth century, however, rice was increasingly shipped westward to feed slaves laboring in the booming cotton industry.

Plantation slavery in the United States crystallized in the form of rice and tobacco plantations in the South during the eighteenth century. These two crops required very different techniques of production that shaped the daily lives of all who were caught in grasp of market agriculture. Well before cotton became the synonymous with slavery in the South, rice and tobacco were king in South Carolina and Virginia, respectively.

BIBLIOGRAPHY

Berlin, Ira. *Many Thousands Gone: The First Two Centuries of Slavery in North America*. Cambridge, MA: Harvard University Press, 1998.

Genovese, Eugene. *Roll, Jordan, Roll: The World the Slaves Made*. New York: Vintage, 1976.

Morgan, Philip D. *Slave Counterpoint: Black Culture in the Eighteenth-Century Chesapeake and Lowcountry*. Chapel Hill: University of North Carolina Press, 1998.

Phillips, Ulrich Bonnell. *American Negro Slavery: A Survey of the Supply, Employment and Control of Negro Labor as Determined by the Plantation Regime*. New York: Peter Smith, 1952.

Wood, Peter. *Black Majority: Negroes in Colonial South Carolina from 1670 through the Stono Rebellion*. New York: W. W. Norton, 1974.

James F. Dator

SEASONAL RHYTHMS OF LIFE

Seasonal changes greatly impacted the lives of Africans and African Americans laboring as slaves in the United States. On plantations, where agricultural work was paramount, the rhythms of life centered on the planting and harvesting of crops such as rice, tobacco, and cotton. Yet the seasons also shaped the experiences of slaves living in cities. In port towns such as New York or Boston, it was not uncommon for icy waters to bring ship-based trade to a halt during the harshest winters. Thus, in the North and the South, the seasons dictated the patterns of labor, shaped access to food, and directly influenced slave health.

Slaves that labored on plantations began to clear the fields for planting new crops in January and February. Planters with enough land at their disposal usually elected to rotate the fields at the beginning of each season so that the upcoming crop would be cultivated in fresh soil. Overgrowth from the previous year was cut down and burned in preparation for the upcoming planting season. On tobacco and cotton plantations, the newly burnt lands were cleared with hoes and sometimes horse or mule driven plows. On rice plantations, slash-and-burn clearing was not as common. Slaves in South Carolina used the tide-flow system, which depended on the careful manipulation of the ebb and flow of the local waterways to flood and drain selected fields. Male slaves were given axes to remove trees from new rice fields, and women and children were assigned the tasks of clearing the brush and shrubs.

Once the lands were cleared, slaves began the back-breaking work of tilling the soil in preparation for planting seed. By March, slaves in tobacco and cotton fields

Slave family in a cotton field. This photograph, circa 1860, shows a slave family in a cotton field near Savannah, Georgia. On plantations, the rhythms of life centered on the planting and harvesting of crops such as rice, tobacco, and cotton. © *Bettman/Corbis.*

began hoeing the soil into small mounds arranged in rows while making sure that the dirt was free of grubs and other nutrient leaching bugs or plants. Most slaves were expected to create at least 350 mounds per day (Morgan 1998, p. 167). In the tidal waters of South Carolina, slaves closed the ruptures along the riverbanks, cleared the drains, prepared sluices, and leveled the fields. Slaves planted the tobacco seed by the end of March, but the intensive labor required to secure the rivers pushed the planting of rice seed into the beginning of April.

Slaves also had to devote what time they could to planting and preparing their provision grounds in the spring. On the largest plantations, slaves often grew their own corn, beans, and yams on small garden plots. In 1732 one onlooker noted that Chesapeake planters allowed slaves "to plant little Platts for potatoes or Indian pease ... on Sundays or [at] night" (Morgan, p. 140).

Food crops such as yams and corn were crucial supplements to the slave's meager rations provided by most masters. Provision grounds, when available, enabled slaves to guard against starvation. With the entire day dedicated to raising their master's crops, nighttime cultivation of communal gardens was a necessity for slaves laboring in the plantation regime.

The long days and hot sun of the summer months contributed to making it the most grueling season for slaves. Rice fields were continually hoed from June through August. Some slaves were forced to wade waist deep in water for hours to stave off birds while others remained on their hands and knees picking weeds and grass from the soil. On tobacco plantations, slaves spent the summer months transplanting tobacco plants and removing ground worms and caterpillars.

The long days, tedious labor, and overt supervision during the summer contributed to slave discontent. In

Virginia, more slaves ran away in April—the height of the planting season. Most runaways in South Carolina elected to flee in June at the beginning of the seemingly incessant period of weeding and tilling. The harvesting of tobacco began at the end of August and usually lasted until late September. The delicate tobacco plants were cut and then hung to dry in the tobacco house. In the fall, the tobacco was carefully inspected, separated into various qualities, and then rolled and packed into hogsheads for shipping abroad. The rice harvest began in September. Slaves drained the fields while others followed with sickles, cutting swaths of rice stalks and stacking them to dry. Rice was processed by hand. Slaves threshed the grain with a flail and removed the husk with a mortar and pestle. After winnowing the chaff from the grain of rice, the kernels were screened of the "rice flour" and broken pieces before being placed in barrels for shipment.

Christmas usually marked the conclusion of the year's labor. On many plantations, slaves expected their masters to allow them "free time"—anywhere from a day to a week—during the holiday. Slaves seized the opportunity to get married, visit relatives on nearby plantations, hold feasts, and plan insurrections. Masters used December 25 to affect benevolence by giving their favored slaves gifts of cloth, rum, and meat. As James Williams recalled, "on Flinchers plantation the slaves had meat but once a year, at Christmas" (1838, p. 65). Frederick Douglass also remarked on the holiday and what it exposed about the seasonal rhythms of life under slavery: "these holidays serve as conductors, or safety-valves, to carry off the rebellious spirit of enslaved humanity" (1845, p. 75).

BIBLIOGRAPHY

Bigham, Shauna, and Robert E. May. "The Time O' All Times? Masters, Slaves, and Christmas in the Old South." *Journal of the Early Republic* 18, no. 2. (1998): 263–288.

Douglass, Frederick. *Narrative of the Life of Frederick Douglass, an American Slave*. Dublin: 1845.

Morgan, Philip D. *Slave Counterpoint: Black Culture in the Eighteenth-Century Chesapeake and Lowcountry.* Chapel Hill: University of North Carolina Press, 1998.

Phillips, Ulrich Bonnell. *American Negro Slavery: A Survey of the Supply, Employment and Control of Negro Labor as Determined by the Plantation Regime.* New York: Peter Smith, 1952.

Williams, James. *Narrative of James Williams: An American Slave who Was for Several Years a Driver on a Cotton Plantation in Alabama.* New York: 1838.

James F. Dator

COTTON PLANTATIONS

During the majority of the seventeenth and eighteenth centuries, cotton was primarily imported to the Northern colonies from the plantations that dotted coastal Demerara, Berbice, and Essequibo in South America. In 1750 most Africans and African Americans slaving in North America labored in the dirt of the tobacco and rice plantations of South Carolina and Virginia. Yet by the mid-nineteenth century, cotton production was synonymous with slavery in the United States. By 1865 cotton plantations dominated the landscape both geographically and socially from the lowlands east of the Appalachians, south of the Ohio River, and all the way west to Texas. The use of plantation slavery to cultivate the textile crop not only redefined what it meant to be enslaved in North America, but also dramatically altered what it meant to be an American in the nineteenth century.

During the crises of war, debt, and slave revolt in the 1730s, plantation owners in South Carolina and Georgia encouraged newly arriving small farmers to grow cotton and corn. The plantation elites, eager to secure the favor of their new neighbors, knew that arrangements with inland farmers might defray some of their costs. Farmers in South Carolina needed the political support of the big planters, who mobilized the militias and controlled colonial legislation. James Oglethorpe, the founder and early leader of the colony of Georgia, encouraged farmers to raise the crop in that state, and the Methodist minister George Whitefield experimented with cottonseed at the Bethesda Orphanage on the eve of the War of Jenkins' Ear. Yet tobacco and indigo proved too profitable for the small farmers who expressed interest in marketing crops. Thus, cotton remained an experimental produce in the lower South for the first three quarters of the eighteenth century.

The nonimportation movement during the American Revolution spurred cotton and cloth production in the colonies. By the 1770s it was not uncommon for slaves to be making cloth to be sold to other plantations on the continent. Plantation owners imported cheap clothing from the New England homespun networks as well. Yet sometimes slaves rejected the cheap, imported clothing given to them by their masters. Slaves on John Channing's plantation refused the "negro clothes" (Chaplin 1993, p. 211). Instead, the male slaves asked for cloth, which they gave to their wives and sisters to fashion, perhaps in African idioms. Starting a plantation was an expensive endeavor. Yet when colonial resistance was met by Parliament's embargo, the children of the elite tobacco and rice farmers found it less so. By the 1790s, Africans and African Americans were increasingly sold by rice and tobacco plantation owners to aspiring cotton masters. The Sea Islands along Georgia's coast became known for the long-staple variety of cotton. In 1793, Whitney's cotton gin forever altered the nature of

Slaves picking cotton in the field. Work lasted from sunrise to sunset, with only short moments of rest, often signaled by a horn. *The Library of Congress.*

slavery in the South. If a farmer could afford the gin, inland farms could yield and rapidly send to market the more delicate short-staple variety of cotton. Tobacco farmers and plantation managers viewed the booming internal cotton trade as an opportunity to become plantation owners. Africans and African Americans from the large plantations were sold, their families divided yet again.

The development of the internal slave trade coincided with the westward expansion of the cotton plantations. Thomas Jefferson's Northwest Ordinance in 1787 guaranteed slave owners the right to reclaim black runaways who fled to the free territories. Later, aspiring cotton planters and frontier farmers benefited directly from Andrew Jackson's bloody military campaigns in Florida and New Orleans during the War of 1812. Old Hickory's fame among whites in the burgeoning cotton belt was central to his presidency. In 1830 he signed the Indian Removal Act, which ushered in an era of forced removal of Cherokee, Creek, and Choctaw and virtually guaranteed federal military intervention on behalf of Southern cotton planters. Total cotton production in the United States increased at least 200 percent every decade between 1810 and 1840 (Phillips 1952, p. 211).

In his narrative, the former slave James Williams remarked on the dismal prospects of being sold to new cotton plantations, noting, "It is an awful thing to a Virginia slave to be sold for the Alabama and Mississippi country." Williams knew that slaves sold westward would "die of grief" and "commit suicide on account" of the news of their sale (1838, p. 32). Sale separated black families—brothers from sisters, wives from husbands, children from parents. Being sold to a new master meant that the slave had to teach oneself new methods of surviving the master's abuse, threats, and labor regime. Running away was common. Africans and African Americans also sought out their kin after they were sold. James Williams' twin brother, who had worked alongside him in Richmond since they were children, was sold to an "Alabama Cotton Planter." Despite the distance, Williams heard that his brother ran away from the new plantation. He discovered that his twin "was seen near the Maryland line" and "escaped into the free states or Canada" (1838, p. 27). More common, however, was the experience of Moses Grandy. His family was "dead or sold away" before he could "remember" (Grandy 1844, p. 5).

Slaves new to cotton production survived by learning the new work regime from their fellow slaves. Owners of large plantations invested in technologies that improved harvesting and finishing of cotton. Masters and drivers allocated tasks based on experience, age, and gender. Unlike slaves on farms, blacks slaving on plantations were assigned specialized tasks that included masonry, blacksmithing, and woodworking. The social division between "domestic" and "field" slaves was greater on large plantations. On the smallest farms, slaves and masters sometimes ate in the same room. On plantations, domestic slaves were expected to remain hidden from public view, use separate entranceways, and sleep in quarters apart from their counterparts in the field. Domestic slaves, often women, raised their master's children, mended clothing, and fixed meals. Sexual exploitation was common. During harvest season, when the need for "field hands" was the greatest, masters did not hesitate to send their "house slaves" into the field. Slaves began to bale cotton toward the end of the harvest season. In the east, slaves might finish the process by December, but in the western states harvesting and baling often extended into March or April. Masters sometimes gave the slaves a few days off during Christmastime. However, even as the harvest season came to a close, slaves began working the fields and preparing for the next year of production. Like tobacco, slaves planted cotton in rows or in linear mounds. Yet masters assigned work according to the task method. Slaves used plows and hoes to turn the soil in the early months of the new year. They removed the old and dead stalks and fertilized the rows with ginned seed or guano, which was imported from South America. Other slaves were ordered to mend the fences or plant corn and wheat in March. In April, black laborers planted the seed by tilling it into the rows of soil. Within three weeks, as the young plants began to sprout, field hands thinned the plants and arranged the plants to grow at intervals of twelve to eighteen inches apart. By midsummer, the plants were left to bloom. Meanwhile, slaves began to harvest the corn and prepare the gin house and bale press for the harvest season.

August and September marked the beginning of picking season. The cotton bolls opened in series, so slaves continued picking for three to four months. Slaves developed rapid techniques for removing the seedy lint from the boll while picking; deft pickers were able to use two hands simultaneously to pick and remove the lint at the same time. Work lasted from sunup to sundown with only short moments of rest, often signaled by horn. Harvest time was the most intense and grueling season for slaves. Drivers and masters often patrolled the task laborers on horseback, usually with a shotgun and whip at their side. Men, women, and children were all ordered to pick as fast as they could in order to beat the planta-

Slaves working on a cotton plantation. Slaves new to cotton production survived by learning the new work regime from experienced slaves. *The Library of Congress.*

tion owner's competitors to the market. Slaves picked hundreds of pounds of cotton from the plants every day, for weeks on end. In 1844, Levin Covington of Natchez, Mississippi, recorded the typical workload of his slaves. Bill averaged 220 pounds of lint per day, Aggy 215 pounds, Dred 205, and Delia 185. Other plantation owners recorded averages of 300 pounds per day (Philips 1952, p. 210). Only rain provided moments of respite for the laborers in the field.

Cotton plantations exhibited features of industrial production and agricultural labor. On the short-staple cotton plantations of the interior, slaves worked in the gin house and the bailing press. Gin houses were typically weatherboard structures, raised about eight feet from the ground. Slaves carted seed cotton from the field to the front of the gin house, where it was weighed and stacked until it could be fed into the gin. Gin rollers separated the seed from the cotton bolls. The seedless lint gathered at the other end of the gin house, where slaves packed into baskets or sacks. They then hauled the sacks to the press, which was used to pack the finished cotton into round or square bales. Slaves carried the ginned cotton to the top of a stepped structure and dumped it into the bale. Mules or horses attached to a long poll moved in a circular motion around the press, which wound the pinion and compacted the lint to the bottom of the bale. They were sealed and set aside until they were ready to be sent to nearest town or port. The average weight of a bale varied from 250 to 500 pounds, depending on the size and quality of the press.

Cotton plantations and slave labor dominated the lives of people living in the South during the nineteenth century. Yet only one-quarter of slaves in the South lived on plantations with fifty slaves or more. Half of the black population in the South lived on small farms with less than twenty slaves (Genovese 1976, p. 7). Most slaveholders owned fewer than five slaves. The majority of blacks lived in the countryside, although some free blacks labored in shipping centers such as Natchez. In 1850, De Bow's Review estimated that of the 3.2 million slaves in the United States, 2.5 million were directly employed in agriculture (Hammond 1897, p. 60). Almost 73 percent of slaves labored in cotton fields. Indeed, the emergence of the cotton plantation in the South forever altered the history of the United States.

BIBLIOGRAPHY

Channing, Joyce E. *An Anxious Pursuit: Agricultural Innovation and Modernity in the Lower South, 1730–1815.* Chapel Hill: University of North Carolina Press, 1993.

Genovese, Eugene. *Roll, Jordan, Roll: The World the Slaves Made.* New York: Vintage Books, 1976.

Grandy, Moses. *Narrative of the Life of Moses Grandy: Formerly a Slave in the United States of America.* Boston, 1844.

Hammond, M. B. *The Cotton Industry: An Essay in American Economic History.* New York: Macmillan, 1897.

Johnson, Walter. *Soul by Soul: Life Inside the Antebellum Slave Market.* Cambridge, MA: Harvard University Press, 1999.

Phillips, Ulrich Bonnell. *American Negro Slavery: A Survey of the Supply, Employment and Control of Negro Labor as Determined by the Plantation Regime.* New York: Peter Smith, 1952.

Williams, James. *Narrative of James Williams: An American Slave Who Was for Several Years a Driver on a Cotton Plantation in Alabama.* New York: 1838. Available online in *Sources in U.S. History Online: Slavery in America.* Gale. Available from http://galenet.galegroup.com/.

James F. Dator

TOBACCO PLANTATIONS

Tobacco has been grown in the Americas for at least two millennia, but European colonization created the conditions for the emergence of cultivators that specialized in large-scale tobacco production. While staple crops such as sugar were readily identified with slave labor in the American colonies, much tobacco was grown by farmers who did not own slaves. However, tobacco's long growing season and its intensive labor requirements meant that it was often produced by enslaved laborers, and the unique nature of its cultivation shaped the work as well as the community of tobacco plantation laborers.

During the American colonial period, tobacco plantations emerged in a variety of places, from parts of Connecticut and New York in the North, south to the Caribbean colonies of Barbados and Jamaica, and as far west as Spanish Louisiana. The largest concentration of tobacco plantations in North America, however, developed in the Chesapeake Bay colonies of Virginia and Maryland. Following the American Revolution, tobacco plantations spread westward to other parts of the upper South, including western Kentucky and Tennessee as well as Missouri.

Successful tobacco cultivation required steady labor from late winter through the fall. The season began in January when laborers cleaned and prepared the beds where tobacco seed was sown, and sowing usually occurred in late February or early March. After significant mid-spring rains, the seedlings would be replanted into hilled rows. One method involved workers using a hoe to gather soil around their leg, which they would remove to create a space for transplanted seedlings. According to historian Philip Morgan, by the mid-eighteenth century Chesapeake tobacco planters expected workers to transplant a seedling every two minutes, and to plant 350 hills per day.

Once transplanted, tobacco seedlings required nearly constant tending until harvest. First, after a certain numbers of leaves appeared, workers would use a small knife or a sharpened thumbnail to cut off the top of each plant to prevent it from flowering. During the summer months, laborers performed three additional tasks: weeding, suckering (or the removal of secondary shoots that would divert energy away from the tobacco leaves), and removing worms and beetles. All three of these tasks required workers to pay close attention to individual plants, to work hunched over, and to perform tasks by hand, all under close supervision. In the mid-nineteenth century, runaway slave John Thompson testified to the nature of the work, and the degree of supervision:

> When the tobacco is ripe, or nearly so, there are frequently worms in it, about two inches long, and as large as one's thumb. They have horns, and are called tobacco worms. They are very destructive to the tobacco crops, and must be carefully picked off by the hands, so as not to break the leaves, which are very easily broken. But careful as they slaves may be, they cannot well avoid leaving some of the worms on the plants. It was a custom of Mr. Wagar to follow after the slaves, to see if he could find any left, and if so, to compel the person in whose row they were found, to eat them. (Thompson, p. 18)

Harvesting the tobacco plants took place as the plants ripened in late August or early September and it was the most labor-intensive part of the crop cycle. The

TOBACCO PLANTATION.

An engraving of a Virginia tobacco plantation, 1855. Slave social activities were structured around the calendar of tobacco production. Summer was filled with work, while winter provided more time for social events such as weddings. *The Granger Collection, New York. Reproduced by permission.*

plants were cut and allowed to wilt in the field for several hours, and then the stalks would be gathered and dried in a barn. After they had dried for a sufficient length of time, the leaves would be stripped from the stalks, and the largest fibers would also be taken out of the leaves, which were then carefully packed into hogsheads. Harvesting, curing and packing tobacco were all delicate operations requiring experience, practice, and close attention.

The nature of tobacco production shaped plantation communities in a variety of ways. Producing significant quantities of quality tobacco was a difficult enterprise because many things could ruin the crop, including pests, disease, weeds, excessive moisture, and improper packaging. Given these dangers slave owners supervised workers quite closely, and typically organized tobacco workers into small teams or squads of a dozen workers or fewer, rather than large gangs. Even slaveholders who owned large numbers of slaves tended to settle them in small groups on different parcels of land. This meant that slave quarters on tobacco plantations were comparatively small, and therefore enslaved men and women often had to look

beyond their own quarters in order connect with kin and friends. Social activities were structured around the tobacco calendar, which meant that there was little slack time in the summer, whereas winter provided more free time for social events such as marriages.

In addition to requiring intensive labor, specialized tobacco production also took a toll on the fertility of the soil. Typically, land would be used for three years, and then allowed to lie fallow for up to twenty so that the land could recover, so this meant that tobacco laborers were required to be more mobile than laborers on rice or sugar plantations. These small squads of workers could be composed of many members of an extended family because men, women, and even very young children were put in the fields to tend tobacco. While the pace of the labor was supervised, the bodily movements of tobacco workers could not be synchronized like they were on sugar plantations, because each plant needed individual attention. But while slaves had some control over their bodily movements, they were still watched closely and struggled to moderate the pace of the labor, as is clear from the testimony of escaped slave Lewis Clark, who recalled his experience on a tobacco plantation in Kentucky:

> When stooping to clear the tobacco-plants from the worms which infest them,—a work which draws most cruelly upon the back,—some of these men would not allow us a moment to rest at the end of the row; but, at the crack of the whip, we were compelled to jump to our places, from row to row, for hours, while the poor back was crying out with torture. (Clarke, p. 24)

BIBLIOGRAPHY

Clarke, Lewis Garrard. *Narratives of the Sufferings of Lewis and Milton Clarke: Sons of a Soldier of the Revolution, during a Captivity of More than Twenty Years Among...* Boston, 1846. "Sources in U.S. History Online: Slavery in America." Gale. Available from http://galenet.galegroup.com.

Morgan, Philip D. *Slave Counterpoint: Black Culture in the Eighteenth-Century Chesapeake and Lowcountry.* Chapel Hill: University of North Carolina Press, 1998.

Thompson, John. *The Life of John Thompson, a Fugitive Slave: Containing His History of 25 Years in Bondage, and His Providential Escape* Worcester: 1856. "Sources in U.S. History Online: Slavery in America." Gale. Available from http://galenet.galegroup.com.

Sean Condon

RICE PLANTATIONS

Rice cultivation was common in the Caribbean and in Africa before it spread along the rivers of South Carolina, North Carolina, and Georgia, as well as the Gulf coast of the United States. Rice cultivation was first developed in what became the United States in South Carolina during the early eighteenth century, by Europeans who brought African slave labor with them from the West Indies. Africans were far more familiar with the product than Europeans, and slaves from West Africa were instrumental in teaching the Europeans about the farming of rice. Rice could be cultivated in swamps or creeks that were diverted to form standing bodies of fresh water. Most rice planters, however, used the waxing and waning tides of rivers for rice farming. The rising tides tended to eliminate other vegetation while giving rice the nourishment it needed, removing the need for slaves to clear the area under cultivation. This reliance on tides severely limited where rice could be grown, however.

Slave labor prepared the growing area. Slaves built the levees and dikes necessary to keep rivers and creeks from overflowing the growing area. They also built irrigation systems, with sluice gates to let the waters in and out. In addition, slaves dug ditches through which the water could flow. The levees required frequent repairs, forcing slaves to work year round. Well-managed rice plantations had redundancies built in such that if one levee failed, the entire crop would not be destroyed. Silt would build up in sluices and ditches, which required the slaves to perform constant maintenance. Thus, whereas during the flood periods slaves could not reach the crop, there was often still a great deal of work for them to do. In addition, the slaves built the residences for their masters and themselves and the buildings for the processing of the rice.

In the spring, slaves would plant the rice seeds. Then the fields would be flooded, allowing the rice to sprout. After this, the growing area would be drained and then hoed. This process of flooding and then hoeing would take place repeatedly, usually four or five times. The slave Charles Ball described the condition of the rice fields: "I saw for the first time, fields of rice, growing in swamps, covered with water. Causeways were raised throug [*sic*] the low-lands in which the rice grew and on which the road was formed on which we traveled. These rice fields, or rather swamps, had, in my eyes, a beautiful appearance" (1859, pp. 49–50). In late summer or early autumn the rice was harvested. Over the course of the autumn and winter slaves prepared the rice for sale. Slaves threshed the rice on hard floors with flails. In 1787 Jonathan Lucas invented a rice mill that could be powered by water. By the nineteenth century the best-financed rice plantations purchased expensive threshing and pounding mills. The rice was polished and then sold. There were few good roads during the early national period, and because rice fields had to be near water in any case, the product was delivered to market, generally Charleston, by boat.

Planters and experts in rice cultivation oversaw the entire production process, but the work was done almost entirely by a slave labor force. The use of fuel and of steam-powered mills to some extent made rice cultivation an industrial process, and illustrates the adaptability of the institution of slavery to processes that were non-agrarian in nature: "The number of hands employed in this threshing-mill is very considerable, and the whole establishment, comprising the fires and boilers and machinery of a powerful steam engine, are all under negro superintendence and direction" (Kemble 1863, p. 100). Those slaves who knew how to use the machinery often received slightly better treatment than field hands.

Rice was a labor-intensive product, though there were periods of less work for the slave labor force when the planting area was flooded. Slaves on rice plantations, therefore, often also tended to corn, potatoes, and other crops, which were their primary food sources, with most rice plantations largely self-sufficient. Rice was produced in an extremely unhealthy environment of swamps, full of mosquitoes carrying malaria and other diseases. Slaves of African ancestry had already developed immunities to many of the dangers present in the swamps, immunities

THE INVENTION OF THE WATER-POWERED MILL

Jonathan Lucas was born in Cumberland, England, in 1754, and trained as a millwright. He found himself in South Carolina along the Santee River after a shipwreck. There were a number of rice planters along the Santee, and Lucas in his time there ascertained that the manner in which rice was detached from its outer hull was inefficient. Slaves used wooden tools to separate the rice. Lucas invented a water-powered mill in 1787, saving the planters manpower and making the product far more profitable. Lucas continued to build mills in the area for a number of planters, continuously improving on his original design to create mills that could be powered by the tide, and much later steam. Lucas eventually settled in the area and became a planter himself, though he continued to build mills for others. His son and grandson continued his mill design work in South Carolina.

Lucas's inventions were essential to the spread of rice cultivation in the region; previous to his invention, indigo was the predominant cash crop for South Carolina. Lucas allowed South Carolina to diversify its agricultural economy and spread rice plantations throughout much of the South.

SOURCE: Dethloff, Henry C. *A History of the American Rice Industry, 1685–1985.* College Station: Texas A & M University Press, 1988.

a white labor force would have failed to possess. Even so, slaves were well aware of the comparative dangers of the climate and work associated with rice plantations. Josephine Brown, in speculating over the potential fate of the brothers of a slave, William, wrote: "If still living, they are lingering out a miserable existence on a cotton, sugar, or rice plantation, in a part of the country where the life of the slave has no parallel in deeds of atrocity. Nothing can be worse than slavery in Louisiana and Mississippi, on the banks of the noblest river in the world" (1856, p. 17).

Rice plantations tended to be quite large, and there were few small independent operators—in part due to the absence of available land, in part due to economic trends that encouraged consolidation. In addition, rice cultivation required large slaveholdings. As a consequence, rice plantations had far larger slave concentrations than plantations raising other products such as hemp and tobacco, though this is also due in part to the fact that large rice plantations were the rule. John George Clinkscales noted the detachment between the owners and the slaves of rice plantations in South Carolina that was one of the hallmarks of rice production: "On many of these slaves were numbered by the hundred; on a few there were more than a thousand. Some of the 'large slave-owners,' that is to say, the owners of more than a thousand did not know their own negroes.

In such cases, master and slave came in touch with each other only through the overseer, or driver" (1916, p. 8). Thus, rice plantations were unlikely to have the evils of the institution of slavery moderated by the paternalism of a personal relationship between master and slave.

Despite the labor-intensive nature of the crop and the dangers of the growing environment, slaves on rice plantations had a far greater degree of freedom than slaves involved in the production of other products. Planters were often absentee owners from spring to late autumn, when tropical diseases were a danger. Plantations were left to an overseer with less authority; as a consequence, rice plantations utilized a task system. Rather than utilizing gang labor, slaves would be assigned a minimum amount of work to do each day. Most slaves would meet their task well before eight or nine hours, leaving them with time of their own for use in hunting, fishing, or garnering their own crops. Young, old, or disabled slaves would be given a fraction of the task that a healthy slave would have to complete. Thus, the work on rice plantations was highly standardized and far more individually oriented than was the case with the gang labor systems used for other products like sugar.

Rice plantations required a large slave labor force and significant capital investment in land and equipment in order to be successful. Given the geographical conditions and the number of slaves involved, rice plantations were an extremely harsh labor environment. At the same time, though, the nature of the product and the absence of owners led to a task system that in many ways gave slaves a far greater degree of agency than was found on plantations that produced other products.

BIBLIOGRAPHY

Ball, Charles. *Fifty Years in Chains, or, The Life of an American Slave.* New York, 1859.

Brown, Josephine. *Biography of an American Bondman.* Boston, 1856.

Clinkscales, John George. *On the Old Plantation: Reminiscences of His Childhood.* Spartanburg, SC, 1916.

Dusinberre, William. *Them Dark Days: Slavery in the American Rice Swamps.* New York: Oxford University Press, 1996.

Heyward, Duncan Clinch. *Seed from Madagascar* [1937]. Columbia: University of South Carolina Press, 1993.

Joyner, Charles. *Down by the Riverside: A South Carolina Slave Community.* Urbana: University of Illinois Press, 1984.

Kemble, Fanny. *Journal of a Residence on a Georgian Plantation in 1838–1839.* London, 1863.

Littlefield, Daniel C. *Rice and Slaves: Ethnicity and the Slave Trade in Colonial South Carolina.* Baton Rouge: Louisiana State University Press, 1981.

Smith, Julia Floyd. *Slavery and Rice Culture in Low Country Georgia, 1750–1860.* Knoxville: University of Tennessee Press, 1985.

M. K. Beauchamp

SUGAR PLANTATIONS

Sugar cane cultivation best takes place in tropical and subtropical climates; consequently, sugar plantations in the United States that utilized slave labor were located predominantly along the Gulf coast, particularly in the southern half of Louisiana. Over the course of the seventeenth and eighteenth centuries, the Caribbean became the largest producer of sugar in the world. The spread of sugar plantations failed to keep pace with demand until the mid-eighteenth century, and European wars disrupted supply lines, keeping demand high. Span- ish and French émigrés from the Caribbean brought sugar production with them when they began to colo- nize the southern United States. In 1795 Étienne de Boré became the first Louisianan to successfully produce sugar. Louisiana could not produce the crop year round as the Caribbean could, but following Louisiana's annexation to the United States sugar production there became lucrative nonetheless, due to protective tariffs that kept the price of Caribbean sugar high. Given the lack of reliable roads in the early national period, planta- tions were generally located near waterways so that sugar could be more easily transported out and the slaves and equipment to manufacture it more easily transported in.

Sugar is a labor-intensive product that required a great deal from the slave labor force. Storms and flooding were a frequent danger to the crop and the facilities of the plantation, requiring slaves to engage in constant

Sugar plantation slaves harvesting sugar cane. Sugar is a labor-intensive product that required a great deal from the slave labor force. Slaves cleared the land, rebuilt and repaired facilities and built a system of dikes and levees to protect the crops from flooding. © *North Wind Picture Archives.*

SUGAR AND THE ATTRITION OF FREEDOM

Sidney Mintz in his work *Sweetness and Power* explores the profound effect sugar had on the modern world. In many ways sugar laid the basis for industrialization. Sugar was one of the first foods to introduce mechanization into its production and it also provided the cheap calories necessary to feed the early proletariat that labored in the cities.

> The track sugar has left in modern history is one involving masses of people and resources, thrown into productive combination by social, economic, and political forces that were actively remaking the entire world. The technical and human energies these forces released were unequaled in world history, and many of their consequence have been beneficial. But the place of sugars in the modern diet, the strangely imperceptible attrition of people's control over what they eat, with the eater becoming the consumer of a mass-produced food rather than the controller and cook of it, the manifold forces that work to hold consumption in channels predictable enough to maintain food-industry profits, the paradoxical narrowing of individual choice, and of opportunity to resist this trend, in the guise of increasing convenience, ease, and 'freedom'—these factors suggest the extent to which we have surrendered our autonomy over our food. (Mintz 1986, p. 211)

SOURCE: Mintz, Sidney. *Sweetness and Power: The Place of Sugar in Modern History*. New York: Penguin, 1986.

rebuilding and repairs. Slaves were responsible for the labor that allowed a plantation to be established. Slaves cleared the land in order to plant sugar cane, cutting down trees and removing their stumps. The slaves also built a system of levees and dikes to protect the growing area from rivers and in some cases seawater. This system would contain redundancies, such that if one levee broke, others would be present to save the sugar crop. Slaves also dug ditches in order to divert water and to drain the area. This was a continuous process, as silt would gradually block the drainage. The work was so constant that some observers doubted the wisdom of engaging in the project at all: "I must confess that there seems to me room for grave doubt, if the capital, labour, and especially the human life, which have been and which continue to be spent in converting the swamps of Louisiana into sugar plantations, and in defending them against the annual assaults of the river, and the fever, and the cholera, could not have been better employed somewhere else" (Olmsted 1861–1862, p. 324). In addition, slaves built the homes for the planters and themselves, as well as the

factory buildings involved in the production of sugar. Joseph John Gurney described the series of buildings found on most of the sugar plantations he observed: "Neat planting settlements visible in various spots; severally consisting of a mansion, a boiling house, a number of negro huts, and a wind mill on some neighboring elevation, for grinding the sugar" (1840, p. 10). Sugar plantations were massive complexes with a series of buildings and a large labor force.

Once land had been cleared and protected from potential flooding, slaves plowed the fields and planted the sugar cane. Sugar quickly robs the soil of nutrients, requiring more and more land to be cleared, the use of animal manure, or crop rotation if production is to keep pace with previous crops. Once planted, however, the crop did not require significant work on the part of the slave labor force. Rather, slaves continued to maintain the levees and drainage ditches, and prepared for the manufacture and packaging of the sugar. Slaves gathered wood for fuel, but also to make the hogsheads in which the sugar was shipped.

During the harvest, the slaves cut the sugar cane and along with beasts of burden transported the cane to the sugar mill. Slaves stored some of the cane under leaves and soil to protect it from the elements, so that it could be used for seeding another crop. Slaves also worked the mill as a sort of protoindustrial labor force. The first sugar mills used manual and animal labor to turn the machinery, but by the mid-eighteenth century planters began to adopt steam-powered sugar mills. If sugar mills were steam-powered, slaves would fuel the fires; if driven by an animal, they would guide it. Once the sugar was ground, slaves transported the syrup to the boiling house, while using the chaff for the fertilization of future crops and as fuel. Slaves also fired the fuel needed to boil the syrup into sugar and oversaw the crystallization process. This process required a specialized knowledge that distinguished the slaves employed in it from field hands involved in the production of other crops: "Negroes bred to mechanical employments, to sugar boiling, and the like, and some domestic slaves, fare much better than those who work in the fields" (Ramsay 1784, p. 82). Slaves would then take the raw sugar to a purgery packed in hogsheads, with holes for molasses to drain out. The extracted molasses would be sold, often for the manufacturing of rum. Once the molasses drained, the sugar was stored in more hogsheads for shipment to market. The entire manufacturing process required specialized knowledge, and would generally be overseen by an engineer or knowledgeable sugar maker. Given the necessary technical knowledge, labor, and machinery, sugar planting required a large capital investment.

Once the sugar was manufactured, slaves generally received a break from work. Then the process would start over again with another planting and the gathering of fuel for the mill and crystallization process. Slaves on sugar plantations had a more difficult labor regimen than slaves farming tobacco, cotton, and most other agricultural products. Fanny Kemble unfavorably compared the slave labor associated with sugar to that associated with these other products: "When I am most inclined to deplore the condition of the poor slaves on these cotton and rice plantations, the far more intolerable existence and harder labour of those employed on the sugar estates occurs to me, sometimes producing the effect of a lower circle in Dante's 'Hell of Horrors,' opening beneath the one where he seems to have reached the climax of infernal punishment" (1863, p. 106). Slave quarters were generally of poor quality—simple shacks—and the food provided was of inferior quality and consisted predominantly of corn and pork. Planters rarely offered any incentives other than the lash. Slaves, however, had many opportunities to escape, and the surrounding swampland made it difficult to recapture runaways.

Sugar plantations required a large investment of both capital and labor. The work that slaves performed in Louisiana and along the Gulf coast was far more rigorous than that found in plantations that produced other crops. Sugar plantations turned large profits, thanks to high demand. The process of making sugar became increasingly technical over time, and represented an early step toward industrialization within agriculture. At the same time, the sugar produced provided cheap calories for the populations of Europe and the United States, making sugar one of the crops most central to the global changes brought about by colonization.

BIBLIOGRAPHY

Dunn, Richard S. *Sugar and Slaves: The Rise of the Planter Class in the English West Indies, 1624–1713.* Chapel Hill: University of North Carolina Press, 1972.

Follett, Richard. *The Sugar Masters.* Baton Rouge: Louisiana State University Press, 2005.

Gurney, Joseph John. *A Winter in the West Indies: Described in Familiar Letters to Henry Clay, of Kentucky.* London: 1840. Available online in *Sources in U.S. History Online: Slavery in America.* Gale. Available at http://galenet.galegroup.com.

Kemble, Fanny. *Journal of a Residence on a Georgian Plantation in 1838–1839.* London: 1863. Available online in *Sources in U.S. History Online: Slavery in America.* Gale. Available at http://galenet.galegroup.com.

Mintz, Sidney W. *Sweetness and Power: The Place of Sugar in Modern History.* New York: Penguin, 1985.

Moody, V. Alton. *Slavery on Louisiana Sugar Plantations* [1924]. New York: AMS Press, 1976.

Olmsted, Frederick Law. *The Cotton Kingdom: A Traveller's Observations on Cotton and Slavery in the American Slave States: Based upon Three Former Volumes of Journeys,* vol. 1. New York: 1861–1862. Available online in *Sources in U.S. History Online: Slavery in America.* Gale. Available at http://galenet.galegroup.com.

Ramsay, James. *An Essay on the Treatment and Conversion of African Slaves in the British Sugar Colonies.* London: 1784. Available online in *Sources in U.S. History Online: Slavery in America.* Gale. Available at http://galenet.galegroup.com.

Whitten, David O. *Andrew Durnford: A Black Sugar Planter in the Antebellum South.* Natchitoches, LA: Northwestern State University Press, 1981.

Michael Kelly Beauchamp

ANIMAL HUSBANDRY

The adaptability of the slaveholding, Southern United States—in terms of geography and climate—to cultivation of crops of various kinds, meant that plantation owners placed much more emphasis on crop production as a market commodity than on animal husbandry. In some places cattle were raised as a profit-making enterprise but generally animal products did not provide the high profit margins as crops such as corn, tobacco, and cotton.

Solomon Northrup, referencing his experiences as a slave on a Louisiana plantation, gave some insight into the low market value of cows in Louisiana around the 1840s. He claimed that the best cows were worth only about five dollars each. In terms of milk as a by-product with possible market potential, he argued that it was "unusual" for a cow to yield as much as two quarts of milk at any one time. Additionally, he said that the small amount of tallow (fat used to make candles, soap, and lubricants) harvested from cows was of a "soft, inferior quality" (Bracey and Sinha 2004, vol. 1, p. 138). Northrup, well known as a writer of a narrative that told about his twelve-year experience as a slave, had been captured into slavery in 1841 after having lived as a free man for all of his life. Northrup contended that the planters in his area chose to purchase cheese and butter shipped to the New Orleans market form the Northern United States, as opposed to commercializing the cow and its by-products. Animal husbandry, in any case, not as labor intensive as crop cultivation, engaged less of the labor of enslaved people than crop production. Northrup measured the labor input expended on corn and cotton production on the plantation where he was enslaved, as opposed to other activities, including caring of hogs. He stated, "Ploughing [*sic*], planting, picking cotton, gathering the corn, and pulling and burning stalks, occupies the whole of the four seasons of the year. Drawing and cutting wood, pressing cotton, fattening

THE FEDERAL WRITERS' PROJECT

The information cited from ex-slaves in this essay was compiled through interviews conducted during the late 1930s, in order to record the memories of the ex-slaves who were then of advanced ages. The interviewers were sponsored by the Federal Writers' Project, which was established during the Great Depression in order to provide jobs for writers, editors, and researchers. The Federal Writers' Project was part of the United States Works Project Administration. The slave narratives were later collected in George Rawick's *The American Slave: A Composite Autobiography*.

SOURCE: Rawick, George, ed. *American Slave: A Composite Autobiography*. 41 vols. Westport, CT: Greenwood, 1972–1979.

and killing hogs, are but incidental labors" (Bracey and Sinha 2004, vol. 1, p. 138).

Among the animals minded by slaves on Southern plantations were hogs, cattle, horses, sheep, goats, chickens, turkeys, and guinea fowls; however, the hog was decidedly the most popular animal on the plantation. Lizzie Farmer, who had been enslaved on a Texas plantation, remembered that her "Massa" had hundreds of beautiful hogs. Hogs were bred primarily to provide food for the inhabitants of the plantations, and became the staple meat in the diet of enslaved people. On plantations, hogs were generally penned, and slaves carried out the routine task of feeding them, sometimes referred to by ex-slaves as "fattening" or "slopping." Bert Mayfield, who had been enslaved in Garrard County, Kansas remembered pulling "pusley"—probably a plant or grass of some kind— from a garden to feed pigs. According to him, the "pigs loved it mighty well" (*Born in Slavery*, Kentucky Narratives, vol. 11, pt. 1).

Bull dogs were put into service to chase down hogs and drive them back into pens when they escaped as communicated by George Henderson from Versailles, Kentucky. Henderson said that his owner had a "very bad male hog" which sometimes broke out of a ten-foot high pen in which it was kept. Henderson quipped humorously, "it would take all the bulldogs in the country to get him back" (*Born in Slavery*, Kentucky Narratives, vol. 13, pt. 1).

It was "hog killin' time" when hogs were slaughtered on the plantations sometime during the fall to winter seasons. The meat was then preserved to be rationed among the occupants of the plantation during the following year. According to Northrup, the slaves began the preservation process by cutting each hog into six pieces, then slating and laying the pieces "one above the other" on tables in a smoke-house. After two weeks, they hung up and smoked the pieces of meat. They continued the smoking process periodically during the year to prevent infesta-

tion of the meat by worms (Bracey and Sinha 2004, vol. 1, p. 138).

Cattle, including cows, steers and oxen, were also bred in plentiful quantities on plantations. Sam Polite from a plantation on St. Helena Island in South Carolina (Gullah country) explained that slaves had to roll cords of mud into the pens where the cows were kept. Women, especially, raked leaves from wood into the cow pens. The mud and leaves, very likely, served as receptacles for the dung of the cows which was used as plant fertilizer.

Care of cattle by slaves also involved driving them to pastures for feeding. Sometimes cattle stampedes would occur as the cattle got out of control, and a "roping" process was used in order to restrain the cattle. Slaves also had to be versed in the technique of "yoking" oxen that were used to pull plows in the fields.

In many places, plantation owners used an unsophisticated method of allowing pigs and cattle to literally raise themselves by roaming around—"free range"—in nearby swamps and woods. Hogs fed on "mast"—the fruit of beech, oak, chestnut, and other forest trees.

As previously indicated, bulldogs played an essential role in hog raising. Northrup explained that around September or October of each year, probably in anticipation of the approaching winter, slaves on the plantation where he was held used the dogs to chase hogs out of the swamps and confine them to pens on the plantation.

With regard to the "free range" cattle, Northrup commented that plantation owners in his area simply marked the ears or branded their initials on the sides of their cattle – a Spanish breed, small and spiked horned— and let them loose into the swamps, "to roam unrestricted within their almost limitless confines" (Bracey and Sinha 2004, vol. 1, p. 138). Northrup speculated that the name Bayou Boeuf, meaning, "the creek or river of the wild ox" most likely originated among the Louisiana French because of the large number of tame and untamed cattle that "swarm[ed] the woods and swamps of Bayou Boeuf" (p. 138). Bayou Boeuf was very likely located close to the plantation where Northrup was enslaved.

Horses were crucial to plantation management because they served as the major mode of transportation, pulling carts, carriages, wagons, and buggies. Evoking a feminist sentiment, Harriett Robinson of Bastrop, Texas boasted that women, perhaps including herself, broke in mules: "thrower 'em down and roped 'em. They'd do it better'n men (Baker and Baker 1997, p. 83).

Horses, sheep, and goats were driven by slaves in herds for "watering" and grazing. Especially in Texas, sheep were raised in large quantities. Andy J. Anderson (formerly Andy Haley), indicated that there were about a thousand sheep on the plantation where he had been enslaved in Williamson County, Texas. Sheep minding was assigned to specific slaves, as were all other jobs on that plantation. Wool was sheared off the sheep twice per year by the slave assigned to that job (Waters 2003, p. 117). Lu Lee, born on a plantation somewhere along the Louisiana/Texas state line, remembered that she and her sister herded sheep in the prairies, and took large shepherd dogs along for protection for wolves, panther and wild cattle (p. 11). Carey Davenport, also a Texas ex-slave, commented jestfully that as a sheep minder, the wolves never "tackled" him because, "They like sheep meat better'n man meat" (Rawick 1972–1979, vol. 4, p. 282). Slaves also provided themselves with additional food supplies by hunting wild chickens and turkeys; and wild game including rabbits, opossums, deer, and cows.

Additionally, slaves were involved in processing by-products from various animals. Alfred Farrell, enslaved in Monticello, Florida, said that the fat of oxen and sheep was melted to make candles, and the leftover grease was put into a large box to be used later for soap-making. The feathers from geese and chickens were used to make mattresses (Rawick 1972–1979, vol. 17, pp. 48–49). Willis Williams from Jacksonville, Florida (born in Tallahassee), remembered that on one occasion he skinned a cow and sold the hide to a man named Pierce who used to buy hides and cure them (p. 5).

In their text *The Sounds of Slavery* (2005), Shane and Graham White emphasize the attention paid by enslaved people to various sounds on the plantation—sounds made by animals, sound coming from spinning rooms, sounds of plantation bells, and the sound made by slave children as they beat clothes with batten sticks on wash-day, for example. White and White also underscore the fact that the enslaved people themselves contributed their own sounds to the cacophony of plantation noises. Indeed, their duties relating to tending animals elicited from the slaves sounds that heralded the traditions of orality of their African heritage. John Davenport told his interviewer that he and other slaves on the plantation yelled, "co-winch, co-winch" to call cows; "co, co" to call mules; and "pig-oo, pig-oo" to call hogs and pigs (White and White 2005, p. 2).

BIBLIOGRAPHY

Baker, Lindsay T., and Julie P. Baker, eds. *Till Freedom Cried Out: Memories of Texas Slave Life*. College Station, TX: A & M University Press, 1997.

Born in Slavery: Slave Narratives from the Federal Writers' Project, 1936–1938. Online collection of the Manuscript and Prints and Photographs Divisions of the Library of Congress. Available from http://memory.loc.gov.

Bracey, John H., Jr., and Manisha Sinha, eds. *African American Mosaic: A Documentary History from the Slave Trade to the Twenty-First Century, Vol. 1: To 1877*. Upper Saddle River, NJ: Prentice Hall, 2004.

Hine, Darlene Clarke, William C. Hine, and Stanley Harrold. *African Americans: A Concise History*. Upper Saddle River, NJ: Prentice Hall, 2004.

Rawick, George P., ed. *The American Slave: A Composite Autobiography*. Vols. 1–19. Westport, CT: Greenwood Press, 1972–1979.

Waters, Andrew, ed. *I Was Born in Slavery*. Winston-Salem, NC: John F. Blair, 2003.

White, Shane, and Graham White. *The Sounds of Slavery: Discovering African American History through Songs, Sermons and Speech*. Boston: Beacon Press, 2005.

Marguerite P. Garvey

CONSTRUCTION AND CLEARING LAND

On both large plantations and smaller farms, slaves worked at a variety of tasks clearing land and constructing buildings and other facilities. Many slaves who worked primarily as field hands nevertheless acquired some basic skills in rough carpentry and other types of labor involved in building and maintaining the structures and roadways needed on a farm or plantation. In some parts of the South, slaves worked several days per year on the public roads. Frederick Law Olmsted (1822–1903), who traveled widely throughout the slave states, reported seeing about thirty male and female slaves working on the roads near a plantation in the Carolinas. He noted, "The women were in the majority, and were engaged at exactly the same labour as the men: driving the carts, loading them with dirt, and dumping them upon the road; cutting down trees, and drawing wood by hand, to lay across the miry places, hoeing, and shoveling" (1958, p. 161). During wartime slaves built fortifications and military camps. In the American Revolution (1776–1783), both British and American forces made use of slave labor for such jobs. During the Civil War (1861–1865), slaves were used to build fortifications for the Confederate army, and runaway slaves or captured contraband slaves were put to work doing similar tasks for the Union forces.

Beyond this kind of basic construction work that most slaves might do on occasion, many slaves were specially trained in building trades such as carpentry and masonry. Slaves built virtually everything on a plantation, from the barns and livestock pens, to their own quarters, to their master's house itself. Historian Adam Rothman cites an advertisement in the *Louisiana Gazette* in 1820 offering a sugar plantation for sale; the ad noted that of the 100 slaves being sold with the land, 40 of them "have callings, such as carpenters, coopers, bricklayers, cabinet makers, plain cooks and pastry cooks, etc." (2005, p. 189). Slaves who worked in skilled trades were often trained by being apprenticed, perhaps informally, to a white tradesman or to an experienced slave who knew the craft. Some were even sent

Chained slaves carrying shovels to work. This undated woodcut shows slaves who are bound by chains and carrying picks and shovels. Slave work teams performed a variety of tasks including building railroads, military camps, maintaining roads and clearing fields. *© Corbis*

overseas to learn trades such as carpentry, cabinetmaking, and landscape architecture.

Historian Charles Joyner, in his study of slavery in the South Carolina low country, notes several examples of highly skilled slave carpenters. Renty Tucker was a slave owned by Plowden C. J. Weston. Tucker built a beautiful chapel known as St. Mary's on Weston's Weehawka plantation, and also a summer home for the Westons on Pawleys Island. A slave carpenter named Richmond who worked on the Woodbourne plantation owned by J. Motte Alston is another example. Richmond built the big house on this plantation almost entirely by himself, requiring help only to move items too large for one man to handle (1985, pp. 72–73).

On the rice plantations in the lowland areas of South Carolina, slaves also built the intricate network of ditches, dikes, and sluice gates that allowed water to

be put on and taken off of the rice crop at the proper times. Tasks such as this, as well as work on roads and railroads, gave some slaves an introduction to some basic aspects of civil engineering.

Many skilled slave builders were hired out to labor for others. Generally, the wages they earned went to the master, although some masters allowed the slaves to keep part of these earnings. Slaves were also hired by state and local governments to work on a variety of public works throughout the South.

Railroads in the South used slave labor in construction. It is common to see slaves listed among the assets owned by railroad companies, but most of the slaves working on railroad construction were hired. Historian Wilma Dunaway notes that by 1860, nearly 600 slaves were at work in western North Carolina on railroad projects. Male slaves were hired to do the construction work, while female slaves cooked and did laundry for the construction crews. Dunaway also notes that the Virginia and Tennessee railroad listed 643 workers in 1856, and two-thirds of these were slaves. On the Virginia Central railroad, sixty slaves worked in two crews to dig a tunnel through the Blue Ridge Mountains, working simultaneously from each end (2003, p. 101). Slaves hired out to work on public works or railroad jobs were often covered by life insurance at the expense of those hiring them, so that the master would be protected from the economic loss if the slave died in an accident.

The work of clearing new land for farming was a very basic but physically demanding type of labor. Many southern farmers continually cleared new lands to replace fields that had been exhausted from overuse. Tobacco was a crop that was particularly hard on the soil; planting was shifted to newly cleared fields every three to four years. John Brown, a runaway slave from Georgia, described clearing tobacco fields for planting:

> In the month of February they begin what is called 'burning the beds,' this is, the dry brush is burnt off from the beds intended to be sown and planted. The ground is then broken up with the grubbing-hoe, an implement something like a pick-axe, only that it is four inches wide, and very heavy. The ground must be well manured before it is broken up, because the tobacco-plant is greedy of food, and likes good living. (1991, p. 149)

Southern farmers often practiced crop rotation, which they called "crop shifting." Land that would no longer grow tobacco might be fruitful for growing grain crops for a few more years. After the grain yields began to decline, the land might be left to lie fallow or unused for several years. A practice known as "long fallowing" involved leaving the land unused (except as pasture) for as long as twenty years. After such a long interval, the land would begin to revert to forest, and if it was to be replanted to crops, it had to be cleared again.

Clearing a field often began with burning off the underbrush and girdling the trees—cutting a deep band around the trunk of the tree, to cause it to die. The first crops might be planted with many of the trees still standing, with the crops simply planted around them. This often made it impossible to use plows drawn by draft animals, therefore, crops were often planted and cultivated with a hoe. Farming with the hoe as the principal tool was a practice many colonial era slaves were familiar with from their African agricultural heritage. Over time, the dead trees in a cleared field would blow down. Getting the stumps out of the ground, often called "grubbing stumps," was particularly difficult, and farmers often simply planted around them, but over time slaves cleared most of the stumps when other tasks were less pressing. Clearing land was the type of work that could be used to fill the downtimes in the agricultural cycle, when the labor of the slaves was not demanded by planting, cultivating, or harvesting the major staple crops. Much of this work was done in the winter. Even at night, slaves sometimes worked burning piles of brush from newly cleared fields.

After the dead trees in a field had fallen, a logrolling might be held, when slaves gathered up the wood. Some of the wood was saved for firewood or lumber, but much of it was burnt in the fields. The term *logrolling* was also used to refer to raising a house, barn, or other type of building. Slaves and their owners from neighboring plantations came together for a big project such as this, and the work was often accompanied by a large meal and became an important social gathering. Historian Eugene Genovese cites the account of Frank Gill, an Alabama ex-slave, about logrollings:

> [D]em was great times, ca'se if some ob dem neighborin' plantations wanted to get up a house, dey would invite all de slaves, men and women, to come wid dere masters. De women would help wid de cookin' an' you may be shore dey had something to cook. Dey would kill a cow, or three or four hogs, and hab peas, cabbage, an' everything lack grows on de farm. (1974, p. 320)

Historians have noted many examples of slave laborers involved in the building trades and other types of skilled craftsmanship. But the toil of the many thousands of anonymous laborers who cleared the land, maintained the roads, and constructed much of the built environment of the slave states has often been described in only the most general terms. Joyner has noted how many of the slaves in the South Carolina rice country, and their descendants, took a measure of well-deserved pride in the work they had done. Even though they did not own the land, they had invested themselves and their skill in it and in the crops it produced. He cites Ben Horry, a former rice plantation slave, who told an interviewer for the Works Progress Administration (WPA) slave narratives in the 1930s, "Missus, slavery time people done something!" (*Born in Slavery*, p. 42).

BIBLIOGRAPHY

Born in Slavery: Slave Narratives from the Federal Writers' Project, 1936–1938. Manuscript and Prints and Photographs Divisions, Library of Congress. Available from http://memory.loc.gov.

Brown, John. *Slave Life in Georgia: A Narrative of the Life, Sufferings, and Escape of John Brown, a Fugitive Slave* [1855], ed. F. F. Boney. Savannah, GA: Beehive Press, 1991.

Dunaway, Wilma A. *Slavery in the American Mountain South: Studies in Modern Capitalism Series.* Cambridge, UK; New York: Cambridge University Press, 2003.

Genovese, Eugene G. *Roll, Jordan, Roll: The World the Slaves Made.* New York: Pantheon, 1974.

Joyner, Charles. *Down by the Riverside: A South Carolina Slave Community*. Urbana: University of Illinois Press, 1985.

Olmsted, Frederick Law. *The Cotton Kingdom: A Traveler's Observations on Cotton and Slavery in the American Slave States* [1861–1862]. Reprint, New York: Knopf, 1958.

Otto, John Solomon. *The Southern Frontiers, 1607–1860: The Agricultural Evolution of the Colonial and Antebellum South*. New York: Greenwood Press, 1989.

Phillips, Ulrich Bonnell. *American Negro Slavery: A Survey of the Supply, Employment, and Control of Negro Labor As Determined by the Plantation Regime* [1918]. Reprint, Baton Rouge: Louisiana State University Press, 1966.

Rothman, Adam. *Slave Country: American Expansion and the Origins of the Deep South*. Cambridge, MA: Harvard University Press, 2005.

Stampp, Kenneth. *The Peculiar Institution: Slavery in the Antebellum South*. New York: Knopf, 1956.

Mark S. Joy

TOOLS AND TECHNOLOGY

The industrial revolution, which began so purposefully in eighteenth-century England, helped to spark a similar revolution in America. The application and use of power-driven machines in manufacturing inevitably produced greater quantities of commodities for a mass market at a cheaper price. In addition, it encouraged the growth of cities and urban areas, which was in conflict with the beliefs of the old Jeffersonian conservatives whose ultimate grand vision for America was the creation of an agrarian republic. Conservative Southern planters and politicians were committed to maintaining an agrarian social order based on slave labor. Some Northern industrialists argued that in a modern industrial economy, slave labor was inefficient and should be abolished. Others took a centrist approach, hoping that some compromise might leave the Southern social order intact while industrialization moved ahead in the South.

The reality is that certain segments in society, for various social, economic, or political reasons, are always unable or unwilling to take advantage of the progress that accompanies technological change. Because slaves were unable to enjoy the fruits of industrialization and because it did not create a better work environment, technological advancement was irrelevant in their daily lives. Moreover, there is a certain irony in that, to a large degree, the Atlantic slave trade fueled the growth of the industrial revolution in both England and America during the eighteenth century. Nowhere was America's role in the process more evident than in the cultivation of tobacco. Slaves in Virginia and Maryland planted, cultivated, and cured tobacco for export and domestic con-

sumption. The trade in tobacco was extremely profitable for the English and many American merchants and investors in the North, although there were periods of overproduction and low prices. Much of the accumulation of capital that resulted was reinvested in modernizing technology, which then sparked a revolution in industry.

Many Southern tobacco planters used their profits to increase their slave populations, but years of growing tobacco had depleted much of the land in the Chesapeake, Tidewater, and Piedmont areas by the early nineteenth century. Moreover, around this time there was a significant decrease in the export of tobacco to European countries, which was partly countered by an increase in domestic consumption, even among slaves. It is impossible to know what impact this had on profits but, apparently, the use of tobacco was widespread among slaves. For example, a posting for the return of a runaway slave in the *Virginia Gazette*, dated May 2 through 9, 1745, describes the slave as a small mulatto man named Peter who "always has a great Quid of Tobacco in his Mouth." Nonetheless, agriculture in the upper South, particularly along coastal areas, continued to suffer from depressed market prices and the soil deterioration that resulted from one-crop farming. The removal of the Creek and Cherokee Indians from their lands in Georgia and Alabama allowed many small farmers access to better farmland in the lower South. Many large planters searched for new crops to replace the cultivation of tobacco.

The industrial revolution in England resulted in the invention of new kinds of mechanical, waterpowered spinning jennies and weavers that revolutionized the textile industry and led to the construction of new textile plants worldwide. In America in 1793, an invention that appeared rather primitive, but that was really a significant technological advancement, would save Southern agriculture. Unfortunately, it would also increase the demand for slave labor. In an effort to revive Southern agriculture some planters had experimented with growing cotton inland away from the coastal lowlands of Georgia and South Carolina. They achieved some success in cultivating a short-staple variety of cotton, but it was inferior to the long-staple variety grown in the lowlands and Sea Islands. While it could be cultivated productively in the interior of Southern states, the problem with the short-staple variety was that the cotton fibers stuck to its green seeds. This made it extremely difficult to prepare the raw cotton for manufacturing into cloth. To ameliorate this problem a young inventor, Eli Whitney (1765–1825), designed a simple machine that he called a cotton gin, which easily removed the fibers from the seeds.

The success of Whitney's invention almost immediately precipitated the spread of the cultivation of cotton across the lower South, where there was ample unspoiled land. This, in turn, led to the increasing need for large numbers of slave laborers. To meet their labor needs, plantation owners purchased more than 300,000 slaves from the Chesapeake colonies, which no longer required large numbers of enslaved laborers for cultivating tobacco. In addition, there was an illegal, but highly profitable and effective, Underground Railroad that smuggled slaves from other Atlantic slave populations into the lower South. It took only about ten years after the invention of the cotton gin for cotton to replace tobacco as the South's most valuable crop. Unlike tobacco, which slave labor cultivated primarily in Maryland and Virginia, planters and small farmers alike grew cotton all across the South. Soon the cotton plant would completely dominate the Southern economy.

As America entered the nineteenth century, Whitney's cotton gin was not the only technological advancement that helped to make cotton such an important agricultural product. There were several others, one of the most important of which was the invention of the sewing machine. Around 1840 Elias Howe (1819–1867), a textile worker who understood the mechanics of contemporary machinery, began to work on a design for a sewing machine. Howe, who had also worked as a precision instrument maker, finally succeeded in constructing a device that mechanically used an eye-pointed needle that could force a piece of thread through a piece of cloth to make a loop that, through a shuttle with another length of thread, passed through to make a lock stitch. Though it enabled a single seamstress to increase her productivity dramatically, Howe's sewing device was extremely expensive and did not sell well. Issac Singer (1811–1875), a mechanic and amateur inventor, added improvements to Howe's device and received a patent in 1851 to manufacture his machine. Like Howe's original sewing machine, Singer's, although much improved, was very expensive. One of Singer's business partners solved the dilemma by allowing the machine to be purchased on installments. This marketing innovation made the sewing machine available to ordinary users, which in turn created a mass market for the cotton that Southern farmers and planters cultivated using slave labor.

Although the plant itself had changed, little else had changed for the slaves who picked cotton. Masters still required slaves to work from sunup to sundown. In fact, all the major cash crops grown in the South, which included tobacco, sugar, rice, and cotton, were labor-intensive and required tedious, backbreaking work. Although the cotton gin allowed a single slave to process far more raw cotton, slaves still had to toil long hours in the hot sun picking cotton. In addition, they often had to drain ditches and clear land of trees, brush, and other debris to free up more land on which to plant cotton. Thus, the cotton gin

did little to make life easier for slaves—though it certainly helped to increase cotton production for a growing international market, which meant substantial profits for the planters.

Those slaves who worked on tobacco plantations and farms had to clear large tracts of land with hoes, scythes, and an assortment of other small tools. The planting, cultivation, and processing of tobacco was tedious, took from dawn until dusk, and frequently required slaves to work under the most adverse conditions. The planting, replanting, weeding, topping, curing, and packing was all done by hand, but was nonetheless profitable for the planter or small farmer. A single slave working daily on a several-acre plot of cleared land could produce more than 1,000 pounds of tobacco, which could be sold at a 200 percent profit.

Slaves who worked on sugar plantations, which were located primarily in Louisiana, cut and hauled sugar cane to the mill, where they were also responsible for grinding and boiling the cane. After the cane had been cooked, refining equipment turned the juice into sugar. However, technology had little or no impact on easing the pain and exhaustion that the slaves suffered from working on sugar plantations. (Often slaves worked from sixteen to eighteen hours per day.)

Working on rice plantations, which were located primarily in the lowlands of South Carolina, was perhaps the most exhausting and dangerous work a slave could do. Rice cultivation required a system of canals, dikes, and gates in order to flood the rice fields. The lowlands were hot and humid, and slaves had to work hours on end in knee-deep, poisonous, snake-infested water and mud, while constantly flailing at disease-carrying mosquitoes. Technology also had little impact on the work of slaves in the rice fields. What did improve conditions for slaves was that Africans had brought with them a knowledge of rice cultivation that enabled them to plant and cultivate rice efficiently. Slaves were able to negotiate a work schedule called the "task system," which meant that they were assigned tasks to complete each day and once they had finished, they had the rest of the day to themselves. Slaves who toiled in the rice fields adamantly refused to work any other way.

For the most part, however, the duties of slaves were far from over at the end of a long day spent toiling in the fields, as Solomon Northup (b. 1808), an ex-slave who worked in the cotton fields, reminds us in his autobiography *Twelve Years a Slave* (1853). Once the fieldwork had been finished for the day the slaves still had additional chores on the plantation, which might include feeding the farm animals, collecting firewood for the master, or doing odd jobs around the master's house. Slaves then returned to their quarters to prepare their daily meal, which usually consisted of salt pork or bacon and cornmeal, and might be supplemented by other foods if the master allowed the slaves to have small garden plots. After preparing for the next day's work and socializing with friends and family for a while, it was off to bed for a few hours sleep.

Advances in science and technology during the nineteenth century had a significant impact on American society in general—especially in the North, where free labor, industrialization, and immigration were moving full-speed ahead. Lowell, Massachusetts, a town of about 17,000, was becoming a model city for the textile industry in the Northeast and cities such as Cincinnati and Columbus, Ohio, were emerging in the Midwest, as technology created more jobs and improved agricultural production. The South, however, remained firmly committed to maintaining a slave society as the Civil War (1861–1865) approached, and no technological advance could change that.

BIBLIOGRAPHY

Bonner, James C. *A History of Georgia Agriculture, 1732–1860.* Athens: University of Georgia Press, 1964.

Daniel, Pete. *Breaking the Land: The Transformation of Cotton, Tobacco, and Rice Cultures since 1880.* Urbana, IL: University of Illinois Press, 1985.

Northup, Solomon. *Twelve Years a Slave, Narrative of Solomon Northup, a Citizen of New York, Kidnapped in Washington, D.C. in 1841, and Rescued in 1853, from a Cotton Plantation Near the Red River in Louisiana.* Auburn, NY: Derby and Miller, 1853.

Reidy, Joseph P. *From Slavery to Agrarian Capitalism in the Cotton Plantation South: Central Georgia, 1800–1880.* Chapel Hill: University of North Carolina Press, 1992.

Young, Jeffrey Robert. *Domesticating Slavery: The Master Class in Georgia and South Carolina, 1670–1837.* Chapel Hill: University of North Carolina Press, 1999.

Donald Roe

HUNTING, TRAPPING, AND FISHING

Although slaves generally worked long hours and many days per year, they often found time for harvesting fish and game. Except in planting or harvest times, most slaves had Sunday as a day without field labor and many masters also gave half of Saturday as free time. Even if slaves worked all day, their nights were usually free. Young slave children spent much time hunting and fishing in the years before they were given heavy workloads. Frederick Douglass (1817–

1895) recalled that on the plantation where he lived as a child, the days between Christmas and New Year's were considered a holiday. "The staid, sober, thinking, and industrious ones of our number would employ themselves in making corn-brooms, mats, horse-collars, and baskets," he recalled, while "another class of us would spend the time hunting opossums, hares, and coons" (1986, p. 114). Many plantations owners countenanced their slaves hunting; but even when it was forbidden, some slaves hunted nevertheless. James Bolton, a former slave in Georgia, recalled that his master forbade hunting, but "jes' the same, we had plenty of 'possums, an no buddy ax' how we cotch them" (Proctor 2002, p. 162).

Slaves sought wild fish and game for all the reasons anyone else did—as recreation, as food, and as a means to get something that might be shared with others, or sold or traded. Historian Nicolas Proctor notes that hunting also provided "a measure of autonomy" for slaves. By providing part of what their own family consumed, or by making a gift of wild game to another slave family, the slave hunter denied the totality of the master's control over his life and labor (2002, pp. 3, 144).

Besides hunting on their own, slaves were often taken hunting along with their master. If a group of white men went on a long hunt, several slaves might accompany them to do the menial labor around the camp, and to serve as beaters or drivers that helped to drive the game toward waiting hunters. At times, masters sent slaves out to hunt on their own, for food that might be used at the master's table, or be used to supplement the rations given to the slaves. Slave hunters, when hunting alone or with their masters, were often entrusted with a firearm within certain limited circumstances. Masters kept close tabs on the amount of shot and powder used, to see if the game brought in matched the ammunition expended. If they did not have access to guns, slaves used traps and primitive weapons. Opossums and raccoons could sometimes be found in their burrows and dispatched with a club; dogs might chase down and kill an animal. Young boys often hunted with slingshots, sticks, or rocks. Former slave Robert Wilson recalled hunting with rocks as a young boy, but admitted to limited success: "Weuns don't kill much of de game but 'twas good fo' to pass de time 'way" (Proctor 2002, p. 147).

Slaves engaged in trapping not just to harvest furs for the market, but also to catch game animals and birds for food. Commercially-made steel traps were sometimes used, but slaves were also ingenious in making a variety of homemade traps, including box traps, snares made of wire or cord, and deadfalls.

Marketable hides and furs that slaves harvested were sold in the informal markets where slaves sold or bartered food from their own gardens, handcrafted items, or fish, game, and other foods gathered from nature.

Fishing was popular among slaves and, as with hunting and trapping, it was both a form of recreation and a way to procure food, or to harvest a resource that could be marketed to others. Fishing was not as gender-specific as hunting, and women, especially young girls, often fished, whereas few hunted. Fish could be caught with simple equipment, and slaves used hooks and lines, gigs or spears, nets, and fish traps. Along the coasts and major river ways, slaves were also heavily involved in commercial fishing. Fish was a major item in the diet of slaves on plantations in the Tidewater region. Historian David Cecelski has noted the large number of slaves involved in the coastal fishing industry in North Carolina; along the Outer Banks, slaves may have made up to as much as 50 percent of the fishermen and women. As Cecelski notes, forced labor seems at odds with the sense of freedom and openness that the maritime life symbolizes in the minds of many people (2001, pp. xix–xx). Like slaves who hunted, slave fishermen often found a measure of independence and autonomy that few other slaves experienced.

BIBLIOGRAPHY

Cecelski, David S. *The Waterman's Song: Slavery and Freedom in Maritime North Carolina.* Chapel Hill: University of North Carolina Press, 2001.

Douglass, Frederick. *Narrative of the Life of Frederick Douglass, an American Slave, Written by Himself* [1845]. Reprint, New York: Penguin, 1986.

Greenberg, Kenneth S. *Honor and Slavery: Lies, Duels, Noses, Masks, Dressing as A Woman, Gifts, Strangers, Humanitarianism, Death, Slave Rebellions, the Pro-Slavery Argument, Baseball, Hunting, and Gambling in the Old South.* Princeton, NJ: Princeton University Press, 1996.

Marks, Stuart. *Southern Hunting in Black and White: Nature, History, and Ritual in a Carolina Community.* Princeton, NJ: Princeton University Press, 1991.

Proctor, Nicolas W. *Bathed in Blood: Hunting and Mastery in the Old South.* Charlottesville: University of Virginia Press, 2002.

Mark S. Joy

SLAVES AND FIREARMS

The fact that slaves sometimes hunted, with their masters or alone with firearms, might surprise some modern readers, but there is much evidence that some slaves used guns in a variety of situations. Most slave states had laws forbidding slaves to bear arms, but these laws usually provided that slaves could carry guns with their master's permission. Certainly there were many masters that never let a slave near a gun. However, when southerners discussed the possibility of slave uprisings, they often assumed that the slaves would find ways to arm themselves. Guns were not the only potential weapon. The average farm or plantation had many tools that might serve as weapons. Although the fear of violence from their slaves haunted some masters, most probably assumed that a rebellious slave would simply run away rather than take up a weapon against the master or his family.

SOURCE: Proctor, Nicolas W. *Bathed in Blood: Hunting and Mastery in the Old South.* Charlottesville: University of Virginia Press, 2002.

***The Rabbits,* 1792.** Young slaves spent much of their time hunting and trapping before they were given heavy workloads. Adults could hunt or fish if they had free time on Sundays or at night. Slaves might hunt small game such as hares, opossum or raccoon. *Private Collection/Bridgeman Art Library.*

Skilled Labor

SKILLED LABOR: AN OVERVIEW

Though slaves in the Americas are typically portrayed as either field hands or domestic servants, many slaves were in fact skilled laborers whose crafts were a vital part of the American economy, particularly in the antebellum South. There is ample evidence for skilled African and African American slave labor, including the manifests of slave ships, which identify artisans such as wood-carvers and metalworkers. Records of sale from the early years of the slave trade through the mid-nineteenth century indicate a higher price for skilled individuals. The narrator of *Fifty Years in Chains; or, the Life of an American Slave*, describing a slave auction, relates the sale of several skilled slaves: "a carpenter ... and a blacksmith [who can] put new steel upon an axe or mend a broken chain ... and a good shoemaker, well acquainted with the process of tanning leather" (Ball 1859, p. 99).

Skilled slaves arrived with knowledge of a wide range of traditional African crafts—pottery making, weaving, basketry, wood carving, metalworking, and building—that would prove valuable in the Americas, particularly during the preindustrial colonial period, when common household goods, such as thread, fabric, and soap, were all made by hand. Colonial labor shortages and a general scarcity of goods intensified the need for skilled slave labor.

Some planters required slaves with specific skills and were willing to pay slave traders a premium for them. Rice planters in the coastal low country of South Carolina and Georgia, for example, were willing to pay more for slaves from Africa's Windward Coast (present-day Senegal to Côte d'Ivoire), as these individuals were skilled in rice cultivation and processing. Their skills included the ability to weave winnowing baskets and to carve wooden mortars and pestles for processing the grains of rice.

During the colonial period, traditional African skills were preserved in some measure, despite the trauma of displacement, largely because of the practical need for handcrafted items. Early pottery from South Carolina often revealed a distinct West African form; winnowing or fanning baskets from the Low Country used both the form and technique of baskets made in Senegambia. In particular, items made by slaves for personal use reflect African tradition; examples include small ceramic face vessels (resembling Kongo pottery) found at burial sites in South Carolina, which are thought to have served a ritual function, and drums made from gourds or wood. (Not surprisingly, few drums survived; many slaveholders prohibited the making or use of drums for fear of their potential use in a rebellion.)

Skilled Slave Labor and Plantation Enterprise

As the plantation economy grew, so too did the need for skilled slave labor. Most plantations had facilities for spinning thread and weaving fabric, as well as for blacksmithing, coopering (barrel making), and carpentry. The list of slaves at Mount Vernon in 1799, the year of George Washington's death, reveals that, of the 184 slaves listed, more than one-quarter were described as skilled workers; they included carpenters, bricklayers, blacksmiths, coopers, millers, distillers, spinners, weavers, and seamstresses. At Thomas Jefferson's plantation at Poplar Forest, Virginia, slaves performed tasks that included brick making, blacksmithing, woodworking, and masonry.

Typically, such skilled labors provided goods for use on the plantation, though in many cases they became profitable enterprises in their own right, providing an additional source of income for the slaveholder, who sold the products made by the slave artisans. Robert Fogel and Stanley Engerman, in *Time on the Cross: The Economics of American Negro Slavery* (1974), have asserted that more than 25 percent of American slaves were craftsmen and semiskilled workers; they suggest as well that many of the leaders of the slave community came from this class of skilled workers and that many became leaders of protests, insurrections, and desertions.

Textile production was a typical plantation enterprise. Female slaves, following their work in the fields or in the slaveholder's household, were often required to spin, weave, or sew at night, usually to fill specific production quotas. The textiles produced by the slaves included cotton, linen, and wool fabrics, as well as embroidered bed coverlets and appliquéd pieced quilts, often made under the supervision of the mistress of the plantation. Sale of the textiles often became a successful business that helped offset fluctuations in a planter's income from crops.

Pottery was another typical enterprise, producing utilitarian wares that in some cases merged Native American and African form and technique. Early pots were hand-built and were fired outdoors, in the African manner; later pots were made in pottery mills owned by planters and were turned on potters' wheels. A prominent pottery-making enterprise, based in part on skilled slave labor, emerged in the Edgefield district of South Carolina (present-day Edgefield, Greenwood, McCormick, Saluda, and Aiken counties) in the early 1800s; the pottery mills

An African American barber. A barber in Richmond, Virginia, 1861. Slaves are typically depicted as farm workers or house slaves, but many had specialized skills. *The Granger Collection, New York. Reproduced by permission.*

relied on the labor of both white potters and skilled slaves. Present-day knowledge of the Edgefield pots may be credited in part to the survival of many signed pots made by a slave named Dave (after Emancipation, Dave Drake), a skilled turner, as potters of the time were called. Dave is believed to have produced hundreds—perhaps thousands—of pots for the Landrum Pottery and later for Miles Mill Factory.

Newspaper advertisements for the return of runaway slaves attest to the value of the skilled slave. There are numerous references to runaway carpenters, seamstresses, joiners, and blacksmiths. For example, in the *Raleigh Register and North Carolina Weekly Advertiser* on April 13, 1807, James Welborn offered a $40 reward for a runaway named Joe, a "good shoemaker, a tolerable cooper." Conceivably, a slave whose skill could provide a potential source of income may have been more likely to flee. A notice in the *Maryland Gazette* posted by the sheriff of Charles County, Maryland, on June 30, 1803, relates that he had taken custody of a "runaway, a stout likely Negro man, who calls himself Jack Turner, and says he is free, a joiner by trade. . . . His master, if any, is requested to take him away, otherwise he will be sold . . . for prison fees and other charges."

Artisans and Maritime Workers

Another area of production of goods by slaves occurred as part of artisanal trades. Throughout the colonies, in the South as well as in the North, a system of apprenticing and hiring out skilled slaves to white and free black craftsmen was a significant part of the production of both utilitarian and decorative items, including furniture, wrought iron grillwork, and jewelry. This system of labor resulted in a higher level of development of skills among enslaved craftspeople while enriching slaveholders. Slaves were apprenticed to cabinetmakers, silversmiths, goldsmiths, printers, and engravers. There was economic benefit for the master craftsmen as well as for the slaveholders; unlike indentured free apprentices, slaves were not released after finishing their apprenticeship but continued to labor—with a higher level of skill yet at the same low rate of pay. Some slaves benefited as well; some were able to purchase their freedom, and others ran away, confident of their ability to earn a living. In the early 1800s in New Orleans, free black artisans and slave apprentices dominated the production of certain fine craft items, such as furniture. Their numbers, in New Orleans and elsewhere, declined by mid-century, following legal restrictions in some states on the numbers of slave apprentices and on the ownership of businesses by free blacks, and as the result of an increase in the development of mechanized industry.

Female slaves were often trained as seamstresses and dressmakers, and their services were hired out as yet another source of income for the slaveholder. Newspaper advertisements indicate that many of these women, who had highly marketable skills, fled. Others, such as Elizabeth Hobbs Keckley (1818–1907), were able to purchase their own freedom by sewing.

Especially during the colonial period, slaves worked in the maritime industries as sailmakers, riggers, boatmen, mariners, and pilots. As scholar Brendan Foley suggested in his essay "Slaves in the American Maritime Economy," one of the paradoxes of American slavery is the degree of freedom that some owners allowed their skilled slaves; some even allowed slaves to sail to foreign ports. Even those slaves whose travels were confined to the rivers of the South came into contact with free blacks and white workers, thus gaining access to information—cultural and political as well as trade-based—that was not accessible to slaves on farms and plantations. Foley also asserts that the economic and cultural contribution of maritime slaves has been largely overlooked and underestimated. Despite the difficulty of documentation, the extent and quality of the work of skilled slaves—in the maritime industries as well as a wide range of arts and crafts—is known to have played a significant role in America's economy and culture.

BIBLIOGRAPHY

Ball, Charles. *Fifty Years in Chains; or, the Life of an American Slave.* New York: H. Dayton, 1859.

Fogel, Robert, and Stanley Engerman. *Time on the Cross: The Economics of American Negro Slavery.* Boston: Little and Brown, 1974.

Foley, Brendan. "Slaves in the American Maritime Economy, 1638–1865: Economic and Cultural Roles." Available at www.mit.edu/people/bpfoley/slavery2.html.

Jackson, Donald, and Dorothy Twohig, eds. *The Diaries of George Washington.* 6 vols. Charlottesville: University Press of Virginia, 1976–1979.

Patton, Sharon F. *African American Art.* Oxford and New York: Oxford University Press, 1998.

Dorothy Bauhoff

APPRENTICESHIP

Apprenticeship, as a concept, is a global phenomenon. Prior to the development of industrial society and wage labor systems, the vast majority of the world developed local economic systems that used local labor, local materials, and local cultural forms to serve local and regional markets. Within this system, what is commonly referred to as "craft guilds" developed to safeguard the knowl-

edge associated with the craft, to protect the interest of those trained in the craft, and to educate young people who were interested in learning the given expertise to earn a living. As an apprentice, a person was required to spend a given amount of time with a master craftsman to learn the skill. In exchange for their labor the apprentices would usually spend three to seven years with the master craftsmen to learn the knowledge base associated with the trade. During that period the apprentices would work exclusively with the master craftsmen. In many cases they would live with their trainers. While learning, they would perform domestic as well as rudimentary skills associated with the given skill. A fraction of the apprentice's time could be spent earning a living. Upon completion of an apprenticeship, the person was considered a novice in the associated craft. After practicing the craft for a number of years and developing a reputation for quality work, a person would eventually earn the title of master craftsman.

During the era of New World slavery, transformations in the economies of Western Europe and Africa distorted, challenged, and in some cases eliminated the guild system. In Western Europe the guild system gave way to mass production in forms such as textile mills. In Africa the most productive and knowledgeable workers and master craftsmen were enslaved to serve on plantations in the Americas. In the North American British colonies the guild system would, to some degree, resurface as the basis for organizing skilled workers in northern industries. With the introduction of chattel slavery, however, the incorporation of enslaved and free African labor would become problematic. Because of both economic insecurity and racism, white workers alienated and resented free African workers, who were relegated to menial labor jobs. They barred them, in most cases, from becoming apprentices to master craftsmen. Organized labor in the southern colonies, in the form of craft guilds, was totally unacceptable for enslaved African workers. Generally those who were enslaved, but skilled, performed specific duties for the plantation owner such as house construction, blacksmithing, house repairs, leatherwork, and shoemaking. Oftentimes those who were skilled were rented out to local businesses and plantations. The master would of course receive the wages for the work performed.

On the eve of emancipation in slave societies throughout the Americas, the apprenticeship concept would resurface in an unusual form. Former slave owners would argue that free African laborers were childlike and required supervision. Without supervision and guidance concerning how to make a living and function as a free laborer, they would become both a burden to themselves and society at large. The apprenticeship program, they argued, was a gradual way to potentially integrate the former slaves into society as potentially free laborers.

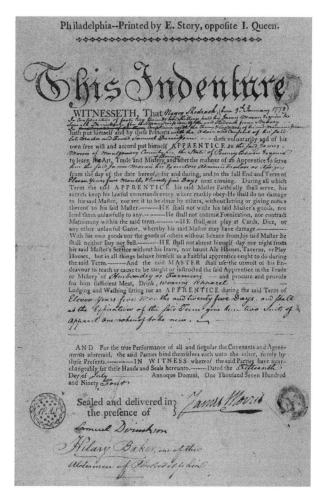

An indentured servitude document from July 15, 1794.
The document is for a former slave, Shadrach, who is to be apprenticed to Pennsylvania farmer James Morris. At the eve of emancipation, slave owners supported an apprenticeship system, arguing that free Africans were child-like and required supervision. *Kean Collection/Hulton Archive/Getty Images.*

In some instances abolitionists, who believed that slave labor created a consciousness in the enslaved that despised productive work and economic activity, advocated for the apprenticeship programs. "Free Negroes," by contrast, maintained a "strong and vibrant" work ethic because they were spared the harshness and oppressive nature of enslaved labor (Alexander 1842, pp. 44–45). In contrast, some pro-slavery advocates would argue that the apprenticeship system actually contributed to the collapse of southern culture and economic activity because it provided the slave with too much freedom. A return to the former days of forced labor and supervision was seen as the only alternative because "without force he (the Negro) will sink into lethargy, and revert to his primitive savage character, and the only feasible and effectual plan to promote his civilization is to persist in those measures that compel him to labour"

(*The South Vindicated from the Treason and Fanaticism of the Northern Abolitionists* 1836, pp. 120–122).

BIBLIOGRAPHY

The Abolitionist; or, Record of the New England Anti-Slavery Society. Boston: Garrison and Knapp, 1833.

Alexander, George William. *Letters on the Slave Trade Slavery, and Emancipation: with a Reply to Objections Made to the Liberation of the Slaves in the Spanish Colonies; Addressed to Friends on the Continent of Europe, during a Visit to Spain and Portugal.* London: C. Gilpin, 1842.

The South Vindicated from the Treason and Fanaticism of the Northern Abolitionists. Philadelphia: H. Manly, 1836.

Kwasi Densu

SLAVE ENTREPRENEURS

The notion of enslaved African Americans employing the principles of capitalism to accumulate wealth might initially seem odd, considering their legal status as property. Yet some slaves, under favorable conditions, accrued capital in the form of currency, commodities, and, on the rare occasion, real estate by providing essential services to the local populace, either by utilizing their artisanal skills or supplying goods for various trade exchanges. One former slave observed that "[t]here were lots of Negroes who had trades. They could make brooms and chair bottoms, and lots of them made a lot of money that way ... and sometimes they would take money and buy their wife and children, and then buy himself" (Rawick 1972–1979, vol. 18, p. 41). These enslaved capitalists peddled handicrafts made in their limited free time and produce from their own gardens in the street markets of such cities as Charleston, Savannah, and New Orleans. They sold goods and bartered in the slave quarters of Southern plantations and they engaged in trade and self-hiring negotiations with white merchants, factory owners, and planters. Like their free counterparts, enslaved entrepreneurs sought to improve the living conditions of themselves and their families, but ultimately their goal was to use the resources of their economic activities to gain their freedom.

During the era of American slavery, a small number of enslaved laborers were able to use their skills to establish businesses with the blessings or at least acquiescence of their slave owners. For example, in 1850 former slave Benjamin Montgomery of Loudoun County, Virginia, was purchased by Mississippi planter Joseph Davis (brother of the future president of the Confederate States of America, Jefferson Davis). On the Davis family's plantation, Davis Bend, Montgomery learned to operate the plantation's steam-powered cotton gin and acquired knowledge in land surveyance and building construction.

In addition, with the help of Joseph Davis, Montgomery established an importing business, providing goods from New Orleans to both white and black consumers. The business prospered, enabling Montgomery to purchase his family's freedom and his own. After the Civil War, Montgomery bought Davis Bend plantation and supervised its operation until his death in 1877. By 1881, however, the Davis family had re-acquired the plantation as a result of foreclosure proceedings against Montgomery's family.

Most enslaved entrepreneurs were artisans. Some enslaved African Americans were taught their skills by family members, but others had been trained by white artisans engaged by slave owners who recognized the high return on hiring out enslaved artisans in a labor-shortage market. They held such occupations as blacksmiths, carpenters, coopers, cooks, seamstresses, ferry operators, wheelwrights, shoemakers, and millers. These were skills in high demand and therefore yielded sustainable livelihoods that could be turned into lucrative businesses. In her autobiography *Behind the Scenes* (1868), Elizabeth Keckley, formerly enslaved in Dinwiddie Court-House, Virginia, and St. Louis, Missouri, told of her mother teaching her to sew as a child and using her skills as a young adult to support the impoverished slaveholding family who owned her as well as her mother. She stated:

> I was fortunate in obtaining work, and in a short time I had acquired something of a reputation as a seamstress and dress-maker. The best ladies in St. Louis were my patrons, and when my reputation was once established I never lacked for orders. With my needle I kept bread in the mouths of seventeen persons for two years and five months (2005 [1868], p. 45).

As a result of the slaveholding family's poverty, Keckley was allowed to hire herself out as a seamstress to the affluent women of St. Louis and thereby began a flourishing dressmaking business. In gratitude for her kind demeanor and superb talent, the "best ladies" of St. Louis loaned Keckley $1,200 in 1855 to purchase her son's freedom and her own. In 1860, she moved her dressmaking business to Washington, DC, and eventually counted among her patrons the wife of Senator Jefferson Davis of Mississippi and the first lady of the United States, Mary Todd Lincoln.

Like Keckley, slave entrepreneurs took advantage of the flexibility and semi-independence that being hired out or self-hired afforded them. It was an accepted practice for slave owners to loan the services of skilled or semi-skilled slaves to local merchants, factory owners, or other planters needing temporary laborers. The terms of the loan were often set out in contracts stipulating housing, food, and clothing provisions for the slave, as well as payment schedules for use of the slave's labor. In self-hire arrangements, however, slave owners left it to the enslaved worker to make his or her own contracts, as

in the case of Keckley. Such hiring practices often led to hired slaves living independent of their masters as nominal or virtually free slaves. Lewis Clarke, a self-hired slave in Kentucky, managed to provide for all his needs even though he had no distinctive skills. In his autobiography *Narratives of the Suffering of Lewis and Milton Clarke* (1846), he explained: "... I hired my time at $12 a month; boarded and clothed myself. To meet my payments, I split rails, burned coal, peddled grass seed, and took hold of whatever I could find to do" (Bland 2001, p. 137).

Although being hired out or self-hired were possible avenues to some degree of economic independence, the possession of qualities deemed necessary for any successful business endeavor were also prerequisites for potential entrepreneurs within the slave community. Risk-taking, ingenuity, business savvy, and aggressiveness were characteristics enslaved children learned from their elders. Slave-born Lunsford Lane recounted his introduction to business in his autobiography *The Narrative of Lunsford Lane* (1842). When he was a child, his father gave him a basket of peaches. He states: "I sold them for thirty cents, which was the first money I ever had in my life" (Bland 2001, p. 94). After several small-scale "money-making" schemes, Lane established a tobacco and pipe manufacturing operation in Raleigh, North Carolina, with his enslaved father as his mentor. Lane was able to purchase his freedom from the proceeds of his venture.

Taking the risk of establishing a business was a precarious undertaking for enslaved African Americans. The act itself was illegal. State slave codes prohibited slaves from entering into business contracts on their own behalf. Enslaved laborers were not allowed to acquire property and were banned from learning to read and write. Furthermore, slaves could not venture beyond their master's property without written permission and were sometimes required to obtain licenses or permits to engage in artisanal endeavors. These were major obstacles for enterprising slaves. Nonetheless, economic agency continued within the slave community. Slave owners utilizing the hiring out time and self-hiring schemes customarily ignored state regulations that conflicted with their profit-making schemes.

Slave entrepreneurship was manifested in a variety of ways, depending on region, temperament of the slave owner, and labor system employed. In urban areas, most slaves were domestics and often were assigned food marketing duties that facilitated opportunities to trade in the marketplace on one's own behalf. While making purchases for the slave-owning family, enterprising slave women sold or bartered pastries, cakes, and handicrafts to make their own money. In addition, enslaved men contributed fish, baked breads and many other items, including the game from hunting trips. Although state slave codes prohibited slaves from carrying guns, slaves were able to circumvent the laws when necessary. According to Mr. Huddleston, a formerly enslaved Tennessean, "Cullud folks been had guns all their life. They kept them hid" (Rawick, p. 36). Some urban slaves also cultivated vegetable gardens on small plots they were allowed to use. Fresh produce flowed into food markets from many of the gardens of enslaved workers.

In the countryside, some plantation owners also allowed their slaves to grow vegetables and raise livestock on small parcels of land and often purchased the produce in surplus after enslaved gardeners had put aside a portion of the harvest for their family's consumption. In one particular case, a planter demanded that his slaves keep chickens on their assigned lots. According to an ex-slave, "each family had a chicken house and they had to raise chickens. They'd (the white people) buy them from you" (Rawick, p. 11).

Allowing slaves the use of small parcels of land was not an act of generosity. Slave owners reduced the food rations of slaves who were permitted to cultivate small lots. Moreover, the enslaved workers had to continue their daily work schedules for the master and only after their work was done could they toil in their private gardens or tend to their livestock. On plantations adopting the gang system of labor, slaves worked from sunup to sundown. Some slaves then worked in their gardens at night and on Sundays, traditionally a day of rest for slaves. Most planters on the outskirts of New Orleans, Savannah, and Charleston, however, used the task system where slaves were assigned individual tasks daily. When their daily chores were completed, the remainder of the day was their own.

Whether residing in the city or countryside and whether skilled or unskilled, enslaved African Americans gained access to exchange networks which facilitated small-scale money-making enterprises. While race and their unfree status significantly hindered the economic agency of bondpeople, market demand for their products sometimes prevailed against the bigotry of white consumers. Moreover, the slaveholders' complicity with the practice of slave self-hiring—a potential stepping stone to economic freedom—conferred legitimacy to the enslaved worker's foray into the free market system. Ultimately, as historian Juliet E. K. Walker suggests in *Black Entrepreneurship*: "the goods and services offered by slave entrepreneurs ... were a necessary and integral part of the antebellum southern economy" (Walker 1983, p. 47).

BIBLIOGRAPHY

Bland Jr., Sterling Lecater. *African American Slave Narratives: An Anthology,* vol. 1. Westport, CT: Greenwood Press, 2001.

Blassingame, John W. *Black New Orleans 1860–1880.* Chicago: University of Chicago Press, 1973.

Keckley, Elizabeth. *Behind the Scenes, Or, Thirty Years a Slave and Four Years in the White House* [1868]. New York: Penguin Books, [2005].

Mintz, S. "African American Voices." Digital History. Available at http://www.digitalhistory.uh.edu.

Rawick, George P., ed. *The American Slave: A Composite Autobiography.* 19 vols. Westport, CT: Greenwood Press, 1972–1979.

Schweninger, Loren. "Black-owned Businesses in the South, 1790–1880." *Business History Review* 63, Spring (1989): 22–60.

Walker, Juliet E .K. "Black Entrepreneurship: An Historical Inquiry." *Essays in Economic and Business History* 1 (1983): 37–55.

Wood, Betty. *Women's Work, Men's Work: The Informal Slave Economies of Lowcountry Georgia.* Athens: University of Georgia Press, 1995.

Carol J. Gibson

FREE FRANK MCWORTER: ENTREPRENEUR EXTRAORDINAIRE

Born a slave in 1777 and manumitted in 1819, "Free Frank" McWorter was the first African American to legally register a town. With profits from various entrepreneurial endeavors, McWorter founded New Philadelphia, Illinois, in 1836 on land purchased from the U.S. government. In 1785, McWorter assisted his master, George McWhorter (who was allegedly his father), in establishing a farm in Pulaski County, Kentucky. When the master moved on to Tennessee to start a new farm, he left McWorter in Kentucky to manage his holdings. McWorter oversaw operations of the farm by day and by night, operated a mining and manufacturing enterprise he had founded during the War of 1812. His business extracted crude niter from nearby caves to produce saltpeter, an essential ingredient in gunpowder. The proceeds from his business and other revenue-generating opportunities he undertook by hiring out his time enabled McWorter to purchase his freedom, whereupon he petitioned the court to have the *h* in McWhorter dropped from his surname and acquired the nickname "Free Frank." Before his death in 1854, McWorter had purchased the freedom of sixteen family members with profits earned through land speculation, commercial farming, and the sale of town lots in New Philadelphia.

SOURCE: Walker, Juliet E. K., *Free Frank: A Black Pioneer on the Antebellum Frontier.* Lexington, KY: University Press of Kentucky, 1983.

CRAFTSMEN

Though countless enslaved craftspeople labored in the Americas from the colonial period until Emancipation, most remain anonymous in the historical record. Yet from the early years of the slave trade, there is evidence of skilled craftspeople, noted on slave ship manifests as metalworkers, woodcarvers, and weavers, among other trades. Such skills were highly valued in the Americas, especially during the pre-industrial colonial period, when household goods such as soap, candles, fabric, and tools were made by hand; a shortage of both skilled labor and goods increased the need for enslaved craftspeople. Slave narratives as well as records of sale indicate that slaves who were skilled craftspeople were sold at higher prices.

Some of the handcraft work by African and African American slaves developed in a regional manner that was related to the plantation economy. In the coastal Low Country of South Carolina and Georgia, for example, crafts that were related to rice cultivation and processing were valued; planters paid higher prices for slaves from the Windward Coast of Africa, who were skilled not only in rice cultivation but also in making the crafted objects necessary for processing, including hand-coiled winnowing or fanning baskets and hand-carved wooden mortars and pestles. The Low Country craft production of fanning baskets and mortars continued throughout the eighteenth and nineteenth centuries, and similar tools were still in use in the early twentieth century on the Sea Islands off the coast of Georgia and South Carolina.

The regional production of ceramics was related to the availability of natural clay. For example, a thriving pottery enterprise developed in the Edgefield district of South Carolina (present-day Edgefield, Greenwood, McCormick, Saluda, and Aiken counties) in the early 1800s using the rich clay deposits of the area to produce stoneware, adding an alkaline glaze made from wood ash or lime. The pottery mills and shops were operated by white planters, who relied on the labor of both white potters and skilled slaves.

There are rare but outstanding examples of signed or attributed works made by enslaved craftspeople. Among the most famous are the works of Dave, an enslaved Edgefield potter who worked for the Landrum Pottery and the Miles Mill Factory from around 1830 through 1864. Remarkably, many of his surviving pots are signed, and many were decorated with inscriptions, often rhymed couplets, by the artist. Scholars have speculated about the reasons that Dave was allowed such artistic freedom at a time when literacy was forbidden to slaves. It has been suggested that there was a significant demand for pots made by Dave, which were distinguished not only by their inscriptions but also by their large size, pleasing proportions, and rich glazes. More than 100 of Dave's surviving pots are preserved in various collections, including those of the Philadelphia Museum of Art and the American Folk Art Museum in New York City.

Many enslaved craftspeople worked as apprentices to white or free black craftsmen, and others were hired out by slaveholders as an additional source of income.

Slave carpenters and cabinetmakers formed a large number of these skilled craftspeople; in New Orleans in the early 1800s, free blacks and slave apprentices dominated the production of fine furniture. A small storage cabinet (c. 1850), considered to be an outstanding example of work by a master cabinetmaker, is attributed to Peter Lee, a slave carpenter from John Collins's Rodney plantation in Alabama.

Henry Gudgell, who was born a slave in 1826 in Kentucky, is believed to be the maker of an ornately carved walking stick, now in the Yale University Art Gallery. The walking stick, made for sale in 1867, is decorated with a lizard, tortoise, and human figure, reflecting a distinctly African aesthetic, and is probably representative of the style of wood carvings made by Gudgell during his enslavement. Gudgell is also identified as a blacksmith, a wheelwright, and a silversmith.

Women slaves often were skilled textile workers. Most plantations had a weaving or spinning building where women slaves were required to spin thread, weave fabric, and sew, usually after a day's work in the fields or in the slaveholder's house. Many of these skilled workers made embroidered bed coverlets and appliquéd pieced quilts. Most of these fragile textiles have not survived, but examples remain. A silk quilt, made by two slaves identified only as Aunt Ellen and Aunt Margaret at the Knob plantation in Kentucky, is dated to the late 1830s. The Bible quilts of Harriet Powers (1837–1910), who was born a slave, are among the best-known African American textile works of the late nineteenth century and may be considered representative of similar works by countless undocumented quilters and seamstresses.

BIBLIOGRAPHY

Lewis, Samella, ed. *African American Arts and Artists*. Berkeley: University of California Press, 1990.

Patton, Sharon F. *African American Art*. Oxford, U.K., and New York: Oxford University Press, 1998.

Vlach, John Michael. *The Afro-American Tradition in Decorative Arts*. Athens: University of Georgia Press, 1990.

Dorothy Bauhoff

INDUSTRIAL WORK

Most slaves in the New World toiled in the fields, but some increasingly worked in industrial occupations, such as the processing of wheat or the manufacturing of iron, as American slavery expanded. This was especially true in Richmond, Virginia, where the slave population continued to increase until 1860 in contrast to other southern cities such as Baltimore, Charleston, and New Orleans, all of which witnessed a corresponding decrease in the late antebellum era. Slave artisans had always been present from the colonial era onward with their craftwork in clay and iron being influenced by western

Slaves working at a tobacco factory. Slaves picking leaves and operating machinery at a tobacco factory, 1754. The tobacco industry in Virginia almost exclusively hired males slaves who would then control the pace and quality of their work. *MPI/Hulton Archive/Getty Images.*

African as well as by western European styles. Industrial Richmond's reliance upon slave labor was relatively new; however; free white labor dominated the city's first workforces for small tobacco and flour mills in the first decade of the nineteenth century. Nevertheless, by 1820, entrepreneurs in Richmond as well as all over the American South quickly began to prefer slave labor over free labor, seeing European immigrants in particular as more expensive and troublesome than bondmen and women.

Canal and railway companies had no other choice but to resort to slaves when immigrants refused to work in unsafe and disease-ridden environments. The tobacco industry in Richmond and nearby Petersburg, for example, almost exclusively came to hire male slaves, who then would go on to control the pace and quality of their production to a remarkable degree. Indeed, the very hallmarks of urban slavery, such as hiring out and living apart, that made slave labor attractive to employers

helped slaves to exercise varying degrees of autonomy both inside and outside the factory. Bans on self-hiring were frequently circumvented by slaves who continued to hunt for jobs with signed permission slips from their owners. This relative freedom came with its own costs; industrial work in the nineteenth century was inherently arduous and dangerous. Slaves in the construction, fishing, canal, steamboat transportation, lumbering, and sugar refining industries put in the longest hours. Their days could exceed the twelve- to sixteen-hour norm, and their owners could preempt any customary breaks for the Sabbath or holidays. Fires and explosions at the workplace prematurely ended many slaves' lives, with mining and transportation the most deadly pursuits of them all.

The hazards and monotony associated with industrial work pushed the hired out to run away for good, even if they had relatively more control over their lives than field hands or domestics. Historians have found that urban, skilled workers were as likely as plantation

RELYING ON SLAVE LABOR

Industrial slave labor encompassed an array of occupations and literally built the American South. Immigrants were seen as less reliable and more expensive in the early nineteenth century, so slaves became the workforces at factories, mines, boats, and shops. Richmond, Virginia, was the epitome of an industrial city reliant upon slave labor with its Tredegar Iron Works eventually becoming the arsenal of the Confederacy. While industrial labor could be especially grim and onerous, the hiring-out and living apart components of industrial slavery allowed bondmen and women somewhat more control over their lives as compared to domestics and field hands.

SOURCE: Starobin, Robert S. *Industrial Slavery in the Old South.* New York: Oxford University Press, 1970.

workers to want to escape and were more likely to succeed in their attempts because of personal connections made alongside the docks and canals. For those left behind, at least in Richmond, industrial slaves became the mainstays of emerging black communities and institutions. Slaves could earn cash, pooling their savings together to build and to purchase churches. This liberating effect of their reliance upon semi-independent laborers was noted by some fearful whites who worried about careless owners sowing the seeds of slave rebellion. In Richmond, many remembered Gabriel Prosser (1776–1800), the hired-out blacksmith at the turn of the century who had plotted to kill all the whites except for poor women, Quakers, Methodists, and Frenchmen. Those qualms had largely subsided by the outbreak of the Civil War (1861–1865), however, as southern nationalists pointed with pride to the economic successes of the industrial and urban slave systems with up to one-fifth of American manufacturing output coming from the Old South.

Ironically, the Civil War would deepen the South's reliance upon industrial slave labor, as the Confederacy needed conscripted workers to build defenses while white male workers joined the army. Wartime provisions tried to restrict the movement and behavior of industrial slave labor more precisely than ever before, but self-interested owners helped their chattel property to avoid such unpleasant jobs as digging trenches or mining lead. Field hands, whom the Confederate government commandeered to build bridges and to unload cargo, used this turn of events to their advantage to plan their escape or to prepare for their emancipation under the Yankees. Eventually, the Confederacy was so desperate to win that it tried to move slaves from being noncombatant support in mobilization to being armed soldiers, but such

virtual abolition was too late to preserve southern independence.

BIBLIOGRAPHY

Boles, John B. *Black Southerners, 1619–1869.* Lexington: University Press of Kentucky, 1984.

Starobin, Robert S. *Industrial Slavery in the Old South.* New York: Oxford University Press, 1970.

Takagi, Midori. *Rearing Wolves to Our Own Destruction: Slavery in Richmond, Virginia, 1782–1865.* Charlottesville; London: University Press of Virginia, 1999.

Charles H. Ford

■ Systems of Work

SYSTEMS OF WORK: AN OVERVIEW
   Jackie R. Booker

TASK SYSTEM
   Kwasi Densu

GANG SYSTEM
   Claus K. Meyer

SYSTEMS OF WORK: AN OVERVIEW

The cultivation of tropical and semitropical crops in the seventeenth-century Caribbean required large numbers of slaves. Initially, Europeans relied on Native American labor, but smallpox decimated the indigenous population. African slaves soon became the laborers of choice in the region. Two labor systems emerged in the Caribbean, and both were eventually transferred to colonial North America, where they became the primary means of extracting labor from African and, later, African American slaves.

Slaves in the Caribbean cultivated sugarcane using gang labor. Groups of male slaves were assigned specific jobs in the process of making sugar. Each gang of slaves performed a specific function; for example, cutting sugarcane, boiling the sugarcane, or packaging the sugar for shipment to Europe. Usually performed by males, gang labor was harsh and demanding, and shortened the life expectancy of slaves. Gang labor tended to result in a disproportionate number of male slaves on sugar estates, with few female slaves present and little interaction between the sexes.

Each gang of slaves operated under the direction of a boss, or manager, who ran the plantation in the absence of the slave owners, who sometimes resided in Europe. Bosses kept careful watch on each gang. Each group of men had the potential to rebel collectively or individually, as one or more slaves could run away from the gang. Managers worked gangs in such a way as to extract the maximum labor from them in each step of the process. Sugar plantation owners migrating to the

Slaves preparing tobacco. An engraving depicting slaves preparing tobacco in Virginia, circa 1790. Newly migrated sugar plantation owners introduced the gang system of labor to the tobacco farms of Virginia and Maryland. *The Stapleton Collection/Bridgeman Art Library.*

Chesapeake colonies of Virginia and Maryland introduced the gang system of labor to the cultivation of tobacco in this region.

Tobacco cultivation was labor intensive, requiring a large number of slaves to produce only small quantities of the product. Groups of male slaves, sometimes numbering 200 or more, performed back-breaking labor: After clearing the land, then preparing the soil for cultivation, they planted the tobacco, weeded the crop, harvested and cured it, and finally prepared it for export to Europe. As with gang laborers in the Caribbean, slaves in the Chesapeake were tightly controlled. Bosses on tobacco plantations told slaves when to get up, what to do, when to eat, and generally micromanaged every aspect of their daily lives. Due to the omnipresent potential for slave rebellions, overseers of gang laborers maintained a watchful eye over their slaves. With the arduous labor required of slaves in gangs, there was perhaps a higher propensity for these slaves to run away or otherwise rebel against their managers.

Gang labor was also the system of choice for the cultivation of cotton in the Deep South, where short-staple cotton had been cultivated for years in small areas, providing English textile manufacturers with ample but not abundant supplies. During the latter half of the eighteenth century, however, cotton growers along the South Carolina–Georgia coastline experimented with long-staple cotton. Its primary drawback was the difficulty involved in separating the seeds from the silky cotton. The invention of the cotton gin in 1793 facilitated the faster removal of seeds from long-staple cotton. This technological advance not only added speed to the production of sea-island cotton, it also resulted in the spread of cotton cultivation to other areas of the Deep South, including Florida, Alabama, Mississippi, Arkansas, Tennessee, Oklahoma, Louisiana, and Texas. As cotton spread into these regions, so did gang labor. Soon after the season's last frost, groups of slaves, including both men and women, began breaking up the ground. Cotton seeds were planted in long rows in fertile soil, and another group of slaves soon began weeding the vast cotton fields that sometimes stretched for miles. During harvest season, gangs of slaves picked the cotton, and, although the cotton gin slowly made its advance into the region, in many cases slave gangs also separated the seeds from the cotton, by hand. Although male slaves predominated in these gangs, female slaves also were involved in the production of cotton. Overall, the creation of long-staple cotton led to the expansion of cotton production, necessitating even more slaves and, with gang labor as the primary system of work, tightened control over hundreds of thousands of slaves from South Carolina to Texas.

Thus, gang laborers had little free time and generally failed to develop any significant skills outside those required for the production of tobacco and cotton. Gang labor increased the already harsh conditions under which slaves operated. Studies show that slaves in regions where gang labor was used had little chance for manumission. Most usually labored under these coerced conditions until their death.

The task labor system also had its origins in the Caribbean, and was transferred to the English North American colonies. Although the task labor system was evident throughout the Southern colonies, it was most common in South Carolina, first with the cultivation of indigo and later with rice cultivation.

During the latter decades of the seventeenth century, indigo became a major crop in the South Carolina colony. Slaves were assigned tasks such as the preparation of the fields, planting, and harvesting during a brief cycle that included the months of July, August, and September. Slaves carried tons of indigo leaves to large vats, where they were boiled, stirred, and beaten. The stench from the preparation attracted millions of flies, driving many slave masters north for the winter, but slaves were required to continue working through the smelly process. Indigo cultivation, which created a dye for export, was based on task labor and a short production cycle, and many slaves on indigo plantations had some free time once their tasks were completed.

The introduction of rice by slaves from the Guinea region of Africa into the South Carolina colony led to a need for more slaves, and it perpetuated the task system. Beginning with the first Carolina rice harvests around 1700, tasking became the labor system of choice for this crop. Once the soil was prepared, slaves usually were assigned one-fourth of an acre to plant, weed, flood, and weed again before harvesting the rice in September. Slaves then would thresh or separate the heads from the stalks, winnow the rice from the chaff, and finally pound the rice by hand before preparing it for shipment to Europe.

The task system as employed in the Carolina and Georgia Low Country gave some slaves free time once

their tasks were completed. Drivers, who oftentimes were experienced slaves, gave daily tasks to each slave. Most assignments were completed by the early afternoon, leaving slaves with time to plant gardens, hunt, fish, tend to chickens, and generally relax after a difficult workday. Some slaves produced enough vegetables to sell in Charleston's marketplaces, earning small profits for themselves.

In an effort to extract even more labor from slaves, some rich planters in the decades before the Civil War switched from the task system to the gang labor system on rice plantations. Accustomed to the little bit of autonomy afforded by the task system, slaves generally resisted gang labor by working slowly, and an increasing number attempted to run away rather than endure the harsher system of labor.

Overall, the type of crop determined whether the gang or the task labor system was used. Regardless of which system slaves operated under, they tried to maintain whatever freedom they could, with slaves in the gang labor system strictly controlled and those under the task system given a minimum of free time to pursue their own activities.

BIBLIOGRAPHY

Carney, Judith A. *Black Rice: The African Origins of Rice Cultivation in the Americas.* Cambridge, MA: Harvard University Press, 2001.

Davis, David Brion. *Inhuman Bondage: The Rise and Fall of Slavery in the New World.* Oxford, U.K.: Oxford University Press, 2006.

Franklin, John Hope, and Alfred Moss. *From Slavery to Freedom: A History of African Americans,* 8th ed. New York: McGraw-Hill, 2000.

Morgan, Kenneth. *Slavery and Servitude in Colonial North America: A Short History.* New York, NY: New York University Press, 2000.

Weir, Robert M. *Colonial South Carolina: A History.* Columbia, SC: University of South Carolina Press, 1983.

Jackie R. Booker

TASK SYSTEM

During the course of the evolution of slavery in the Americas, two methods of labor organization developed within the context of the plantation system: gang labor and task labor. The gang labor system was the most popular form. Most contemporary images of slavery emerge out of this experience. The gang labor system organized field hands into work gangs. Members of the work gangs were chosen based on physical health, age, skill level, and gender. Gang labor was popular in the United States, particularly on cotton and tobacco plantations. Within this system, field hands would perform various agricultural tasks, depending on the season, throughout the day. The season would also determine the length of the day. Typically, during the summer months, field hands would work between fourteen and eighteen hours per day. This is the origin of the popular notion of working from sunup to sundown.

The task system, unlike the gang system, was not based on a set number of working hours. Within the task system, field hands were assigned certain tasks based on the production needs of a given plantation system, and the average length of time a task took to complete. For instance, because a strong male field hand could hoe eight to ten rows of cotton across a fifteen-acre field in one day, that amount of hoeing was considered both a day's work and a set task. For women, the task would require seven to eight rows per fifteen-acre field (Brown 1855, p. 196). Various work tasks on the plantation were divided in this manner. The task system was popular in the coastal areas of the United States and in the Caribbean, where rice and sugarcane were important cash crops. Coastal rice plantations, for instance, developed three distinctive systems of rice production: (1) the upland or rain-fed system; (2) the tidal water system; and (3) the swampland system. Each system required specific tasks. The upland system required the clearing of forests and the construction of fields similar to those found in most rain-fed agricultural systems. Both the tidal water and swampland systems required the building of channels and dikes as part of an elaborate flood irrigation system. Rice plantation owners paid high prices for slaves taken from the African region that would come to be known as the *rice coast*, where indigenous rice cultivation was extremely developed. This stretches from present-day Senegal to present-day Liberia.

Unlike the gang system, the task system in some cases gave slaves a degree of autonomy. After completing a given task, field hands would frequently have time to cultivate private fields and gardens, spend time with family, or rest. This degree of autonomy, particularly in areas where enslaved Africans were the numerical majority, led to strong retention of indigenous knowledge and cultural norms in the areas of language, religion, craft production, social organization, the arts, and agricultural production. The Gullah cultures of the Georgia and South Carolina Sea Islands are one such example. In addition, it allowed enslaved persons to participate in market activity, which permitted them to purchase provisions and in some cases freedom and land in the postemancipation period. Because of this, plantation owners often argued that the task system was potentially more profitable, given that it in some ways mimicked free labor (Conder 1833, p. 75). The assumption was that if field hands were happier and perceived that they had

more control over their time and space, they would work harder. This would become an important argument for the elimination of chattel slavery and the promotion of wage labor under the infamous sharecropping system.

BIBLIOGRAPHY

Brown, John. *Slave Life in Georgia: A Narrative of the Life, Suffering, and Escape of John Brown, a Fugitive Slave, Now in England.* London: W. M. Watts, 1855.

Conder, Josiah. *Wages or the Whip: An Essay on the Comparative Cost and Production of Free and Slave Labor.* London: Hatchard and Son, 1833.

Kwasi Densu

GANG SYSTEM

The term *gang system* denotes a particularly exacting mode of labor widespread on slave plantations in the United States. The gang system is based on key factors, including division of labor and the strict supervision of slaves working together in groups. In its fully developed form, gang labor requires the synchronic or coordinated (hence interdependent), mechanical performance of relatively simple, repetitive tasks at a high, regular work pace. In these respects, gang labor on U.S. plantations anticipated the regime of the industrial assembly line.

The gang system was first developed on the sugar plantations of the Caribbean. In the United States, it was particularly widespread on the tobacco plantations in Maryland and Virginia, in the Cotton Belt, and on the sugar plantations of the Gulf coast.

Forms and Extent

At its simplest, gang labor involved the supervised synchronic work of a group of field hands. A carefully selected worker set the pace; the others were required to follow his or her example, urged on by the whip and yells of a white overseer or a black driver. This mode of work was common; for example, in the hoeing of cotton, in which several dozen slaves could be employed together on large plantations. At times, hoe gangs were used in tandem with plow gangs, for whom they set the pace of work.

A more complex form of gang labor assigned different tasks to workers within the same gang. In sowing cotton, slaves chosen for their skill and experience drilled the holes for the seed. (This was the most important part of the work as the spacing and depth of the openings played a key role in the success of the crop.) The weakest or poorest workers dropped the seed into the ground, others followed and closed the holes. Thus each gang consisted of groups of three workers, the most dexterous of whom set the speed for the two others. The leaders of the groups, in their turn, followed the movement of a pacesetter. Because of the mechanical nature of the

A chain gang in Richmond, Virginia, circa 1860s. The slaves suffered from the brutal enforcement of gang discipline. But working as a group gave them strength as well. Slave gangs often sang while they worked, which eased the monotony of the work and could serve to slow down the pace. *The Library of Congress.*

work, gang labor reminded observers of military formations or machines.

A sizeable number of slaves was required to realize the full potential of gang labor with its differentiation of the workforce. In their 1974 work on the economics of American slavery, the historians Robert Fogel and Stanley Engerman suggested that, on average, only holdings of sixteen and more slaves comprised enough able field hands for the deployment of the gang system. However, not all large plantations relied primarily on gang labor. In the low country of coastal South Carolina and Georgia, in particular, planters generally preferred the task system. But the forced mobility of slave labor meant that most likely a majority of antebellum slaves experienced gang labor at some point in their lives.

Even on those plantations that made heavy use of the gang system, labor was organized differently on many occasions. Gangs proved especially efficient in the simple repetitive tasks that formed part of the cultivation of sugar, cotton, and tobacco. They were also used in raising provisions. But much work both in the production of the slave staples themselves and in other parts of the plantation economy was not congenial to the gang system. Moreover, some evidence suggests that the use of gang labor declined during the antebellum period as slaves opposed the rigors of the regime and mechanization changed the work requirements on large plantations.

Gang Labor and Slave Life

Work dominated slave life, and gang labor was one of its most oppressive and monotonous forms. A former slave recalled that, as a large gang of cotton pickers pushed ahead to finish their rows before dinner, "not a sound could be heard, only a steady click, click, click, click of the fingers of three hundred Negros [*sic*] splitting cotton pods, with the heavy tread of half a dozen Negro drivers just behind them" (Gaines 2003, p. 17). Invariably, the black drivers or the white overseers supervising the gangs carried whips, and the image of large groups of slaves working uniformly under the whip struck travelers and, to the twenty-first century, dominates the public perception of slave work.

The slaves suffered from the brutal enforcement of gang discipline. Their role, however, cannot be reduced to that of parts of a machine, passive in themselves, but driven to do their work until they broke. Gang labor, for one, was a communal experience. Working together at the same pace put the slaves under pressure, but also gave them some strength. Often slave gangs accompanied their work with songs, which eased the monotony of their toil and could also serve to slow down the rhythm of the work. One master reported that he forbid his slaves to sing *drawling* tunes ... for their motions [were] almost certain to keep time with the music" ("Management of Negroes," 1850, p. 163). Apparently, however, such policies could not always be implemented or enforced (Mead 1820, pp. 13–14).

The individual worker within a gang was not altogether powerless either. The slaves could cause irrecoverable damage to the plants or their yield even when they worked under supervision, and it was not always easy to trace back the damage to the perpetrator. A cotton planter of the South Carolina Upcountry lamented: "The slave ... by experienced craft, unless your eye is on the very stalk at the time, can cut it up, so that you will not be able to find whence it came" ("Cotton Culture," 1839, p. 359). This vulnerability of the crops put some check on the use of brute force and made concessions to the workers necessary even under the strict regime of the gang.

On gang-system plantations, slaves generally had to work from sunup to sundown. Gang laborers, therefore, had as a rule no incentive to work fast and often seemed lazy and listless to white observers. But the significance of the gang system went beyond the setting of the fields. Overworking of pregnant women and young mothers was common and led to very high infant-mortality rates on gang-labor plantations. Unlike the task system, the exhausting regime of the gang left the field hands hardly any room to work on their own account and limited the time for communal activities. The gang system also stood for the classification of slaves by age and gender, strength and skill. It contributed to the stratification of the slave community and thus helped planters to establish a set of incentives, which, while not inextricably linked with gang labor, derived particular resiliency from it. The gang system was a key element of the plantation regime. Its combination of ruthless coercion and calculated regimentation helped make many slave plantations remarkably productive. The slaves highly resented gang labor and the oppressive plantation regime associated with it. Once emancipated, southern freedmen refused to work in gangs whenever possible.

BIBLIOGRAPHY

"Cotton Culture." *Southern Agriculturalist* 12, no. 7 (July 1839): 358–360.

CONVICT LABOR

Forced labor did not disappear with the end of the Civil War. The Thirteenth Amendment, which abolished slavery, expressly exempted convicted felons from its provisions. Convict labor was not limited to the South, but both symbolically and numerically it gained special significance in the region.

In the postbellum period, the southern states began to lease out convicts to private businesses, which at times employed the men in agricultural operations, but more often in the production of turpentine, in industrial establishments, or in railroad construction. Both task and gang systems were used in the exploitation of convict labor. The convict-lease regime provided a cheap substitute for regular state prison systems and served, at the same time, to control the recently emancipated African American workforce. Many states formally abolished leasing out convicts as early as the 1880s, but the practice continued well into the twentieth century until it was no longer perceived to be fiscally profitable.

About the turn of the twentieth century, chain gangs appeared in a new context when southern states began to employ convicts systematically in the construction of public roads—a form of gang labor that had largely ended by the 1940s. In the mid-1990s, however, chain gangs employed in public work were reintroduced by several jurisdictions, most notably by Maricopa County, Arizona, where the system continues in the twenty-first century.

BIBLIOGRAPHY

Lichtenstein, Alex. *Twice the Work of Free Labor: the Political Economy of Convict Labor in the New South.* New York: Verso, 1996.

Mancini, Matthew J. *One Dies, Get Another: Convict Leasing in the American South, 1866–1928.* Columbia: University of South Carolina Press, 1996.

Fogel, Robert William. *Without Consent or Contract: The Rise and Fall of American Slavery.* New York: W. W. Norton, 1989.

Fogel, Robert William, and Stanley L. Engerman. *Time on the Cross: The Economics of American Negro Slavery.* London: Wildwood House, 1974.

Gaines, Thomas S., ed. *Buried Alive (Behind Prison Walls) for a Quarter of a Century: Life of William Walker.* Chapel Hill: University of North Carolina, 2003.

"Management of Negroes." *Southern Cultivator* 8, no. 11 (November 1850): 162–164.

Mead, Whitman. *Travels in North America.* New York: C. S. Van Winkle, 1820. Available from http://hdl.loc.gov.

Moore, John Hebron. *The Emergence of the Cotton Kingdom in the Old Southwest: Mississippi,*

1770–1860. Baton Rouge: Louisiana State University Press, 1988.

Morgan, Philip D. "Task and Gang Systems: The Organization of Labor on New World Plantations." In *Work and Labor in Early America,* ed. Stephen Innes. Chapel Hill: University of North Carolina Press, 1988.

Roberts, Justin. "Working Between the Lines: Labor and Agriculture on Two Barbadian Sugar Plantations, 1796–97." *William and Mary Quarterly* 63, no. 3 (July 2006): 551–586. Available from http://www.historycooperative.org.

Claus K. Meyer

Family and Community

Family and Community Overview

Historians have argued about the slave family and the slave community, especially since the 1960s. The black family has especially been an area where historical interpretation has intersected with the public policy and reached into popular literature and public discussions. Both the general public and historians have argued and used interpretations of the enslaved black family in an attempt to explain current problems and even as an argument for reparations for enslavement.

The Jamaican-born African American sociologist, Orlando Patterson (1998), illustrates this extreme passion. He pointed to contemporary problems in the African American family and looked to slavery as the origin of the black matriarchy. According to the historical literature, under slavery black men became emasculated and powerless because white plantation owners were the patriarchs. Therefore, the slave family, as such, differed from what was considered the norm. Males were absent from the family, and women headed the household of children. It is somewhat ironic that in the 1970s, at about the time that a number of male scholars were arguing there was no black matriarchy, feminists, turning to African American women as exemplars of strength, argued that matriarchy, far from implying cultural inferiority, was a good thing. Patterson asserted that revisionist arguments contesting the matriarchy thesis are "an intellectual disgrace, the single greatest disservice that the American historical profession has ever done to those who turn to it for guidance about the past and the etiology of present problems. Indeed, in many ways this denial of the consequences of slavery is worse than the more than two centuries of racist historiography that preceded it" (1998, p. xiii).

Because states did not recognize the legal marriage between enslaved peoples, for decades historians assumed that there was no marriage, and hence no slave family as one would understand it in more modern times. In the 1960s and 1970s, however, a group of social historians and others interested in the family, especially labor historian Herbert Gutman, investigated plantation records, census documents, naming patterns, slave autobiographies, and former slave narratives. They found compelling evidence of strong African American families even within the horrible constraints of slavery. In slavery, African Americans maintained both marriages and family, and the recognition of the father-husband by both the enslaved people and the white community was evident. The enslaved people's commitment to family against all odds can only be described as truly heroic.

Demographic studies exploring the natural increase in the population of slaves concluded that slaves in the southern United States had a strong social base. Only in the United States did a slave population ever reproduce itself, and the birthrates for enslaved peoples approached that of the white population. Stable families provided physical, emotional, and cultural support for childbirth and child rearing. Yet slaves understood the tenuous position of their families. Members could be punished or sold at the owner's discretion or whim. Still, families remained a central institution and integral to the slave community. The two-parent family was a common form of slave family in a variety of locations and sizes; unions between husbands and wives and parents and children often endured for many years. African American parents headed these families; they loved and cared for their children and each other.

Although slaves arranged themselves in family units, they differed from white families in significant ways. Although not legally recognized, planters did allow marriage as a social institution, and slaves themselves chose to live in couples and family units. U.S. senator and pro-slavery advocate, James Henry Hammond (1807–1864), wrote in his rules for governing slaves that "Marriage is to be encouraged as it adds to the comfort, happiness & health of those who enter upon it, besides insuring a greater increase" (1831–1855, p. 36).

A slave family outside their cabin on a southern plantation. The two-parent slave family was a common form of slave family in a variety of locations, and unions between husbands and wives and parents and children often endured for many years. © *North Wind Picture Archives.*

Slave families also differed from white southern families because, by law, the slave father was not the legal head; the slave owner was, a situation impossible to compare to the white family. Also different from the white situation, the law gave the slave mother rather than the slave father the determining role in ascribing the status of the children. In the mid-1600s, when so many of the fathers were free and white, various colonies decided that "all children born in this country shall be held bond or free only according to the condition of the mother" (Stevenson 1993, p. 1045). This goes against the patriarchal notion that fathers owned the children, but the legal ownership was still, usually, that of a male, only it was the white male.

African Americans under slavery had divorce as an option, which was usually withheld from white southerners. Some owners made it harder than others. "When sufficient cause can be shown on either side, a marriage

may be annulled, but the offending party must be severely punished," wrote Hammond in his Edgefield plantation rule book (1831–1855, p. 36). Churches were integrated in the South before the Civil War (1861–1865) and some churches even allowed for divorce for enslaved people, especially when a spouse was sold away. Thus, whereas whites could not obtain a divorce, slaves were able to obtain church-sanctioned separations.

While many scholars agree that some slaves lived in families, the extent of such family life is still a cause of debate. Studies of slave communities have shown a wide variety of family structures and dynamics, and more is needed of these local and regional studies. One scholar of low-country rice plantations in South Carolina, Leslie A. Schwalm (1997), found a predominance of extended families and extrafamilial relationships rather than male-headed nuclear families. In a study of slavery in colonial and antebellum Virginia, another scholar concluded "neither monogamous marriages nor nuclear families dominated slave family forms" (Stevenson 1995, p. 52). Still other historians hold that slaves formed male-headed households to the extent their situation allowed.

The slave family itself was a major source of solace for slaves and the basis of community. Using more African American testimony, especially the New Deal Works Progress Administration former slave narratives, a group of historians responded to critiques of slavery as totally repressing the enslaved peoples so that their culture only mimicked white society. By looking at the enslaved people and describing their modes of resistance and formation of a unique culture, historians such as John Blassingame argued for cultural resiliency, separate spheres, and strong slave families. People who lived under the bonds of slavery still lived outside the control of whites. Africans and their descendants, despite difficulties, created a community that provided some protection from the worst abuses of slavery. They, or their forbearers, had once been members of widely disparate African ethnic groups—speaking a variety of languages and coming from different social backgrounds. They incorporated elements of their own traditions with European languages, religions, and cultures—and with some American Indian ingredients as well—and laid the foundations for the vibrant African American community that would see its members through the vicissitudes of American history. They found ways to offer resistance (both active and passive) to have family lives, spirituality, and community—not just to persevere, but to live, in the harshest of circumstances. Enslaved people were more than slaves; they were mothers, fathers, aunts, preachers, artisans, rebel, rogue, and a myriad of other identities that made up a slave community.

Historians do agree that masters and slaves struggled over the boundaries of slavery and freedom. Recently historians teeter between victimization, the cost of slavery to enslaved people and to American society, and the resilience and accomplishments of enslaved peoples. Historian Ira Berlin wrote, "the slaves' history—like all human history—was made not only by what was done to them but also by what they did for themselves" (2003, p. 4). While not ignoring slavery's harshness, and not contending that the cultural achievement of the slaves was an easy one, this group of slave community scholars found that, within the unfreedom of slavery, enslaved men and women created areas of control outside of white supervision.

BIBLIOGRAPHY

Berlin, Ira. *Generations of Captivity: A History of African American Slaves.* Cambridge, MA: Belknap Press of Harvard University Press, 2003.

Hammond, James Henry. "Silver Plantation Stock and Crop Book." In *Papers of James Henry Hammond and Hammond and Beech Island Farmer's Club.* Columbia: University of South Carolina, 1831–1855.

Patterson, Orlando. *Rituals of Blood: Consequences of Slavery in Two American Centuries.* Washington, DC: Civitas/CounterPoint, 1998.

Schwalm, Leslie A. *A Hard Fight for We: Women's Transition from Slavery to Freedom in South Carolina.* Urbana: University of Illinois Press, 1997.

Stevenson, Brenda. "Slavery." In *Black Women in America: An Historical Encyclopedia*, ed. Darlene Clark Hine. Brooklyn, NY: Carlson, 1993.

Stevenson, Brenda. "Black Family Structure in Colonial and Antebellum Virginia: Amending the Revisionist Perspective." In *The Decline of Marriage among African Americans: Causes, Consequences, and Policy Implications*, ed. M. Belinda Tucker and Claudia Mitchell-Kernan. New York: Russel Sage Foundation, 1995.

Orville Vernon Burton

■ Family Structure

FAMILY STRUCTURE: AN OVERVIEW

Ex-slave Harriet Jacobs recounted a horrific scene she witnessed of a mother and her seven children being sold separately at a slave auction:

> I saw a mother lead seven of her children to the auction-block. She knew that some of them would be taken from her; but they took all. The children were sold to a slave-trader, and their mother was bought by a man in her own town. Before night

THE SLAVE FAMILY

The horrors African Americans faced under slavery created several obstacles for those who desired to maintain stable family structures. Slaves who wanted to preserve stable family units were at the complete mercy of masters who considered slaves their personal property, and therefore could at any time disrupt the family lives of their slaves: Husbands could be sold away from wives, wives away from husbands, and children from their parents; also, family members could be abused by their masters and other whites with impunity.

Despite these challenges slaves strived to form stable family units. Historians such as Herbert Gutman and Ann Patton Malone have presented evidence that the majority of slaves grew up in households where both parents were present in the lives of their children. Slaves also maintained extended, multigenerational family units that included grandparents, aunts, uncles, cousins, and siblings. Finally, slaves who were not related often looked after one another. For example, a child who had been separated from his or her parents might be raised by someone unrelated. Slaves also went to great lengths to keep loved ones close, including running away to find estranged family members. The families that slaves formed provided a source of strength and hope for the majority of those in bondage.

SOURCE: Genovese, Eugene. *Roll, Jordan, Roll: The World the Slaves Made.* New York: Vintage, 1976.

her children were all far away. She begged the trader to tell her where he intended to take them; this he refused to do. . . . I met that mother in the street, and her wild, haggard face lives to-day in my mind. She wrung her hands in anguish, and exclaimed, 'Gone! All gone! Why *don't* God kill me?' I had no words wherewith to comfort her. Instances of this kind are of daily, yea, of hourly occurrence (2001, p. 17).

The scene recounted by Jacobs vividly describes the difficulties of forming a stable family life under slavery. Slaves were at the complete mercy of their masters: slaves could not marry without the consent of their masters; children and spouses could be punished or abused without consideration for the feelings of parents, wives, and husbands; and family members could be sold away from one another at any time without promise of ever being reunited. Ex-slave Mary Armstrong remembered one slave owner who seemed to delight in splitting up slave families, "He was so mean that he would never sell the man an' woman an' chillen to the same one. He would sell the man here, an' the women there, an' if they was chillen, he would sell them some place else. Oh, old Satan in torment wouldn' be no meaner than he . . . was to the slaves" (Rawick 1972–1979, vol. 2T, p. 66). However, despite these daily reminders of the horrors of slavery, African Americans strived to develop communities with coherent family structures; amazingly, they were often successful in doing so.

Family Stability, Patriarchy, and Related Issues

For at least a century after the end of American slavery there persisted a common belief that the slave family was a weak institution. The dislocation caused by the business concerns of one's master might force wives to take new husbands, force husbands to take new wives, and children might have to suddenly adapt to new family units. By charging that slaves changed partners often and abandoned children easily, some observers have asserted that slaves did not value their families as much as whites. There was also a self-serving motive on the part of whites to condemn the morals of slaves: this allowed whites to claim that the separation of families or the sexual exploitation of black women by white men had little effect on slaves (Genovese 1976, p. 461). In truth, ex-slave William Wells Brown's account of a mother pleading for the return of her child after it was given away better demonstrates the reality of the commitment slaves had for their families: "The mother as soon as she saw that her child was to be left, ran up to Mr. Walker [the slave trader who gave away her child], and falling upon her knees begged him to let her have her child; she clung around his legs, and cried, 'Oh, my child! My child! Master, do let me have my child'" (Osofsky 1969, pp. 191–192).

The reality that many male slaves were sold away from their wives and children, thereby in many cases diminishing the chance for a stable family unit that consisted of a mother, father, and children, has led some to assert that most slave families consisted primarily of a matriarch with a largely absent father. However, many historians have found that the majority of slave children grew up in families that included both a father and a mother. So for most slave children the reality was that a father was present in their lives. Ex-slave Will Adams remembered his father fondly, "I 'members when I was just walking good that pa would come in from the fiel' at night and take me out of bed, dress me, feed me, then play with me for hours" (Rawick 1972–1979, p. 10). Will Adams' experience was more common than not as slave parents sought to form stable families for their children.

During the late twentieth century historians began a revolution in thinking about the role of the family in the lives of slaves. Herbert Gutman found that by studying the birth records on a large South Carolina plantation, most of the slaves residing there came from multigenerational families and that most families consisted of a father, mother, and children. He also found that most of these marriages were long lasting, therefore enabling children to grow up in stable two-parent families. A similar study of Louisiana slaves, conducted by Ann Patton Malone, found that during the 1840s almost half of all slave households included children with a mother and father present. Both Gutman and Eugene Genovese have also concluded that by examining the black family in the postbellum South historians can demonstrate that the black family was a strong institution during slavery; according to Genovese, even stronger in the South than in the urban North. Therefore, both historians argued that by examining the strength of the black family after emancipation one may conclude that this stable structure did not instantly develop after emancipation. Instead, it reflects the strength of family ties during slavery. Genovese also wrote that the desire to maintain strong family bonds was reflected in the motivation of many runaway slaves, "Almost every study of runaway slaves uncovers the importance of the family motive: thousands of slaves ran away to find children, parents, wives, or husbands from whom they had been separated by sale (Genovese, p. 451).

John Blassingame described the slave family as "one of the most important survival mechanisms for the slave. In his family he found companionship, love, sexual gratification, sympathetic understanding of his sufferings; he learned how to avoid punishment, to cooperate with other blacks, and to maintain his self-esteem" (Blassingame 1972, p. 78). The owner of slaves had a pecuniary interest in allowing and even encouraging slaves to form family units. For one thing the children of these families would be his property and could be used as future laborers when they became old enough to perform labor. They could also be sold as human chattel to earn him a profit. Another incentive for the owner of slaves to support the creation of slave families was that stable family units made it less likely that slaves would escape. Genovese wrote, "The masters understood the strength of the marital and family ties among their slaves well enough to see in them a powerful means of social control (Genovese, p. 452). A father or mother with children would probably be less likely to run off and leave his or her spouse and children behind. Running away with a spouse and children in tow would have made recapture nearly assured as most areas of the South had slave patrols that were dedicated to catching runaways. Finally, slaves with families were more likely to be compliant. For example, owners were able to use the threat of selling a slave's spouse or children if the slave did not behave according to his or her master's wishes.

Slave Marriages

Even though the formation of family units was often encouraged, slave marriages were not recognized by the law. Despite this, slaves formed marriages with other slaves as well as with free blacks. After gaining permission from one's master the marriage ceremony was rather simple. Ex-slave Cora Armstrong recalled the ceremony, "The way slaves married in slavery time they jumped over the broom and when they separated they jumped backward over the broom" (Rawick 1972–1979, vol. 8B, p. 75). Of course the marriage of a slave

couple was a precarious bond, fraught with potential peril. Henry Bibb, in his autobiography about his life as a slave in Kentucky, described the difficulties slave marriages faced: "There is no legal marriage among slaves of the South; I never saw or heard of such a thing in my life … every slaveholder is also the keeper of a house or houses of ill-fame. Licentious white men, can and do, enter at night or day the lodging places of slaves; break up the bonds of affection in families; destroy all their domestic and social union for life; and the laws of the country afford them no protection" (Osofsky, pp. 77–78). So even though slave owners had pecuniary incentives for encouraging stable family units they often disrupted these liaisons through their own sexual interactions with slaves, as well as the sale of spouses and children. Former slave Ruth Allen recalled, "My mother was a slave an' me daddy, the ol' devil was her ol' white master. My mammy didn' have any more to say about what they did with her than the rest of the slaves in them days … they kept mu mammy and me til' I was 'bout three years old, an' then when they saw I was goan 'a be much whiter and better lookin' than his own chilern' by his own wife, they sold me and mammy, an' got rid of us for good" (Rawick 1972–1979, vol. 2S, p. 101). The children resulting from these unions often grew up without the support of their father but, if lucky, might be looked after by an uncle or other male slave.

While many slave owners encouraged their slaves to marry within their own plantation community, many slaves married slaves and free blacks off the plantation. Such marriages created a looser family structure with the mother and children on one plantation and the father in another location. These partnerships were often called "abroad marriages," and sometimes resulted from a lack of possible mates on a slave's own plantation or the desire by a particular slave to select the mate of his or her own choice. Of course, abroad marriages had to be approved by the masters of both slaves. Abroad marriages also created the stress of not knowing how one's spouse was faring on a day-to-day basis. If a husband did not appear for a scheduled visit it might mean he was merely delayed, but it could also mean he had been sold away, never to be seen again. Abroad marriages also created a type of family structure that was more matrifocal in nature, with the mother bearing more responsibility for childrearing. Husbands and wives lacked the ability to see each other frequently, and their children grew up with a largely absent father.

Alternate Family Structures

Abroad marriages, slave sales, and other grim realities of slavery created a need for slaves to form alternative family structures. Many slave children were partly raised by aunts, uncles, older siblings, step-parents, and other slaves who were not relatives. Ex-slave Barney Alford recalled an older slave woman who looked after the slave children, "Ole Mammy 'Lit' wus mity ole en she lived in one corner of de big yard en she keered fur all de black chilluns..." (Rawick 1972–1979, vol. 6S, p. 23). Martha Griffith Browne, a former slave, recounted the first view of her new quarters when she, as a young girl, was sold away from her family: "There resting upon pallets of straw, like pigs in a litter, were groups of children ... How strange, lonely, and forbidding appeared that tenement" (Browne 1969, p. 20). These children and the older woman who lived with them would become the child's new family. Many plantations also included multigenerational families, which meant that uncles, aunts, cousins, and grandparents were available to provide family support.

Slavery created incredible stresses on the slave family. However, despite the challenges, slaves created strong family bonds, and in many cases slaves were able to form two-parent households for raising children. Evidence of the strong bonds of families during slavery could be found in the immediate aftermath of the Civil War as African Americans traveled throughout both the North and South in search of children, spouses, and siblings that had been separated from them while in bondage. Many white contemporary observers were surprised at the commitment of African Americans to find these separated loved ones. Much of their surprise resulted from the widespread racist beliefs in the white community about the lack of strength of family bonds among slaves. Fortunately, through the reconstructive work of modern historians, one is able to see that slaves created strong family structures that helped them persevere.

BIBLIOGRAPHY

Blassingame, John. *The Slave Community.* New York: Oxford University Press, 1972.

Born in Slavery: Slave Narratives from the Federal Writers' Project, 1936–1938. Online collection of the Manuscript and Prints and Photographs Divisions of the Library of Congress. Available from http://memory.loc.gov.

Browne, Martha Griffith. *Autobiography of a Female Slave.* New York: Negro Universities Press, 1969.

Genovese, Eugene. *Roll, Jordan, Roll: The World the Slaves Made.* New York: Vintage, 1976.

Gutman, Herbert G. *The Black Family in Slavery and Freedom, 1750–1925.* New York: Vintage, 1976.

Jacobs, Harriet. *Incidents in the Life of a Slave Girl.* New York: W. W. Norton, 2001.

Malone, Ann Patton. *Sweet Chariot: Slave Family and Household Structure in Nineteenth-Century Louisiana.* Chapel Hill: University of North Carolina Press, 1992.

Osofsky, Gilbert, ed. *Puttin' On Ole Massa: The Slave Narratives of Henry Bibb, William Wells Brown, and Solomon Northup,* New York: Harper and Row, 1969.

Rawick, George P., ed. *The American Slave: A Composite Autobiography.* 19 vols. Westport, CT: Greenwood Press, 1972–1979.

Steven Barleen

FATHERHOOD

The language of fatherhood became central to the ideological debate over slavery in the United States, while biological paternity and the contested power dynamics of parenthood were defining features of American slavery.

For their most persistent defense of legal bondage, proslavery ideologues in the antebellum South argued that the relationship of master to slave was analogous to that of husband to wife or father to child. The argument was grounded in the belief that a patriarchal model of family was sanctioned by the Christian Bible and constituted the basic unit of all government. According to this model, the male served as the head of household—as did the Old Testament patriarchs—whereas wives and children were his subordinate dependents. By arguing that slaves constituted part of the master's extended household, slaveholders and politicians, wrote historian Stephanie McCurry, "attempted to endow slavery with the legitimacy of family" (1992, p. 1251). Indeed slaveholders frequently employed the term "our family, white and black," to suggest an ideology of slaveholding paternalism so pervasive that nineteenth-century legal codes concerning masters and slaves were grouped under the category of "domestic relations" along with the legal headings of "husband and wife," "parent and child," and "guardian and ward" (Genovese 1991, p. 69; Bardaglio 1995, p. xi).

The term "our family, white and black" and the analogy of slaves as children served as political propaganda that concealed the violence and power dynamics inherent to the master-slave relationship. But it also resonated literally in the biological paternity of children conceived through slaveholders' sexual exploitation of slave women. As abolitionist and ex-slave Frederick Douglass wrote, the slaveholder "*may* be and often *is* master and father to the same child.... thousands [of slaves] are ushered into the world annually, who—like myself—owe their existence to white fathers, and most frequently, to their masters" (2003 [1855], pp. 18–19).

In the American colonial period, colonists initially followed English tradition by which a child born of a slave parent and a free parent inherited the status of the father. But beginning with a 1662 Virginia law, children of slave women followed the condition of their mother. The law addressed the increasing difficulty of determining the children's paternity; it also reinforced the power and property rights of the master by assuring him chattel ownership of his slave descendants. In addition, slaveholders' estates were shielded from any legal claims by slave mothers or their children. "This

A SLAVE FATHER SOLD AWAY FROM HIS FAMILY.

A father sold away from his family.   An illustration from the 1860 *Child's Antislavery Book* showing a slave father being sold from his family. Facing the threat of separation, slave fathers might run away and send word to their masters that they would return if the threat abated. In this way, slave fathers used their own labor to negotiate the preservation of families.   © *Corbis.*

arrangement," wrote Douglass in his 1855 autobiography, "admits the greatest license to brutal slaveholders, and their profligate sons, brothers, relations, and friends, and gives to the pleasure of sin, the additional attraction of profit" (2003 [1855], p. 18).

Moreover, the arrangement mystified the parentage of slave children such as Douglass. Though his master was rumored to have been Douglass's father, his actual paternity remained his entire life "shrouded in a mystery I have never been able to penetrate" (2003 [1855], p. 14). Slave mothers were often forbidden to name their baby's fathers or feared the repercussions of doing so. This could include sale or reprisals from jealous mistresses who misdirected their wrath over their husbands' infidelities to the slave women on whom the slaveholders forced intercourse. Children were taught not to inquire about their paternity or told incredible stories to account for human reproduction. When a planter's son was introduced as her father, one child replied, "I ain' got no father . . . buzzards laid me an' de sun hatch me; an' she [mother] came' long an' pick me up" (Schwartz 2000, p. 100).

Annie Burton knew of her father, a neighbor of her master and mistress, though she only saw him about a dozen times around the age of four when he was driving by her master's. Whenever Burton's mistress saw the man going by, she would take the child's hand, run to the piazza and shout, "Stop there, I say! Don't you want to see and speak to and caress your darling child? She often speaks of you and wants to embrace her dear father. See what a bright and beautiful daughter she is, a perfect picture of yourself. Well, I declare, you are an affectionate father." Years later in her autobiography, Burton recalled, "I well remember that whenever my mistress would speak thus and upbraid him, he would whip up his horse and get out of sight and hearing as quickly as possible. My mistress's action was, of course, intended to humble and shame my father. I never spoke to him, and cannot remember that he ever noticed me, or in any way acknowledged me to be his child" (1909, p. 8).

Burton's recollection of her father demonstrates the unwillingness of white fathers to acknowledge slave children. According to historian Marie Jenkins Schwartz, slave-owning fathers rarely favored their multiracial children. To the abhorrence of slaves, who believed fathers should take responsibility for their children, most slaveholders sold or simply ignored their slave progeny.

Depending on whether slave family relationships had been disrupted by sale or whether slave couples had chosen partners who lived abroad or who were owned by the same slaveholder, enslaved fathers might or might not live in the same household as their children. Those who lived at home shared family responsibilities with their partners. Fathers might supplement the family's rations by fishing. Because mothers could only breastfeed infants during scheduled rest periods from their field labor, fathers shared in the childcare by bringing water to their nursing partners. Facing the threat of family separation, slave fathers might run away and send word to their masters that they would return if the threat abated. In this way, slave fathers used their own labor to negotiate the preservation of families.

Elijah Knox was the enslaved father of John and Harriet Jacobs, both of whom published slave narratives in 1861. Knox was a skilled carpenter, and though owned by a different slaveholder than his wife and children, he was allowed to hire out his time and live in the same household as his family. But that arrangement changed with the capriciousness of the family's owners. The children's mistress took Harriet into her lodgings and sent John to work in the office of her son-in-law. Harriet was nine; John was ten. Three months later, Knox was forced to move from his home in Edenton when his mistress married a man who forbade him to hire out his time. John Jacobs later recalled of Knox, "The knowledge that he was a slave himself, and that his children were also slaves, embittered his life, but made him love us the more" (1861, pp. 85–86).

Not only could families be separated at the slaveholder's whim, but the power of the slaveholder and the authority of enslaved parents held competing claims over the loyalties of enslaved children. Harriet Jacobs recalled a childhood incident in which John (called William in her narrative) was summoned simultaneously by his mistress and the children's father: "[H]e hesitated between the two; being perplexed to know which had the strongest claim upon his obedience." When he was reproved by his father for answering the call of his mistress, the boy replied, "You both called me, and I didn't know which I ought to go to first" (1987 [1861], p. 9).

Slave parents such as Elijah Knox had to walk a fine line between teaching children to privilege their mother's and father's authority without drawing the ire of their master or mistress. The complicated reality that probably contributed to John Jacobs's confusion was that slave children were subject to the punishment of slaveholders with little ability of parents to intervene. Henry Bibb recounted how, as an enslaved father, he was unable to shield his infant daughter from the cruel-

ties of their mistress, in whose care the child was necessarily left while her parents performed the master's labor. When he recalled seeing the mark of his mistress' hand on his daughter's cheek, Bibb lamented, "Who can imagine what could be the feelings of a father and mother, when looking upon their infant child whipped and tortured with impunity, and they placed in a situation where they could afford it no protection. But we were all claimed and held as property" (1849, p. 49).

When he published his own autobiography in 1861, John Jacobs did not recount the childhood incident of confused allegiances recorded in his sister's narrative. But the politics represented by that incident were reflected in his conception of slavery. In his first chapter, Jacobs provided an indictment of slavery based on the same patriarchal model of family invoked by slavery apologists. Yet Jacobs rebutted the proslavery paternalism by implicitly arguing that the institution of slavery, along with the power of the slaveholder, obliterated for slaves the very model of family on which rests the notion "our family, white and black":

> To be a man, and not to be a man—a father without authority—a husband and no protector—is the darkest of fates. Such was the condition of my father, and such is the condition of every slave throughout the United States: he owns nothing, he can claim nothing. His wife is not his: his children are not his; they can be taken from him, and sold at any minute, as far away from each other as the human fleshmonger may see fit to carry them. Slaves are recognized as property by the law, and can own nothing except by the consent of their masters. A slave's wife or daughter may be insulted before his eyes with impunity. He himself may be called on to torture them, and dare not refuse. To raise his hand in their defense is death by the law (1861, p. 85).

Jacobs defined fatherhood in terms of one's ability to wield authority and protection over one's family, in whom he must possess some figurative sense of belonging. And he literally must be able to own property and to be autonomous. "To be a man, and not to be a man" suggests that a bondman is biologically male but cannot conform to the definitions of manhood and fatherhood outlined here because slavery and the master's power deprives them of parental authority. Like the pro-slavery argument Jacobs intended to refute, this indictment of slavery rests on an adherence to gendered power relations within the family. Together, these arguments illustrate how the rhetoric of paternalism and fatherhood were employed and contested in the ideological debates over antebellum slavery.

BIBLIOGRAPHY

Bibb, Henry. *Narrative of the Life and Adventures of Henry Bibb, An American Slave, Written by Himself.* New York, 1849. "Documenting the American

South." University Library, University of North Carolina at Chapel Hill. Available from http://docsouth.unc.edu.

Bardaglio, Peter. *Reconstructing the Household: Families, Sex, and the Law in the Nineteenth-Century South.* Chapel Hill: University of North Carolina Press, 1995.

Burton, Annie. *Memories of Childhood's Slavery Days* Boston: Ross Publishing Company, 1909. "Documenting the American South." University Library, University of North Carolina at Chapel Hill. Available from http://docsouth.unc.edu.

Clinton, Catherine. *The Plantation Mistress: Woman's World in the Old South.* New York: Pantheon Books, 1982.

Clinton, Catherine. "Southern Dishonor: Flesh, Blood, Race and Bondage." *In Joy and Sorrow: Women, Family, and Marriage in the Victorian South,* ed. Carol Bleser. New York: Oxford University Press, 1991.

Douglass, Frederick. *My Bondage and My Freedom* [1855]. Reprint with notes by John Stauffer. New York: Random House, 2003.

Genovese, Eugene. "'Our Family, White and Black': Family and Household in the Southern Slaveholder's Worldview." *In Joy and in Sorrow: Women, Family, and Marriage in the Victorian South,* ed. Carol Bleser. New York: Oxford University Press, 1991.

Jacobs, Harriet A. *Incidents in the Life of a Slave Girl* [1861], Jean Fagan Yellin, ed. Cambridge, MA: Harvard University Press, 1987.

Jacobs, John S. "A True Tale of Slavery." Published serially in *The Leisure Hour: A Family Journal of Instruction and Recreation,* February 7, 14, 21, and 28, 1861, (nos. 476–479), pp. 85–87, 108–110, 125–127, 139–141. "Documenting the American South." University Library, University of North Carolina at Chapel Hill. Available from http://docsouth.unc.edu.

McCurry, Stephanie. "The Two Faces of Republicanism: Gender and Proslavery Politics in Antebellum South Carolina." *Journal of American History* 78, no. 4 (March 1992): 1245–1264.

Schwartz, Mary Jenkins. *Born in Bondage: Growing Up Enslaved in the Antebellum South.* Cambridge, MA: Harvard University Press, 2000.

Yellin, Jean Fagan. *Harriet Jacobs: A Life.* New York: Basic Civitas Books, 2004.

Christina Adkins

MOTHERHOOD

Children born to slave mothers were slaves, regardless of the father's status, whether black or white, free or slave. Laws regarding the status of slave children—called the "increase" or "issuance" of the mother—varied from state to state, though all revolved around the fact that, as spelled out by Jacob Wheeler in his 1837 treatise on slavery, "the child before born is part of the mother, and its condition the same; the birth does not alter its rights" (p. 323). In some states even if the mother was freed soon after the birth of a child, the child was required to be in servitude for the same number of years as she was before her emancipation.

Slave mothers faced the constant worry that they or their children could be sold at any time. Women used as breeders of slaves were forced into pregnancy again and again; both they and their offspring were prized commodities at the slave markets, crushing any development of the natural attachment between mother and child. Families were routinely separated; husbands and wives had no true status as a couple, and mothers were rarely allowed to stay with their children. A slave mother's worth was tied to her productivity in the fields or as a servant: if her skills waned or someone was willing to pay a good price, she was sold at the annual auction regardless of whether she had young children.

Many small children fended for themselves. Once they reached the age of three or four and could complete simple tasks, they were considered valuable enough to warrant some attention. George Taylor Burns, a former slave from Vanderburgh County in Arkansas, related to an interviewer a memory from his second or third year:

> Nothing impressed the boy with such unforgettable imagery as the cold which descended … one winter. Motherless, hungry, desolate and unloved, he often cried himself to sleep while each day he was compelled to carry wood. One morning he failed to come when the horn was sounded to call the slaves to breakfast. 'Old Missus went to the negro quarters to see what was wrong,' and 'she was horrified when she found I was frozen to the bed.'" (*Born in Slavery*, Indiana Narratives, vol. 5, p. 37)

For slave mothers who were allowed to raise their children, care was a constant worry. Many lost children within the first year of life to croup, fever, or other ailments. Conditions varied from homestead to homestead, but most new mothers were allowed to nurse their babies three or four times daily. At larger plantations, babies and young children were cared for in nurseries within the slave quarters or a shack close to the fields. At smaller plantations where there were few infants, the small children were usually left alone in their parents' cabins. Kate E. R. Pickard, a teacher in the Female Seminary of Tuscumbra, Alabama, wrote about slave mothers at a Lawrence County plantation:

> At that time there was no old woman on the place to take care of the children; and every mother, when she went to the field in the morning, locked her little ones in her cabin, leaving some bread where they could get it when they became hungry.

Or, if there was one too small to help itself to the bread, the thoughtful mother tied a little mush in a rag upon its finger, so that when, as babies will, it thrust its finger in its mouth, it could suck the mush through the rag, and that would keep it quiet (1856, p. 163).

As slave children usually had little or no clothing, their mothers often made shifts from flour or grain sacks or pieced together tiny swatches of cloth. All sewing and laundry took place at night or on the weekends.

Slave mothers provided their children with chunks of bread and soup or gruel made from flour, wheat, water, or milk, sometimes sweetened with molasses. The family of Alice Wright, an Alabama-born slave, lived in the yard of their slaveholders; children were fed by a "trough on the floor with wooden spoons and as many children as could get around that trough got there and ate" (Arkansas Narratives, vol. 2, part 7, p. 245).

Although motherhood for slaves was a wrenching situation, children were celebrated as a gift from God. Pickard wrote of Vina's joy over her firstborn son: "She knew her babe was born to slavery—and sorrow; but oh! so dearly did she love it!" (p. 191).

BIBLIOGRAPHY

Born in Slavery: Slave Narratives from the Federal Writers' Project, 1936–1938 Manuscript Division, Library of Congress. Arkansas Narratives, vol. 2, part 7. Indiana Narratives, vol. 5. Available from http://memory.loc.gov.

Pickard, Kate E. R. *The Kidnapped and the Ransomed: Being the Personal Recollections of Peter Still and His Wife "Vina," After Forty Years of Slavery.* 3rd ed. Syracuse, NY, 1856. (Repr., Lincoln: University of Nebraska Press, 1995.)

Wheeler, Jacob D. *Practical Treatise on the Law of Slavery.* New York: A. Pollock, 1837.

Nelson Rhodes

CHILDHOOD AND ADOLESCENCE

By the end of the U.S. Civil War (1861–1865), 4 million people in the United States were slaves. Of this number, more than 1 million were children under the age of sixteen. Those that grew up within the system of slavery were denied access to many of the benefits of a real childhood. Put to work at an early age and subjected to arbitrary punishments and separations, enslaved children's experiences forced them to become adults well before their time.

Conditions under slavery impacted child development at every stage. Poor prenatal care, heavy workloads, and poor diet all contributed to high infant mortality rates among enslaved populations. If babies did survive the first few months, they would soon experience separation from mothers who were expected to return to work shortly after giving birth. Under these circumstan-

A slave family in Beaufort, South Carolina. Several generations of a slave family in Beaufort, South Carolina. Many former slaves testified to working as soon as they were old enough to perform simple tasks. *The Library of Congress.*

ces, the primary responsibility for child care fell onto others within the slave community. In small households, children might be permitted to accompany their parents to work or, alternatively, be placed in the care of domestic servants. On larger plantations, children attended nurseries staffed by slaves who were either too old or too young to perform other forms of work. The relationships developed between these caregivers and enslaved children were often significant.

Evidence also suggests that important distinctions existed between enslaved children's experience based on the labor system. The task system—adopted in the rice cultivating areas of South Carolina and Georgia—afforded workers a degree of flexibility and autonomy that ensured parents more time with their children and extra money for the provision of clothing and food. This was important, as many slaveholders were less concerned with the comfort of enslaved children than with frugality. Though conditions varied, most children were provided with only one or two garments made from cheap fabric and often went without shoes until the coldest months, when cheaply made brogans were provided. A little extra income allowed enslaved people to provide extra clothing to their children, affording a greater degree of comfort and dignity. In parts of the South, where gang labor predominated, longer workdays and heightened surveillance inhibited these types of activities.

During their earliest years, enslaved children were not expected to work full time on the plantation. However, it was common for even the youngest children to perform menial chores in preparation for their future roles. Many former slaves testified to working as soon as they were old enough to perform simple tasks. Andrew Moss, a former slave from Georgia, explained that his owner "had little hoes" with "handles 'bout de size of my arm for de little fellers." Moss recalled walking "up and down de rows, followin' de grown folks, an chopping wid de hoe" (*Born in Slavery* 2001, vol. 15, p. 50). While Moss was responsible for basic agricultural tasks, other small children took on domestic chores within the home. James Monroe Abbott was employed as a house servant at the age of seven. One of his primary duties was to care for his dying owner by standing at the side of his bed "keepin' de flies offen him." When the man finally died, Abbot was "so glad to be out" that he ran about telling everyone "By God, he's daid" (vol. 10, p.1).

During their preteen years, children began to perform more routinized domestic, agricultural, or industrial jobs. The vast majority of slaves in the U.S. South were field hands. Enslaved children worked alongside family members in the field planting, cultivating, and harvesting a variety of crops. Others were sent out as apprentices to learn craft skills by working alongside older blacksmiths, masons, and carpenters. Girls had less opportunity in this area because the apprenticeships were reserved for men and childbearing was considered disruptive to craftwork. Some children performed domestic work, including: food preparation; washing clothes; cleaning living quarters; and caring for children. Other chores might include the production of household items such as clothing and soap, or the gathering of eggs and milking of cows. In contrast to craft apprenticeships, both boys and girls performed these forms of labor. For example, Nelson Birdsong, a former slave from Alabama, remembered that his first work was "nussing a baby boy" (*Born in Slavery* 2001, vol. 1, p.33). In *Ar'n't I a Woman: Female Slaves in the Plantation South*, Deborah Gray White suggests that the similarity in enslaved boys' and girls' labor is indicative of their future roles within the plantation economy. "Since both girls and boys were expected to become field hands," White contends, "it is not surprising that as children they did the same chores" (1985, p. 94).

Despite their heavy workload, enslaved children also found some time to play. Sundays, evenings, and holidays offered an important respite and the opportunity for recreation and amusement. Popular games such as hopscotch, hide-and-seek, and marbles tested children's skills and put them into competition against others.

AS WE FOUND THEM.

These children were owned by Thomas White, of Mathews Co., Va., until Feb. 20th, when Capt. Riley, 6th U. S. C. I., took them and gave them to the Society of Friends to educate at the Orphan's Shelter, Philadelphia.

Profits from sale, for the benefit of the children.

Portrait of former slaves who are brother and sister. An 1864 photograph of a brother and sister who are former slaves. The Union Army captured them and turned them in to an orphanage in Philadelphia. Enslaved children's experiences forced them to become adults well before their time. *Peregrine F. Cooper/George Eastman House/Getty Images.*

Winning boosted self-esteem and promoted positive affirmation from peers. Charlie Davenport, a former slave from Natchez, Mississippi, described how after performing their tasks the little children played together in the street. "Us th'owed horse-shoes, jumped poles, walked on stilts, an' played marbles," Davenport said (*Born in Slavery* 2001, vol. 9, p. 34). Lacking the money to purchase the more traditional toys possessed by their white counterparts, enslaved children imaginatively fashioned their own playthings out of the material world around them. Marbles were molded from clay and baked in the sun. Dolls were made from rags and string. Others made toy horses out of branches and small tree limbs that could be ridden around the plantation. Evidence suggests that there was little distinction in the types of games played by boys and girls. In the world of play, as in the world of work, gender roles were less distinct for enslaved children.

Distinctions in gender roles became more evident during adolescence. Though boys and girls continued to perform similar types of labor they now dressed differently. Girls wore calico dresses that were rendered more elaborate for special occasions through the use of brightly colored dyes and hoops. However, the physical changes associated with adolescence brought considerable anxiety to the mothers and caregivers of enslaved girls. As Harriet Jacobs (1813–1897) explained in *Incidents in the Life of a Slave Girl* (first published in 1861), after enslaved girls reached their teens, mothers lived "in daily expectation of trouble" (2001, p. 48). Protecting young women from the sexual impulses of black and white men was considered critical. Mothers sought to delay courtship for as long as possible and when relationships did develop, a complex set of rules regulated their maintenance. Trash gangs—a predominantly female workforce that performed tasks around the plantation—provided an important space for socialization. While working with the trash gang, young women would be educated about sexuality and childbirth and provided with advice on how to escape sexual abuse. Protection was not reserved for girls alone. Enslaved children lived in a world of arbitrary violence that their parents were often powerless to protect them from. Learning to handle volatile situations was a critical skill that children had to learn at an early age. Through the guidance of kin and community, enslaved boys and girls survived childhood through learning to resist the worst aspects of slavery and preserve their own integrity.

BIBLIOGRAPHY

Born in Slavery: Slave Narratives from the Federal Writers' Project, 1936–1938. Library of Congress, Manuscript Division. 17 vols. Washington, DC, 2001.

Jacobs, Harriet. *Incidents in the Life of a Slave Girl*, eds. Nellie Y. McKay and Frances Smith Foster. New York: Norton, 2001.

King, Wilma. *Stolen Childhood: Slave Youth in Nineteenth-Century America*. Bloomington: Indiana University Press, 1995.

White, Deborah Gray. *Ar'n't I a Woman? Female Slaves in the Plantation South*. New York: Norton, 1999.

Kerry L. Pimblott

FAMILY SEPARATION AND REUNION

Slaves were oftentimes separated from family members and friends for a variety of reasons. For example, they could be sold to liquidate estates, to settle debts, or because they were considered incorrigibly defiant, or they could be given as wedding presents.

Research by several scholars provides further details about how African and African American slaves families were broken up. One scholar found that forcible separations ended about 19 percent of all slave marriages. Another study suggests that 13 percent of all slave marriages were broken with the sale of one partner (Gutman 1976, p. 147). Still another work shows that slaves were sold on average about five times during their lifetimes, with males separated from their families twice as often (Davis 1993, pp. 658–659).

Based on an analysis of 634 bills of sales from slave traders, one scholar concluded that 7 percent of all slave children in the eight to eleven age cohort were removed from their families. Another 14 percent of slave children aged twelve to fourteen were sold and children in the eight to fourteen age cohort were involved in 25 percent of all sales. These figures indicate that there was a preference for younger slaves on the part of buyers, especially those between eight and fourteen years of age (Tadman 1989, pp. 141–142, 151).

Masters and slaves each had their own concept of family and what it meant within the system of slavery. Masters had absolute authority over their slaves, including the right to sell family members at the slightest whim. Masters also believed they had the best interest of the slave family at heart. Slaveholders sold slaves for economic reasons and there were no laws concerning human civilities that prevented the breakup of any slave family. Husbands were separated from wives and mothers distanced from their children. Planter paternalism—having the best interest of the slave family in mind—was not always evident. Masters argued that slaves had little attachment to family members and therefore suffered little when family members were sold.

Slaves, in truth, looked to their extended family for support and strength as a means of survival. They dreaded the sale of one or both parents or the dissolution of their family. Masters used the threat of selling a slave to coerce submission or obedience from slaves. Because of the omnipresent threat of separation, slaves developed extended relationships by bringing close relatives into the family bond. Slaves often named their children after close relatives as a way of extending kinship and memory. They dreaded the auction block and the prospect that they or a family member would be sold away, perhaps into the Deep South never to be seen again. Thus, contrary to the belief system of their masters, slaves had a deep attachment to family members and this affection extended to close relatives within the extended family.

Evidence of slave family separations became more apparent as the Civil War (1861–1865) drew to a conclusion. In 1863, the U.S. Congress created the Freedmen's Inquiry Commission to hear testimony regarding the separation of slave families. Testifying before the commission was Solomon Bradley, a former slave from South Carolina who had enlisted in the South Carolina Colored

A painting of a slave family being sold to pay a master's debts, circa 1800. Scholars estimate that between 13 and 19 percent of slave marriages were broken up by sale or forced separations. *Michael Graham-Stewart/Bridgeman Art Library.*

Regiment. After he joined the Union army, his wife and two children were sold away. He told commission members he had not seen his family in more than one year and did not expect to be reunited with them. Robert Smalls (1839–1915), another ex-slave who distinguished himself during the Civil War by stealing a Confederate ship, testified that slave families were always close-knit. Slaves, he commented, regarded their family connections with much love, so much so that some blacks would walk fifteen miles on a Saturday night to see a cousin. These and other statements convinced commission members and Congress to pass the Freedmen's Bureau Act.

Created in March 1865, the Bureau of Refugees, Freedmen, and Abandoned Lands, commonly known as the Freedmen's Bureau, became the first federal social welfare agency. Although the agency was not tasked with finding and reuniting ex-slave families, the overwhelm-

ing demand for reunions led agents to send telegrams, write letters, provide transportation vouchers, and wherever possible work to reunite ex-slave families.

In some cases, ex-slaves who joined the Union army reported that masters sold their family members as retribution for their enlistment. A Freedmen's Bureau agent in St. Louis complained that he received daily reports from field officers who had black soldiers requesting protection for their families. In one such example, slave traders in Kentucky threatened to sell family members because their father enlisted in the Union army. Some family members of black enlisted men reported being sold, while others said that they were forced off plantations and became destitute. On other occasions, the Union army caused black family separations, by recruiting black men and using other ex-slaves as laborers.

*— The husband and wife, after being sold to different pur-
chasers, violently separated....never to see
each other more.*

A husband and wife being sold to different buyers.   An engraving from an 1804 abolitionist
publication showing a husband and wife being separated after being sold to different buyers. Slaves could
be sold to liquidate estates, settle debts, or given as wedding presents.   *The Granger Collection, New York.
Reproduced by permission.*

Poignant testimony from Freedmen's Bureau records attests to the separation and reunion of countless black families during slavery and their efforts, along with that of the bureau agents, to find and reunite family members. Anne Rowe, a slave on a plantation near Baton Rouge, ran away to Boston in 1848. Twenty years later, she asked the Freedmen's Bureau for help in locating her two brothers, Joseph and George Rowe, who had joined the Union army (Rowe 1868). In Columbia and Spartanburg, South Carolina, bureau agents looked for Susan Jenkins and offered to transport her to Columbia where her mother had been located (Jenkins 1866). In Montgomery, Alabama, Polly Bates asked agents to find her son, named John Patterson. During the Civil War, his master had carried him away to Mississippi. Although bureau records do not always indicate if attempts at family reunion were successful, these and countless more examples illustrate how ex-slaves often turned to the Freedmen's Bureau for assistance (Bates 1868).

Bureau agents reunited Charity Cox, an eighty-year-old former slave, with her family by providing transportation. She traveled via stagecoach from Charlottesville, Virginia, to Shelbyville, Tennessee (Cox 1866, pp. 404–405). The bureau issued transportation vouchers to a family of nine ex-slaves who journeyed from Mecklenburg County, Virginia, to join relatives in Washington County, Mississippi. Bureau agents in Richmond, Virginia, transported Richard Jones to Petersburg, Virginia, reuniting a son with his mother. Jones had had both legs amputated at a Richmond hospital and needed his mother's assistance (Jones 1866, pp. 721–722). Rueben Willis, his wife, three adult daughters, and five small children were all transported from Washington, DC, to London, Ohio, where they joined other relatives in their extended family. These and numerous other examples of successful family reunions can be found throughout the Freedmen's Bureau documents (Willis , p. 459).

Overall, although many ex-slaves turned to the Freedmen's Bureau for assistance in relocating family members, most were not successful in finding their loved ones. Time and distance operated against many ex-slaves seeking family reunions. Without modern means of communication, family bonds created during slavery were in freedom forever broken.

BIBLIOGRAPHY

Bardaglio, Peter W. *Reconstructing the Household: Families, Sex, and the Law in the Nineteenth-Century South*. Chapel Hill: University of North Carolina Press, 1995.

Bates, Polly. Polly Bates to the Montgomery, AL, Bureau of Refugees, Freedmen and Abandoned Lands, February 20, 1868. Record group 105, entry 167, box 34.

Berlin, Ira. *Many Thousand Gone: The First Two Centuries of Slavery in North America*. Cambridge, MA: Belknap Press of Harvard University Press, 1998.

Cox, Charity. Agent M. M. Kennil to Lt. Joyce, Superintendent, March 9, 1866. Richmond, VA. M1048, roll 11, pp. 404–405.

Jenkins, Susan. H. W. Smith to J. Mansfield, May 28, 1866. Bureau of Refugees, Freedmen and Abandoned Lands. Record group 105, entry 3156.

Jones, Richard. D. P. Bowe to Captain James McDonald, Superintendent, June 15, 1866. Richmond, VA. M1048, roll 11, pp. 721–722.

Gutman, Herbert G. *The Black Family in Slavery and Freedom, 1750–1925*. New York: Pantheon, 1976.

Rowe, Anne. C. Robbins to Lt. F. D. Garraty, Baton Rouge, LA, Bureau of Refugees, Freedmen, and Abandoned Lands. Record group 105, entry 1516.

Tadman, Michael. *Speculators and Slaves: Masters, Traders, and Slaves in the Old South*. Madison: University of Wisconsin Press, 1989.

Wood, Betty. *Slavery in Colonial America, 1619–1776*. Lanham, MD: Rowman and Littlefield, 2005.

Willis, Rueben. Agent's Report of Investigations of Destitute Freedmen, Washington, DC. M1055, roll 17, p. 459.

Jackie R. Booker

ELDER AND OLD AGE

"God ain't ax about your color, God ax about your heart" (Rawick 1977, vol. 11, p. 194). These words were spoken by Ben Horry when he was eighty-five years old. Horry was born a slave in South Carolina. He was one of many former slaves interviewed by a member of the Federal Writers' Project (FWP), a Works Progress Administration (WPA) relief program that was later collected and published by George Rawick in the 1970s and later made available online by the Library of Congress. Many of the elderly interviewed during the 1930s project reflected on their experiences during their enslavement: "I got the scars on my body to show to this day," stated Louisiana-born Mary Reynolds, age 105 (Rawick 1972, vol. 5, p. 238). Charity Anderson, age 101, remembered being one of the house servants (Rawick 1977, vol. 1, p. 15). North Carolina-born Sarah Gudger, age 121, stated that she "never knew nothing but work" (Botkin 1989).

Slaves who lived on plantations and performed the laborious tasks dictated by the nature of slavery ceased to be useful laborers once they reached old age. Some of these wise and "tried by the fire" individuals settled among the younger slaves and served as human warehouses of information with remarkable memory. Taken from the narrative of Henry Clay Bruce (1836–1902) is a description of elderly slaves, often called sages:

> Then there were a great many old men among them that might be called sages, men who knew the number of days in each month, in each year, could tell the exact date when Easter, Whit[e] Sunday would come, because most masters gave

GROWING OLD

What happened in the life of an American slave who reached old age? The elderly slave's fate depended much on the character of his or her master. If the master was kind, the elderly slave may have retired from hard labor and began to watch over the small children who were too young to labor in the fields of the plantation. Conversely, an elderly slave may have been esteemed for his or her memory and ability to archive facts about birth and death places, as seen in the life of Henry Clay Bruce. Bruce was considered particularly fortunate in all his surroundings during slavery. His narrative of his experience is written from the perspective of being a slave for twenty–nine years and then from the perspective of being a free man for twenty–nine years.

Frederick Douglass's narrative, by contrast, may respond to the question about the fate of the elderly with a less positive reflection. The fate of Douglass's grandmother after the death of several generations of her slave owners left Douglass with the opinion, "If any one thing in my experience, more than another, served to deepen my conviction of the infernal character of slavery, and to fill me with unutterable loathing of slaveholders, it was their base ingratitude to my poor old grandmother" (p. 375).

SOURCE: Gates, Henry Louis, ed. *Classic Slave Narratives*. New York: New American Library, 1987.

Monday following each of these Sundays as a holiday to slaves ... These old sages determined dates by means of straight marks and notches, made on a long stick with a knife, and were quite accurate in arriving at correct dates (1969, p. 13).

Naturally, all slaves after becoming elderly were not as fortunate as Bruce recalls and many suffered a different fate. Following is a very passionate account given by Frederick Douglass (1817–1895) concerning the fate of his grandmother as an elderly slave:

...she had served her old master faithfully from youth to old age. She had been the source of all his wealth; she had peopled his plantation with slaves; she had become a great grandmother in his service. She had rocked him in infancy, attended him in childhood, served him through life, and at his death wiped from his icy brow the cold death sweat, and closed his eyes forever. She nevertheless was left a slave—a slave for life—a slave in the hands of strangers (Gates 2002, p. 375).

Douglass's pain and agony over his grandmother's fate continued to be revealed later in the narrative:

And to cap the climax of their base ingratitude and fiendish barbarity, my grandmother, who was now very old ... her frame already racked with the pains of old age, and complete helplessness fast stealing over her once active limbs, they took her

to the woods, built her a little hut, put up a little mud chimney, and then made her welcome to the privilege of supporting herself in perfect loneliness (Gates 2002, p. 375).

Another image of the elderly and old age is seen through the narrative of A. C. Pruitt who was a slave in St. Martinsville, Louisiana:

Dey have 'nother old woman what do nothing on de scene but weave on de loom ... One old lady what am mos' too old to git 'round, she take care de chillen and cook dere food sep'rate ... I have de old gramma what come from Virginny. Her name Mandy Brown. Dey [the master] 'low her hire own time out. She wasn't freeborn but dey give her dat much freedom. She could go git her a job anywhere jes as long as she brung de ole missy half what she done made. Iffen she made $5.00, she give Miss Frances $2.50 (*Born in Slavery*, Texas Narratives, vol. 16).

BIBLIOGRAPHY

Born in Slavery: Slave Narratives from the Federal Writers' Project, 1936–1938. Manuscript and Prints and Photographs Division, Library of Congress. Texas Narratives, vol. 16. Available from http://memory.loc.gov.

Bruce, Henry Clay. *The New Man: Twenty-Nine Years a Slave, Twenty-Nine Years a Free Man*. Miami, FL: Mnemosyne, 1969.

Botkin, B. A., ed. *Lay My Burden Down: a Folk History of Slavery*. Athens: University of Georgia Press, 1989.

Douglass, Frederick. *Narrative of the Life of Frederick Douglass, an American Slave*. Boston: Anti-Slavery Office, 1845.

Gates, Henry Louis, Jr., ed. *Classic Slave Narratives*. New York: New American Library, 2002.

Rawick, George P., ed. *American Slave: A Composite Autobiography*. Westport, CT: Greenwood Press, 1972.

Rawick, George P., ed. *American Slave: A Composite Autobiography*. Supp., Series 1. Westport, CT: Greenwood Press, 1977.

Johnnie M. Maberry-Gilbert

MEALTIMES

Researcher James Walvin, author of *Slavery and the Slave Trade* (1983), believes that no generalization can adequately convey the full reality of slavery because of the diversity of the slave experience. Walvin also points out that slaves owned by impoverished masters or those living in harsh climates or locales would suffer accordingly. Determining how climate and locale determine or encourage inhumane treatment may be a subject for another debate. One may argue the point when assessing the similarity of meals and mealtime of slaves from various geographical locations and climates.

Frederick Douglass (1817–1895) describes the typical mealtime for slaves in *Narrative of the Life of Frederick Douglass, an American Slave* (1845):

> Our food was coarse corn meal boiled. This was called mush. It was put into a large wooden tray or trough, and set down upon the ground. The children were then called like so many pigs, and like so many pigs they would come and devour the mush; some with oyster shells, others with pieces of shingles, some with naked hands, and none with spoons. He that ate fastest got the most; he that was strongest secured the best place, and few left the trough satisfied (Gates 1987, p. 359).

In the narrative *To Be a Slave* (1853) Solomon Northup gives a description of mealtime with bacon:

> ... Each one received, as his weekly allowance, three and a half pounds of bacon, and corn enough to make a peck of meal. That is all—no tea, coffee, sugar, and with the exception of a very scanty sprinkling now and then ... no salt. When the corn is ground and fire is made, the bacon is taken down from the nail on which it hangs; a slice is cut off and thrown upon the coals to broil. The majority of the slaves have no knife much less a fork. They cut their bacon with the axe at woodpile. The corn meal is mixed with a little water, placed in the fire and baked. When it is "done brown" the ashes are scraped off being placed upon a chip which answers for a table, the tenant of the slave hut is ready to sit down upon the ground to supper ([1853] 1968, p. 73).

Interviewed in 1937 by Works Progress Administration (WPA) recorder Ruth Thompson, Richard Toler admitted that he did not know his exact age but he was sure that he was at least half a century and that slavery was not a pleasant time: "Ah never had no good times till ah was free," he said, "Ah was bo'n on Mastah Tolah's (Henry Toler) plantation down in ole V'ginia, near Lynchburg in Campbell County" (Rawick 1972, p. 97). Toler was very certain about the kind of meals he had on his master's plantation: "We had very bad eatin'. Bread, meat, water. And they fed it to us in a trough, jes like the hogs" (Rawick 1972, pp. 97–101).

A. C. Pruitt, a slave of the Magill family located in Martinsville, Louisiana, recalls a more pleasant mealtime experience: " ... Come five in de evenin' us have de bigges' meal, dat sho' seem like a long time 'cause dey ain't feed us but two meal a day, not countin' de eatin' us do enduring de day" (*Born in Slavery*, Texas Narratives, vol. 16, part 3).

BIBLIOGRAPHY

Born in Slavery: Slave Narratives from the Federal Writers' Project, 1936–1938, Library of Congress. Texas Narratives, vol. 16, part 3. Available from http://memory.loc.gov.

MEALTIME ON THE PLANTATION

Imagine it is mealtime and you have not eaten all day. Now imagine hearing a loud clanging that signals that it is the mealtime hour (or few minutes). You see children and adults rushing to a feeding trough at the sound of the clanging. The trough may not be big enough to accommodate all the hungry stomachs that pressed forward when the signal was given. There may be pushing and shoving. Perhaps now is not the time to worry about table manners (especially when there is no table). It is the time, however, to worry about getting close enough to the trough in order to get the only food that you are allowed to have in a twenty–four–hour period. *The Life of Frederick Douglass* details the content of such a meal.

SOURCE: Tyler, Ronnie C., and Lawrence R. Murphy, eds. *Slave Narratives of Texas*. Austin, TX: Encino Press, 1974.

Douglass, Frederick. *Narrative of the Life of Frederick Douglass, an American Slave*. Boston: Anti-Slavery Office, 1845.

Gates, Henry Louis, Jr. ed. *The Classic Slave Narratives*. New York: Signet, 1987.

Northup, Solomon. *To Be a Slave* [1853], ed. Julius Lester. New York: Dial Press, 1968.

Rawick, George P. *American Slave; a Composite Autobiography*. Westport, CT: Greenwood, 1972.

Walvin, James. *Slavery and the Slave Trade: A Short Illustrated History*. Jackson: University Press of Mississippi, 1983.

Johnnie M. Maberry-Gilbert

CHILD REARING AND EDUCATION

Slaves of the antebellum South rarely obtained any sort of formal education. This was in part the result of strict antislavery laws that had been enacted in most Southern states—Alabama, Georgia, Louisiana, Mississippi, Missouri, North Carolina, South Carolina, and Virginia—that made it illegal for masters and mistresses to teach their bondmen even the rudiments of reading and writing. As a result, by 1860, it is estimated that only approximately 5 percent of slaves were literate. Slaveholders and state legislators alike held fast to the belief that any slave who could read and write posed a great threat to the survival of the institution of slavery. For example, if a slave could read he might interpret the Bible in ways that could bring him to the conclusion that slavery was both immoral and un-Christian. In addition, a literate slave could read newspaper accounts that discussed the growing abolitionist activity in the North. And, at the most extreme level, the empowered literate slave, reacting to what he or she had read, could be rendered capable of instigating slave insurrections.

REBECCA, AUGUSTA and ROSA.
Slave Children from New Orleans.

A portrait of three slave girls from New Orleans, 1863. Slaves of the antebellum South rarely received any formal education. Slave holders and legislators believed that slaves who could read or write were dangerous to the institution of slavery. *MH Kimball/George Eastman House/Getty Images.*

There were, however, despite the legal constraints and general fears, a very few notable slaveholders who did teach favored slaves how to read and write.

Despite the legal restrictions, many slaveholders, especially mistresses, chose to religiously educate their bondmen. Plantation mistresses typically emphasized aspects of the Bible that encouraged slave subservience. They were particularly inclined to introduce to their slaves the Ten Commandments, the Lord's Prayer, the Apostles' Creed, and various catechisms prepared specifically for slaves. Many bondmen fully recognized the overhanded purpose of their owners' efforts to interject Christianity into their lives, characterizing such behavior as manipulative and self-serving. Slaves often noted what they construed to be a contradiction between God's Word and mistress's cruelty and inhumanity. Former bondman William Wells Brown declared that "slavehold-

ers hide themselves behind the Church," adding that "a more praying, preaching, psalm-singing people cannot be found than the slaveholders of the South." The Reverend William H. Robinson, another former slave, substantiated Brown's observation by mocking his white family's daily prayer which included the line, "grant us all a large increase of slaves …" Furthermore, he belittled his mistress's sermon to her slaves in which she included the line, "God's wisdom is displayed in the system of slavery." In many cases, white-provided religious education, instead of improving them, provided them with evidence that slavery was an immoral and unconscionable institution.

Slaveholders further "improved" slaves by providing them practical educations. Masters, mistresses, or overseers relayed knowledge related to agriculture, carpentry, masonry, blacksmithing, cooking, sewing, child-care, first aid, and other plantation-related activities. However, these activities were self-serving for the white population that was exquisitely aware of the relationship between slave efficiency and profit.

Although slaves could not depend upon the white community to provide them with the types of educations that they may have desired, they did attain "educations" (education being defined differently than it is in the twenty-first century) via other means, specifically their families, their peer groups, and religious leaders within their community. Although many persons within the slave community contributed to the education of any given member, it was the slave's family—both immediate and extended—that was the seminal provider of instruction in his youth. As a result of parental influence and the child-rearing practices of their elders, enslaved children learned slave resistance while, at the same time, maintaining their integrity. Bondmen—through their complex kinship networks—effectively transmitted displeasure about slavery and the lifestyle it perpetuated from one generation to another; this sometimes resulted in successful slave resistance to white cultural domination.

In order to survive physically and psychologically, even on the most basic of levels, a slave needed to internalize many important concepts. These included: (1) solidarity and communality within the slave community; (2) distrust and/or suspicion of their owners; (3) their own feeling of black superiority; (4) the relative autonomy of their owners and the government; and (5) the significance and importance of their own black/African religions.

In elaboration, slaves recognized the unending value of solidarity and communality. First, slaves came to view themselves as a member of a social group, whose components shared a common lifestyle, common interests and problems, and a common need to stand as one. At very young ages, bondmen understood that their fellow enslaved members were mutually dependent on one another. As a consequence, they learned never to betray their fellow slaves, nor to steal from them, nor to fight with them. In addition, they were expected to provide aid to fugitive slaves, to take pride in the accomplishments of community members, and to sub-stitute their services for their injured or sick counter-parts. Susan Davis Rhodes, who had been a slave in North Carolina, recalled: "People in my day didn't know book learning but dey studied how to protect each other, and save 'em from such misery as they could."

Second, the slave community also instilled within the minds of young slaves the reality that the interests of whites were inimical to those who were relegated to the slave quarters. Thus, from a very early age, most blacks were suspicious of whites. Blacks viewed whites, in many instances, as liars and hypocrites, especially as they related to, and interacted with, the African American community. Although there were a few kind and well-intentioned slaveholders, slave youth, except in very special circumstances, were told to never fully trust their masters, mistresses, and overseers. Despite such suspicion and distrust, both the slave of his master and the master of his slave, plantation dynamics were far too complex to conclude that many bondmen were not victimized by conflicted feelings. Former slave Austin Steward recalled that when his mistress died "the slaves were all deeply affected by the scene; some doubtless truly lamented the death of their mistress; others rejoiced that she was no more, and all were more or less frightened [about being sold off the plantation]. One of them I remember went to the pump and wet his face, so as to appear to weep with the rest."

Slave youth were also taught that the members of their community should view themselves superior to whites both morally (because they opposed enslaving others) but behaviorally as well. In particular, slave children, by virtue of discussion which they overheard and by behaviors which they observed themselves, were easily brought to the point that they viewed their white owners as lazy, incompetent, and unable to physically engage themselves in farming, cooking, cleaning, carpentry, laundry, or any other type of physical task. Slave children were made to understand that many masters passed their lives traveling, engaging in phony business, gambling, and fretting about money and that mistresses, as a group, were weak, spoiled, histrionic, naïve, delicate creatures unwilling or unable to participate in daily household chores. In extension, the slave community schooled its younger members in those ways by which they could outwit their white owners. For example, young bondmen were taught by their elders how to forge passes, how to rub garlic or red onion on their feet in order to keep dogs off their trail, and how to escape from having been locked in their slave cabins by climbing up the chimney. And finally, slave youth were taught that they could effectively deceive the white community via a carefully crafted secret language, songs, and gestures imparted to them by their family and others.

Concurrently, as young slaves learned of effective ways by which they could outwit their masters, their black elders made them acutely aware of the relative autonomy of their owners. Most significantly for the bondman, slaveholders possessed absolute and final authority over their slaves and at any time could dismantle slave families by selling off members and could inflict punishment for any perceived offense. Consequently, despite slaves' concerted efforts to resist the proverbial chains of slavery, they always lived in fear. Despite having been "educated" in the ways of resistance, ultimately elders in the slave community at large felt forced to warn their youth that there were consequences attached to challenging white power. Younger slaves were further reminded that the local and state governments as well as the judicial system were positioned to uphold the hegemony of the white planter class.

And, finally, many African American slaves labored to instill into the minds of their youth an appreciation for the black/African spirit world. Elderly bondmen, especially, felt it was their responsibility to educate the younger generations about important aspects of their native African animistic religions and the significance of witches, ghosts, Voodoo, hoodoo, haints, curses, conjuring, and spirits, which were all components of their belief systems. Slaves melded many of those and other aspects of their African religions with chosen aspects of Christianity to form a syncretic Afro-Christianity. This Afro-Christianity that was widely taught provided members of the slave community an emotional escape from their dreary day-to-day lives and, more importantly, an identity that transcended anything created by the white planter class.

In summation, the education and child-rearing of a slave child was no easy feat, either for those who provided it or for those who received it. There were many lessons and skills to be learned for any slave child to function practically and emotionally as a member of his own black community and as a functionary in the white plantation world. Every slave was indebted to members of his nuclear family, his extended family, and his fellow community members to provide him practical skills and a psychological compass to carry him through the trials of a life in bondage.

BIBLIOGRAPHY

Brown, William Wells. *Narrative of William W. Brown, A Fugitive Slave, Written by Himself.* Boston: 1847.

King, Wilma. *Stolen Childhood: Slave Youth in Nineteenth-Century America.* Bloomington: Indiana University Press, 1995.

Palmer, Colin A. *Passageways: An Interpretive History of Black America*, Vol. 1: *1619–1863.* Fort Worth, TX: Harcourt Brace College Publishers, 1998.

Raboteau, Albert J. *Slave Religion: The "Invisible Institution" in the Antebellum South.* New York: Oxford University Press, 1978.

Robinson, Reverend William H. *From Log Cabin to the Pulpit, or, Fifteen Years in Slavery,* 3rd ed. Eau Claire, WI: 1913.

Schwartz, Marie Jenkins. *Born in Bondage: Growing Up Enslaved in the Antebellum South.* Cambridge, MA: Harvard University Press, 2000.

Webber, Thomas L. *Deep Like the Rivers: Education in the Slave Quarter Community, 1831–1865.* New York: W. W. Norton, 1978.

Williams, Heather Andrea. *Self-Taught: African American Education in Slavery and Freedom.* Chapel Hill: University of North Carolina Press, 2005.

Katherine E. Robrer

SLAVE QUARTERS

Little physical evidence of the nature of slaves' quarters was recorded or has survived. Generally speaking, however, it is known that housing for slaves was of poor quality. Slaves typically lived in small log houses coated with a plaster made of mud and other materials to keep out the wind, rain, and snow; a brick fireplace was centered in the largest part of the structure. Dirt floors were most common, and wooden chimneys that could be moved as needed were attached. The door was usually centered on one side, and if there was a window, it was typically unglazed. Archaeological evidence of duplex-like cabins shared by two or more families has also been discovered. On the largest plantations, housing for slaves was often a large barracks-like structure fitted with bunks and occupied solely by men; women, children, and the elderly lived some little distance away in mean, small wood cabins. Black overseers on the largest plantations sometimes occupied a small one-room cabin by themselves.

Historians and archaeologists have also found some interesting variables in slave housing. In the coastal regions of Georgia and South Carolina, slaves' houses were sometimes built to mimic various styles of West African architecture. These homes would be a reflection of the socioeconomic status of the slaves' African ancestors, which would determine the shape of the house, the placement of rooms, and the design of the courtyards. Moreover, religious beliefs and practices of African ancestors would figure prominently in the type of dwelling built.

Furthermore, archaeologists have discovered evidence of slave quarters built that mimicked construction techniques still used in West Africa. For example, American slaves constructed roofs from thatch or a clay mixture. Excavations have also unearthed wooden shingles and clay roofs that were reinforced by timber.

There are records showing that early in the nineteenth century many slave owners had the slaves' quarters arranged in a circular pattern around the masters' houses. This duplicated the practices of many African tribal chiefs, which may have comforted many slaves.

A group of African Americans standing in front of a shack. A photograph, circa the mid-1850s, of a group of African Americans, presumably slaves, standing in front of a wooden cabin in the South. Slaves typically lived in small log houses coated with a plaster made of mud and other materials to keep out the wind, rain and snow. *Hulton Archive/Getty Images.*

However, the planter elite used this system because they found it easier to control their slaves when they lived in close proximity to the masters' houses.

The amount and quality of furniture, cooking utensils, and other household amenities found in slave quarters varied depending on the size of the plantation, the largesse of the owners, and the status of individual slaves. Most slaves' cabins would have been outfitted with pallets for the adults to sleep on—children often slept on the floor—and perhaps wooden boxes or stools for sitting. There might be some rudimentary utensils used for cooking, and bowls or gourds from which to eat. Wooden buckets were used to carry water for cooking, drinking, and bathing. Some slaves were lucky enough to acquire castoffs from their masters; archaeological excavations at Mount Vernon, owned by George Washington (1732–1799), have unearthed dishes of various materials, glassware, and pewter utensils.

Finally, many slaves planted small vegetable gardens around their cabins, and often acquired small barnyard animals, such as chickens. This provided them not only with extra food, but goods that they could sell or exchange to acquire additional clothing, foodstuffs not provided by the master, or other amenities they deemed important.

BIBLIOGRAPHY

Genovese, Eugene. *Roll, Jordan, Roll: The World the Slaves Made*. New York: Pantheon, 1974.

Singleton, Theresa, ed. *"I, Too, Am America": Archaeological Studies of African American Life*. Charlottesville: University of Virginia Press, 1999.

Marilyn K. Howard

■ Relationships among Slaves

RELATIONSHIPS AMONG SLAVES: AN OVERVIEW

A special relationship existed in the slave communities between and among males, females, parents, and children. Social relations among slaves enabled them to affirm their humanity, and most importantly, served as a conveyor of culture and survival skills that aided in the resilience and ability of slaves to endure the harshness of the institution of slavery. These relationships gave slaves a sense of self-worth and belonging that often prevented them from fleeing.

Slaves formed friendships and highly emotional attachments and displayed loyalty to one another while forced to live in this institution. Despite having most every aspect of their lives controlled by whites, they were still able to create a viable social world with its own array of shared beliefs, customs, interaction patterns, and social arrangements.

The relationships among slave men and women had to conform to the rigorous controls of the work and social patterns established by the system of slavery. Nevertheless,

Two slave boys. A photograph of two slave boys, circa 1870. Social relations among slaves enabled them to affirm their humanity and aided their ability to endure the harshness of the institution of slavery. *Hulton Archive/Getty Images.*

love and affection played a large part in male-female relationships. Slaves, with the permission of their owners, married or formed common law unions. However, when slaves married, these unions were performed by their owners. As recounted by ex-slave Harriet McFarlin Payne:

> When two of de slaves wanted to get married, they'd go up to de big house and de master would marry them. They'd stand up before him and he'd read out of a book called the disciple and say, Thou shalt love the Lord thy God with all thy heart, all thy strength, with all thy might and thy neighbor as thyself. Then he'd say they were man and wife and tell them to be honest and kind to each other.

Although the slave's social standing in society was deemed culturally and socially beneath that of the southern class structure, they nevertheless built strong family relationships within these constraints. These relationships existed from one generation to the next. Owners encouraged the slave women to bear children because they were regarded as future laborers. In most assessments, because of the labor requirements of parents,

SOCIAL INTERACTION AMONG SLAVES

Although theoretically and legally—except for some humane restrictions—the slaves were not persons but utilities with no will of their own, social interaction within their own world on the plantation created a social life among them with nearly all of the features of any society.

Tinie Force and Elvira Lewis of LaCenter, Kentucky, were very familiar with the slavery period, as they were both slaves, and witnessed the social interaction among the slaves:

Ring dancing was largely practiced during the slavery period. The general procedure was to draw a ring on the ground, ranging from 15 to 30 feet in diameter. The size of the ring to be used was determined by the number of persons who were engaged in the dancing ring. The youngsters would congregate within the ring and dance to the rhythmic hand clapping and rhythm of the tambourine.

Also the darkies were very fond of sports, such as hurdle racing. The contestants would leap over hurdles that were placed at regular intervals apart. There was a kind of jumping too, which was called hurtling pole, which was a small rigid pole about 12 feet in length. The jumper would take a long running start, which would enable him to take an additional momentum; and with the assistance of the hurtling pole, would leap over a hurdle that was placed a considerable elevation above the ground. (Rawick 1972–1979, Vol. 18, p. 300)

SOURCE: Rawick, George P. *The American Slave: A Composite Autobiography,* 19 vols. Westport, CT: Greenwood Press, 1972–1979.

children suffered from the lack of care and attention. James W. C. Pennington recalls his revelations of slavery at four years old. He said he was robbed of the adequate care and attention of his parents during the day and he suffered miserably. He felt as though he had been thrown in a world without a social circle to flee for comfort.

Furthermore, female bondwomen had ample time to develop consciousness grounded in their identity as females, thus female bonding to female conflict was not uncommon. The social stratus created an atmosphere rife with smoldering jealousies and antipathies. In addition, women regularly vied for the attention of men. When a husband or boyfriend switched his affection from one woman to the other, altercation between the women involved was likely. As in the case of a slave named Molly, the cook in June Chestnut's household, Molly attacked a woman whom her husband had given her calico dress to, and tried to burn the dress off of the woman with a red hot poker (Woodward 1981).

The elder slaves were highly regarded in the slave community. As recalled by Fredrick Douglass (1817–1895) about the slave community at large, he said, "There is not to be found, among any people, a more rigid enforcement of the law of respect of elders, than they maintain" (1987, p. 49). Moreover, the relationship between the elder slaves and the slave community was one of admiration. The elder slaves served as repositories of cultural tradition from which the younger generation drew. The elderly slaves through such activities as child care, storytelling, procurement of food, and religious leadership helped to build slaves' self-esteem and self-worth, thereby creating slave communities with positive images of themselves.

The storytelling in particular was an important entertainment, educational, and coping mechanism. The old men were able to recount elements of the tales and stories in their own languages, thus giving their tales an African flair. The elder slaves contributed substantially to the perpetuation of the African American slave community. They also provided the slave communities with religious leadership, which provided the elderly males with the greatest opportunities for influence over other slaves (Close 1997)

Moreover, old bondwomen served a crucial role in the slave community as well. They were likely to attend all slave births and all of the slave deaths. Their accumulated knowledge delivered one into life, helped one survive it, and sometimes, as can be said of many physicians of the period, helped one to an early grave. As midwife and doctor she embodied the link between the generations and it was partly through her that a central aspect of black culture, the secret of the herbs, was transmitted (White 1985).

Hence, the relationships that existed between men and women, children, parents, and the elders of the slave community functioned like those in other societies throughout history. These associations made it possible for slaves to develop a sense of identity and communal values, and laid the foundations for the formation of families whose kinship ties spread from one generation to the next. These relationships enabled slaves to negotiate some autonomy within the restraints imposed upon them by enslavement. Within these social constructs slaves flourished and created a sense of community among themselves, social organization, and culture.

BIBLIOGRAPHY

Close, Stacey K. *Elderly Slaves of the Plantation South.* New York and London: Garland, 1997.

Douglass, Frederick. *My Bondage and My Freedom.* Urbana: University of Illinois Press, 1987.

Durant, Thomas J., and J. David Knottnerus. *The Plantation Society and Race Relations: The Origins of Inequality.* Westport, CT: Prager, 1999.

Finkelman, Paul. *Women and the Family in a Slave Society: The Negro Slave Family.* New York and London: Garland, 1989.

Pennington, James W. C. *The Fugitive Blacksmith, or Events in the History of James W. C. Pennington: Pastor of a Presbyterian Church, New York, Formerly a Slave in the State of Maryland, United States,* 3rd ed. London: C. Gilpin, 1850.

White, Deborah Gray. *Ar'n't I a Woman?: Female Slaves in the Plantation South.* New York and London: Norton, 1985.

Woodward, C. Vann, ed. *Mary Chestnut's Civil War.* New Haven, CT: Yale University Press, 1981.

Deliah Brown

KINSHIP

In the face of sometimes insurmountable odds, enslaved people made great efforts to maintain family ties. Because men and women were property within the U.S. slave-holding system, they could be bought, sold, or given away on a whim. Slave marriages were not legally binding under the law. Instead, men and women had to establish consensual unions that could be dissolved at any time. Husbands and wives faced constant threat of being sold away from each other. Similarly, enslaved children belonged not to their parents, but solely to the master. However, enslaved men and women did not rely solely upon these familial relationships. Instead, the descendants of African men and women maintained a cultural tradition of intricate extended family networks. Father, mother, and siblings were not the only measure of the concept of family.

Enslaved people maintained a broad network of equally important blood and fictive kin ties. Blood kin were relatives who were directly related to an individual. This extended family consisted of parents, siblings, aunts, uncles, cousins, grandparents, great-grandparents and, in the case of the iconic photograph of the family on Smith's Plantation in Beaufort, South Carolina, great-great-grandparents. Fictive or "play" kin were nonblood kin who were treated like blood kin. These men and women were addressed by names generally reserved for family, such as "Mama," "Papa," "Uncle," "Aunt," "Brother," "Sister," and "Cousin."

Although the terms *Uncle* and *Aunt* are the same ones used by whites, they are emblematic of a lack of respect for enslaved men and women. All black men and women were "Aunt" and "Uncle" because they could not be referred to as "Mrs.," "Mr.," or "Miss." However, in the enslaved community, the bonds of fictive kin meant something entirely different. Fictive kin were closer than friends. In some cases, they were able to stand in for blood kin and were respected as such for taking care of children to whom they were not related, and when necessary disciplining them as well. Former

slave Allen Allensworth related to his biographer that his fictive aunt Phyllis stood in for his mother when he was sold from the Upper South to the Lower South as a child. She volunteered to care for him like a mother as he had been, for all practical purposes, orphaned by law. As a result, young Allensworth felt an attachment to Aunt Phyllis for the rest of his life. Similarly, Harriet Jacobs spoke fondly of her fictive uncle Fred, who wished to learn to read the Bible. He had no money, but gave Jacobs fruit as payment for her instruction.

Extended families could be maintained because of the housing arrangements of the enslaved on plantations. At Monticello, the enslaved lived in houses along the south side of Mulberry Row. At the Hermitage, the duplex style homes of the Field Quarters housed many family groups. These homes were separated by a thin wall with separate entrances. Family groups lived on either side. Edmund Jenings's plantations had "dwelling houses" and "quarters" both of which housed large groups of enslaved people. On the Sea Islands, a style of enslavement had developed wherein the master of the plantation remained in Charleston during the summer months to avoid the unhealthy atmosphere; the duplex style of home was used to keep large groups of enslaved people together and, with an absentee master, families prospered.

These kinship ties did not stop at the property lines of plantations. Extended kinship groups spread from plantation to plantation. Ex-slave and abolitionist Frederick Douglass remembered fondly that his mother, who lived on another plantation, walked 12 miles each way at night to tuck him into bed. She would stay with him through the night and leave early in the morning to walk back to her plantation in time for work the next day. As a result, Douglass recalled that he never saw his mother's face by the light of day.

Historian Herbert Gutman wrote one of the definitions of kin involved being shaped by "[f]amily and kinship patterns of belief and behavior associated with traditional West African tribal societies" (1977, p. 223). Although Gutman did not go into great detail about the topic in his text, he said that West African societies from which the enslaved men and women of America were descended placed high value on extended family and family ties. In the United States nuclear families were disrupted frequently because of sale or other factors, and the extended family was created by enslaved African American men and women using wisps of the West African family structure as a way to maintain family ties.

Recent scholars dispute Gutman's argument. Instead of having a broad-minded way of looking at family and kinship ties—acknowledging that a nuclear family headed by a father is not the only type of family organization that exists—historians have narrowly defined the family. In earlier scholarship, historians were concerned with recreating and identifying all members

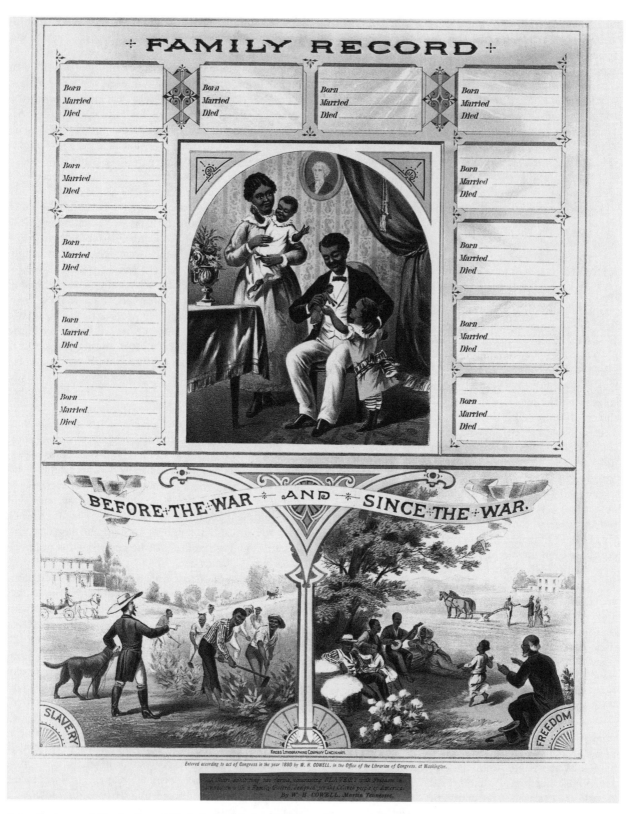

A family tree and illustration of life before and after the Civil War. A 1880 family tree featuring an African American family. The bottom shows the difference in African American family life before and after the Civil War. Slave families could be separated at any time and enslaved people made great efforts to preserve family ties. © *Corbis.*

of the enslaved nuclear family. An unrecorded father was written off as "not listed," and his absence was given as evidence of the weakness of the African American family under enslavement. West African family structures do not look like Western European family structures. In West African cultures there is a long tradition of extended family relationships. Family ties were centered on extended family with male and females as coheads instead of a family group based upon immediate family with a father as head of household. Additionally, as Gutman noted, maternal uncles and aunts were generally at the heads of these family groups rather than fathers and mothers. The West African model of family was secondary to the extended family network.

As a result, contemporary scholarship has suggested that earlier scholars were incorrect in their assumptions that extended families replaced nuclear families for enslaved people. Extended families were not an adaptive form of family groups because the notion of extended family was not a foreign one to people of African descent in America. Their ancestors brought this cultural tradition with them from the West African nation-states from which they came. Therefore the notion of African Americans scrambling to create a family structure as a result of enslavement is not entirely accurate. Europeans could not destroy a family structure that was not the norm for enslaved families of African descent.

These notions of the value of extended family from West Africa and valuing this system over the system of a nuclear family promoted the extended family system, which provided a built-in safety net for enslaved people who could be separated from either blood or fictive kin at the whim of their masters. The bonds of kinship were so sound that to avoid separation, men and women escaping slavery often went to live with kin on other plantations. Children escaped to be with their parents, husbands and wives escaped together, and, in the cases of enslaved people who were particularly skilled at running away, they would frequently return to the plantations from which they had come.

Certain other traditions of kinship were not developed or transformed in America, but instead brought from Africa and manifested in the New World. In traditional West African societies, status comes with age. The older a person is, the more respect they are owed. Elders are closest to ancestors and, because of their life experience, are entitled to esteem. In the New World masters noted that a disapproving look from an elder in the enslaved community was more effective than a beating to keep young people in line. Elders in the community were responsible for maintaining order. Jacobs wrote of her grandmother, who was called Aunt Marthy in the enslaved community, and was well known and respected in among them for her intelligence, skills in food preparation and cheery personality. Moses Roper's grandmother visited him every day and brought him food

while he was imprisoned for escaping. Grandy's elderly mother had food brought to her by her children and "other near relations" nightly.

Furthermore, intergenerational bonds were strengthened by naming practices. Enslaved people named their children after fathers, grandparents, and, infrequently, mothers. Children were also given the name of cousins.

Having a large extended family had many benefits and few drawbacks. Family provided refuge from the cruelties of slavery. Kin networks supported and promoted mutual obligations. These obligations ensured that children were clothed, fed, loved, and cherished, the elderly were taken care of, and people of all ages had a sense of connection and nurturing in a community larger than themselves.

BIBLIOGRAPHY

Douglass, Frederick. *Narrative of the Life of Frederick Douglass, an American Slave, Written by Himself, with Related Documents*, [1845] ed. David W. Blight. Boston: Bedford/St. Martin's Press, 2003.

Franklin, John Hope. *From Slavery to Freedom: A History of African Americans*. New York: Knopf, 2000.

Gutman, Herbert George. *The Black Family in Slavery and Freedom, 1750–1925*. New York: Vintage, 1977.

Joyner, Charles W. *Down by the Riverside: A South Carolina Slave Community*. Urbana: University of Illinois Press, 1984.

Morgan, Philip D. *Slave Counterpoint: Black Culture in the Eighteenth-Century Chesapeake and Lowcountry*. Chapel Hill: University of North Carolina Press, 1998.

Tanya Mears

SKIN COLOR

For proponents of slavery, the darker a person's skin, the more savage was such a person's nature—hence the "right" of whites to subjugate people of dark skin. Many Southerners believed that the Bible sanctioned enslaving dark-skinned people. In the Book of Genesis, the descendants of both Cain and Ham (son of Noah) are cursed to serve others in perpetuity. The Canaanites, distinguishable by their skin tone and hair, were to be "hewers of wood and drawers of water." In his *Apology for Slavery* (1977), Alexander Geddes asks, "If *Heaven* then had doomed the posterity of Ham to be slaves, what presumption . . . is it [of] *Man,* to assert their freedom?" (p. 27). Geddes asserted that slavery was not only a biblical edict but also one "authorized by the Law of Nations . . . A *Black* and a *Slave* have become synonymous terms; and *African freedom* would be a [falsity of] language" (p. 24).

Such a literal reading of the Bible even persuaded some slaves. Gus Rogers, born in Alabama, referred to the Canaanites when explaining slavery to an interviewer:

SKIN COLOR AND THE CENSUS

Near the end of the nineteenth century, as the vagaries of slavery faded in the South and elsewhere in America, the United States Census Bureau began the laborious process of trying to account for the mixed races of ex-slaves. To gain an accurate snapshot of racial ancestry, in terms of lineage and skin color, census takers were told to use the following descriptors when gathering information for the 1790 census: "The word 'black' should be used to describe those persons who have three-fourths or more black blood; 'mulatto,' those who have three-eighths to five-eighths black blood; 'quadroons,' those persons who have one-fourth black blood; and 'octoroons,' those persons who have one-eighth or any trace of black blood" (United States Bureau of the Census 2002, p. 27).

SOURCE: United States Bureau of the Census. *Measuring America: The Decennial Censuses from 1790 to 2000.* Washington, DC: U.S. Department of Commerce, Economics, and Statistics Administration, 2002.

"So, Miss, there we are, and that is the way God meant us to be. We have always had to follow the white folks and do what we saw them do, and that's all there is to it. You just can't get away from what the Lord said" (*Born in Slavery*, Alabama Narratives, vol. 1, p. 336).

Opponents of slavery, too, cited the Bible as supporting their view, arguing that as all mankind was created in God's image, no man should be in bondage to another. They turned to science to explain variations in skin color. The darkness or lightness of skin was attributable to a person's proximity to the equator. People located close to the equator had darker skin, those farther away, lighter skin. As Thomas Clarkson noted in his essay on slavery, "It is evident, that if you travel from the equator to the northern pole, you will find a regular gradation of colour from black to white. Now if you can justly take [a man] for your slave who is of the deepest dye, what hinders you from taking him also, who only differs from the former but by a shade?" (1788, p. 132).

On Southern plantations and homesteads, slaves with fairer complexions as a result of miscegenation were a prickly subject. Such slaves held a precarious position. They were sometimes treated well by their slaveholders as part of the family (though still servants), but they were sometimes hated by the mistress and her children as the product of an illicit and sinful act by the master. Light-skinned slaves were sometimes ostracized by their fellow slaves because of their special privileges. As William Wells Brown, writing in 1863, noted, "My fair complexion was a great obstacle to my happiness.... Often mistaken by strangers as a white boy, it annoyed my mistress very much." When a visiting stranger commented on Brown's likeness to his master, his mistress "ordered me out of the room.... After the stranger left, I was flogged for his blunder" (pp. 17–18).

BIBLIOGRAPHY

Born in Slavery: Slave Narratives from the Federal Writers' Project, 1936–1938, Library of Congress. Alabama Narratives, vol. 1. Available from http://memory.loc.gov.

Brown, William Wells. *The Black Man: His Antecedents, His Genius, and His Achievements.* Boston: T. Wells, 1863.

Clarkson, Thomas. *An Essay on the Slavery and Commerce of the Human Species.* 2nd ed. London, 1788.

Geddes, Alexander. *An Apology for Slavery; or, Six Cogent Arguments Against the Immediate Abolition of the Slave-Trade.* London, 1792.

Nelson Rhodes

SLAVE BODIES

For slavery to function as an effective system of compelled labor and social control, it had to inflict itself upon black bodies and transform them to its needs. This process demeaned the humanity of African "chattels"; debased their bodies as brutish, ugly, and inherently servile; divided and segregated them one from another to maximize profits and productivity; terrorized, violated, and disciplined them to the crucial tasks of labor and reproduction; and bought, sold, swapped, rented, and gifted them to serve the economic and cultural interests of the master class. Millions of Africans and African Americans were victims of this process of corporeal enslavement, yet they were implicated in it as well, as were the abolitionists who sought their emancipation. That terrible contradiction is a story historians are only beginning to explore. More positive are the ways blacks in bondage used their bodies to reject slavery and affirm their own humanity. As with most flesh-and-blood choices, however, such victories seldom came without grievous costs.

As the historian Winthrop Jordan has shown, Europeans since at least the sixteenth century viewed African bodies as naturally suited to slavery. The double debasement of Plato's equation of the body with the slave, the soul with the master seemed fully realized here: the dark skin, the supposedly coarse and animalistic features, the limbs and trunk that departed from the proportions of Renaissance perfection, all provided corporeal justification for the decision to enslave. To those blacks who tumbled down gangways in Charleston, Savannah, or the Chesapeake at the end of the Middle Passage, near-naked, weakened, sickly, and reeking, it was easier still to ascribe servile status. Africans became slaves at least partly because their bodies, to European senses, looked and smelled slavish.

Conversely, from the moment black captives arrived on the African coast to be sold, their bodies showed signs of ethnicity and lineage that were important in

Determining selling price. A woodcut showing a slave being weighed to determine her weight and, thus, her price, 1834. Traders on both sides of the Atlantic carefully considered skin color, facial features, body structure and stature when choosing slaves. © *Corbis.*

determining potential market value. Traders on both sides of the Atlantic carefully considered skin color, facial features, stature, and body structure to reckon whether captives were Coromantee or Ibo, Ashanti or Yoruba, and well-suited to labor in malarial rice swamps, to minding cattle, to corn and tobacco tillage, or to some other culturally familiar task. More than this—and more dubious—white buyers viewed physical characteristics as indications of cultural or tribal character. The planter looking to purchase a stoic, brawny plow hand or a prompt and submissive house slave came to auction armed with prejudices about the supposedly inherent traits each African ethnic group possessed. As well, buyers and sellers ascribed to particular ethnicities reputations for fractiousness or docility, intelligence, rectitude or duplicity, all of which were supposedly reflected in a slave's form and features.

Upon arrival in the New World, black bodies underwent a complex process of transformation intended to fit them to their new lives in bondage. Some had already been branded, scarred, or tattooed with the marks of their purchasers. Nearly all had been denuded of clothing and ornamentation that identified their previous social status and cultural origins. In their place were shackles, rags, and little more. Following sale, blacks were marked as no longer African by the new clothes they were forced to wear and the hairstyles they were compelled to adopt, and their particular cultural practices came to precipitous ends. How and why ritual behaviors such as female circumcision and facial scarification failed to persist under slavery remains obscure, but their passing was an important step in the destruction of cultural particularism among the enslaved and the creation of a racial slave identity. Though enslaved Africans in colonial America preserved cultural ties first by "reading" common tribal identities in other black bodies, ethnic intermarriage blurred stark lines with the passage of generations. With the closing of the transatlantic slave trade to America in 1808 and the forced migration of hundreds of thousands of blacks after 1820 from coastal farms and plantations to the riches of the Mississippi Valley and beyond, memories faded and physical distinctions grew less clear. By 1860, when blacks in bondage looked around them they saw, first and last, other slaves. That common identity provides an especially monstrous measure of slavery's success.

Slave bodies in the Old South were continually disciplined by violent punishment—real, threatened, and imagined. For the black abolitionist Frederick Douglass, it took four years of brooding "over the scars which slavery and semi-slavery had inflicted upon his body and soul" before he rose up against bondage (1855, p. xxi). Most bondpeople passed all their lives without taking that vital step. The odds were too long, the physical pain resistance risked too great. This was the source of the master's power, far into the antebellum period: the willingness and ability to scourge and mutilate, to cut and burn, to beat and kill. In the colonial and Revolutionary eras in particular, slaves were subject to a range of horrific punishments limited only by the sadistic imagination of the planter class. Troublemakers were broken on the wheel, burned alive, drawn and quartered, emasculated, maimed, and crippled. With the spread of paternalist ideology after 1820, such vicious modes of retribution grew rarer, replaced by the near universal use of the whip as a measured, rational, and educative means of punishment. Of course it never achieved those ends, but whipping offered a superb means of marking slaves' bodies with signs of masters' power. In this sense, it violently and indelibly forced political relations upon the public gaze, inflicting wounds that could never be completely erased.

In the hegemonic conflict between masters and slaves, black female bodies became a crucial site of struggle. The construction of slave families and communities represented a hard-fought political compromise between planters and their human property, accomplished over the course of generations. This achievement depended on the presence of fertile female black bodies, ready both to work and to reproduce. In many cases, masters employed the right to marry as a reward for faithful work, exacting a steep economic price in return for legitimating sexual access to female bodies. Though abolitionists sometimes claimed too much, arguing that upper South owners "bred" their slaves like horse or mules, with an eye to selling their progeny away at steep prices, it was true that masters implicitly controlled slave sexuality, sundering black marriages at will through sale or gift, and not infrequently creating them as well, in hopes of promoting profitable reproduction. Such strategies, to be sure, did nothing to deny white men sexual access to black bodies, and by 1860 perhaps one-quarter of American slaves had mixed-race ancestry. "Like the patriarchs of old, our men live all in one house with their wives and their concubines," South Carolina's Mary Chesnut complained, "and the mulattoes one sees in every family exactly resemble the white children." Every white woman knew the paternity of light-skinned slave children in neighboring households, she sniffed, "but those in her own she seems to think drop from the clouds, or pretends so to think" (Woodward 1981, p. 29).

As corrosive as miscegenation was to paternalist ideology, it exacted a greater toll still on black families. The untold millions of rapes the mulatto presence symbolized indicate the centrality of white violence against black women in establishing slaveholders' hegemony. They also signify the existence of relationships of a more complex sort, where female slaves employed their bodies to gain heightened status within the slave community, to exact a material quid pro quo from their overlords, or to pursue the affections of their own hearts across racial lines. Faced with the overwhelming power of the planter class and living with the daily prospect of violence and violation, many women doubtless made the best bargains they could for themselves, yielding their bodies in hopes of meager benefit.

For some, the benefits of this sort of partial identification with the master class were significant, for others they were transitory, hollow, selfish, and destructive. Interracial sexual relations were an important path to voluntary emancipation for slave women and their offspring across the South. They also laid the foundation for a system of status hierarchy based on skin color, both within the slave community and outside it. By 1860, exclusive urban clubs and voluntary associations open only to light-skinned free people of color were establishing a brown elite dedicated to perpetuating the racial prejudices of their white forefather-masters. How far enslaved blacks came to internalizing the atrocious body politics of white society and its zealous brown acolytes is

a subject requiring further analysis. Abolitionist slave narratives, interviews with ex-slaves conducted by the Works Progress Administration in the 1930s, and other sources reveal a range of contradictory and often self-serving biases. More telling, perhaps, is evidence of contemporary black behavior. Antebellum travelers wrote endlessly about slaves who clothed their bodies, as best they could, in fashions emulating the power and status of their white overlords. When they lashed out in violence, too, slaves more commonly struck black bodies, not white ones. This, too, was a behavioral identification with the master class, achieved through violent assault on other slaves. Blacks in bondage fought each other, beat their wives, children, and elders, and killed other slaves no more frequently than working people in other settings have done, but the meaning of this violence was dramatically different. The bondman who lashed out at a fellow slave both reproduced the action of his master and, conversely, struck indirectly at the master's power by damaging his human property. Both aspects of black violence affirmed individual freedom by attacking slave bodies. Historians have done little to date to assess the cost of such ambiguous efforts.

Other slaves made the same political point in different ways, both more and less damaging. From the beginning of the Middle Passage to the last days of the Civil War, some blacks who refused to suffer bondage destroyed the slave bodies that imprisoned them. For every suicide, there were many more blacks who pursued other sorts of self-destructive behavior, particularly alcohol-fueled, or simply retreated inward. Where opportunity presented itself and conditions became intolerable, others attempted a more hopeful tactic of survival, "stealing themselves" through projects of self-emancipation. This group was small in the years before secession, and most fugitives returned voluntarily after several days or weeks, rendering up their bodies to punishment and confirming themselves as slaves. During the Civil War, however, perhaps one slave in eight denied the Confederacy his or her crucial labor power by "stealing themselves."

By 1860, white Americans had become virtually obsessed with the presence of black bodies in their midst. Economically, they were crucial. If cotton was king, as slaveholders boasted, it was the labor of slave bodies that rendered them rich. More than this, slave bodies were employed to secure mortgages, pay debts, and serve as gifts and dowries. In the North, antislavery forces increasingly came to lean upon the pornographic depiction of slave bodies in pain and sexual defilement to prove their arguments about the evils of the peculiar institution. The success of these graphic depictions of slavery's corporeal horrors was ambivalent at best. On one hand, works such as *American Slavery As It Is* (1839) and *Uncle Tom's Cabin* (1852) made plain the suffering bondage inflicted on black bodies. On the other hand, abolitionist propaganda often portrayed black bodies as ugly and inferior, stirring racist loathing at the same time it won converts to the antislavery cause. Ultimately, it would require the sacrifice of black men in Union blue rendering up their bodies—and their lives—in battle at Fort Wagner, Port Hudson, the Crater, and elsewhere to begin to challenge those stereotypes.

BIBLIOGRAPHY

Douglass, Frederick. *My Bondage and My Freedom*. New York: Miller, Orton, and Mulligan, 1855.

Gomez, Michael A. *Exchanging Our Country Marks: The Transformation of African Identities in the Colonial and Antebellum South*. Chapel Hill: University of North Carolina Press, 1998.

Johnson, Walter. *Soul by Soul: Life inside the Antebellum Slave Market*. Cambridge, MA: Harvard University Press, 2001.

Jordan, Winthrop D. *White over Black: American Attitudes toward the Negro, 1550–1812*. Chapel Hill: University of North Carolina Press, 1968.

Reid-Pharr, Robert F. *Conjugal Union: The Body, the House, and the Black American*. New York: Oxford University Press, 1999.

Roberts, Dorothy. *Killing the Black Body: Race, Reproduction, and the Meaning of Liberty*. New York: Vintage, 1998.

Schroeder, Lars. *Slave to the Body: Black Bodies, White No-Bodies, and the Regulative Dualism of Body-Politics in the Old South*. New York: Peter Lang, 2003.

Stowe, Harriet Beecher. *Uncle Tom's Cabin; or, Life among the Lowly*. Boston: J. P. Jewett, 1852.

Weld, Theodore D. *American Slavery As It Is: Testimony of a Thousand Witnesses*. New York: American Anti-Slavery Society, 1839.

Woodward, C. Vann, ed. *Mary Chesnut's Civil War*. New Haven, CT: Yale University Press, 1981.

Lawrence T. McDonnell

GENDER ROLES

Race and gender roles were integral to the patriarchal institution of slavery in America from colonization until the conclusion of the Civil War in 1865. Beginning in the 1640s and coming to fruition by the 1680s, slavery in America shifted from a more diverse institution, including large numbers of black and Indian slaves as well as white English indentured servants, to a far stricter racially divide convention along a black and white binary. Gender roles shifted to maintain the patriarchal establishment in America, redefining both male and female expectations through social and linguistic practices. Challenges to slavery often used gender discourse to frame both supporting and opposing arguments until

emancipation. Although racial difference was instrumental in the perpetuation of slavery, gender roles contributed equally to the continuance and contestation of this institution.

Scholarship on Virginia explores the ways gender roles shifted to preserve the patriarchal system in response to opposition from lower white males and slave unrest from the 1660s to the 1680s. The ensuing rebellion lead by Nathaniel Bacon in 1676 resulted in a distinct shift in the pool of available labor. What started as a system reliant on English white indentured servants and convicts, Native Americans, and free and bound blacks shifted to depend overwhelmingly on an enslaved black population, in part because they seemed to be the least difficult to control due to the ease in distinguishing them from the majority of the free population and lack roots in the region. Gender discourse proved essential once this division emerged. Race began to define both free and slave peoples and served as a way to differentiate and justify these new categories. The House of Burgesses passed legislation denying black men their manly roles as providers and protectors, limiting their access to property and guns. Using maternal lineage to determine blacks' status as slaves, "the refusal of social rights of fatherhood to enslaved men emphasized that slaves could not form their own households … but were incorporated into their owners' households" (Scully 2005, p. 5). Gendered terminology, such as the use of the word *wench*, shifted from representing a lower class or morally depraved woman to representing black women. Furthermore, "discourses of racial difference and masculinity also addressed the need of elite Anglo-Virginians to fashion a distinct colonial identity" (Brown 1996, p. 184). This perception decreased the authority of the British Crown over the settlers who as a result of masculinity increasingly opposed to the policies of the Crown that were received as an attempt to feminize or undermine the white male population.

Unlike agricultural labor in both Europe and Africa, plantation economies in America rarely maintained a strict gendered division of labor. In all locations women could be found working in the fields along with the men. "From the planters' perspective, this denial of women's performance of agricultural labor involved a denial of their femininity and thus emphasized both racial difference and inferiority" (Scully 2005, p. 6). This repudiation of gendered roles further served to establish a differentiation between whites and blacks as only white men and women possessed what amounted to proper gender roles. This is not to refute that some specialized tasks were reserved for individuals of a particular sex. In a discussion of slavery in Pennsylvania, Edward Turner commented that male slaves were occupied as "bakers, blacksmiths, bricklayers, hammermen, refiners, sail-makers, sailors, shoemakers, tailors and tanners"

Female slaves sitting by a fireplace in a cabin. An undated woodcut showing two female slaves sitting by a fireplace in a slave shanty near Petersburg, Virginia. Plantation economies in America rarely maintained a strict gendered division of labor. In many locations, women could be found working in the fields along with the men. *© Bettman/Corbis.*

while the women "cooked, sewed, did housework, and at times were employed as nurses" (1911, p. 41). Writing about slavery in Mississippi, Charles Sydnor commented that "it is noticeable that indoor occupations of the men and women differed rather widely" as women performed spinning, weaving and making or mending clothes while men shelled corn or repaired equipment. Sydnor explained, however, that "outdoors the women and boys were occasionally . . . assigned the lighter tasks. But women seem usually to have done about as much plowing as men and on one large estate did most of this work" (1933, p. 12).

While support for slavery appeared in gendered terms, so did challenges that focused on the ill effects of slavery on the family. Many abolitionists concentrated on the assault adulterous relationships between black women and white men raised to the family. George Bourne stated that the slave states "are one vast brothel, in which multiform incest, polygamy, adultery, and other uncleanness are constantly perpetrated" (1837, p. 27). Bourne, like others, defended the integrity of the family because it was "the appointed school for the discipline of the race" ("Native of the Southwest," p. 13). Bourne's solution to this issues rested on southern white women, as only through their initiative could the bonds of slavery be shattered. An analysis of works by both those for and those against slavery, it is evident that gender roles were central to the creation and dissolution of American slavery.

BIBLIOGRAPHY

Bourne, George. *Slavery Illustrated in Its Effects upon Women and Domestic Society.* Boston, 1837.

Brown, Kathleen M. *Good Wives, Nasty Wenches, and Anxious Patriarchs.* Chapel Hill: University of North Carolina Press, 1996.

"Native of the Southwest." *The Family and Slavery.* Cincinnati, OH, n.d.

Scully, Pamela, and Diana Paton, eds. *Gender and Slave Emancipation in the Atlantic World.* Durham, NC: Duke University Press, 2005.

Sydnor, Charles Sackett. *Slavery in Mississippi.* New York, 1933.

Turner, Edward Raymond. *The Negro in Pennsylvania: Slavery—Servitude—Freedom, 1639–1861.* Washington, DC, 1911.

Damian Nemirovsky

SEXUALITY AND REPRODUCTION

The experience of bondage for slave women was largely distinguished from that of slave men by the commodification of sexuality and reproduction. Each time an enslaved woman gave birth, the slaveholder acquired additional human property. This fact gave rise to a deeply gendered system of slavery. Just like slave men, slave women were expected to work, often performing arduous labor. But where slaveholders most valued the brawn of slave men and their ability to perform back-breaking physical labor, masters were most concerned with the fertility of slave women. According to historian Deborah Gray White, "Once slaveholders realized that the reproductive function of the female slave could yield a profit, the manipulation of procreative sexual relations became an integral part of the sexual exploitation of female slaves" (1985, p. 68).

Some male slaveholders coerced sexual relationships with slave women and increased their capital by fathering slaves. But slaveholders tried other ways to manipulate what they considered their reproductive domain, though slaves' efforts to preserve sexual and reproductive autonomy meant that these were areas over which the master-slave power dynamic was constantly being renegotiated.

Such was the case for Harriet Jacobs, who famously lived in her grandmother's garret for seven years to avoid sexual assault from the man who owned her. The harassment Jacobs endured began when she was fifteen and the man, represented in her narrative as Dr. Flint, began whispering obscenities in her ear and passing her licentious notes. When Jacobs wanted to marry a free man, Flint responded, "I'll soon convince you whether I am your master" and decreed that if Jacobs was determined to marry, she should marry one of Flint's male slaves (Jacobs [1861] 1987, p. 39). As a free man, Jacobs's fiancé lived beyond Flint's authority. Had she married another of Flint's slaves, Jacobs would have been further in the power of the slaveholder, who wanted to seclude her in a cabin and make her his concubine. According to Jacobs, Flint "claimed the right to rule me body and soul" (p. 38). But it was also her submission Flint wanted. And by maintaining control of her sexuality, Jacobs denied Flint's authority. Seeing marriage as an impossibility, she entered a sexual relationship with a local white politician. She later reflected, "If slavery had been abolished, I, also, could have married the man of my choice; I could have had a home shielded by the laws." But as that was not the case, Jacobs found, "There is something akin to freedom in having a lover who has no control over you, except what he gains by kindness and attachment" (p. 55). By her own characterization, Jacobs's affair was a careful political calculation that allowed her to exert agency against Flint by preserving her sexual autonomy. Before long, though, she was the mother of two children, both legally Flint's property. And to her struggle for personal autonomy was added her struggle for the care and protection of her children.

As with Flint, who had refused Jacobs's request for marriage to a free man and ordered her to choose a husband from among his slaves, slaveholders felt it within their purview to regulate marital relations of slaves, usually by granting or withholding permission for courtship or marriage. In Hannah Crafts's *The Bondwoman's Narrative*, the imminent coerced marriage of the narrator precipitates her decision to run away. But such cases were rare. As historian Marie Jenkins

Schwartz noted, "The extensive effort that would have been required to force sexual partners upon slaves and ensure that the couple stayed together deterred all but the most ardent of would-be breeders." But knowledge that pairings were occasionally coerced, however infrequently, "worried slaves and pushed them into early marriages of their own making, rather than marriages arranged by their owners" (2000, p. 188).

Even then, the fact that marriage between slaves had no legal sanction meant that the union could be broken up. Suggesting the degree to which the sexuality of the married couple was commodified, Annie Burton recalled that where she spent her enslaved childhood, if no children were born within the first year of a marriage, slave couples usually were separated by the sale of one or both slaves.

Because slaveholders profited from the labor as well as the fertility of female slaves and because arduous labor threatened the health and stamina of expectant mothers, the work routines of pregnant women became a major point of concern. According to Marie Jenkins Schwartz, "the desire to increase their human property and to appear humane made owners reluctant to deny pregnant slaves relief from difficult work assignments for fear they would miscarry or produce a sickly or stillborn baby" (2000, p. 27). But cases where women failed to produce a child—either after falsely claiming pregancy or failing to report a miscarriage—led most owners to wait until the advanced stages of pregnancy, when imminent childbirth was clearly visible, to lighten workloads. And even then, slaveholders had differing ideas about what constitued heavy labor. The families of expectant women could negotiate the terms of treatment either by running away or refusing to work until slaveholders agreed to accommodations. But the reduced workloads had to be renegotiated with each instance of pregnancy.

Similarly, breastfeeding tended to interrupt the work routines of new mothers, who had to remain close to their nursing infants. This meant that during daylight hours mothers either had to be assigned work that allowed them to remain close to their infants or, for those mothers assigned fieldwork, that babies had to be carried to the field and nursed during scheduled periods of rest. Slaveholders generally preferred that children be weaned as soon as possible, usually between the ages of eight months and one year. Some imposed daytime regulations on the practice, particularly for fieldworkers. In another instance, Harriet Jacobs recalled that her mother, a twin, had been weaned at three months old so that Jacobs's grandmother could provide sufficient nourishment for her mistress's baby, whom she also nursed. More often, though, slaveholders' practice of withholding family rations for children under the age of two, meant that "many—probably most—mothers found it desirable to continue breastfeeding a baby through the child's second year" (p. 68).

The physical demands of labor and childbearing exacted a toll on the bodies of slave women, as Frances Kemble, an English native married to Georgia planter Pierce Butler, recorded in her journal. Chief among the entreaties of Butler's slaves was the extension of mothers' lying-in time after the birth of a child. The rule and custom of the plantation required that women return to their field labor three weeks after giving birth. After observing Kemble's own "tenderly watched confinement and convalescence" the slave women requested an additional week of recuperation before their mandatory return to hoeing the fields, a request Butler denied. Kemble also recorded a catalog of the women's gynecological complications and noted the high mortality rate of their childen: Fanny gave birth to six children, of whom only one survived; Nanny had three children, two of whom died; Leah, six children, three of whom died; Sophy, ten children, five of whom died; and Sally, in addition to two miscarriages, gave birth to three children, one of whom died. Kemble wrote of the slave women, "I think the number they bear as compared with the number they rear a fair gauge of the effect of the system on their own health and that of their offspring" (1984, p. 231).

To remedy these effects, many slaves took steps to regulate their own fertility. As most bondpeople highly valued children and motherhood, their efforts were not meant to prevent pregnancy altogether but to space pregnancies far enough apart that they did not "exhaust [mothers'] strength or interfere with their ability to care for older children" (Schwartz 2006, p. 94). Prolonged breastfeeding provided for the nuture of infants but was also understood to reduce the possibility of additional pregnancy, though its specific role in supressing ovulation was not known. Despite slaveholders' insistence on early weaning, slave mothers were likely to continue nursing their children in private until the age of two or beyond. In addition, many plants were known to have useful medicinal qualities. The root of the widely available cotton plant, as well as dogwood or dog-fennel root, could be chewed or boiled into a tea to induce menstruation. Slave women employed these herbal medicines to prevent conception or cause miscarriage. When they wanted to become pregnant, they simply ceased the treatments. Slaveholders attempted to quash the practice by punishing women found to employ these methods of reproductive control, but masters had a difficult time regulating what was largely practiced in secret.

BIBLIOGRAPHY

Burton, Annie. *Memories of Childhood's Slavery Days* [1909]. Chapel Hill: University of North Carolina, 1996.

Clinton, Catherine. *The Plantation Mistress: Woman's World in the Old South*. New York: Pantheon Books, 1982.

Crafts, Hannah. *The Bondwoman's Narrative,* ed. Henry Louis Gates, Jr. New York: Warner Books, 2002.

Jacobs, Harriet A. *Incidents in the Life of a Slave Girl* [1861], ed. Jean Fagan Yellin. Cambridge, MA: Harvard University Press, 1987.

Kemble, Frances. *Journal of a Residence on a Georgian Plantation in 1838–1839,* ed. John A. Scott. Athens, GA: University of Georgian Press, 1984.

Schwartz, Marie Jenkins. *Born in Bondage: Growing Up Enslaved in the Antebellum South*. Cambridge, MA: Harvard University, 2000.

Schwartz, Marie Jenkins. *Birthing a Slave: Motherhood and Medicine in the Antebellum South*. Cambridge, MA: Harvard University Press, 2006.

White, Deborah, Gray. *Ar'n't I a Woman?: Female Slaves in the Plantation South*. New York: W. W. Norton, 1999.

Christina Adkins

GIFT EXCHANGE

Cultural anthropologists and sociologists specializing in gift studies have long been interested in the socioeconomic importance of practices of giving, receiving, and reciprocating. The field owes a great debt to Marcel Mauss (1872–1950), who, in *The Gift: The Form and Reason for Exchange in Archaic Societies* (1925), argued that prestations and counter-prestations (including the exchange of ceremonies and feasts), particularly in societies and cultures without formal economic markets, formed complete social systems in their own rights. More recently, scholars such as Mark Osteen (2002) have examined the motives and meanings behind money and material exchanges, arguing that they are the building blocks of social life and interaction.

These activities call for particular attention from historians of slavery in the United States. Certainly, several scholars have focused on how, during the Christmas season, slaveholders bestowed feasts, presents, and days off from labor upon slaves. Yet, as authors Shauna Bigham and Robert E. May have observed, those historians have also "treated Christmas celebrations as one of several manifestations of planter paternalism" (1998, p. 265). To focus merely on one-way channels of gift-giving is to overlook not only the meanings Christmas held for slaves, but also the extent to which slaves themselves exchanged gifts with one another on holidays and other occasions. Indeed, an analysis of these rites can offer insight into the social, cultural, and economic lives and influence of Africans and their descendants in the United States.

For many enslaved blacks, gift-giving and commodity exchanges were instrumental to the building and maintenance of their social ties and contributed in important ways to the stability of their communities. In her essay on slaves' constructions of masculinity and ethnicity in French colonial New Orleans, for example, Sophie White shows how male slaves in the region could steal and distribute clothing in order to cement social relationships, especially with the women in their lives. "Thus," according to White, "in the case against Jupiter belonging to Sr Pradel, and Alexandre belonging to Sr Dumanoir, they each admitted to giving items of apparel to their mistresses, claiming to be motivated by the desire for sexual favors" (Gunning, Hunter, and Mitchell 2004, p. 136).

Although White's analysis is based on an examination of eighteenth- and nineteenth-century criminal cases, male slaves in the United States gained access to desirable goods through other means as well. With enslaved families frequently forced to live on separate plantations, many husbands and fathers nurtured ties to their wives and children by bestowing gifts upon them. Van Moore, who as a child had been kept as a slave on a plantation in Galveston, Texas, recalled a time when his father visited his family from a neighboring plantation. "He rid all the way on a mule, carryin' a wallet what was thrown over de back of de mule like a pack saddle, and he gives it to mammy. You know what was in dat wallet? He brung a coon and possum and some corn dodger, 'cause he thinks we don't have 'nough to eat down there" (*Born in Slavery*, Texas Narratives, vol. 16, part 3).

Men who were unable to deliver such goods in person could find other ways to send gifts to their families, thanks in large part to individuals known as "runners" who made trips back and forth between plantations. According to one former slave's recollection, "If [the husband and father] was smart enough to have a little garden or make little things like little chairs for his chillum to sit in or tables for 'em to eat on and wanted you to have 'em fore he could get back to see you, they would be sent by the runner" (*Born in Slavery*, Georgia Narratives, vol. 4, part 4). For these men, gift-giving provided a way for them to act as patriarchs and heads of the household, even when they could not reside in or operate traditional households with their wives and children.

As recipients of such gifts, enslaved women (who slaveholders certainly defined by their capacities for reproduction and labor) were able to adapt notions of femininity to their own realities. And while they may not have had the same access to material goods as their male counterparts, many female slaves used the skills and resources that were available to them to nurture ties to their loved ones. According to historian Jacqueline Jones, "while the act of cooking might not differ in a technical sense when performed for blacks as opposed to whites, it certainly assumed heightened emotional significance for the black women involved, and, when carried out in such subversive ways, political significance for social relations on the plantation" (1986, p. 31).

In considering the ways in which slaves cultivated and maintained social ties through gift exchanges, one can add texture to their understanding of how African American men and women responded to the limitations slaveholders imposed upon them. Moreover, by paying attention to gift exchanges, one can see how slaves understood, adapted to, and even challenged ideas about labor, family, and gender.

BIBLIOGRAPHY

Bigham, Shauna, and Robert E. May. "The Time O' All Times? Masters, Slaves, and Christmas in the Old South." *Journal of the Early Republic* 18, no. 2 (Summer 1998): 263–288.

Born in Slavery: Slave Narratives from the Federal Writers' Project, 1936–1938, Library of Congress. Georgia Narratives, vol. 4, part 4. Available from http://memory.loc.gov.

Born in Slavery: Slave Narratives from the Federal Writers' Project, 1936–1938, Library of Congress. Texas Narratives, vol. 16, part 3. Available from http://memory.loc.gov.

Gunning, Sandra; Tera W. Hunter; and Michele Mitchell, eds. *Dialogues of Dispersal: Gender, Sexuality, and African Diasporas.* Malden, MA: Blackwell, 2004.

Jones, Jacqueline. *Labor of Love, Labor of Sorrow: Black Women, Work, and the Family from Slavery to Present.* New York: Vintage, 1986.

Mauss, Marcel. *The Gift: the Form and Reason for Exchange in Archaic Societies* [1925]. Trans. W. D. Halls. New York: Norton, 1990.

Osteen, Mark, ed. *The Question of the Gift: Essays across Disciplines.* New York: Routledge, 2002.

Tamara Walker

COURTSHIP AND MARRIAGE

Marriage among slaves was permitted at the discretion of owners, sometimes arranged by them, and sometimes simply forbidden. For slaves who were allowed to marry, their status was neither respected nor sanctioned by law because they were the property of their owners. Some slaveholders, however—usually those with strict religious beliefs—encouraged their slaves to be monogamous and marry in the eyes of God.

Slaves had little time and even less freedom for courting. When slaveholders did not choose mates for their slaves, those slaves could select from among the owner's other "holdings" or sometimes from the slaves of nearby or neighboring estates. If a slave chose to court someone on another homestead, he or she was required to get permission to visit on weekends and holidays. Slaveholders who believed that a happy slave was a productive slave would not

A slave marriage ceremony, circa 1800s. Marriage among slaves was permitted at the discretion of masters, sometimes arranged by them and sometimes forbidden. *© Bettman/Corbis.*

only agree to the courtship but try to buy the intended bride or groom.

Courtship was generally brief, with the exchange of small gifts or poems for those who could read and write, and visits among the families. Ex-slave Rhodus Walton recollected courtship on a Georgia plantation to an interviewer, who noted that "gifts to one's sweetheart were not permitted, but verses such as: 'Roses are red / Violets are blue / I don't love / No one but you' were invariably recited to loved ones. Young negro men always 'cocked' their hats on one side of their heads when they became interested in the other sex" (*Born in Slavery*, Georgia Narratives, vol. 4, part 4, p. 124).

Camilla Jackson, born in Decatur, Georgia, was owned by Dr. Peter Hoyle, a deeply religious man who considered courtship and marriage a sacred rite. Camilla recited her story: "Dr. Hoyle never selected the mates for his slaves but left it to each person to choose whomever he wished . . . from among the slaves on some of his friends' plantations. The person

chosen was allowed to call on Sundays after getting a 'pass' from his master. A young man courted the girl in the presence of her parents. . . . When the master was notified of the intended marriage, he would prepare a feast and call in his own preacher to perform the ceremony" (*Born in Slavery*, Georgia Narratives, vol. 4, Part 2, p. 296).

Some slave owners who scorned the notion of courtship and marriage among slaves took a different approach. Their goal was simply to keep up male slaves' spirits (and thus enhance their ability to work) by arranging to satisfy their sexual needs. John Campbell, a self-proclaimed researcher of the races, referred to "an intelligent American planter" who told him "that he had found the most beneficial effects from the judicious admixture of a proportion of one 'lively wench' to five males in a gang" (Campbell 1851, p. 493).

Slaveholders who chose mates for their slaves usually based the decision on convenience or productivity.

They considered females from twelve to fifteen years old and males thirteen or older of marrying age. Some owners chose mates simply because the slave was old enough, some out of spite (knowing a slave had feelings for someone else), and some in view of the potential progeny, matching the strongest males with the hardiest females. Berry Clay explained: "Courtships were very brief, for as soon as a man or woman began to manifest interest in the opposite sex, the master busied himself to select a wife or husband and only in rare cases was the desire of the individual considered. When the selection was made, the master read the ceremony and gave them a home. He always requested, or rather demanded, that they be fruitful. A barren woman was usually separated from her husband and sold" (*Born in Slavery*, Georgia Narratives, vol. 4, pt. 1, p. 191).

Marriage ceremonies varied from a few spoken words to an actual service and celebratory feast. Some slave owners took marriage vows seriously, bringing in a justice of the peace to issue a marriage license. Others performed the rites themselves, reciting a few sentences, then having the couple jump over a broom. Peter and Lavinia Still's marriage in Alabama was recounted by Kate E. R. Pickard, a friend and teacher in the region: "Old Cato Hodge, a Baptist preacher belonging to one of the neighbors, performed the ceremony. That over, a merry company, consisting of all Vina's fellow-servants, and a few of Peter's best friends from his master's plantation, enjoyed a substantial supper in the kitchen" (Pickard 1856, p. 112). Other marriages were far less ceremonious. Alice Wright, a slave born in Taylor County, Kentucky, discussed her father's choice of a bride: "My father tended the white folks' mules … When he married my mother, he was only fifteen years old. His master told him to go pick himself out a wife from a drove of slaves that were passing through, and he picked out my mother. They married by stepping over a broom. The old master pronounced them as master and wife" (*Born in Slavery*, Arkansas Narratives, vol. 2, pt. 7, p. 245).

Marriages offered a secure refuge for some slaves. But few marriages were allowed to thrive, as couples were frequently separated at slave markets and their children sent to homesteads throughout the South. Very few slaves grew up with two parents.

BIBLIOGRAPHY

Born in Slavery: Slave Narratives from the Federal Writers' Project, 1936–1938. Manuscript Division, Library of Congress. Arkansas Narratives, vol. 2, part 7. Available from http://memory.loc.gov.

Born in Slavery: Slave Narratives from the Federal Writers' Project, 1936–1938. Florida Narratives, vol. 3. Available from http://memory.loc.gov.

Born in Slavery: Slave Narratives from the Federal Writers' Project, 1936–1938. Georgia Narratives, vol. 4, parts 2 and 4. Available from http://memory.loc.gov.

Campbell, John. *Negro-mania: Being an Examination of the Falsely Assumed Equality of the Various Races of Men*. Philadelphia, 1851.

Pickard, Kate E. R. *The Kidnapped and the Ransomed: Being the Personal Recollections of Peter Still and His Wife "Vina," After Forty Years of Slavery*. 3rd ed. Syracuse, NY, 1856.

Nelson Rhodes

CONFLICT BETWEEN SLAVES

For decades, historians have stressed slaves' ability to overcome adversity through their reliance on religion, family, and culture. Conflict nevertheless wracked the slave community from the introduction of American slavery to its abolition. Rivalries and mistrust routinely disrupted the harmony and solidarity of the quarters. Such conflicts played an ambiguous role in the lives of slaves, both constituting and corroding their sense of community.

A number of cleavages among bondpeople had the potential to shatter the unity of the slave community. During the colonial period, Philip D. Morgan observed, "Frictions among African ethnic groups or between Africans and creoles" pitted some slaves against their fellow bondpeople (1998, p. 614). Other divisions persisted after the closing of the transatlantic slave trade. Although bondpeople conferred status on skilled slave craftsmen, preachers, and conjurors, others did not earn such universal respect. On the largest plantations, occupational stratification fostered distinctions among slaves. Domestic servants at times considered themselves the so-called slave aristocracy and adopted an attitude of superiority toward their counterparts laboring in the fields. Field slaves might reciprocate by regarding house servants with resentment, suspicion, and mistrust for appearing too closely allied with the master. Likewise, the occupational hierarchy slaves constructed held black drivers in low esteem. Appointed by some slaveholders, especially in the Carolina Lowcountry, slave drivers found themselves in the psychologically ungratifying position of having to enforce the master's dictates by directing the labor of bound family, friends, and acquaintances, wielding the whip as necessary. Drivers who too eagerly did the master's bidding risked ostracism in the slave quarters. Conflicts resulted not only from occupational fissures, however, but also from skin color. Lighter-skinned slaves (who were also more likely to serve as house servants) sometimes internalized white standards by ranking themselves superior to

West Indies as They Are. An engraving from Richard Bickell's 1825 book *West Indies as They Are* depicts male slaves holding down a female slave and beating her as the master looks on. In some areas, such as the Carolina Lowcountry, black slave drivers found themselves in the position of having to enforce the master's rules and dole out punishments. © *Corbis.*

darker-skinned slaves, although Eugene D. Genovese emphasized that "more fraternity than hostility" marked their relations (1976, p. 429).

In part, conflicts among slaves determined the contours of a particular slave community. The domestic slave trade routinely disrupted slave communities and necessitated continual social re-creation. Newcomers needed to earn their welcome into a new plantation family. Henry Haynes' newly purchased slave woman "quarreled with the other Negroes" in the quarters and hence remained a perpetual outsider (Johnson 1999, p. 196). Slaves who too frequently shirked work by feigning illness, repeatedly thrusting greater burdens of work on their comrades, might also become outcasts; so too might bondpeople who betrayed their fellows by informing the master of slave thefts, conspiracies, or other crimes. As outsiders, fugitive slaves might not automatically expect sympathy or assistance from enslaved strangers they encountered during flight.

Verbal quarrels and physical confrontations erupted frequently in the quarters. Many slaves recalled that, as children, they ate from a common trough filled with corn bread and sweet milk or clabber. Slave children jostled with their peers to fill their bellies and engaged in other scraps typical of childhood, often simply for sport. As adults, slave men challenged one another to physical contests. Masters seemed to delight in the spectacle. Some even orchestrated more formalized violence among slaves, wagering on wrestling and boxing matches that pitted slaves from one plantation against their enslaved neighbors.

Adult female and male slaves committed violent acts of their own accord as well. One slave recalled "his mother and another woman ... fighting over their children," while another remembered that a "woman cussed my mother and it made her mad and they had a fight" (Rawick 1977, vol. 7, pt. 2, p. 732; vol. 7, p. 94). Among antebellum whites, slave women gained a reputation for frequently committing infanticide, but these reports were wildly exaggerated. Far more evidence survives documenting the violence of slave men. Drunkenness often played a role in such violent confrontations. Fights erupted at dances and frolics—wherever liquor flowed freely. Urban slaves had somewhat greater access to alcohol than rural bondpeople, yet slaves in the countryside imbibed with the master's consent at cornshuckings, logrollings, and other events in the agricultural calendar, clandestinely at many other times. Slaves' brief taste of liberty, their ability to travel and pursue leisurely pastimes, and their relative lack of physical exhaustion meant that Saturday nights, the Sabbath, and holidays hosted most of the violent contests among slaves. Weekend gambling, one slave admitted, prompted "disagreement[s] wid a few fights" (vol. 9, pt. 4, p. 1,433).

Slaves often fell out over property disputes. Most bondpeople lacked any secret or safe repository for their possessions, so any cash or valuable commodities were vulnerable to theft. In South Carolina, the bondman Wiley reportedly stole "some Tobacco and half a dollar in mony" from another slave. George smote Sam fatal blows with an axe after Sam accused him of "taking his hammer," and Toney struck Dick after Dick accused him of stealing "more leather than his back could pay for." "In Georgia," wrote Genovese, "a blacksmith killed a fellow slave for stealing the keys to his shop" (p. 607). Like male slaves, enslaved girls and women clashed over the possession of goods as well. In Mississippi, one slave girl jealously guarded her dresses by force, while a slave woman became angry when her spouse gave her clothes to "other gals fer to dance in" (Rawick 1977, vol. 7, pt. 2, p. 623; vol. 7, p. 163). The theft of foodstuffs prompted harsh reprisal. Three bondpeople in South Carolina attacked J. W. Norris's slaves over some stolen bacon, while slaves John and Dave accosted Dan for stealing corn. In both of these instances, slaves relied on violence as a means of self-preservation. The theft of bacon or corn threatened to reduce their own rations, so slaves willingly fought to safeguard their provisions. To avoid punishment for the loss of pilfered goods, slaves also defended masters' property even if it had no immediate value to them. Six slaves in South Carolina ran off another bondman named Ned lurking about their master's blacksmith shop trying to steal iron. Slaves also engaged in violent confrontations over the repayment of debts they had contracted with one another. Amos and Andrew, for instance, "fell out about a debt" incurred in the purchase of bread.

In addition to economic matters, issues of love and family sparked violent confrontations among slaves. Slave men vied with one another for desirable bondwomen at home or on nearby plantations. Two South Carolina slaves fought because they were both apparently in love with the same woman, while another male slave thrashed a competing admirer about the face with a switch of grapevine to warn him away from his beloved. After North Carolina bondwoman Dicey refused to let Edmund court her daughter Deely, the despondent slave slit the protective mother's throat.

Despite their lack of force in law, slave marriages were widely recognized as fact by both masters and slaves. Yet domestic quarrels sometimes disrupted the harmony of the slave cabin. Some slave men employed spousal abuse to affirm and maintain their position as head of the household, and masters created an environment conducive to domestic violence when they matched slave couples with callous disregard for the bondpeople's personal preferences. One Alabama slave remembered that the overseer "useta whip mammy an' pappy, 'ca'se day fight so much" (Rawick 1977, vol. 6, p. 216).

Slave men used violence to protect and defend the women they claimed as their own and to jealously guard slave women against the sexual overtures of other bondmen. Nelson struck fellow North Carolina slave Gabriel a mortal blow with a fence rail after the latter insulted his wife. In South Carolina, one slave struck another with a large stick because he felt the man was bothering his wife. But slave men could not provide foolproof protection, if the slave women in question even wanted it. Adultery marked a leading cause of marital difficulties for slave couples, and cuckolded slave men often craved revenge against the slave interloper. A slave named George in South Carolina found himself in the middle of several conflicts at once. At the same time a slave named Tom sought revenge against George for breaking up Tom's marriage, a bondman named Ed also accosted George, pulling a pistol on him because George was sleeping with Ed's wife. Cases of adultery also drove enraged slave wives to violence. A Baptist church in South Carolina disciplined bondwoman Betsey for striking her cheating husband.

Masters disapproved of conflicts and fights in the quarters, which jeopardized plantation harmony and produced unwelcome economic effects. Injured slaves might require time off work, not labor as quickly or efficiently, or lose monetary value if their wounds proved serious enough. One Georgia slave described the rules on many plantations when he reported, "We were not even allowed to quarrel among ourselves" (Rawick 1977, vol. 12, pt. 2, p. 75). When fights did erupt, masters drew upon a number of punishments: placing transgressing slaves in stocks or chains, locking them in a gin house or other outbuilding, or, most frequently, whipping them. If conflicts among slaves produced a permanent disability, a severe maiming, or death, and especially if the combatants belonged to different masters, the aggrieved slaveholder might seek redress through the Southern court system. Slaves put on trial for crimes against fellow bondpeople stood better odds than if the victim were white. A guilty verdict was not automatic, and those convicted typically escaped with a whipping and/or short jail term. In Georgia, slaves accused of murder of another bondperson were typically found guilty of the lesser charge of manslaughter and punished through a combination of lashes and branding.

Across the South, transportation out-of-state and executions proved exceptionally rare when slaves were both the perpetrator and the victim of the crime.

BIBLIOGRAPHY

Genovese, Eugene D. *Roll, Jordan, Roll: The World the Slaves Made*. New York: Vintage, 1976.

Griffin, Rebecca. "Courtship Contests and the Meaning of Conflict in the Folklore of Slaves." *Journal of Southern History* 71 (November 2005): 769–802.

Harper, C. W. "Black Aristocrats: Domestic Servants on the Antebellum Plantation." *Phylon* 46 (June 1985): 123–135.

Harper, C. W. "House Servants and Field Hands: Fragmentation in the Antebellum Slave Community." *North Carolina Historical Review* 55 (January 1978): 42–59.

Johnson, Michael P. "Runaway Slaves and the Slave Communities in South Carolina, 1799 to 1830." *William & Mary Quarterly* 38 (July 1981): 418–441.

Johnson, Michael P. "Smothered Slave Infants: Were Slave Mothers at Fault?" *Journal of Southern History* 47 (November 1981): 493–520.

Johnson, Michael P. "Work, Culture, and the Slave Community: Slave Occupations in the Cotton Belt in 1860." *Labor History* 27 (Summer 1986): 325–355.

Johnson, Walter. *Soul by Soul: Life Inside the Antebellum Slave Market*. Cambridge, MA: Harvard University Press, 1999.

Kaye, Anthony E. "Neighbourhoods and Solidarity in the Natchez District of Mississippi: Rethinking the Antebellum Slave Community." *Slavery & Abolition* 23 (April 2002): 1–24.

Kolchin, Peter. *American Slavery, 1619–1877*. New York: Hill and Wang, 1993.

Kolchin, Peter. "Reevaluating the Antebellum Slave Community: A Comparative Perspective." *Journal of American History* 70 (December 1983): 579–601.

McDonnell, Lawrence T. "Money Knows No Master: Market Relations and the American Slave Community." In *Developing Dixie: Modernization in a Traditional Society*, ed. Winfred B. Moore, Jr., Joseph F. Tripp, and Lyon G. Tyler. Westport, CT: Greenwood Press, 1988.

Morgan, Philip D. *Slave Counterpoint: Black Culture in the Eighteenth-Century Chesapeake and Lowcountry*. Chapel Hill: University of North Carolina Press, 1998.

Morris, Christopher. "Within the Slave Cabin: Violence in Mississippi Slave Families." In *Over the Threshold: Intimate Violence in Early America*, ed. Christine Daniels and Michael V. Kennedy. New York: Routledge, 1999.

Penningroth, Dylan C. *The Claims of Kinfolk: African American Property and Community in the Nineteenth-Century South*. Chapel Hill: University of North Carolina Press, 2003.

Penningroth, Dylan C. "My People, My People: The Dynamics of Community in Southern Slavery." In *New Studies in the History of American Slavery*, ed. Edward E. Baptist and Stephanie M. H. Camp. Athens: University of Georgia Press, 2006.

Rawick, George P., ed. *The American Slave: A Composite Autobiography*. 19 vols. Westport, CT: Greenwood Publishing Company, 1972.

Rawick, George P., ed. *The American Slave: A Composite Autobiography, Supp., Series 1*. 12 vols. Westport, CT: Greenwood Press, 1977.

Stevenson, Brenda. "Distress and Discord in Virginia Slave Families, 1830–1860." In *In Joy and in Sorrow: Women, Family, and Marriage in the Victorian South, 1830–1900,* ed. Carol Bleser. New York: Oxford University Press, 1991.

Stevenson, Brenda. *Life in Black and White: Family and Community in the Slave South*. New York: Oxford University Press, 1996.

West, Emily. "Tensions, Tempers, and Temptations: Marital Discord Among Slaves in Antebellum South Carolina." *American Nineteenth Century History* 5 (Summer 2004): 1–18.

Jeff Forret

■ Relationships between Masters and Slaves

POOR WHITES
Jeff Forret

FREE BLACKS
Jocelyn M. Cuffee

RELATIONSHIPS BETWEEN MASTERS AND SLAVES: AN OVERVIEW

Masters and slaves in the Old South were never separate entities. "They belong to us. We also belong to them," wrote Rev. John Adger: "They are divided out among us and mingled up with us and we with them in a thousand ways" (1998, p. 167). Bound by conflict and common purpose both, linked by powerful, insolubly contradictory emotions of love and hate, blacks in bondage and whites who held them in thralldom derived economic and political status, social identity, and cultural and moral imperatives from the struggle they waged against each other. Historians still violently disagree over the character of this conflict, and have not nearly begun to explain its trajectory with regard to time and place. Virtually all, however, agree that the national political conflict that eventuated in civil war in 1861 had its foundation in the ambivalences of the master-slave relation.

Certainly there was nothing distinctly American—much less southern—about that bond before the antebellum era. Slavery is a system of social organization and labor control found in virtually all cultures across the past two millennia. Though commonly employing ritual mechanisms of denigration or social death, there is nothing essentially racial about the peculiar institution as it existed in the American South or elsewhere. Indeed, the forced importation and sale of Africans was resorted to only as a consequence of the failure of white indentured servitude and enslavement of Native Americans. Initially, free, indentured, and enslaved workers of various races labored alongside each other in the seventeenth-century Chesapeake, and even more complex and overlapping social identities emerged in the decades before secession. In general, however, relations between masters and slaves in America between 1620 and 1865 fall into two broad political categories: the so-called warfare state and the regime of paternalist hegemony.

The Warfare State

That naked antagonism should govern the terms of bondage seemed perfectly obvious to both blacks and whites throughout the colonial era. Southern planters were economic men-on-the-make, risking heavily in hopes of turning big profits fast. Treatment of slaves necessarily involved a complex cost-benefit analysis, shaped both by considerations of bondpeople as social capital and tokens of honor, and by pragmatic political calculations. Working hands hard in the fields and cutting costs to near subsistence level promised rich rewards. But pushing slaves too hard might send them over the brink into violence and rebellion. Legal codes and daily practice reflected colonial planters' unrelenting search for the limits to their mastery, hemming in black self-activity, curbing access to the Gospel, and complicating private projects of emancipation. Again and again, overlords fell back on the tools of open violence to secure subservience, beating and mutilating slaves, raping and selling them, and murdering their human chattel in a dozen legal and horrifying fashions.

Slave conspiracies, uprisings, and acts of day-to-day resistance punctuated early American history, culminating in the Stono revolt in South Carolina in 1739 and the plot—real or imagined—to burn New York in 1741. Hopeful blacks confounded white Revolutionary ideology during the War of Independence by insisting that any struggle for freedom and sovereignty necessarily involved them as well as their owners. Freedpeople from Crispus Attucks (c. 1723–1770) onward played an important, if marginalized, role in the patriot cause. Conversely, tens of thousands of enslaved blacks took heed of Lord Dunmore's Proclamation (1775), which offered freedom to slaves who joined Dunmore's army (although after his retreat, he resold them back into servitude). The Declaration of Independence itself, silent on slavery's place in the new republic it created, reflected the internal divisions and indecision within the planter class and its northern allies about how best to secure bondpeople to "good and faithful" labor. Increasingly, worried masters described their human chattel as the "Jacobins of the country," bent on murderous self-liberation. They sought to defeat such schemes through rigorous laws, harsh treatment, and fierce reprisals. Like ruling classes everywhere, however, slaveholders fretted whether the path of safety was one of tighter discipline or of gradual amelioration. When bondpeople in Haiti rose up in bloody—and successful—revolution in the 1790s, the days of the American slaveholding republic looked numbered as well. As Thomas Jefferson put the problem, Americans held the "wolf" of slavery "by the ears," and seemed unable either to hold it for long or to let it go.

Republican fears of creeping tyranny and a seemingly inevitable race war culminated in a two-pronged scheme to restrict slavery politically and geographically, eradicating it across the course of generations. From 1787 to 1819, state and federal lawmakers steadily barred slavery from Western territories and newly admitted states, simultaneously enacting provisions for gradual emancipation of bondpeople in the northern states. Equally important, they blocked access to fresh importations of Africans by closing the transatlantic slave trade to America after 1800 (though South Carolinian protests gained their state congressional dispensation to import slaves until 1808). Both parts of this strategy were predicated on whites' realistic calculation that the warfare state that existed eternally between masters and slaves could be reined in for a time, but never finally mitigated.

With no more blacks making the Middle Passage, slavery's ranks would gradually dwindle—all slave populations had shown a steady tendency to decline over time without fresh imports—, its territory would shrink, and eventually, effortlessly, bondage would disappear from the American republic.

The terrible irony was that, across the next three generations, slavery did not die. On the contrary, it exploded, both territorially and demographically. Jefferson's Louisiana Purchase of 1803 vaulted the peculiar institution across the Mississippi River and laid the basis for five decades of sectional controversy. More astounding still, between 1800 and 1860, the number of enslaved blacks in the United States did not dwindle—it quadrupled, from 1 to 4 million souls, outpacing the rate of population increase among whites and free blacks both. The sources of this remarkable, perplexing turn of events remain understudied, but leading slavery scholars to attribute it to changes in the political character of the master-slave relation itself, a shift from the so-called warfare state to what historian Eugene Genovese has called an ideology of paternalism.

Paternalism

Whereas colonial slavery essentially depended on the ability to beat blacks into submission, paternalism relied upon the political and psychological power of the blow that did not fall. Pre-revolutionary overlords had been tyrants in the truest sense, accepting—and demonstrating—few or no limits to their terrifying power. For eighteenth-century elites, steady profits and obedient labor, white and black, had provided ethic enough to justify this brutal course of action. By perhaps 1820, however, Anglo-American ruling classes had increasingly turned toward abstract equations of right, duty, and submission that denied class antagonism between rich and poor, slave and free, and described a harmonious—if rigorous—interaction that pleased God and served all. "That an inscrutable Providence will eventually work out [the slave's] moral elevation, through the agency of the white man, I have not a doubt," one master told the *Southern Cultivator*, "but it must be done by 'moral suasion,' coupled with a smart sprinkling of that great civilizer—the cow hide" (Hurricane 1860, p. 276). There were ethical limits to what overlords and underlings might demand from each other, a paternalist bargain of rewards and punishments, constantly renegotiated, that seized and surrendered measures of freedom in exchange for mites of order and security.

In justifying themselves to themselves, however, masters accorded slaves an elevated status and an enlarged sphere of rights and customs. Blacks were not brutes to be compelled and restrained by vigilance and violence, southerners now declared: They existed interdependently with their overlords, combining their brawn with the master's brain—and heart—to the mutual benefit of all.

The slave owed the master faithful labor and due submission under this scheme; the master provided all the gifts of law, material security, moral guidance, and managerial direction. Just as the bondman might err in a score of ways, including sloth, sauciness, willful obtuseness, or "drapetomania" (the supposed tendency of blacks to run away), masters might wrongly give way to tyrannous passions or an equally egregious spirit of inconsistent leniency. Though never realized in practice, and spelled out only in piecemeal fashion in political, agricultural, and religious documents of the antebellum era, paternalism held both master and man to a doctrine of reciprocal rights and duties.

Paternalism became pervasive especially in the seaboard South and on smaller slaveholding units where such personalism was unavoidable, not simply because of the material prosperity it generated. Cotton's kingdom made slaveholders incomparably the richest segment of the American ruling class, then or thereafter. It also materially improved the lives of slaves themselves over their colonial counterparts, as far as surviving evidence shows. Slave houses became more substantial and often larger. Black diets improved. Family units grew in size and complexity, marriages were more frequently respected, and many slaves managed to acquire skills, property, and even a smattering of education. Whites on occasion still betrayed jittery nerves about the possibility of massive slave revolt, but with the passage of time those fears came to seem increasingly unrealistic, not least because nothing more than the most disorganized, localized, and suicidal risings ever took place.

The success of paternalism as a political strategy, the failure of blacks to emancipate themselves through violence in the antebellum era, and the improvement of blacks' material lives under antebellum slavery all derive finally from the judicious and unrelenting struggle over the rightful limits of the masters' power. When planters portrayed themselves as good masters, blacks struggled to hold them to that ideal. In doing so, however, they were compelled to identify with the master, performing in rough outline the characteristics of the good slave. By a constant work of artifice, negotiation, bluff, and self-deception, masters and slaves struggled for hegemonic control of day-to-day life in the antebellum South.

It is inevitable and obvious that this political coupling of love and hate—real, feigned, self-contradictory, and half-realized—created enormous strife, tension, and torment among and between enslaved blacks and enslaving whites. Historians have done much to ponder—and avoid pondering—just what the master-slave relation cost Americans and how it shaped generations to come. For Ulrich Phillips, a pioneer of modern slavery studies, bondage was usually mild and educative for blacks; it was white masters who were truly liberated by emancipation. Writing forty years later, Kenneth Stampp accentuated the enduring brutality of slavery, suggesting that nothing like a paternalist bargain was ever played out in practical terms. Indeed, writers such as Stanley Elkins and Willie Lee Rose chimed in, the infantilization Phillips described and the cruelty Stampp discovered were two sides of the same coin: Slavery had been more horrific than elites let on, and the consequences left blacks scarred, socially, culturally, and psychologically, long after emancipation. In response to this damning—and depressing—indictment, an outraged circle of white and black liberal researchers described how slaves avoided cultural damage by creating their own world of the slave community beyond the master's control, where a countervailing ethos reigned from sundown to sunup. Most complex of all has been Genovese's view, detailed in *Roll, Jordan, Roll* (1974), that paternalism did spread broadly across the South by the 1850s, and that it exacted perilous costs and yielded ambiguous benefits to both blacks and whites, ultimately leading to secession and civil war.

Nothing like consensus currently exists among scholars on these questions, and much closer consideration of the warfare state, paternalism, and the transition between the two—if such indeed took place—is needed. Beyond these broad considerations, closer attention to how the master-slave relation was shaped by region, crop choice, farm unit size, race, gender, market access, and many other factors will focus research in years to come. Likewise, greater attention to questions of attachment and loss generated by object-relations theorists, kinship and property considered by anthropologists, and the formation of social movements, debated by political scientists and sociologists, will enrich discussion. Despite a century of research, scholarly understanding of the master-slave relation, its meanings, changes, and consequences, remains in its infancy.

BIBLIOGRAPHY

Adger, John B. *My Life and Times, 1810–1899* [1899]. Spartanburg, SC: Reprint Company, 1998.

Blassingame, John M. *The Slave Community: Plantation Life in the Antebellum South.* New York: Oxford University Press, 1979.

Elkins, Stanley M. *Slavery: A Problem in American Institutional and Intellectual Life.* Chicago: University of Chicago Press, 1959.

Genovese, Eugene D. *Roll, Jordan, Roll: The World the Slaves Made.* New York: Vintage, 1974.

Genovese, Eugene D. *The Slaveholders' Dilemma: Freedom and Progress in Southern Conservative Thought, 1820–1860.* Columbia: University of South Carolina Press, 1992.

Hurricane. "The Negro and His Management." *Southern Cultivator* 17 (1860): 276.

Morgan, Philip D. *Slave Counterpoint: Black Culture in the Eighteenth-Century Chesapeake and Low Country.* Chapel Hill: University of North Carolina Press, 1998.

Patterson, Orlando. *Slavery and Social Death: A Comparative Perspective.* Cambridge, MA: Harvard University Press, 1982.

Phillips, Ulrich B. *American Negro Slavery: A Survey of the Supply, Employment, and Control of Negro Labor as Determined by the Plantation Regime.* New York: D. Appleton, 1918.

Rose, Willie Lee. *Slavery and Freedom.* New York: Oxford University Press, 1982.

Stampp, Kenneth M. *The Peculiar Institution: Slavery in the Antebellum South.* New York: Vintage, 1956.

Lawrence T. McDonnell

THE MASTER

The meaning and power of the word *master* during the years of slavery perhaps depended on the character of those who bore the title. The various masters portrayed in a number of slave narratives and slave autobiographies evoke a range of emotions from admiration to utter disgust.

The Autobiography of a Female Slave (1857), a novel and pseudo-slave narrative written by Mattie Griffiths (d. 1906) to press the cause of abolition, is written in the voice of a slave girl called Ann. Griffiths was the owner, by inheritance, of six slaves. She hated the peculiar institution and moved north to get away from it. She details bondage under a master of horrific temperament and deeds. The reader is drawn to a place and time full of brutalities that no human being should have to endure. Before introducing the cruel master, however, the author provides a glimpse into the character of a kinder master. Life under the first master was ideal and very different from the life of most slaves in southern Kentucky. Ann (Griffiths) describes the first master, Mr. Nelson, as "a large venerable-looking man, with scanty, gray locks floating carelessly over an amplified forehead, a wide, hard featured face, with yet a kindly glow of honest sentiment; broad, strong teeth, much discolored by the continued use of tobacco"(p. 9). This master promised to give Ann "a good thrashing at some future period," but never did. Ann remembers that "as a token of good-will, he always presented us (the slave children) with a slice of buttered bread" (p. 9).

Ex-slave George Fleming expressed fond memories of his master: "I longed [belonged] to Marse Sam Fleming. Lawd chile, dat's de best white man what ever breathed de good air. ... On the plantation we lived jes' like a great family wid Marsa de daddy of 'em all. ... When any slaves got sick, Marse took care of em till they got well" (*Born in Slavery*, 2001, South Carolina Narratives, statement no. 2, n.p.). Henry Bibb (b. 1815), author of *Narrative of the Life and Adventures of Henry*

Labor Issues. A cartoon from 1824 showing a master relaxing and pontificating about labor issues while his slaves work in the fields. The slave holders are generally rich, aristocratic, overbearing; they look with utter contempt upon a poor laboring man, wrote Henry Bibb in Narrative of the Life and Adventures of Henry Bibb, An American Slave. *© Bettman/Corbis.*

Bibb, an American Slave (originally published in 1849), offers a less affectionate characterization of slaveholders (masters):

> The slaveholders [masters] are generally rich, aristocratic, overbearing; they look with utter contempt upon a poor laboring man, who earns his bread by the "sweat of his brow," whether he be moral or immoral, honest or dishonest. No matter whether he is white or black; if he performs manual labor for a livelihood, he is looked upon as being inferior to a slaveholder, and but little better off than the slave, who toils without wages under the lash. (1969, p. 25)

Griffiths writes, in *Autobiography of a Female Slave*, about her confusion over the master's lack of concern for maintaining slave families as a unit of support: "Why, I remember that when master sold the gray mare, the colt went also. Who could, who would, [and] who dared, separate the parent from her offspring?" (1857, p. 16). Perhaps if the author had not allowed the old, kindly master to die suddenly, the life of her main character would have taken on a different twist. The estate had to be settled and as a consequence the young master, the son of Mr. Nelson, sold Ann: "a

tall, hard-looking man came up to me, very roughly seized my arm, bade me open my mouth; examined my teeth; felt of my limbs; made me run a few yards; ordered me to jump; and being satisfied with my activity, said to Master Edward, 'I will take her.'" Ann then recalls her mother's pain: "my mother's ... whole frame was distorted with pain. ... No, no, I can't do it. ... [R]ocking her body back and forward in a transport of agony, she gave full vent to her feelings in a long, loud, piteous wail." It was that cry of grief, that "knell" of a breaking heart, that rang in Ann's ears for many long and painful days (p. 12). Ann was filled with a new horror as she witnessed the anguish of her relatives: "and forgetful of the presence of Peterkin [the new master], I burst into tears: but I was quickly recalled by a fierce and stinging blow from his stout riding whip" (p. 16). Thus the character of the new master is established.

Charity Morris was interviewed by Parnella Anderson for the Works Progress Administration (WPA) Writers' Project. She gives this account of her master's death: "When de ole haid [master] died out dey chillun get de property. You see we slaves wuz de property. Den we got separated. Some sent one way and some another. Hit jes happent dat Marse Jim drawed me" (*Born in Slavery* 2001, p. 2, document 30005, p. 149). Norrece Jones compiled, in *Born a Child of Freedom, Yet a Slave*, evidence from various sources that masters relied far more heavily on punishments than on rewards to keep slaves working. Jones adds: "the former ranged from physical torture to psychological terror, and all segments of white society concurred that some form of either, if not both, was essential" (1990, p. 72). William Colbert was born in 1844 in Fort Valley and remembered his master as "a mean man": "Jawsuh, he warn't good to none of us niggers. All de niggers hated to be bought by him kaze he wuz so mean. When he wuz too tired to whup us, he has the overseer to do it: and the overseer was meaner dan de massa" (*Born in Slavery*, 2001, Alabama Narratives, vol. 1, item 3, p. 1).

The words *master* and *control* may have appeared synonymous in *Autobiography of a Female Slave*, as slaves endured degradation and brutality under the rule of master Peterkin. The harshness of southern slavery is suggested by the author's remark that she did not believe that slavery existed in a more brutal and cruel form anywhere else than in Kentucky where she lived (Griffiths 1857, p. 103).

Having been taught how to read by her former owners, Ann was a Bible scholar who asked questions pertaining to the treatment of the slaves by her master:

> We are told to love our master. Why should we? Are we dogs to lick the hand that strikes us? Or are we men and woman with never dying souls—men and women unprotected in the very land they have toiled to beautify and adorn (Griffiths 1857, p. 125).

Later in the novel she explains: "The masters who instruct their slaves in religion, could be numbered, and I will venture to assert that, if the census were taken in the State of Kentucky the number would not exceed twenty" (p. 209).

BIBLIOGRAPHY

Bibb, Henry. *Narrative of the Life and Adventures of Henry Bibb, an American Slave* [1849]. New York: Negro University Press, 1969.

Born in Slavery: Slave Narratives from the Federal Writer's Project, 1936–1938. Library of Congress, Manuscript Division. Washington, DC, 2001. Available online from http://icweb2.loc.gov.

Griffiths, Mattie. *Autobiography of a Female Slave*. New York: Redfield, 1857.

Jones, Norrece T. *Born a Child of Freedom, Yet a Slave: Mechanisms of Control and Strategies of Resistance in Antebellum South Carolina.*

Middletown, CT: Wesleyan University Press, 1990.

Johnnie M. Maberry-Gilbert

THE MISTRESS

While many slaves called the slaveholder's wife the *mistress* of the plantation or homestead, the word *mistress* also referred to a slave woman forced into a sexual relationship with the slave owner. On the majority of homesteads, female slaves were always at the mercy of their masters who could either force them to breed with other slaves or would choose one or more for themselves.

Slave mistresses were commonplace and prevalent in the South. White women either ignored the situation or were resigned to it, knowing there was little they could do to change the relationship. They often blamed the mistresses, choosing to believe the slaves seduced their husbands, brothers, and sons—rarely acknowledging that the young women were regarded as property and had no rights whatsoever.

One of the more cited cases of a slaveholder/mistress relationship was that of Thomas Jefferson (1743–1826), author of the Declaration of Independence and the nation's third president. Jefferson had many slaves at his Monticello, Virginia, mansion and was particularly fond of the light-skinned, pretty Sally Hemings. Hemings was reportedly his mistress for years, and historians believe Jefferson may have fathered several of her six children.

Slaveholders' Wives

While many slaveholder wives were acutely aware of their husbands' sexual conquests, others chose to turn a blind eye. Wives found their husbands' liaisons disgraceful and sinful, but slave women didn't really count as human beings, let alone rivals. If a slave owner had sexual relations with a white woman, it was a far greater offense to the family and the community. Turnabout, however, was never fair play. Though rare, slaveholders' wives had dalliances of their own; it was considered far beyond shameful and kept quiet when and if it occurred. As Hortense Powdermaker commented in her book *After Freedom: A Cultural Study in the Deep South* (1939), "Any self-respecting woman ... tries to observe strict secrecy about her extra-marital relations. Whatever 'disgrace' is connected with them lies in being talked about" (p. 163).

Some wives had no control over their husbands and feared them almost as much as the slaves. In *Born in Slavery: Slave Narratives from the Federal Writers' Project, 1936–1938*, John Henry Kemp, known as "Prophet," related that his father and master John Gay was known throughout Mississippi as one of the cruelest and most vengeful slaveholders. When Gay had set his sights on Kemp's mother (as a teen), she begged Mrs.

A woman whipping a slave girl, 1934. Slave mistresses were commonplace in the South. White women often blamed the slaves for white male infidelity, rarely acknowledging that the young women were regarded as property and had no rights whatsoever. *MPI/Hulton Archive/Getty Images.*

Gay to intervene. "So great was the fear in which Gay was held that when Kemp's mother, Annette Young, complained to Mrs. Gay that her husband was constantly seeking her as a mistress, and threatening her with death if she did not submit, even Mrs. Gay had to advise the slave to do as Gay demanded, 'My husband is a dirty man and will find some reason to kill you if you don't'" (*Born in Slavery*, vol. 3, p. 186).

The same was true of the Donaldson plantation in Florida, where Sarah Rose and her mother lived. According to Sarah's reminiscences in *Born in Slavery*, "Donaldson was a very cruel man and frequently beat Sara's mother because she would not have sex with the overseer..." (p. 168). Additionally, "Donaldson's wife committed suicide because of the cruelty not only to the slaves but to her as well" (p. 169).

Conditions

While all female slaves could be forced into sex—with other slaves for breeding programs, into arranged mar-

riages, or as sexual conquests for the slaveholder, his overseers, or his sons—the lot of a mistress could be particularly brutal. Slaveholders sometimes chose girls barely into puberty, especially if they were physically attractive. If they thwarted the advances of their owners, they could be beaten, whipped, hung by the wrists, sold, or mysteriously disappear. Slave mothers dreaded the onset of adolescence for their daughters, but had little or no control of the future.

Not all slave mistresses, however, lived in misery. Some slaveholders genuinely cared for their mistresses, providing them many comforts. For the very fortunate, chores were decreased or done away with completely, extra food and nice clothing was provided, and they lived in furnished cabins away from slave quarters—mostly so the owner could come and go as he pleased in private. The downside to such amenities was the resentment of their fellow slaves, and the vitriolic hatred of the white women on the homestead.

Not surprisingly, the results of slaveholder-slave liaisons were mixed-race children. Sometimes these children were prized for their light coloring and supposed intelligence (most slaveholders believed the lighter the skin the higher the intellect) and raised alongside their white siblings. Other times, the mixed race offspring were sold as house servants or gotten rid of very quickly if they looked too much like the slaveholder.

BIBLIOGRAPHY

Born in Slavery: Slave Narratives from the Federal Writers' Project, 1936–1938. Online collection of the Manuscript and Prints and Photographs Divisions of the Library of Congress. Available from http://memory.loc.gov.

"Thomas Jefferson: A Biography," and "Sally Hemings." Monticello: The Home of Thomas Jefferson. Available from http://www.monticello.org.

Powdermaker, Hortense. *After Freedom: A Cultural Study in the Deep South.* New York: Viking Press, 1939.

Nelson Rhodes

THE MASTER'S FAMILY

Information about the families of slave masters appears in bits and pieces in the narratives of slaves. In his autobiography, *The Life of Moses Grandy*, one slave describes some of his interactions with his master's family, beginning with his master's attempt to sell him to another slaveholder:

> But, at length, persons came who agreed to give the prices he set on us. His wife, with much to be done, prevailed on him not to sell me. ... My young master and I used to play together; there was but two days difference in our ages. My old master always said he would give me to him.

A plantation owner visiting the slave quarters on his Virginia plantation, circa 1700s. In his 1847 autobiography, *Narrative of the Life of William Brown*, William Brown writes about a nephew, William Moore, who was brought into the Master's Family. "His name being that of my own, mine was changed, for the purpose of giving precedence to his, though I was the senior by ten or twelve years." © *North Wind Picture Archives.*

When he died, all the colored people were divided amongst his children, and I fell to young master; his name was James Grandy. ... When my master came of age, he took all his colored people to himself. Seeing that I was industrious and persevering, and had obtained plenty of work, he made me pay him almost twice as much as I paid Mr. Furley. (1844, p. 9)

William Wells Brown (1815–1884), author of *Narrative of William W. Brown*, speaks of being taken from the fields to work in the master's house: "I was taken out of the field to work in the house as a waiter. Though his wife was very peevish, and hard to please, I preferred to be under her control than the overseer's" (1847, p. 35). When Brown's master moved to the city he brought with him other family members:

They brought with them Mr. Sloan, a Presbyterian minister; Miss Martha Tulley, a niece of theirs from Kentucky; and their nephew William. The latter had been in the family a number of years, but the others were all new comers. ... My master and mistress were great lovers of mint julep, and every

morning, a pitcher-full was made, of which they all partook freely, not excepting little master William. After drinking freely all round, they would have family worship, and then breakfast. ... My master's family consisted of himself, his wife, and their nephew, William Moore. He was taken into the family when only a few weeks of age. His name being that of my own, mine was changed, for the purpose of giving precedence to his, though I was the senior by ten or twelve years (p. 38).

Other sources that provide some information about the master's family are found in the Works Progress Administration (WPA) narratives. Ex-slave George Fleming recalls his master's family affectionately:

Missus Harriet, dat Marse Sam's wife, she give us a looking glass so we could see how to fix up. Lawd a mercy, Missus Harriet was one fine woman. She allus after us to see dat we didn't suffer nothing. Marse Sam's boys, Lyntt and Frank, sho was tigers, but cose dey wasn't mean tigers. They had real long beards. Marse Lyntt was my young master, and he the bestest man I ever know'd, cepting his daddy. He allus doing something to have fun outen us lil' niggers, 'cause we got fun outen it too. I member how he used to sot us in the hog pen, but we wasn't scared as we 'lowed we was (*Born in Slavery,* 2001, South Carolina Narratives, entry 11).

In fact, the slave and his family and the master and his family were, more often than not, a team, sharing the burden of work together in the field. Unfortunately, the partnership did not extend to sharing profits.

BIBLIOGRAPHY

Born in Slavery: Slave Narratives from the Federal Writers' Project, 1936–1938, Library of Congress, Manuscript Division. Washington, DC: 2001. Available online from http://icweb2.loc.gov.

Brown, William Wells. *Narrative of William W. Brown, a Fugitive Slave.* Boston: Anti-Slavery Office, 1847.

Five Slave Narratives: A Compendium. New York: Arno Press, 1968.

Goodwin, C. James, and Thelma Kirpatrick. *Official Manual State of Missouri, 1973–1974.* Jefferson City, MO: Von Hoffman Press, 1974.

Grandy, Moses. *Narrative of the Life of Moses Grandy; Late a Slave in the United States of America.* Boston: O. Johnson, 1844.

Johnnie M. Maberry-Gilbert

BLACK SLAVE OWNERS

Despite the popularity of the novel *The Known World* (2003) by Pulitzer Prize-winning author Edward P. Jones, the phenomenon of slaveholding among African Americans, of black people owning other black people as slaves, has not received widespread attention. However, historians and other scholars have discovered records of slaveholding among blacks dating from the colonial period through the antebellum era. Such records include wills in which black slave owners left slave property to family members or friends; deeds of emancipation required when slave owners manumitted their slaves; bills of sale recording the purchase and sale of slaves; court records detailing suits disputing ownership of slave property; and personal papers referring to slave ownership. Some early historians saw free black slave ownership as positive because it meant that free blacks had the economic and legal ability to own slaves. In general, there were two categories of slaveholding by African Americans: benevolent and commercial.

Benevolent slave ownership among African Americans is characterized by the purchase of relatives or friends. For instance, a free African American woman might purchase her husband in order to remove him from the threat of a cruel master. Or a parent might purchase his or her children for the same reason. Because some state legislatures, such as the 1806 Virginia legis-

lature, required emancipated slaves to leave the state, a woman's continued ownership of her spouse, or a parent's continued ownership of his or her children, was often the only way for a family unit to remain intact within the state. Some free African Americans purchased slaves with the understanding that the enslaved person would then purchase his or her freedom over time in installments. Or a slave might accumulate his or her purchase price through the practice of hiring out and approach a free black person to buy him or her with that money with the understanding that the slave would live as a free person. Thus, these African American owners were not necessarily enslaving people for their labor, but purchasing relatives or friends to keep families together or to help people move out of slavery.

Scholars of African American history argue about whether commercial slaveholding was more or less common than benevolent slaveholding among blacks, but all would agree that there were at least some black slaveholders who held slaves for precisely the same reason as their white counterparts—to earn money.

One of the best documented cases is that of William Ellison, a cotton gin maker from South Carolina. Ellison did not consider himself a black man but a man of color, a mulatto. At a time when the vast majority of blacks in the South were slaves and almost all free blacks were poor, Ellison was one of the wealthiest free persons of color in the South and wealthier than most whites. Ellison owned a large cotton plantation and more slaves than any other free person of color in the South outside of Louisiana, even more than all but the richest white planters. In 1840 Ellison owned thirty slaves. By 1847 Ellison's property grew to 350 acres and thirty-six slaves. And on the eve of the Civil War, he owned sixty-three slaves. His slaves toiled in fields and were trained to make and repair cotton gins. They were unlikely to describe their owner as benevolent.

BIBLIOGRAPHY

Johnson, Michael P., and James Roark. *Black Masters.* New York: W. W. Norton, 1984.

Fay A. Yarbrough

NATIVE AMERICANS AND SLAVERY

Bondage was not a new concept to Native Americans in the South. Long before the arrival of Europeans, most tribes in the region had practiced a traditional form of kinship slavery. This type of slavery differed significantly, however, from that practiced by the Europeans who first witnessed it. As was often the case, white observers were influenced by their own cultural experience and tended to view native practices through the same lens. Hence, when explorers from Hernando de Soto on encountered kinship-based bondage, they described it according to the master-slave paradigm they knew themselves.

Although incorrect in describing kinship slavery in the sixteenth and seventeenth centuries, the European-style slavery paradigm would be an apt portrayal of the form of plantation slavery that American Indians were practicing in the southeastern United States by the nineteenth century.

Traditional Indian Slavery

Most Native American communities in the South were defined by kinship. An individual was either related to the group, and therefore acceptable, or was an outsider and a potential enemy. Diplomatic and trade relations with other groups often involved ceremonies "adopting" outsider representatives into the kinship circle. Outsider captives taken in warfare, however, were a different story. They might be adopted into the tribe to replace lost kinsmen; they might be executed, in revenge for lost kinsmen; or they might become slaves. The choice, once captives entered the village, was usually made by the women. Almon Wheeler Lauber observes that, compared to the potentially grisly alternative, enslavement was "in itself a kindly act on the part of the captors" (Lauber 1915, p. 292).

Enslaved captives were not considered part of the kinship circle, but rather existed outside it at the whim of their masters. As enemies, their lives were forfeit; they could be killed at any time. Because there was no commercial agriculture, these slaves were not cogs in a profit-earning machine, but rather worked alongside their masters at their daily chores. Their condition as slaves—*atsi nahsa'i* to the Cherokee, a nonhuman possession—was not hereditary, nor was it necessarily permanent. They could be adopted into the tribe at any time, and often were. Generally speaking, notes the historian Claudio Saunt, "they cooked, cleaned, collected firewood, farmed, provided sexual services, and were a lot like any other family member" (Saunt 2005, p. 17). Theda Perdue argues in her 1979 study that slaves played an important role in Cherokees' concept of identity. She notes that, because of the Cherokees great emphasis on individualism and lack of a centralized government, an outsider group was necessary to help define the boundaries of community. The same could be said of the many other Native groups throughout the South who practiced a similar form of slavery.

The Indian Slave Trade

Native Americans' first experiences with the style of bondage common in the English colonies would come not in the role of master but in that of victim. Colonists began to enslave Indians within a few years of their first encounters with them. After the Powhatans under Opechancanough struck at Jamestown in 1622, killing as many as a third of the colonists, the English sought a bright side to the disaster. Lauber's volume reprints a tract originally published in London, which notes that Indians "who before were used as friends, may now justly be compelled to servitude in mines, and the like, of whom some may be sent for the use of the Summer Islands" (1915, p. 370).

Before long, the use of Indians as slaves extended beyond merely those individuals who engaged in combat against English settlers. Colonial powers traded with various tribes, offering them commercial goods in return for their own captives taken from other Indians. These captives would be sent to plantations in the eastern colonies or in the Caribbean. Competing European powers encouraged their Indian allies to raid the allies of their colonial counterparts. The prospect of wealth spurred many whites and Indians to escalate warfare to unprecedented heights. One raid by South Carolinians and their Indian allies in the Yamassee War led to the enslavement of, according to Lauber, "almost the entire population of seven towns, in all, some 1400 persons" (1915, p. 121). Captives were no longer a by-product of war, but the focus of it—slaves were no longer just an "other" against whom to define one's community, but a marketable commodity. The resultant enterprise system was, according to the historian Alan Gallay, "inextricably connected to the growth of the plantations," and was, in fact, "at the center of the English empire's development in the American South" (Gallay, 2002, p. 7). He estimates that between 24,000 and 51,000 American Indians were enslaved in the South from 1670 to 1715, making the slave trade "the most important factor affecting the South" in that period (2002, p. 299).

Indians and African Americans were both initially victimized by slavery, working together and often intermarrying; eventually, however, chattel slavery became an exclusively African American experience. Several factors may have influenced the gradual decline in the Indian slave trade. Native Americans were ultimately judged to be comparatively unsuited for plantation labor, with higher death and desertion rates than that of their black counterparts. Lauber ascribes this phenomenon to the assumption that "the dominant idea of Indian life was the love of liberty. Heredity and environment cooperated to make the Indian a creature opposed to all restraint when exercised by an exterior force" (1915, p. 140). Another element may have played a larger role: the traditional gendered division of labor among most Southern Indian tribes. Agricultural work was the realm of women, whereas hunting was the responsibility of men. Forcing Native American men to do field work not only restricted their freedom, it challenged their gender roles. Whatever the motivation, Indians were more likely to die and much more likely to escape. Further, it was more practical from a safety standpoint to enslave people whose relatives were an ocean away, as opposed to only a few miles away and armed.

An Indian sent into Slavery.

A Native American being sold as a slave. Native Americans' first experiences with slavery in the colonies were as victims, not masters. Later, slavery began to be more associated with African Americans and the elite Native Americans adopted European practices, including slavery. *Mary Evans Photo Researchers, Inc.*

A New Approach

The basic concepts of chattel slavery had certainly begun to take shape in the minds of Indians in the South by the late eighteenth century. The slave trade had introduced the commodification of human beings; this was no doubt reinforced by the practice of colonial officials rewarding Indian allies with African slaves and paying bounties for the return of runaways. Events set in motion by the American Revolution would lead to Indian adoption of not only the concept but the institution itself.

The Revolution was a watershed for Native Americans east of the Mississippi. Indian leaders had for centuries been able to play various colonial powers against each other, retaining a considerable amount of autonomy and political leverage. Even with the decline of French power, Indians had still been able to turn to the British government to protect their interests against encroaching settlers. The Treaty of Paris, in 1783, changed everything. Now, with the occasional exception of the Spanish (whose southeastern holdings were minimal compared to those of the United States, and would not last long), Native Americans had only one white government to deal with. Indians were no longer really needed as allies against European powers, and the declining deerskin trade limited

their economic strength. Further, by the 1790s it had become apparent to Indians in the South that they had little hope of besting the new federal government militarily. A new approach was called for.

Many Southern Indian leaders believed they would have to defend their lands not with physical weapons, but by adopting European approaches. Prominent Indians in many tribes married their daughters to white traders, thus making those traders part of their kinship circle and cementing a commercial relationship with them. Elite Indian youths, many of them the offspring of those mixed marriages, were attending American schools and universities by the nineteenth century. For those unable to leave their lands to get an education, some tribes—such as the Choctaw—invited Christian missionaries into their territory, often with more of an eye toward gaining a formal education for their children than for religious conversion. Within the space of a generation or two, the largest Southern tribes—Cherokees, Choctaws, Creeks, Chickasaws—saw an increasing trend toward "Americanization," at least among their elites. One of the most significant aspects of this Americanization was the development of plantation agriculture, and with it large-scale chattel slavery.

Native Americans as Plantation Owners

The 1830 federal Choctaw census showed that, of 17,963 inhabitants of Choctaw land in Mississippi, 512 were slaves. There were sixty-six slave owners, of whom only twelve were white. Chief Greenwood LeFlore owned thirty-two slaves, Chief David Folsom owned ten. Joseph and James Perry owned fifty-one. Nor were the slaveholders all biracial—prominent "full blood" chief Mushulatubbee owned ten slaves. Other tribes were proportionately similar in the number of slaves held in comparison to their population.

Owners tended to be elites—but not always. Small farmers who owned slaves were often more traditional in their general outlook than were the elites. As a result, black slaves' experience on such small farms differed quite a bit from their counterparts on larger farms or plantations (which operated in much the same way as those owned by the Indians' white neighbors). Small slaveholders were more likely to treat their human property in a way that closely mirrored the traditional handling of kinship slaves; working closely with them, sometimes behaving as if they were family. Many white travelers of the time commented on the "lax" treatment slaves received from such owners, and many blacks would later claim to have received much better care from their Indian masters than did the slaves of whites. This pattern persisted into Indian Territory after Removal but became increasingly rare. By the time of the Civil War, a slave's lot in Indian hands was little different from that of slaves anywhere else.

In an undated narrative recorded when she was eighty-three, Polly Colbert, an ex-slave whose masters had been Choctaw, tells of an existence that seems closer to traditional practices than to chattel slavery:

> I reckon it was on account of de rich land dat us niggers dat was owned by Indians didn't have to work so hard as dey did in de old states, but I think dat Indian masters was just naturally kinder any way, leastways mine was. My mother, Idea, was owned by de Colbert family and my father, Tony, was owned by de Love family. When Master Holmes and Miss Betty Love was married dey fathers give my father and mother to dem for a wedding gift. I was born at Tishominge and we moved to de farm on Red River soon after dat and I been here ever since. I had a sister and a brother, but I ain't seen dem since den. My mother died when I was real small, and about a year after dat my father died. Master Holmes told us children not to cry, dat he and Miss Betsy would take good care of us. Dey did, too. Day take us in de house wid dem and look after us jest as good as dey could colored children. We slept in a little room close to them and she allus seen dat us was covered up good before she went to bed. I guess she got a sight of satisfaction from taking care of us 'cause she didn't have no babies to care for. (*Born in Slavery: Slave Narratives from the Federal Writers' Project, 1936–1938.*)

After Removal to the West, plantation slavery became even more firmly entrenched among the aforementioned tribes. Native American political leaders wanted no interference with their practice of the institution; this led to years of controversy centered on the missionaries they had invited into their midst. The Choctaws passed laws forbidding anything that even hinted at abolitionism—including teaching blacks to read, sing, or even eating at the same table with masters—and any non-Indian engaging in such behavior was liable for expulsion from the Choctaw nation. Although few missionaries rocked the boat on the issue, Northern church members who funded the missionaries were uncomfortable with, and in some cases incensed by, the pollution of their activities through close association with slavery. "Christianity has been represented as the warrant for a system of slavery which offends the moral sense of the Christian world," one official lamented to the American Board of Commissioners for Foreign Missions (Whipple 1859, p. 20).

Leaders of the Five Civilized Tribes felt so strongly about their rights as slaveholders that they were increasingly sympathetic to their neighboring white Southerners who had begun to call for secession from the Union. Once secession had become a reality, the Confederate government sent officials to negotiate with the Indians. As noted by Annie Heloise Abel in her 1919 study, native leaders were warned that a Northern victory would result in the freeing of their slaves and the loss of their lands. Although there were large pro-Union minorities in several of the tribes, and even some abolitionist groups, the Five Tribes' political leaders eventu-

ABOLITION CONTROVERSY IN INDIAN TERRITORY

In 1854 Choctaw leader George Harkins complained in a press release that white abolitionist missionaries were educating slaves in his nation:

> What are we to infer from this, but that they have their secret designs, and a greater feeling for the welfare of the slave among us, than for the Indian? There is no State in the South that would be willing for the Abolitionists to teach their slaves; and in fact they dare not attempt it; and it is because we are *Indians* that they suppose they can have this privilege among us. If the Abolitionists are not satisfied to teach our children alone, then I say for once, let the connection between us and the American Board be dissolved and every Abolitionist be driven out of the nation at once. (*New York Observer and Chronicle*, December 14, 1854, p. 398)

An editorial in the *Boston Atlas*, reprinted soon afterward in *The Liberator*, attacked Harkins's racial views. Ironically, the white editorialist's anti-Indian racist terms were even more disturbing than Harkins's comments:

> Harkins has very pretty notions of civilization . . . perhaps it has never occurred to him, that for one oppressed people to oppress another is a bad way of awakening sympathy . . . perhaps, however, he still takes an aboriginal view of the subject, and means to follow up the pursuit of civilization by the revival of scalping, burning at the stake, and other agreeable Indian diversions. If so, he ought to put a ring in his nose and red-ochre his cheeks without delay. (*The Liberator*, December 29, 1854, p. 206)

BIBLIOGRAPHY
The Liberator, December 29, 1854, p. 206.
New York Observer and Chronicle, December 14, 1854, p. 398.

ally entered an alliance with the Confederate States and provided troops for the war effort. The Southern diplomats' warnings at the beginning of the conflict proved true, even if they were a self-fulfilling prophecy; the Indian alliance with the Confederacy led to further loss of territory when their cause was defeated, and the federal government forced all the tribes to abolish slavery and make their former slaves tribal citizens.

BIBLIOGRAPHY

Abel, Annie Heloise. *The American Indian as Participant in the Civil War* [1919]. Lincoln: University of Nebraska Press, 1992.

Born in Slavery: Slave Narratives from the Federal Writers' Project, 1936–1938. Manuscript Division,

Library of Congress. Narrator "Polly Colbert." Available from http://memory.loc.gov.

Gallay, Alan. *The Indian Slave Trade: The Rise of the English Empire in the American South, 1670–1717.* New Haven, CT: Yale University Press, 2002.

Lauber, Almon Wheeler. *Indian Slavery in Colonial Times within the Present Limits of the United States.* New York: Columbia University, 1913.

Perdue, Theda. *Slavery and the Evolution of Cherokee Society, 1540–1866.* Knoxville: University of Tennessee Press, 1979.

Porter, Kenneth W. "Relations between Negroes and Indians within the Present Limits of the United States." *Journal of Negro History* 17, no. 3 (1932): 287–293.

Saunt, Claudio. *Black, White, and Indian: Race and the Unmaking of an American Family.* New York: Oxford University Press, 2005.

Sources in U.S. History Online: Slavery in America. Gale. Available from http://www.gale.com/pdf/facts/Slavery.pdf.

Whipple, Charles K. *Slavery and the American Board of Commissioners for Foreign Missions.* New York and Boston: American Anti-Slavery Society, 1859.

Troy D. Smith

SEXUAL EXPLOITATION AND MISCEGENATION

The term *miscegenation* entered the American lexicon during the election of 1864, when a group of Democrats circulated an anonymous tract suggesting that the Republican Party "advocated sex and marriage across the color line" (Hodes 2003, p. 115). Intended as political sabotage, the pamphlet exploited white anxieties about the potential for interracial relationships to disrupt an American class system that was inextricably entwined with ideologies of race. The construction of this social hierarchy, along with racial categories, began in the seventeenth century when new colonial laws increasingly transformed servitude from a multiracial system of fixed-term indenture to one of lifelong race-based slavery. As Elise Lemire writes, prohibitions on interracial sex and marriage "ensured that social and economic equality would not occur between whites and blacks and that slavery would be perpetuated as a race-based system by making interracial marriage illegal." These laws also "legally substantiated" ideologies of white racial superiority, and "made the children of inter-racial couples bastards and thereby concentrated freedom [*sic*] and wealth in white families by not allowing these illegitimate children to inherit" (2002, p. 2). Antimiscegenation legislation and attempts by white male legislators to control the sexuality of African American men and white women helped construct and reify a social hierarchy that ensured the power of a white male patriarchy. As historian Peter Bardaglio writes, Southern white men "viewed female sexuality as property that they owned, like slaves, and protection of this property was a key to preserving their position in society" (1995, p. 65).

In colonial South Carolina, men and women of European, African, and Native American descent frequently had relationships with a person of different ancestry. Only with the passage of a 1717 law did it constitute a punishable offense for a white man or woman to conceive a child with a partner of African descent. The penalty, whether the accused was a white man or woman, or free or indentured, was a fixed period of seven years servitude (Wood 1996, p. 99). In Virginia and Maryland, antimiscegenation legislation was adopted much earlier. Because white women constituted a small percentage of the colonial population, legislatures tried to prevent interracial marriage and childbearing by making both punishable with fines, indenture, banishment, or incarceration (Clinton 1991, p. 56). As historian Peter Wood writes, the emergence of antimiscegenation laws suggests the frequency with which multiracial children were born into the population, "only to have their descendants sifted back into the ever more arbitrary and rigid 'black' and 'white' categories of later times" (1996, p. 99).

Evidence of the social stratification that emerged with antimiscegenation laws was also evident in Southern rape law, which meted out unequal punishment for those convicted of sexual assault. For white men the penalty was typically incarceration. For black men, the penalty in the colonial period was castration, whereas in the antebellum period it became death. Mostly concerned with the rape of white women, the legal codes were largely silent on the rape of black women. Though a white man could be convicted of raping another master's slave, the assault was considered by the courts a crime against the slaveholder for violating his property. A Mississippi law prescribed punishment for male slaves' rape of female slaves only in cases involving children under the age of twelve (Bardaglio 1995, p. 68).

An 1861 Georgia law demonstrates how prolonged resistance was to regarding the sexual assault of slave women as a crime. According to the statute, rape was defined as "the carnal knowledge of a female whether slave or free, forcibly and against her will." But drafters of the law justified the inclusion of slaves in the law on the grounds that it would "preserve the integrity of the statute books." As for the sexual abuse of a slave woman, the legislator believed that "the occurrence of such an offense is almost unheard of" (Bardaglio 1995, p. 68).

Indeed, this legislator's position mystifies the frequency with which enslaved women endured sexual exploitation by slaveholders. Antimiscegenation laws made interracial sex a criminal offense, but these laws were aimed at preserving white men's assertion of

SLAVERY IN THE UNITED STATES. — THE TRAGEDY OF PAULINE.

A illustration of Pauline, the first slave in New Orleans, June 6, 1846. Paulina was killed by her mistress after being impregnated by her master. White men created a legal and social milieu in which they were virtually uninhibited to sexually exploit their bondwomen. *Mary Evans Photo Researchers, Inc.*

ownership over white female sexuality and reproduction. At the same time, white men created a legal and social milieu in which they were virtually uninhibited to sexually exploit their bondwomen. These relationships of interracial sex, rather than challenging white male power in the racialized and gendered social hierarchy, reinforced its hegemony.

Ex-slave Louisa Picquet (2003) recounted in her as-told-to autobiography how at the age of fourteen she became the object of sexual advances by her owner, Cook, the man she also presumed to be the father of the three children her mother bore while owned by Cook. Picquet evaded Cook's advances but was flogged so unmercifully for it, she resigned herself to resisting no more. Her seizure by the sheriff to pay Cook's debts seemed a temporary reprieve until she was bought by Williams, who made her his concubine. Picquet had four

children, of whom Williams was the biological father, a fact he never acknowledged.

Though slaveholders rarely acknowledged their paternity of slave children, the sexual exploitation of female slaves was known by diarist Mary Chesnut (1823–1886) as a common practice. "Like the patriarchs of old," Chesnut wrote, "our men live all in one house with their wives and their concubines, and the mulattoes one sees in every family exactly resemble the white children—and every lady tells you who is the father of all the mulatto children in everybody's household, but those in her own she seems to think drop from the clouds, or pretends so to think" (1981, p. 29).

Ella Gertrude Clanton Thomas, married to a Southern planter, also criticized the sale of slave women as concubines in an an 1858 journal entry: "Oh is it not enough to make us shudder for the standard of morality in our Southern homes?" (1990, p. 168). As a "most striking illustration of the general feeling on the subject," Thomas cited the case of George Eve, who carried a slave woman north with him to live as his concubine. "It was well known," Thomas recalls, "that he lived with her constantly violating one of God's ten commandments, yet nothing was thought of it." But when Eve's family received a report that a marriage ceremony had taken place between Eve and the woman, "public opinion was outraged" and Eve's father, who was "terribly mortified," attempted to have the groom declared insane (p. 168). For Thomas, the case clearly illustrated the hypocrisy of religious and social mores. The Eve family and the general public would tolerate the woman's concubinage but leveled a charge of insanity when the son dared violate the cultural taboo against interracial marriage.

But despite her frank criticism of these sexual mores, Thomas herself was not immune. Her musings on the subject were prompted by the entrance of the slave Lurany and her daughter Lulah, whom Thomas described as "white as any white child" (p. 167). "There is some great mystery about Lurany's case," Thomas wrote, "How can she reconcile her great professions of religion with the sin of having children constantly without a husband?" (p. 167). If Thomas deduced that Lurany's children might have been the product of a forced sexual union, she nevertheless adhered to the custom of many mistresses, who blamed female slaves for the exploitation committed by slaveholders.

Such was the case for Harriet Jacobs (1813–1897), who famously lived in her grandmother's garret for seven years to avoid sexual assault by the man who owned her. The harassment Jacobs endured began when she was fifteen and the man, represented in her narrative as Dr. Flint, began whispering obscenities in her ear and passing her licentious notes. Knowing of her husband's base designs, Mrs. Flint regarded Jacobs as an object of "constant suspicion and malevolence." Jacobs recalls many nights waking to find Mrs. Flint bending over her or reenacting Dr. Flint's harassment: "She whispered in my ear, as though it was her husband who was speaking to me, and listened to hear what I would answer" (1987, p. 34). Jacobs eventually made her way to New England, but the seven years she spent hiding in the cramped crawl space of her grandmother's attic in order to resist Flint's abuse left her physically impaired for the rest of her life.

Cherry Loguen chose a different method of resistance. She used a stick to beat her knife-wielding attacker unconscious (White 1999, p. 78). But there could also be serious reprisals for women who defended themselves with violence or otherwise resisted would-be rapists. Frederick Douglass's aunt Esther rebuked the sexual advances of her master Anthony and defied his orders against accepting the courtship of another slave. According to Douglass, Esther was "evidently much attached to Edward, and abhorred—as she had reason to do—the tyrannical and base behavior of old master. . . . His attentions were plainly brutal and selfish, and it was as natural that Esther should loathe him, as that she should love Edward" (2003, pp. 37–38). For her assertion of sexual autonomy, Esther was tortured with severe and repeated floggings, which assumed an explicitly sexualized quality. Though it is unclear whether she continued to resist Anthony, Douglass writes, the physical abuse was "often repeated in the case of poor Esther, and her life, as I knew it, was one of wretchedness" (p. 38).

Slaveholders also tried to manipulate sexual relationships between slaves, sometimes by forbidding courtship, as in the case of Esther and Edward, but more often by encouraging relationships that would likely produce children. According to historian Marie Jenkins Schwartz, "Efforts by slaveholders to foster childbearing ranged from subtle persuasion to outright force" (2000, p. 188). The latter tactic was extremely rare, but Sam and Louisa Everett, a Florida couple who legally married after the Civil War (1861–1865), told an interviewer in 1936 that they had been forced together by a slaveholder. Louisa told the interviewer that because the union produced healthy children, "I never had another man forced on me, thank God" (*Born in Slavery*, Florida Narratives, vol. 3). Though such cases constituted rare exceptions, Schwartz notes, "the knowledge that forced pairings occurred occasionally worried slaves and pushed them into early marriages of their own making, rather than marriages arranged by their owners" (2000, p. 188).

While some bondpeople found ways to resist sexual exploitation, these means were generally confined to the master-slave relationship, as the law offered little protection or recourse to slaveholders' sexual abuse. In fact, the law legitimized and reified the gendered, racialized caste system that condoned the sexual exploitation of slaves. Long after slavery's demise, these racialist ideologies remained sanctioned in law. Legal prohibitions on racial intermarriage persisted until 1967, when they were finally declared unconstitutional (Lemire 2002, p. 2).

BIBLIOGRAPHY

Bardaglio, Peter. *Reconstructing the Household: Families, Sex, and the Law in the Nineteenth-Century South.* Chapel Hill: University of North Carolina Press, 1995.

Born in Slavery: Slave Narratives from the Federal Writer's Project, 1936–1938. Library of Congress, Manuscript Division. Florida Narratives, vol. 3.

Chesnut, Mary. *Mary Chesnut's Civil War.* Ed. C. Vann Woodward. New Haven, CT: Yale University Press, 1981.

Clinton, Catherine. "Southern Dishonor: Flesh, Blood, Race, and Bondage." In *In Joy and in Sorrow: Women, Family, and Marriage in the Victorian*

South, ed. Carol Bleser. New York: Oxford University Press, 1991.

Douglass, Frederick. *My Bondage and My Freedom* [1855]. Reprint, New York: Modern Library, 2003.

Hodes, Martha. "Wartime Dialogues on Illicit Sex: White Woman and Black Men." In *Sexual Borderlands: Constructing an American Sexual Past*, ed. Kathleen Kennedy and Sharon Ullman. Columbus: Ohio State University Press, 2003.

Jacobs, Harriet A. *Incidents in the Life of a Slave Girl: Written by Herself* [1861]. Reprint, Cambridge, MA: Harvard University Press, 1987.

Lemire, Elise. *"Miscegenation": Making Race in America*. Philadelphia: University of Pennsylvania Press, 2002.

Picquet, Louisa, and Hiram Mattison. *Louisa Picquet, the Octoroon: A Tale of Southern Slave Life* [1861]. Chapel Hill: University of North Carolina Press, 2003.

Schwartz, Marie Jenkins. *Born in Bondage: Growing Up Enslaved in the Antebellum South*. Cambridge, MA: Harvard University Press, 2000.

Thomas, Ella Gertrude Clanton. *The Secret Eye: The Journal of Ella Gertrude Clanton Thomas, 1848–1889*. Chapel Hill: University of North Carolina Press, 1990.

White, Deborah, Gray. *Ar'n't I a Woman?: Female Slaves in the Plantation South* [1985]. Reprint, New York: Norton, 1999.

Wood, Peter. *Black Majority: Negroes in Colonial South Carolina from 1670 through the Stono Rebellion* [1974]. Reprint, New York: Norton, 1996.

Christina Adkins

OVERSEERS AND DRIVERS

Overseers were agents employed by Southern slaveholders to supervise the daily affairs on a plantation. These individuals often came from a class of landless young men, some of whom were the sons of well-established slaveholders. Over time, however, a professional class of managers also developed to meet the needs of the ever-expanding plantation economy of the South during the antebellum era.

An overseer's duties on the farm were manifold. Their primary task was to insure the timely production of cash crops such as cotton, tobacco, rice, and sugar cane. Because these were such labor-intensive crops, an overseer was also responsible for directing the activities and living conditions of slaves, who were the backbone of the region's workforce.

On some farms overseers were given a great deal of license to carry out their duties as they saw fit. For example, on absentee plantations, where the owner was gone for months at a stretch, agents sometimes held a virtual free reign over the plantation. More typically, however, slave owners were physically present at least part of the time on the farm. As a result, owners monitored closely the activities of their hired agents and laid out all manner of rules regarding everything from the proper feeding, clothing, and housing of slaves to the exact dates for which the crops should be sown, weeded, and harvested.

Such close oversight could breed resentment between slave owners and overseers. While overseers chafed at any perceived interference, owners insisted on complete obedience from their agents. Overseers were therefore expected to abide by all plantation regulations or else face dismissal for insubordination. Complicating this relationship was also the matter of class distinctions. As members of the Southern landholding class, plantation owners tended to snub non-slaveholders as their social inferiors. This was a point that did not go unnoticed by either party. In fact, slaves sometimes adopted the same attitude of superiority toward their managers. One servant reminisced with a decided degree of satisfaction, for example, that her overseer had always been "nothin' but white trash" (Rawick 1972–1979, vol. 6, p. 120).

Beyond occasional quibbles with the master, however, overseers maintained the most contact with slaves. Living in adjacent quarters and working side-by-side in the fields on a daily basis, managers and slaves developed close working relationships. Yet, as often as not, these relationships were highly contentious. Slaves distrusted white authority figures in general, especially those who were not their owners. Thus, resentments might grow quickly against overseers that wielded the whip too often. Another source of conflict was the systematic sexual abuse of female slaves by overseers. This sort of exploitation was commonplace, according to one former agent. He recalled, for example, how in his neighborhood overseers "took … [few] pains to conceal their habits of licentious intercourse with the female slaves" (Roles 1864, p. 14).

Such endemic tension between overseers, masters, and slaves, coupled with the fact that overseeing was not a relatively high-paying profession, led to a high turnover rate on many plantations. In fact, some managers remained on the same farm only for the duration of one growing season before seeking their fortunes elsewhere. Regardless, as the cotton economy continued to prosper demand for overseers remained high in all areas of the South for decades during the antebellum era.

Slave Driver

A driver was a slave appointed by an owner to maintain discipline and supervise the cultivation of crops on the plantation. Typically drawn from the ranks of the most experienced hands, a driver was usually an older male slave with a well-established reputation for obedience and due diligence. On large plantations a slave driver functioned as an assistant to the overseer. In this role, he

An overseer at work. An overseer monitors field hands cutting sugar cane on a southern plantation, circa 1800s. Overseers were employed by southern slaveholders to supervise the daily affairs on a plantation. They often came from a class of landless young men, some of whom were the sons of well-established slaveholders. © *North Wind Picture Archives.*

helped direct the activities of field hands and administer punishments to slaves who refused to work. On smaller farms cost-conscious owners sometimes utilized slave drivers in lieu of overseers. In this situation, drivers assumed many of the same duties as a paid agricultural agent. They were responsible not only for managing the labor force but for rationing out food and clothing and maintaining tools and housing.

Because drivers enjoyed the confidence and trust of the master, they occupied a relatively privileged status on the plantation. Some benefits could accrue as a result. For example, slave drivers in charge of rationing out foodstuffs and clothing could appropriate the best and biggest shares for their family members. Likewise, with regard to fieldwork, drivers could favor their friends and family by allocating the easiest tasks to them.

A driver's influence also extended to the slave community at large. Some were held in very high esteem among the slave population. For example, many of these men served as preachers. Or, they were

sometimes called upon to mediate disputes between slaves. Yet, as often as not, drivers were reviled by their fellow slaves. Their position as favored servant could generate intense resentment, especially if a driver profited materially from his position at the expense of other slaves. More importantly, because one of a driver's main duties was to discipline his fellow slaves, he could quickly earn the enmity of others by asserting this authority too often.

BIBLIOGRAPHY

Bassett, John S. *The Southern Plantation Overseer as Revealed in His Letters.* Northampton, MA: Smith College, 1925.

Genovese, Eugene. *Roll, Jordan, Roll: The World the Slaveholders Made.* New York: Random House, 1976.

Rawick, George P., ed. *The American Slave: A Composite Autobiography.* 41 vols. Westport, CT: Greenwood Press, 1972–1979.

Roles, John. *Inside Views of Slavery on Southern Plantations.* New York, 1864.

Scarborough, William K. *The Overseer: Plantation Management in the Old South.* Athens: University of Georgia Press, 1984.

Van Deburg, William L. *The Slave Drivers: Black Agricultural Labor Supervisors in the American South.* Westport, CT: Greenwood Press, 1979.

Amy Crowson

POOR WHITES

For much of the twentieth century, historians insisted that mutual hatred and animosity characterized the relationships between slaves and poor whites. More recent scholarship has complicated and refined that picture, uncovering a broad and complex range of relations among the South's dispossessed, both black and white. At times, shared economic deprivation and impoverishment tempered racial hostilities and drew slaves and poor whites together into civil, cordial, and even intimate and loving relationships. On a daily basis, slave and poor white interaction both reinforced and challenged Southern racial boundaries.

Ample evidence from travelers' accounts and slave narratives supports the assertion of slaves' and poor whites' mutual resentment and contempt, but loathing coexisted with friendship and camaraderie. In childhood, poor white boys and girls sometimes played with slave youngsters. "We thought well of the poor white neighbors," remembered one North Carolina slave. "We colored children took them as regular playmates" (Rawick 1972, vol. 15, pt. 2, p. 345). Occasionally, however, childhood fun could take a menacing turn as white children imitated masters by tormenting blacks their own age. One former bondperson resented how the "po' white kids" beat the slave children and "make us call dem marser" (Rawick 1972, vol. 16, Ohio Narratives, p. 40). The complexity of slave-poor white relationships in childhood continued into adulthood.

Labor Relations

Poor white men and women sometimes worked together with slaves, either as agricultural laborers in the fields, as domestics, or as industrial workers in textile mills and other establishments. Sometimes they labored harmoniously, sometimes not. At the conclusion of the workday or on weekends, however, slaves and poor whites might relax with one another in their leisure time, occasionally in evangelical churches but more frequently in the more profane and overwhelmingly male subculture of the southern grog shop. There, slave and poor white men together drank "spirituous liquors" and gambled at seven up, rattle-and-snap, pitch-and-toss, or chuck-a-

RHODES V. BUNCH (1825)

Enraged at the thriving underground trade between slaves and poor whites, frustrated planters united to oust irksome poor whites from the community. In the mid–1820s, neighbors in Charleston District, South Carolina, cooperated to evict the poor white shopkeeper Andrew Rhodes from the insubstantial shack he rented because "he was dealing with their negroes and was a troublesome neighbor" (Forret 2006, p. 110). Rhodes was regarded as "a nuisance in the parish, and a great vagabond, with whom no white man associated, and who cultivated no land, and owned ... property ... only fit for negro trading" (p. 110). Rhodes had spent several years in the Charleston jail, mostly for perjury. Charleston authorities had also imprisoned him briefly for uttering incendiary comments during the Denmark Vesey rebellion of 1822. (Reportedly, Rhodes had expressed his opinion to three free black men that "the negroes ought to fight for their liberty" [p. 151].) Fearing the poor white man's corrupting influence on their slaves, neighbors entered the shack during Rhodes's absence, meticulously removed his meager belongings ("suitable only for the lowest retail grog shop" [p. 110]), and, with the owner's consent, systematically dismantled the humble dwelling. Upon his return, Rhodes, stunned, sued his neighbors for trespassing. The defendants vindicated themselves, saying, "The object in pulling down the house was to prevent ... Rhodes, [from] getting possession again, and to expel him thereby from the neighborhood; as he was trading illicitly with the negroes" (p. 110). Clearly siding with the vigilantes, the sympathetic judge awarded Rhodes one paltry cent in compensation.

BIBLIOGRAPHY

Forret, Jeffrey. *Race Relations at the Margins: Slaves and Poor Whites in the Antebellum Southern Countryside.* Baton Rouge: Louisiana State University Press, 2006.

Kennedy, Lionel H., and Thomas Parker. *An Official Report of the Trials of Sundry Negroes, Charged with an Attempt to Raise an Insurrection in the State of South Carolina: Preceded by an Introduction and Narrative; and in an Appendix, a Report of the Trials of Four White Persons, on Indictments for Attempting to Excite the Slaves to Insurrection.* Charleston, SC: James R. Schenck, 1822.

luck. In Yorkville, South Carolina, for example, poor white mattress maker "Ptolemy Funk did game with Cards with two negro men slaves" in 1856 (Forret 2006, p. 59).

More than any other activity, a thriving underground trade brought slaves and poor whites together. In their illicit economic exchanges unsanctioned by the master, slaves most frequently purchased or traded for alcohol, poor whites for food. While men proved the more active participants in these surreptitious networks of exchange, slave and poor white women were also involved. In South Carolina, for instance, the poor and

Preparing the family meal. A woodcut based on an E. W. Kemble illustration featuring a poor white woman cooking in front of her rural cabin in Georgia, circa 1800s. Poor whites often worked with slaves in the fields, as domestics, and as industrial workers. *© North Wind Picture Archives.*

illiterate Sarah and Jemima Woodward purchased "a quantity of meat and flour of the value of one dollar" from a female slave named Bet (Forret 2006, p. 87). Because goods stolen off the plantation fueled much of the trade, slaveholders bristled at the clandestine traffic. But despite their efforts to curb it through the passage of laws, community censure, and the creation of vigilance associations, the covert slave-poor white economy continued unabated until emancipation.

Poor whites played a contradictory role in regulating the slaves of the Old South, both sustaining and subverting planter authority and the Southern social order. As overseers and patrollers, spies and slave hunters, poor white men performed vital roles for slave owners and, by extension, the slave system. Through these functions, they kept slaves in their oppressed condition as they reassured slaveholders of their own allegiance to the Old South's racial hierarchy. Slaves frequently complained about "poor white trash" overseers and "patterollers" who treated them cruelly. Masters likewise lamented the quality of white men they relied upon for these crucial services. Poor white patrollers, explained one anonymous correspondent to the *Richmond Enquirer,* "glory in this sort of temporary military authority . . . and, making it the

occasion of a *frolic,* their bad passions stirred up by drink, they maltreat the quiet, inoffensive, home staying negro." In no official capacity, many poor whites kept a vigilant eye on slaves and reported transgressions to the master. A few even made a living as professional slave catchers assigned to track down runaways. William Blackledge of Richland District, South Carolina, remembered ex-slave Jacob Stroyer, was illiterate, "very poor, and had a large family," including "a wife, with eight or ten helpless children." He hunted fugitive slaves with dogs and a gaunt, decrepit horse. Blackledge overstepped his authority, however, when he fatally shot a fugitive who had killed several of his canines. Authorities apprehended Blackledge and hanged him for the slave's murder (Katz 1996, pp. 198–201).

Poor whites possessed the means to subvert the slave system masters expected them to enforce. Poor whites sometimes falsified passes and free papers for slaves. One South Carolina master swore an affidavit in 1832 that one of his slaves by the name of Jacob ran off, aided by "a ticket" forged by a poor white man. Other poor whites harbored fugitive slaves or conveyed them away. When North Carolina slave Allen Parker ran away, he found shelter at "the house of a poor white woman who had been a friend to my mother" (Parker 1895, p. 82). During Moses Roper's escape, he encountered "a poor man" in North Carolina who "took me up in his cart" and conducted the fugitive northward (Roper, 1970 [1838], p. 30). Although a few poor whites assisted slaves out of friendship or as a means to attack the slave system, most expected compensation in goods or labor for the favors they provided. Fugitive slave John Brown recorded that he "obtained a forged pass from a poor white man, for which I gave him an old hen" (Chamerovzow 1855, p. 72). A tiny number of poor whites hoped to profit from slave stealing. Some quickly resold as their own the slaves they abducted; others waited patiently until the master advertised a reward, then produced the hostage and collected the money.

The only offense a poor white could commit that alarmed masters more than slave stealing was joining with bondpeople in outright rebellion, and in each of the most famous slave conspiracies and rebellions of the nineteenth century, including those of Gabriel, Denmark Vesey, and Nat Turner, slaves either predicted that poor whites would side with them or received encouragement or assistance from them. Although most poor whites made no attempt to assist slave runaways and rebels, those who did undermined the very social structure slaveholders expected them to defend and implicitly called poor whites' commitment to the slave regime into question.

Social Interaction

More often than not, slaves and poor whites in the antebellum South coexisted peacefully, at times even amiably, but violence nevertheless frequently erupted between them, and while mutual hostility and resentment accounted for much of that violence, slaves' and poor whites' own routine interracial fraternization fostered some of the physical conflicts between them. Erstwhile amicable socializing in the masculine interracial subculture of drinking, gambling, and carousing could quickly descend into violence. Slave and poor white men marinated in alcohol and playing games of chance frequently came to blows. In South Carolina, one poor white gambler, likely enraged by losing money to a slave, "beat and wound[ed]" the bondman Jacob "by knocking him with a Stool and Stab[b]ing him with a dirk in the back" (Forret 206, p. 171). For the infraction, he earned a twenty-dollar fine, two weeks in jail, and twenty lashes. Misunderstandings in the underground economy also provoked violence between slaves and poor whites. In North Carolina, the slave George attacked an "old, infirm & poor" white man who "kept a grog shop" for failing to trade him shoes and rum, and Gilbert Fanny followed through on his vow to harm the bondman Jet for informing local whites that Fanny had weighed plundered meat for the slave (Forret 2006, p. 176). As these

examples demonstrate, slave and poor white men together inhabited a shadowy subculture of conviviality and violence. The lower orders of southern society shared a rough-and-tumble culture in which camaraderie and play could suddenly turn into rivalry and animosity. That slaves and poor whites careened erratically between friendship and violence suggests the tensions underlying their social interactions.

Sexual Relations

Slaves and poor whites engaged in a range of sexual contacts, from voluntary to involuntary and everything in between, but the experiences of poor white women and men contrasted markedly by sex. Poor white women sometimes found companionship across the color line. The *Richmond Enquirer* recorded the case of poor white Susan Percy, who ran off with a slave named John in 1857. When apprehended, Susan confessed "that an intimacy had grown up" between them, and together they resolved "to make their escape to a free State," giving John his freedom and Susan the chance to "hide her shame" for falling in love with a slave. In another extraordinary case, the slave Bay Ben absconded from North Carolina "in company with a white woman who has several children" by him. According to the *Raleigh Register*, "The woman calls her name GATSY TOOTLE, and considers herself the wife of Ben." Many of these apparently consensual affairs between poor white women and slave men originated in their close working contact. In North Carolina, for example, an affinity developed between Abraham Peppinger's poor white servant girl Polly Lane and his slave Jim in 1825.

Poor white women's working lives, however, also made them vulnerable to sexual assault. Mary Dunn reported a rape committed by the slave Warrick, with whom she had spun cloth in the slave quarters. Accusations of interracial rape met with skepticism in Southern courtrooms, however, as elite white men considered poor white women promiscuous, sexually depraved, and less worthy of legal protection than economically valuable slaves. The young poor white woman Rachael Holman struggled to establish her good character in court when she brought a charge of attempted rape against the slave Lewis. Rachael promptly reported the assault and had bruises on her throat and arms and a torn dress, but she also had a reputation for being "too familiar with the colored population," allegedly having a relationship with a bondman named Elias. As a result, the court found Lewis not guilty.

Poor white men confronted far fewer restrictions on their sexual behavior with slave women. Like poor white women, poor white men engaged in a wide array of sexual relationships with slaves. As overseers, they sometimes used their authority over slave women to extract sexual favors. But even poor white men not in positions of power exercised sexual dominance over female slaves.

When Thomas D. Foy wanted sex, he "went out to where some negro Girls were washing," approached a slave woman, and "retired to a hog pen" (Forret 2006, p. 218). In contrast to poor white women, poor white men successfully capitalized upon the privileges of their race and sex to transcend their class status and appropriate the bodies of slave women for their own libidinous purposes. The gendered experiences of poor white women and men in their sexual encounters with slaves reflected and affirmed the sexual double standard in southern society. Scholars have often asked why slaves and poor whites failed to forge a class-based coalition and offer a biracial challenge to planter dominance in the Old South. The nature of the relationship between slaves and poor whites itself supplies one response to the question. Slaves and poor whites engaged in such competing and contradictory types of relationships that it would have been incredibly difficult for them to unite unequivocally.

BIBLIOGRAPHY

Arroyo, Elizabeth Fortson. "Poor Whites, Slaves, and Free Blacks in Tennessee, 1796–1861." *Tennessee Historical Quarterly* 55 (Spring 1996): 56–65.

Bolton, Charles C. *Poor Whites of the Antebellum South: Tenants and Laborers in Central North Carolina and Northeast Mississippi*. Durham, NC: Duke University Press, 1994.

Bolton, Charles C., and Scott P. Culclasure, eds. *The Confessions of Edward Isham: A Poor White Life of the Old South*. Athens: University of Georgia Press, 1998.

Cecil-Fronsman, Bill. *Common Whites: Class and Culture in Antebellum North Carolina*. Lexington: University Press of Kentucky, 1992.

Chamerovzow, L. A., ed. *Slave Life in Georgia: A Narrative of the Life, Sufferings, and Escape of John Brown, a Fugitive Slave, Now in England*. London, 1855.

Forret, Jeff. *Race Relations at the Margins: Slaves and Poor Whites in the Antebellum Southern Countryside*. Baton Rouge: Louisiana State University Press, 2006.

Genovese, Eugene D. "'Rather Be a Nigger Than a Poor White Man': Slave Perceptions of Southern Yeomen and Poor Whites." In *Toward a New View of America: Essays in Honor of Arthur C. Cole*, ed. Hans L. Trefousse. New York: Burt Franklin & Company, Inc., 1977.

Genovese, Eugene D. *Roll, Jordan, Roll: The World the Slaves Made*. New York: Vintage, 1976.

Harris, J. William. *Plain Folk and Gentry in a Slave Society: White Liberty and Black Slavery in Augusta's Hinterlands*. Baton Rouge: Louisiana State University Press, 1998.

Hodes, Martha. *White Women, Black Men: Illicit Sex in the Nineteenth-Century South*. New Haven: Yale University Press, 1997.

Katz, William Loren, ed. *Flight from the Devil: Six Slave Narratives*. Trenton, NJ: Africa World Press, Inc., 1996.

Lockley, Timothy James. *Lines in the Sand: Race and Class in Lowcountry Georgia, 1750–1860*. Athens: University of Georgia Press, 2001.

Parker, Allen. *Recollections of Slavery Times*. Worcester, MA: Chas W. Burbank & Co., 1895.

Rawick, George P., ed. *The American Slave: A Composite Autobiography*. 19 vols. Westport, CT: Greenwood Press, 1972–1979.

Roper, Moses. *A Narrative of the Adventures and Escape of Moses Roper, from American Slavery; with a Preface, by the Rev. T. Price, D.D.* [1838]. New York: Negro Universities Press, 1970.

Jeff Forret

FREE BLACKS

Since the mid-1600s, free people of African descent have been in America. It is a common misperception that only enslaved black people were in America from the earliest days of exploration and colonization until the final abolition of slavery at the close of the Civil War. Although the majority of black people came to America as captive slaves, there were free people of African descent who lived and worked with early explorers and colonists in the American colonies. For example, the first documentation of free blacks in America was dated around 1644. The Dutch West India Company seized Spanish ships with captive African slaves and used them as the primary source of labor in the New Netherlands colony (present-day New York). "An Act of the Director of New Netherlands" dated February 25, 1644, freed eleven "Company Negroes" with "nineteen years of faithful service" to the Company (Williams 1998, p. 5). In 1644, some black slaves also obtained their freedom by petitioning the company with the assistance of white citizens of New Netherlands who were opposed to slavery.

In New Netherlands there were three categories of people of African descent: slaves, half-slaves, and freemen. Half-slaves were similar to indentured servants; after they obtained freedom from the Company, these half-slaves had continued financial and work obligations to the Dutch West India Company including having to agree that their children "born or yet to be born" would still be slaves of the company (Higginbotham 1980, pp. 107–108). The manumitted blacks essentially paid for their continued freedom through their labor for their former masters. Their freedom was conditional, and they could be returned to slavery if they did not meet the obligations that the company imposed on them. One example of a manumission agreement from Dutch West

India Company details the conditions of a former slave's freedom:

> Therefore we, the Director and Council do release, for the terms of their natural lives, the above named an [*sic*] their wives from Slavery, hereby setting them free and at liberty, on the same footing as other free people here in New Netherlands, where they shall be able to earn their livelihood by Agriculture, on the land shown and granted to them, on the condition that they, the above named Negroes, shall be bound to pay for the freedom they receive each man for himself annually, as long as he lives, to the West India Company for its deputy here, thirty skepels (barn baskets-22 ½ bushels) of Maize, or Wheat, Pease or Beans, and one Fat Hog, valued at twenty guilders, which thirty skepels and the hog they, the Negroes, each for himself, promises to pay annually, beginning from the date hereof, on pain, if anyone of them shall fail to pay the yearly tribute, he shall forfeit his freedom and return to slavery (Williams, p. 15).

These freed black people were not truly free because of these impossible conditions. They did not achieve true freedom until after the Dutch West India Company failed in 1664; at that time the former slaves did not have any further obligations to the defunct company. After 1664 when the English took over New Netherlands and renamed it New York, there was no middle ground of being a half-slave: a person of African descent could only be categorized as free person or a slave under English law. The status of a black person's mother was the determinative factor in deciding whether a person of African descent was born free or in bondage. This maternal line of descent was contrary to English common law in which the status of one's father determined free status. This change was made in the American colonies to combat the problem of mixed children who were born as a result of the frequent unions between black female slaves and free white men (Higginbotham and Higginbotham 1993, pp. 1242–1245).

Because of the presumption that people who were white or Native American were free, and people of African descent were slaves, many free African Americans had to sue for their freedom to prove that they were free people. One example of this type of freedom suit was the Virginia case of *Hudgins v. Wright* (1806). In the *Hudgins* case, the plaintiffs sued for their freedom because they claimed that they were American Indians because their mother was an American Indian. The court determined that they were free Native Americans based on their appearance and outside evidence that their mother and maternal grandmother were of Indian descent. The author of the *Hudgins* opinion, Judge George Tucker of the Virginia Court of Appeals, helped to solidify the practice that people of African descent were presumed to be slaves, primarily based upon physical appearance.

Negro Expulsion from a Railway Car, Philadelphia. From the *London News*, 27 Sept 1856. *Library of Congress, Washington, DC/ Bridgeman Art Library.*

Tucker restated the presumption that white people and Native Americans were free and that people with typical African features were presumed to be slaves. According to Tucker:

> Nature has stampt [*sic*] upon the African and his descendants two characteristic marks besides the difference of complexion, which often remain visible long after the characteristic distinction of colour either disappears or becomes doubtful, a flat nose and woolly head of hair . . . so pointed is this distinction between the natives of Africa and the aborigines of America, that a man might as easily mistake the glossy, jetty clothing of an American bear for the wool of a black sheep, as the hair of an American Indian for that of an African, or the descendant of an African (*Hudgins v. Wright*, 11 Va. 134 (1806).

Before the Emancipation Proclamation of 1863 and the end of the Civil War in 1865, many slaves gained their freedom through manumission. After the Revolutionary War, some slave owners manumitted slaves who had served as soldiers in the Revolutionary War; other slaveholders freed their slaves because human bondage was contrary to the precepts of the Declaration of Independence and the United States Constitution. By the early 1800s, there were more than 20,000 free blacks

PAUL CUFFEE

Paul Cuffee was a free African American who was prominent in gaining civil rights for African Americans in the early days of the United States. He was born in Cuttyhunk, Massachusetts, near New Bedford, in 1759. His parents were Kofi, a former slave from Ghana, and a Wamponoag Indian woman.

He was a successful businessman and captain who owned a shipping company, whaling ships, and a large amount of property in Westport, Massachusetts. Cuffee opened the first integrated school in Massachusetts in 1797 after his children were denied admission to the local public elementary school because of their race.

Cuffee was instrumental in winning the right to vote for free African American property owners. Cuffee and his brother John petitioned the Massachusetts legislature in 1780 to protest the taxation without representation of free black people. Although Cuffee's efforts were not successful initially, his actions led to free African American citizens winning the right to vote through an act of the legislature.

Cuffee was also an advocate of the Back to Africa movement and helped finance a trip to Sierra Leone for African Americans who wanted to return to Africa because of racial discrimination in the United States. He shipped thirty-eight African Americans to Sierra Leone in 1815. Cuffee had planned more voyages to Africa for free blacks who wanted to emigrate, but he died in 1817.

BIBLIOGRAPHY

Hope Franklin, John, and Alfred A. Moss Jr. *From Slavery to Freedom: A History of African Americans.* New York: Random House, 2004.

Nell, William Cooper. *The Colored Patriots of the American Revolution, with Sketches of Several Distinguished Colored Persons, To which Is Added a Brief Survey of the Condition and Prospects of Colored Americans.* Boston: Robert F. Wallcut, 1855.

living in the slave state of Virginia. Manumission was not a viable option for many black slaves and some escaped from slavery, sued for their freedom via freedom lawsuits, or purchased their freedom from their masters (Higginbotham and Higginbotham 1993, pp. 1220–1222, 1237–1242).

The experiences of each of these groups were different depending on whether they lived in an abolitionist state or slave state. Some other factors that determined the quality of life of free African Americans included the manner in which they obtained their freedom and the attitudes and beliefs of White society in particular geographic locations in the United States before 1865.

In the Southern slaveholding states, there were free blacks but their situations were quite different from similarly situated free blacks in the Northern states and northwestern territories. These African Americans lived a precarious existence in a Southern society that still held thousands of their brethren in human bondage. Proslav-

ery white citizens did not readily accept the concept of free blacks and often harassed, humiliated, and killed them. These free black people were constantly in danger of being kidnapped and sold into slavery illegally and had to constantly prove that they were free men and women. For example, in 1800, more than 20,000 free people of African descent lived in Virginia. Because Virginia was one of the Southern states with the most slaveholders and black slaves, it was very difficult for free blacks to prove that they were free. In Southern states such as Virginia, there was a presumption that people with darker skin and other African physical characteristics were slaves. Free black people who had African features had the burden of proving that they were truly free and not slaves. People with white or light skin were presumed to be free (Higginbotham and Higginbotham 1993, pp. 1237–1242).

Even if an emancipated slave could prove that he or she was free, it was not a guarantee of absolute freedom in the Southern states and the person could be resold into slavery under certain conditions. For example, under Virginia law, "any emancipated slave remaining in the state more than a year, may be sold by the overseers of the poor for the benefit of the literary fund." In North Carolina, a 1799 statute declared that "any slave set free, except for meritorious service ... may be seized by any free holder, and sold to the highest bidder." Conditions were even worse for free African Americans in South Carolina where "any person may seize such freed man and keep him as his property" (Davis 1845, p. 3).

Free African Americans lived in the Northern United States before the American Revolutionary War. The experiences of northern free people of African descent were quite different than the experiences of free Blacks who lived in the slaveholding states. Although they were free, most White Americans still did not consider free African Americans to be their equals and they were often denied the rights and privileges of white citizens and had to fight for their civil rights, including the right to obtain a public education and the right to vote. Despite these social, political, and legal inequities, there were many successful free African Americans in the non-slaveholding states. For example, even though they lived and worked in the free states, free African Americans were still in danger of being kidnapped into slavery after the passage of the federal Fugitive Slave Act of 1850. This federal law gave federal marshalls and their deputies the authority to pursue, capture, and return any escaped slave to their owner. Just like in the South, many free African Americans did not have proof of their free status and might be captured and sent to a life of human bondage in a slave state. As a result of the Fugitive Slave Act of 1850, many free African Americans and slaves migrated to Canada and established communities in the Canadian provinces. Whether free African Americans lived in a slave state or a free state, they were not truly free until the passage of the Thirteenth Amendment to the U.S. Constitution on December 18, 1865. Even after the passage of this constitutional amendment that abolished slavery, the newly freedmen still did not enjoy the rights and privileges of white citizens until nearly a century later.

BIBLIOGRAPHY

Berlin, Ira. *Slaves without Masters: The Free Negro in the Antebellum South.* New York: Pantheon, 1974.

Davis, Edward M. *Extracts from the American Slave Code.* Philadelphia: Philadelphia Female Anti-Slavery Society, 1845.

Franklin, John Hope, and Alfred A. Moss, Jr. *From Slavery to Freedom: A History of African Americans.* New York: Random House, 2004.

Green, Robert, P., Jr. ed. *Equal Protection and the African American Constitutional Experience: A Documentary History.* Westport, CT: Greenwood Press, 2000.

Higginbotham, Jr., A. Leon. *In the Matter of Color, Race and the American Legal Process: The Colonial Period.* New York: Oxford University Press, 1980.

Higginbotham, Jr., A. Leon, and F. Michael Higginbotham. "Yearning to Breathe Free: Legal Barriers Against and Options In Favor of Liberty in Antebellum Virginia." *68 New York University Law Review* 1213, 1220–1222, 1237–1245 (1993).

Hudgins v. Wright, 11 Va. 134 (1806).

Nell, William Cooper. *The Colored Patriots of the American Revolution, with Sketches of Several Distinguished Colored Persons, To Which Is Added a Brief Survey of the Condition and Prospects of Colored Americans.* Boston: Robert F. Wallcut, 1865. "Documenting the American South." University Library, University of North Carolina at Chapel Hill. Available from http://docsouth.unc.edu/nell/nell.html.

Williams, Oscar. *African Americans and Colonial Legislation in the Middle Colonies.* New York: Garland Publishing, 1998.

Jocelyn M. Cuffee

■ Internal Economy

INTERNAL ECONOMY: AN OVERVIEW

Enslaved people in both the Caribbean and in the United States participated in what historians call the "slaves' internal economy." This phrase refers to an informal economic system that operated within or underneath legally sanctioned systems of economic exchange. As property, slaves could not legally make contracts, thus negating any sort of legal personal trade. Yet, abundant evidence from narratives, court cases, plantation records, and even legal statutes themselves indicate that slaves actively engaged in economic activity outside the labor completed for their masters. The inherent contradictions of the internal economy make it fruitful territory for explorations of master-slave relations, enslaved life and culture, and the economy of slave societies.

The ways in which scholars have interpreted the internal economy not only reflect predominating historiographic trends, they also reveal the process by which historians have attempted to cope with the seeming paradox of property ownership by chattel. In the Caribbean, anthropologists were at the forefront of this discussion. Seminal work by Sidney Mintz and Douglas Hall in the mid-1950s paved the way for later efforts to ascertain the mechanics and meaning of slaves' economic behavior among the varied labor systems of the eighteenth- and nineteenth-century Caribbean.

In the United States, early twentieth-century historians such as Ulrich Phillips (1877–1934) and Lewis Gray (b. 1881) grappled with the paradox of the internal economy indirectly, establishing the extent to which such activity occurred and considering the meaning of such activity to the master class. The synthetic works of the 1970s fit slaves' economic activity within the context of larger interpretations of master-slave relations and slave culture. Robert Fogel and Stanley Engerman (1974) characterized the internal economy as part of a system of rewards and incentives, whereas Herbert Gutman and Richard Sutch considered it as part of a set of customary rights and concessions. John Blassingame (1979) argued that slaves' economic behavior increased communalism and solidarity, whereas Eugene Genovese's (1976) precapitalist characterization of the South held that market systems in the South were not developed fully enough for internal economic activity to have significant impact on slaves' life and culture.

The first detailed studies of internal economies in the antebellum South emerged in the early 1980s. In 1982 and 1983 Philip Morgan published two essays exploring the nature of the task system in Low Country South Carolina and Georgia. According to Morgan, the internal economy allowed slaves to earn cash and accumulate property, thus inculcating in slaves a "quasi-proprietorial attitude" (1983, p. 401). Moreover, the decisions that slaves made regarding the management and sale of their goods "fed individual initiative and sponsored collective discipline and esteem" (Morgan 1982, p. 597). Slaves, according to the interpretation put forward by Morgan and others, were empowered by such economic activity, their behavior being an assertion of their agency. Other scholars, among them Lawrence McDonnell, Peter Coclanis, and Peter Kolchin, challenged this prevailing interpretation, wondering whether the introduction of market behavior into the slave community introduced dissent and, ultimately, tied slaves more closely to their masters. More recently, Dylan Penningroth (2003) has attempted to straddle these conflicting interpretations, arguing that though conflicts often emerged in the slave community, property and kinship were inextricably linked.

Though scholars continue to differ over the meaning of slaves' economic behavior, most agree on its importance for understanding slave societies as a whole. The major themes that predominate in slavery historiography emerge starkly in focused study of internal economies in the South and the Caribbean. With the emergence of social and cultural history, for example, historians have focused not simply on the ways in which masters managed their slaves, but on the ways in which bondpeople created their own lives within a system of bondage. Historians have established the presence of active economic networks within slave communities and have explored the interplay of gender, family structure, religion, and African traditions within them. Questions asked by historians interested in slave life and culture include: To what extent did market participation solidify ties in the slave community?; did family structure affect conceptions of property ownership?; and what roles did women play in the internal economy?

In addition to relationships within the slave community, considering the internal economy helps scholars think productively about slaves' connections with the surrounding nonslave community, particularly with free persons of color and poor whites. Bondpeople did not restrict their trade to their fellow enslaved. Rather, they forged economic and concomitant social ties to members of the surrounding community. United, in many respects, by class but differentiated by race, poor whites and slaves both competed and collaborated in economic affairs. Scholarship in this area has been particularly insightful but—especially with regard to relationships with free blacks—much ground has yet to be covered.

Finally, work on the internal economy reminds scholars that slaves' lives were not divorced from their masters. The economic behavior of enslaved people occurred within the context of white management and governance. Among the more important questions addressed within the historiography is whether or not the internal economy served as a means of resistance or accommodation to the slave system. On the one hand, bondpeople developed skills and behaviors that challenged the mastery of the slaveholding class. On the other, participation in the internal economy offered a level of satisfaction that may have allayed long-term dissent and resistance to the system.

Scholars interested in the slaves' internal economy find a wealth of sources available to them. The Works Progress Administration interviewed elderly ex-slaves in the 1930s—these oral histories provide a wealth of information about everyday life, particularly the presence of money in the slave community. Planters' journals reveal management techniques and economic accounts with slaves. Court records detail aspects of underground or illicit economic activity. Travelers' narratives, among them Frederick Law Olmsted's (1822–1903) *Cotton Kingdom*, provide a useful outsider's perspective on the economic relationships among members of slave-based societies.

Published memoirs, particularly those written by ex-slaves, have proven significantly useful as they detail the minutiae of everyday life in slavery. Authors such as Charles Ball (b. 1781), Henry Clay Bruce (1836–1902), Frederick Douglass (1817–1895), Lunsford Lane (1803–1863), and many others detail the independent economic activities in which they participated while enslaved.

BIBLIOGRAPHY

Ball, Charles. *Slavery in the United States. A Narrative of the Life and Adventures of Charles Ball, a Black Man, Who Lived Forty Years in Maryland, South Carolina, and Georgia, as a Slave under Various Masters, and Was One Year in the Navy with Commodore Barney, during the Late War.* New York: John S. Taylor, 1837.

Ball, Charles. *Fifty Years in Chains; or, The Life of An American Slave.* New York: H. Dayton, 1859.

Berlin, Ira, and Philip Morgan. *The Slaves' Economy: Independent Production by Slaves in the Americas.* London: Frank Cass, 1991.

Blassingame, John W. *The Slave Community: Plantation Life in the Antebellum South.* New York: Oxford University Press, 1979.

Fogel, Robert, and Stanley Engerman. *Time on the Cross: The Economics of American Negro Slavery.* Boston: Little and Brown, 1974.

Forret, Jeff. "Slaves, Poor Whites, and the Underground Economy of the Rural Carolinas." *Journal of Southern History* 70, no. 4 (November 2004): 783–824.

Genovese, Eugene. *Roll, Jordan, Roll: The World The Slaves Made.* New York: Vintage, 1976.

Hudson, Larry. *To Have and To Hold: Slave Work and Family in Antebellum South Carolina.* Athens: University of Georgia Press, 1997.

Lockley, Timothy. *Lines in the Sand: Race and Class in Low Country Georgia, 1750–1860*. Athens: University of Georgia Press, 2001.

McDonnell, Lawrence T. "Money Knows No Master: Market Relations and the American Slave Community." In *Developing Dixie: Modernization in a Traditional Society*, eds. Winfred B. Moore Jr., Joseph F. Tripp, and Lyon G. Tyler. New York: Greenwood Press, 1988.

Mintz, Sidney, and Douglas Hall. "The Origins of the Internal Marketing System." *Yale University Publications in Anthropology* 57 (1960): 3–26.

Morgan, Philip D. "Work and Culture: The Task System and the Work of Low Country Blacks, 1700–1800." *William and Mary Quarterly* 4 (1982): 563–599.

Morgan, Philip D. "The Ownership of Property by Slaves in the Mid-Nineteenth-Century Low Country." *Journal of Southern History* 49, no. 3 (1983): 399–420.

Olmsted, Frederick Law. *The Cotton Kingdom: a Traveler's Observations on Cotton and Slavery in the American Slave States: Based upon Three Former Volumes of Journeys and Investigations by the Same Author.* New York: Mason Brothers, 1861–1862.

Penningroth, Dylan C. *The Claims of Kinfolk: African American Property and Community in the Nineteenth-Century South.* Chapel Hill: University of North Carolina Press, 2003.

Kathleen Hilliard

SLAVE GARDENS

To supplement basic provisions provided by their master, some bondpeople grew their own foodstuffs and staple crops for personal consumption or sale. Enslaved men and women typically tended these gardens or "patches" after they had finished their daily or weekly work for their master.

For some slaves, these gardens provided crucial supplements to an otherwise nutrient-deprived diet. The extent to which bondpeople and their masters relied on slave gardens for basic provisioning depended on the type of labor system employed and the region in which the plantation was situated. In Jamaica, for example, slaves cultivated "provision grounds," which were, according to traveler Zachary Macaulay, their sole means of subsistence. Elaborating on this system, Macaulay explained that "[i]f, therefore, they neglected to employ in their provision-grounds a sufficient portion of the Sunday, to secure to them an adequate supply of food, they might be reduced to absolute want" (Macauly 1824, p. 39).

In the United States slave gardens were often less extensive, as slaveholders often provided basic, albeit meager, provisions. In two narratives detailing his life

in bondage, the ex-slave Charles Ball (c. 1780–?) described the role such small-scale agriculture played in the slaves'" daily lives. In *Fifty Years in Chains* (1859), Ball assured readers that bondpeople subsisted on more than a small allotment of corn and salt from their master, by supplementing their diet with produce from their own gardens. In *Slavery in the United States* (1853) he elaborated further, explaining, "the people are allowed to make patches, as they are called—that is, gardens, in some remote and unprofitable part of the estate, generally in the woods, in which they plant corn, potatoes, pumpkins, melons, and others for themselves" (p. 166).

As important to slaves in both the Caribbean and in the United States were the opportunities gardens provided for market participation. Frederick Law Olmsted (1822–1903) explained that slaves on a South Carolina plantation were "at liberty to sell whatever they choose from the products of their own garden" (Olmsted 1861–1862, p. 251). Opportunities for market sale of produce were naturally greater where slaves had larger land allotments and more time to cultivate and then sell their crops. Because provision grounds were more extensive in many parts of the Caribbean, Sunday markets were an important component of slaves'" economic lives there. In Grenada, for example, the Reverend Benjamin Webster complained that slaves there rarely attended church services because Sunday was the only "day on which slaves have an opportunity of bartering the produce of the provision grounds allotted to them by their masters" (Riland 1827, p. 99). Such a practice was common in areas of the Low Country South as well, where the task system allowed slaves to spend greater time and energy in crop cultivation and market participation in cities such as Savannah and Charleston.

But foodstuffs could provide only a limited amount of cash, and many slaves were interested in earning larger amounts of money. Some slaveholders recognized such acquisitiveness and allowed slaves to grow staple crops such as cotton, rice, corn, and tobacco for sale. Henry Clay Bruce explained how this process worked on his master's Virginia plantation:

> Each man was allowed one acre of ground to raise his own little crop, which, if well cultivated, would produce nine hundred pounds of tobacco. We used his horse and plow, and worked our crop as well as we did his in the daytime, and when ready for market, he sold our crop with his, giving each one his share. This was our money, to be spent for whatever we wanted aside from that given by him (1895, p. 84).

Slaves aimed to add variety to their diets and wealth to their households though the cultivation of foodstuffs and staple crops. As with other activities associated with the internal economy, however, such practice held ambivalent meaning, by both promoting opportunities for wealth and independence and simultaneously attaching slaves more firmly to the plantations.

BIBLIOGRAPHY

Ball, Charles. *Slavery in the United States: A Narrative of the Life and Adventures of Charles Ball, a Black Man, Who Lived Forty Years in Maryland, South Carolina, and Georgia, as a Slave under Various Masters, and Was One Year in the Navy with Commodore Barney, during the Late War.* New York: John S. Taylor, 1853.

Ball, Charles. *Fifty Years in Chains; or, The Life of an American Slave.* New York: H. Dayton, 1859.

Bruce, Henry Clay. *The New Man: Twenty-Nine Years a Slave, Twenty-Nine Years a Free Man.* York, PA: P. Anstadt, 1895.

Macaulay, Zachary. *Negro Slavery, or, A View of Some of the More Prominent Features of That State of Society: As It Exists in the United States of America and in the Colonies of the West Indies, Especially in Jamaica.* London: Society for the Mitigation and Gradual Abolition of Slavery throughout the British Dominions, 1824.

Olmsted, Frederick Law. *The Cotton Kingdom: A Traveller's Observations on Cotton and Slavery in the American Slave States: Based upon Three Former Volumes of Journeys and Investigations by the Same Author.* New York: Mason Brothers, 1861–1862.

Riland, John. *Memoirs of a West-India Planter.* London: Hamilton, Adams, 1827.

Kathleen Hilliard

HIRING TIME FOR WAGES

Within the system of slavery, the meaning of hiring time varied according to place and situation. According to his or her master's discretion, a slave might hire his own time for compensation outside of the time allotted for work for his master. Likewise, a master might hire out or rent his slave to another master. In one variant of this system of slave hire, wages for labor performed were paid directly to the slave, a portion of which was given to the master.

Though, legally, their lives and labor were not their own, some enslaved people seized opportunities to earn wages for themselves during time in which they were not engaged in labor for their masters. A crucial component of the internal economy, this system of wage work allowed bondpeople to accumulate small amounts of cash and property as a means of supplementing their allowances. The amount of free time available for hire depended upon the type of labor in which a slave was engaged for his or her master. In the gang system of labor, generally seen in interior cotton and tobacco plantations, bondpeople commonly worked from sunup to sundown with Sundays allowed for rest. Under the task system, slaves were assigned a task to be completed by the end of the day. If slaves completed their tasks early, the rest of the day was theirs to spend as they chose

(as sanctioned by the master). During this free time, many slaves performed additional labor for compensation in the form of cash payment or in-kind goods.

In *Fifty Years in Chains* and *Slavery in the United States*, Charles Ball (c. 1780–?) explained the "universally" followed practice of "working on Sunday for wages," describing a typical Sunday on a South Carolina plantation:

> At the time I rose this morning, it wanted only about fifteen or twenty minutes of sunrise; and a large number of the men, as well as some of the women, had already quitted the quarter, and gone about the business of the day. That is, they had gone to work for wages for themselves—in this manner: our overseer had, about two miles off, a field of near twenty acres, planted in cotton, on his own account... About twenty of our people went to work for him to-day, for which he gave them fifty cents each. Several of the others, perhaps forty in all, went out through the neighbourhood, to work for other planters. (1859, p. 128)

It is important to note that although slaves such as Ball benefited materially from overwork opportunities, such labor was often performed after a hard day's or week's labor, often taking the place of rest and recreational time.

Slaves might also receive wages through the hiring out system. Masters hired out or rented their slaves to other masters. While, in some cases, the slave owner received sole payment for labor performed, it was common for bondpeople to receive a wage as well. Frederick Law Olmsted (1822–1903) observed this phenomenon in a coal mine in Virginia: "The slave[s] are, some of them, owned by the mining company; but the most are hired of their owners, at from $120 to $200 a year, the company boarding and clothing them." But, according to Olmsted, these Virginia slaves earned compensation as well. He noted, "it was customary to give them a certain allowance of money and let them find their own board" (1861–1862, p. 54).

In some cases, particularly in cities such as Savannah and Charleston, bondpeople were responsible for finding work for themselves. Here, slaves earned wages for labor performed, provisioning themselves and paying a monthly or annual share of these wages to their master. Ex-slave Lunsford Lane (1803–1863) described this process for the readers of his narrative: "I hired my time of her [his mistress], for which I paid her a price varying from one hundred dollars to one hundred twenty dollars per year. This was a privilege relatively few slaves in the south enjoy; and in this I felt truly blessed" (1845, p. 15). Ball noted a similar practice in Savannah where he "saw many black men who were slaves, and who yet acted as freemen so far that they went out to work, where and with whom they pleased, received their own wages, and proved their own subsistence; but were obliged to pay a certain sum at the end of each week to their masters" (1859, p. 287).

The notion and practice of receiving wages for hire complicated the relations between slaveholder and slave. For slave owners, this system of payment challenged lines of authority, their mastery threatened by employers willing to compensate slaves for their labor. Likewise, slaves hiring time for wages acted with a degree of choice and independence rarely seen in work for their masters and, in fact, some bondpeople used these opportunities as justification and means of resistance to their enslavement. In the end however, masters allowed slaves to hire time for wages in the hope that short-term economic opportunities would allay long-term discontent.

BIBLIOGRAPHY

Ball, Charles. *Slavery in the United States: A Narrative of the Life and Adventures of Charles Ball, a Black Man, Who Lived Forty Years in Maryland, South Carolina, and Georgia, as a Slave under Various Masters, and was One Year in the Navy with Commodore Barney, during the Late War.* New York: John S. Taylor, 1837.

Ball, Charles. *Fifty Years in Chains; or, The Life of An American Slave.* New York: H. Dayton, 1859.

Lane, Lunsford. *The Narrative of Lunsford Lane, Formerly of Raleigh, N.C., Embracing an Account of His Early Life, the Redemption by Purchase of Himself and Family from Slavery, and His Banishment from the Place of His Birth for the Crime of Wearing a Colored Skin.* Boston: Hewes and Watson, 1845.

Olmsted, Frederick Law. *The Cotton Kingdom: A Traveler's Observations on Cotton and Slavery in the American Slave States: Based upon Three Former Volumes of Journeys and Investigations by the Same Author.* New York: Mason Brothers, 1861–1862.

Kathleen Hilliard

EXCHANGE RELATIONS

Exchange relations within the slaves' internal economy can be characterized in economic, social, and racial terms. Fundamentally, however, exchange relations are about issues of power and are thus political.

In economic terms, bondpeople functioned according to the market roles of producers, sellers, consumers, and middlemen. The most optimistic (or perhaps naïve) slaves expected prices and wages to fluctuate according to laws of supply and demand, but narrative accounts and memoirs reveal the creation of a much more thorny set of relationships when slaves entered the marketplace. Slaves, poor whites, storekeepers, free blacks, and slaveholders engaged in trade cagily, constantly evaluating the advantages or disadvantages that their race, status, or social connections conferred upon them.

Slaveholders were wary of slaves' participating in dealings beyond their range of surveillance. State statutes and local slaveholder customs prohibited unregulated trade; in many cases slaveholders required that their charges carry tickets or written permission allowing them to exchange specific goods. The rationale was both practical and political. Slaveholders worried constantly that their charges might steal from their stores, then slip off to trade stolen goods such as corn or cotton for cash or manufactured goods. Storekeepers and, especially, transient peddlers and wagoners were subject to particular suspicion because of the large variety of goods they could offer—including alcohol—and the temptation they offered to acquisitive servants. "The storekeepers are always ready to accommodate the slaves," Charles Ball (c. 1780–?) declared, "who are frequently better customers than any white people; because the former always pay cash, whilst the latter almost always require credit" (1859, p. 130).

But did slaves receive a fair price for their goods? Ball continued: "In dealing with the slave, the shopkeeper knows he can demand whatever price he pleases for his goods, without danger of being charged with extortion; and he is ready to rise at any time of the night to oblige friends who are of so much value to him" (Ball 1859, p. 130). Herein lay the crux of the problem for both storekeeper and slave: In engaging in trade not sanctioned by the master, shopkeepers risked fines from local authorities and the ire of their slaveholding customers. As Ball explained, however, there were risks for slaves too. Storekeepers could easily report such activity to masters, losing a sale but gaining the favor of a wealthier patron. In most cases, mutual interest and wary trust made for uneasy and sometimes risky exchange. Sales need not have occurred in formal consumption venues such as taverns and local merchants. If the trade was illicit in the eyes of the master, the same risks and benefits characterized less formal transactions with poor whites and free blacks as well.

At risk for the master in these transactions was bond labor and human capital both and he had to carefully consider local market opportunities and temptations in the management and regulation of his workforce. Slaveholders were wary of the relationships that market participation engendered. Collaboration between social inferiors, no matter what their race, challenged the mastery of the slaveholding class. Yet, the material desires of their charges were real and to deny them risked dissatisfaction and, perhaps, resistance. As a result, many slaveholders promoted, or at least permitted, participation in the internal economy. The ex-slave Henry Clay Bruce (1836–1902) observed this practice in Virginia, explaining "[t]he practice of allowing slave ground to raise a little crop obtained generally among slave owners, but most of them had to work their crop of tobacco after sundown, and without plowing" (1854, p. 84). Who

SELLING SWEET POTATOES IN CHARLESTON.

Slaves selling sweet potatoes on the street. A woodcut showing slaves selling sweet potatoes on a Charleston, South Carolina, street, 1861. Slaveholders were wary of slaves participating in dealings beyond their surveillance. *The Granger Collection, New York.*

profited, then, from the slaves' hard work? Bruce minced no words: "The master got the benefit of money after all, because the slave spent it for his own pleasure and comfort, which was a direct advantage to the master" (1854, pp. 84–85).

Slaveholders not only recognized the potential benefit of a carefully regulated internal economy, they also deployed examples of slaves' money-making activities in their defense of the peculiar institution against abolitionist attacks. Commenting on the economic difficulties of a northern, wage-earning seamstress, Nehemiah Adams (1806–1878) commented, "A vast many slaves get wages in a better form than this, in provision for their support for the whole of life, with permission to earn something, and more or less to the disposition of the masters and the ability of the slaves" (1854, p. 51). It is worth noting that few proslavery advocates acknowledged the declining fortunes of nonslaveholding whites in their own communities during this same period.

In participating in the internal economy, bondpeople not only wrestled with the contradictions of their own enslavement, they also negotiated the tenuous relationships of power that marked slave society. Though mutual interest facilitated much of this economic activity, self-interest, jealousy, and the desire for political and social advantage made exchange relations among and with slaves particularly tenuous.

BIBLIOGRAPHY

Adams, Nehemiah. *A South-Side View of Slavery; or, Three Months at the South, in 1854.* Boston: T.R. Martin, 1854.

Ball, Charles. *Fifty Years in Chains; or, The Life of an American Slave.* New York: H. Dayton, 1859.

Bruce, Henry Clay. *The New Man: Twenty-Nine Years a Slave, Twenty-nine Years a Free Man.* Boston: T.R. Marvin and B.B. Mussey, 1854.

Kathleen Hilliard

PROPERTY ACCUMULATION

Those implicated in slavery, the "peculiar institution," daily wrestled with its many contradictions. In no area was this more apparent than the realm of the internal economy. Slaves, as legal chattel, could not, logically, hold chattel themselves. Yet, evidence shows that slaves went to sometimes extraordinary lengths to acquire and accumulate cash and property.

Though no law sanctioned slaves' economic activity, the statutes themselves implicitly acknowledged its existence. In the United States, as the antebellum period progressed, legislation appeared that explicitly prohibited the ownership of certain types of property. Some of these prohibitions were obvious: Slaves could not possess firearms, for example, for fear of resistance and insurrection. Similarly, most areas prohibited slaves' ownership of boats and horses, as they might facilitate running away. Still other codes included sumptuary legislation, which regulated the type of clothing worn by slaves. But these legal restrictions often fell before local custom, and historians have found that slaveholders consented and often promoted property accumulation by their charges.

The amount of property slaves were able to accumulate depended greatly on the type of labor system operated by their master and the skills held by the individual slave. By and large, slaves' ability to accumulate property was based on an economy of time—the more time slaves spent away from labor for their master, the more time they could devote to productive activity. For that reason, bondpeople engaged in task work, especially in the Low Country regions of South Carolina and Georgia, tended to accumulate more property than those who worked as gang laborers or house servants. Frederick Law Olmsted (1822–1903) noted the taxing but flexible nature of the task system while traveling through South Carolina: "In the woods I saw a negro by a fire, while it was still night, shaving shingles very industriously. … No doubt he was a slave, working by task, and of his own accord at night, that he might have the more daylight for his own purposes" (1861–1862, p. 215).

Though Olmsted did not speculate on the "purposes" to which the South Carolina slave would devote himself during the day, his narrative details the many ways in which bondpeople put their time to economic activity. Though slaves might accumulate property by inheritance from other slaves or gifts from their masters, most bondpeople accumulated property via productive money-earning activity. For example, many slaves planted personal gardens or raised chickens, often selling excess produce, eggs, and fowl. Others sold baskets or other handmade goods. Still others sold their time, hiring themselves for wages as either agricultural labors or skilled tradesmen.

Bondpeople spent their money, according to accounts from the early nineteenth century, on both "necessities" and "luxuries," the definitions of which varied according to individual tastes and desires. In *Slavery in the United States*, Charles Ball explained this process of consumption and property accumulation:

> The money procured by these, and various other means, which I shall explain hereafter, is laid out by the slaves in purchasing such little articles of necessity or luxury, as it enables them to procure. A part is disbursed in payment for sugar, molasses, and sometimes a few pounds of coffee, for the use of the family; another part is laid out for clothes for winter; and no inconsiderable portion of his pittance is squandered away by the misguided

slave for tobacco, and an occasional bottle of rum. Tobacco is deemed so indispensable to comfort, nay to existence that hunger and nakedness are patiently endured to enable the slave to indulge in this highest of enjoyments (1853, pp. 190–191).

For some bondpeople, especially those who purchased items such as foodstuffs, liquor, or tobacco, the process of property accumulation was slow—immediate needs, wants, and desires took precedence over long-term property accrual. Others, however, laid aside money, looking for ways to increase wealth for themselves and their families. The historian Philip Morgan examined internal economies in Low Country South Carolina and Georgia and noted that bondpeople there took advantage of the flexible nature of the task system to accumulate significant amounts of property such as cattle, horses, and even carts and carriages (Morgan 1983, pp. 399–420). Still others put off even these more durable investments in hopes of accumulating enough to acquire yet more valuable pieces of "property—their own bodies. Lunsford Lane, for example, accumulated few luxuries, instead dedicating himself to acquiring enough wealth to purchase his freedom. He explained this process to the readers of his narrative:

> Fearful that the accumulation of so much money might prove disastrous to my hopes, should it be known, I deemed it politic, during all this time, to go shabbily dressed, and to appear as poor as possible, but to pay my mistress for my services promptly. My funds I kept hid, never venturing to lend or invest a penny in anything likely to create suspicion; nor did I let any one but my wife know that I was making any. (1845, p. 48)

Property accumulation via participation in the internal economy was a double-edged sword for both slaves and masters. Slaves could vastly improve the material quality of their bonded lives, and in so doing, develop a sense of pride and accomplishment as they watched the accumulation of the fruits of their labor. Slaveholders were wary of the sense of independence this sort of economic activity engendered, but recognized that those with significant property interests were bound more tightly to their plantations.

BIBLIOGRAPHY

Ball, Charles. *Slavery in the United States: A Narrative of the Life and Adventures of Charles Ball, a Black Man, Who Lived Forty Years in Maryland, South Carolina, and Georgia, as a Slave under Various Masters, and Was One Year in the Navy with Commodore Barney, during the Late War*. New York: John S. Taylor, 1837.

Lane, Lunsford. *The Narrative of Lunsford Lane, Formerly of Raleigh, N.C., Embracing an Account of His Early Life, the Redemption by Purchase of*

*Himself and Family from Slavery, and His
Banishment from the Place of His Birth for the Crime
of Wearing a Colored Skin.* Boston: Hewes and
Watson, 1845.

Morgan, Philip D. "The Ownership of Property by Slaves
in the Mid-Nineteenth Century Lowcountry."
Journal of Southern History 49, no. 3 (1983):
399–420.

Olmsted, Frederick Law. *The Cotton Kingdom: A
Traveller's Observations on Cotton and Slavery in the
American Slave States: Based upon Three Former
Volumes of Journeys and Investigations by the Same
Author.* New York : Mason Brothers, 1861–1862.

Kathleen Hilliard

SLAVE MONEY

"If there is money in the world, I must manage to have
a part of it" (Atwater 1857, p. 24). So explained a
Georgia slave to Northern traveler Horace Cowles
Atwater in the winter of 1856 to 1857. Prior to his
three-month Southern tour, Atwater might have been
surprised by such a statement, assuming, as many
others outside of the South did, that enslaved people
had no access to or use for cash money. Like many
other chroniclers of the South during the antebellum
period, Atwater, once enlightened, devoted significant
attention to slaves' money-making activities, noting,
"The slaves, in favorable localities, have more opportunities for earning money to furnish themselves with
necessaries and luxuries, than one would at first suppose" (1857, p. 24). Earning and spending money
formed a crucial component of the slaves' internal
economy.

Slaves throughout the United States earned money
through productive activity undertaken during their "off
time"—the evenings and Sundays when they were not
working for their masters. Bondpeople could earn cash
in any number of ways: by selling foodstuffs or staple
crops from personal gardens or provision grounds; raising and selling poultry and eggs; selling crafted goods
such as woven baskets or brooms; and hiring their time
for wages. Slaves might also receive small tokens of
money as "rewards" for good behavior from their masters at Christmas, as a sign of approval upon a marriage,
or at the birth of a child.

In *Slavery in the United States* (1853), the ex-slave
Charles Ball explained that slaves' money was "spent in
various ways; sometimes for clothes, sometimes for better food than was allowed by the overseer, and sometimes for rum; but those who drank rum, had to do it by
stealth" (p. 157). As Ball explained, bondpeople could
spend their money on basic necessities such as blankets
and coarse clothing; on more luxurious items such as

molasses, sugar, or white flour; or on fine clothing that
would allow them to distinguish themselves from their
homespun-clad peers (p. 157). Money could be spent in
more unconventional ways as well. Henry Bibb, for
example, paid cash to a conjurer for a potion to prevent
his master from whipping him (1849, p. 27). Other
slaves saved their money in hopes of one day accumulating enough money to purchase their freedom. Lunsford
Lane worked diligently to acquire cash for this purpose:
"These sums, and the hope that then entered my mind
of purchasing at some future time my freedom, made me
long for money; and plans for money-making took the
principal possession of my thoughts" (1845, p. 8).
Other slaves, such as those described in Benjamin
Drew's *A North-Side View of Slavery* (1856), found cash
money particularly useful as they made their escape
north to freedom in the antebellum period.

In addition to its exchange value, money served
social purposes. Cash-strapped merchants, accustomed
to extending lines of credit to local whites, often were
eager to accept currency from bondpeople, thus promoting economic relationships off the plantation. Likewise,
the fungibility of currency facilitated theft as slaves
appropriated goods and sold them for less conspicuous
cash. Accumulated money and property conferred elevated social status as well, and melded notions of moral
and political economy.

BIBLIOGRAPHY

Atwater, Horace Cowles. *Incidents of a Southern Tour:
or, The South, as Seen with Northern Eyes.* Boston:
J. P. Magee, 1857.

Ball, Charles. *Slavery in the United States: A Narrative of
the Life and Adventures of Charles Ball, a Black
Man, Who Lived Forty Years in Maryland, South
Carolina, and Georgia, as a Slave under Various
Masters, and Was One Year in the Navy with
Commodore Barney, during the Late War.* New
York: John S. Taylor, 1837.

Bibb, Henry. *Narrative of the Life and Adventures of
Henry Bibb, an American Slave, Written by Himself.*
New York: H. Bibb, 1849.

Drew, Benjamin. *A North-Side View of Slavery: The
Refugee, or, The Narratives of Fugitive Slaves in
Canada.* Boston: J. P. Jewett and Company, 1856.

Lane, Lunsford. *The Narrative of Lunsford Lane,
Formerly of Raleigh, N.C., Embracing an Account of
His Early Life, the Redemption by Purchase of
Himself and Family from Slavery, and His
Banishment from the Place of His Birth for the Crime
of Wearing a Colored Skin.* Boston: Hewes and
Watson's, 1845.

Kathleen Hilliard

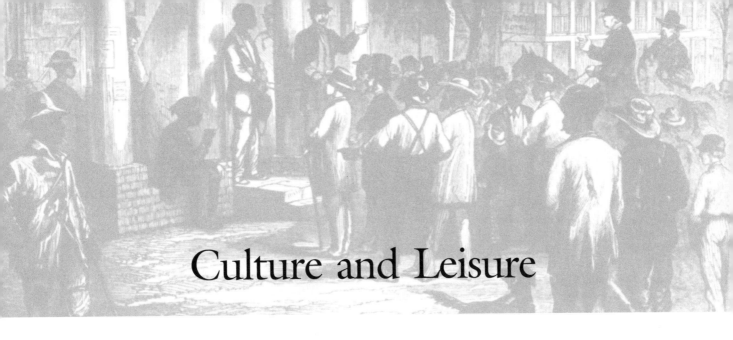

Culture and Leisure

■ Culture and Leisure Overview

What was the nature of slaves' leisure time, and what kinds of cultural institutions did they craft therein? Or, as historian Kenneth Stampp asked in *The Peculiar Institution*, "What else was there in the lives of slaves besides work, sleep, and procreation? What filled their idle hours? What occupied their minds?" (1956, p. 361). This is a difficult question, an answer for which has only slowly, and recently, emerged through the careful study of slave folklore and narratives.

In early twentieth-century interpretations of slavery, the space of the plantation allowed for little leisure time or cultural formation, but much work and white domination. Historians such as Ulrich Phillips (1877–1934) posited the plantation as a sort of slave school run by white masters, an engine of acculturation that trained African American men and women for a subordinate place in modern society. Even more sympathetic historians such as Stampp, writing during the civil rights era of the 1950s, lamented that little would ever be known about slave culture, because of the paucity of sources. However, as John Blassingame (1972) and other scholars of slave culture have shown since the 1970s, there was a slave community, and important elements of that community were formed in leisure time.

The work of the plantation did consume a tremendous amount of slaves' time and energy, and therefore leisure activities were usually limited to the nighttime, holidays, and Sundays. Typically slaves received two or three days off at Christmas, a holiday usually accompanied by gifts, feasts, dances, weddings, and athletic contests; in John Canoe (or John Kunering) festivals, especially in North Carolina, slaves dressed in elaborate masks and wigs. In a particularly ironic turn, considering their bondage as chattel laborers, the Fourth of July was another festival time for plantation slaves. The fall harvest was an important time of work as well as recreation, as slaves sang corn-shucking songs, barbecued, and drank alcohol in a carnival-like atmosphere. Harvest was also a time for celebrating fertility. Although slave weddings were not legally binding, marriage rituals such as "jumping the broom" were essential for creating and preserving the slave community.

On a more regular basis, Sunday was an important day of rest and worship, as many slaves put away their bland work clothing and donned their nicest apparel. Women wore dresses dyed in bright colors, and some former slaves recalled that girls occasionally fashioned hoops of grapevine to make their skirts fuller. Although many plantations required slaves to attend white churches, a number of slaves developed their own forms of worship that embodied syncretic religiousbeliefs. In emotional sermons and hymns, slaves expressed their desire for freedom and found a therapeutic release that white religion did not embody.

In slave music—and life in general—there was not a clear divide between the sacred and the secular. As Charles Joyner (1999) has shown, songs were sometimes ironic and sometimes literal, but in either case music was an important coping mechanism for the harsh realities of slave life; sometimes, moreover, song lyrics also enabled clandestine communications about secret meetings. During holiday festivals, slaves sang, danced, or patted juba, using hands, knees, and shoulders to create elaborate, syncopated clapping patterns. They also played instruments such as gourd fiddles and banjos crafted from sheep hides, as well as drums, tambourines, and flutes. A number of these instruments had their origins in Africa, like much of slave culture in general. However, like African American cultural forms in general, music did not pass across the Atlantic without important transformations.

Enslaved peoples began to shape a distinct culture during the Middle Passage, and this cultural transformation was continued in America. As historian Sterling Stuckey (1987) has shown, the counterclockwise dance ceremony, or ring shout, was an important space for creating a pan-African consciousness and establishing crucial relationships with ancestral spirits. Another important space for the continued shaping of culture was the slave quarters, the relative privacy of which allowed a place for slaves to interact on their own terms beyond the overseer's watchful eye. Women created quilts that were valued both for their utility and their decoration, and sometimes were able to grow gardens of potatoes, pumpkins, and other fruits and vegetables, to supplement meager rations. Likewise, in their spare time men often provided food by hunting or fishing in nearby wooded areas.

A pervasive element of slave culture was the telling of stories, which included morality tales that warned against working on Sunday or talking too much. A distinct genre of slave tale, though, was the trickster narrative, which typically admired smaller or weaker protagonists who outwitted larger, or stronger, opponents. In this way, tellingly, slaves inverted white society's interpretation of the trickster's significance. During the antebellum period, sentimental culture warned against the confidence man, the urban trickster who took advantage of others by earning their trust. However, slaves, locked into unfavorable power relations, crafted stories that admired legerdemain employed for the benefit of the powerless. For example, artful and quick-witted heroes such as Br'er Rabbit outsmarted their ponderous opponents, using trickery for good. Similarly, stories about John (or Jack) showed a common slave using rhetorical skill and guile to make fools of whites and to escape his master's punishment.

Power relations between slaves and masters were shaped at a young age, even during play. Slave children typically had more freedom than their elders, and sometimes played marbles or hide-and-seek. In some instances, slave children played with planters' children, and remarks and actions by the white children ultimately demonstrated the subordinate place of slaves on the plantation. As children grew older, the cessation of integrated play invariably indicated a line of demarcation between the innocence of childhood and the realities of adult life; according to Eugene Genovese (b. 1930), "[t]he etiquette of race relations began early" (1974, p. 516).

As these examples demonstrate, although the oppressive nature of slavery cannot be overlooked, it is important to understand how leisure activities and cultural forms permeated the otherwise stifling peculiar institution. As Blassingame has noted, "The slave's culture bolstered his self-esteem, courage, and confidence, and served as his defense against personal degradation" (1972, p. 56). Ultimately, slaves' leisure and culture helped them to survive the ordeal of their bondage.

BIBLIOGRAPHY

Blassingame, John W. *The Slave Community; Plantation Life in the Antebellum South.* New York: Oxford University Press, 1972.

Fox-Genovese, Elizabeth. *Within the Plantation Household: Black and White Women of the Old South.* Chapel Hill: University of North Carolina Press, 1988.

Genovese, Eugene. *Roll, Jordan, Roll: The World the Slaves Made.* New York: Pantheon, 1974.

Gomez, Michael A. *Exchanging Our Country Marks: The Transformation of African Identities in the Colonial and Antebellum South.* Chapel Hill: University of North Carolina Press, 1998.

Joyner, Charles. *Shared Traditions: Southern History and Folk Culture.* Urbana: University of Illinois Press, 1999.

Kolchin, Peter. *American Slavery, 1619–1877.* New York: Hill and Wang, 1993.

Levine, Lawrence. *Black Culture and Black Consciousness: Afro-American Folk Thought from Slavery to Freedom.* New York: Oxford University Press, 1977.

Stampp, Kenneth M. *The Peculiar Institution: Slavery in the Antebellum South.* New York: Knopf, 1956.

Stuckey, Sterling. *Slave Culture: Nationalist Theory and the Foundations of Black America.* New York: Oxford University Press, 1987.

White, Deborah Gray. *Ar'n't I a Woman? Female Slaves in the Plantation South* [1985]. New York: Norton, 1999.

Brian M. Ingrassia

■ Song and Dance

SONG AND DANCE: AN OVERVIEW

"For the African," historian Sterling Stuckey once said, "dance was primarily devotional, like a prayer" (Stuckey 1987, p. 25). Dance, for those first slaves introduced into the New World, was a vehicle of community; it was a way of communicating with one's ancestors, one's gods, and one's universe in toto. "Because the emotions of slaves were so much a part of dance expression," Stuckey further wrote, "the whole body moving to complex rhythms, what was often linked to the continuing cycle of life, to the divine, was thought to be debased" in the eyes of whites. That a dance could be sinful would have been a foreign idea to Africans (Stuckey 1987, p. 25).

Thomas Wentworth Higginson (1823–1911), colonel in command of a Union regiment composed of black soldiers (many of them ex-slaves), was drawn to the periphery of his men's circle on more than one night. He was enrapt by the sound of their singing, and often by the dances that accompanied those songs. He realized that song and dance were closely connected—a combination of methods by which those soldiers fostered unity and spirituality in the face of hardship. Some younger troops affected a cynical attitude toward the activity, but even they were drawn into the moment when an especially urgent and passionate song, *Room in There*, was sung: then, "every man within hearing, from oldest to youngest, would be wriggling and shuffling as if through some magic piper's bewitchment." Higginson was affected by the song, but could not be a part of it (Stuckey 1987, pp. 28–30).

Singing and dancing were an integral part of plantation life for slaves. Former slave Fanny Randolph recalled the dances of her youth, during a corn shucking festival:

> Us 'ud all git ter-gether at one uv de cabins an us 'ud have er big log fire an' er room ter dance in. Den when us had all shucked corn er good while ever nigger would git his gal an' dey would be some niggers over in de corner ter play for de dance, one wid er fiddle an' one ter beat straws, an' one wide r banjo, an' one ter beat bones, an' when de music 'ud start up (dey gener'ly played 'Billy in de Low Grounds' or 'Turkey in de Straw') us 'ud git on de flo'. Den de nigger whut called de set would say: 'All join hands an' circle to de lef, back to de right, swing corners, swing partners, all run away!', An' de way dem niggers feets would fly! (Georgia Narratives, p. 196).

Some of the social dances would be very familiar to whites of the time, or even of the early twenty-first century. Waltzes, square dances, the Virginia reel, the schottische, polkas, quadrilles, and cotillions were common. Julia Blanks recalled a dance called the "gallopade—and that's what it was, all right; you shore galloped. You'd start from one end of the hall and run clear to the other end" (Texas Narratives, p. 99). Sara Colquitt slyly added to Works Progress Administration

***The Old Plantation*, folk art by Abby Aldrich, 1800.** This illustration shows plantation slaves by their slave quarters celebrating with music and dance. Their instruments include hollowed-out gourds and banjos. Historian Sterling Stuckey once said, "For the African, dance was primarily devotional, like a prayer." *MPI/Hulton Archive/Getty Images.*

(WPA) reporters in the 1930s that "us sho'did more'n dance, I'm telling you" (Alabama Narratives, p. 89).

Other dances had uniquely African elements of music and rhythm. One popular party game involved dancing with a glass of water on one's head, to see who could dance the most energetically without spilling any. Another popular form was clapping juba (or patting juba). Solomon Northup, a former slave who escaped to freedom, described this as "striking the hands on the knees, then striking the hands together, then striking the right shoulder with one hand, the left with the other—all the time keeping time with the feet, and singing" (Northup 1853, p. 322).

Although one slave preacher said that "Yer'll neber git ter hebben by loafin', pitchin' cents, and dancin' juba," many slaves at least found some pleasure in their earthly sojourn by engaging in the latter, and other forms of dance. Jane Smith Hall Harmon, eighty-eight years old at the time of her interview, expressed her view of dancing:

I allus could dance, I cuts fancy steps now sometimes when I feels good. At one o' dem big old country breakdowns (dances), one night when I was young, I danced down seben big strong mens, dey thought dey wuz sumpin'! Huh, I danced eb'ry one down! (Georgia Narratives, p. 196)

Former slave Tom Mills put it more succinctly. "I was a dancin' fool," he said. "I wanted to dance all the time" (Texas Narratives, p. 91).

BIBLIOGRAPHY

Higginson, Thomas Wentworth. *Army Life in a Black Regiment.* Boston: Osgood & Co., 1870.

Northup, Solomon. *Twelve Years a Slave.* Auburn, NY: Derby and Miller, 1853.

Stuckey, Sterling. *Slave Culture: Nationalist Theory and the Foundations of Black America.* New York: Oxford University Press, 1987.

Works Progress Administration Slave Narrative Project. "Fanny Randolph." *Georgia Narratives.* vol. 4, part 3, p. 196.

Works Progress Administration Slave Narrative Project. "Jane Smith Hall Harmon." *Georgia Narratives.* vol. 4, part 2, p. 99.

Works Progress Administration Slave Narrative Project. "Julia Blanks." *Texas Narratives.* vol. 16, part 1, p. 99.

Works Progress Administration Slave Narrative Project. "Sara Colquitt." *Alabama Narratives.* vol. 1, p. 89.

Works Progress Administration Slave Narrative Project. "Tom Mills." *Texas Narratives.* vol. 16, part 3, p. 91.

Troy D. Smith

SPIRITUALS

In the early nineteenth century, white travelers—both American and European—began to write accounts of hearing very affecting religious songs sung by slaves.

The lyrics of many such songs began to appear in books and journals in the mid-1830s, and their popularity with white audiences grew after the Civil War (1861–1865). One of the earliest descriptions of spirituals was recorded in 1816, by George Tucker (1778–1861):

... my ears were assailed by the voice of singing... I saw a group of about thirty Negroes, of different ages and sizes, following a rough looking white man ... As they came nearer, I saw some of them loaded with chains to prevent their escape; while others had hold of each others hands ... They came along singing a little wild hymn of sweet and mournful melody; flying by a divine instinct of the heart, to the consolation of religion ... "It's nothing at all but a parcel of Negroes sold to Carolina, and that man is their driver, who has bought them." ...The truth is, they feel, and exquisitely too ... Even in the land of their banishment, it is said, they ... have several little wild songs which they sing with tears, recalling the images of past felicity, their cabins and their cornfields. (Epstein 1965, p. 203)

"Spirituals were born as the religious vision of the larger society was caught," historian Sterling Stuckey wrote, "as by centripetal force, drawn to the innermost regions of black spiritual consciousness and applied to what blacks were experiencing in slavery" (Stuckey 1987, p. 25). These were not the same hymns sung by white worshippers; in some cases slaves would sing the more traditional hymns when whites were nearby, but reserve the more emotional—and more Africanized—songs for themselves alone, perhaps because some whites questioned the propriety of what they considered simplistic lyrics and overly passionate delivery for religious songs. Nevertheless, slaves felt that their own songs had "more religion than those in the books" (Epstein 1965, p. 205). The songs, and the emotions behind them, demonstrated both a sustained sense of spirituality and community carried from Africa and perhaps the best parts of Christianity. According to Eugene Genovese, slave religion "stretched a universalist offer of forgiveness and ultimate reconciliation to white America" (Genovese 1974, p. 278).

Thomas Wentworth Higginson (1823–1911) recorded the words to a spiritual sung by his black troops which demonstrates all the above-mentioned elements and more:

I know moon-rise, I know star-rise,
Lay dis body down.
I walk in de moonlight, I walk in de starlight,
To lay dis body down.
I'll walk in de graveyard, I'll walk through de graveyard,
To lay dis body down.
I'll lie in de grave and stretch out my arms;
Lay dis body down.
I go to de judgment in de evenin' of de day,

A prayer meeting of fugitive slaves from the South in Washington, DC, circa early 1860s. In some cases, slaves would sing the traditional hymns around white people and reserve the more emotional and Africanized hymns for themselves. © *Mary Evans Picture Library/The Image Works.*

When I lay dis body down.
And my soul and your soul will meet in de day
When I lay dis body down (Higginson 1870, p. 55)

The song speaks of a yearning for peace, of faith, of hope for a better world beyond the veil, of harmony, and of reconciliation. As, indeed, most spirituals did and do.

BIBLIOGRAPHY

Epstein, Dena J. "Slave Music in the United States Before 1860." *Music Library Association Notes* 20 (1965): 195–212, 377–390.

Genovese, Eugene. *Roll, Jordan, Roll: the World the Slaves Made.* New York: Pantheon Books, 1974.

Higginson, Thomas Wentworth. *Army Life in a Black Regiment.* Boston: Osgood & Co., 1870.

Stuckey, Sterling. *Slave Culture: Nationalist Theory and the Foundations of Black America.* New York: Oxford University Press, 1987.

Troy D. Smith

WORK SONGS

"Of the many forms of black music extant in this century," Paul Oliver wrote in 1982, "the work songs appear to have had the longest history" (Oliver 1982, p. 188). George Tucker (1778–1861) commented on corn shucking songs in 1824 (in a novel set in 1796 titled *The Valley of the Shenandoah; or, Memoirs of the Graysons*); their origins and structure can be traced to Africa. Gang-singing among working blacks can be heard still from the Ivory Coast to Jamaica. It was commonly heard throughout the antebellum South among field-workers, stevedores, railroad workers, and boatmen—the words differed, but the form was consistent. In a pattern whose source can be attributed to the savannah region of West Africa, a lead singer calls out a phrase and the work group sings a reply. This call-and-response form would also become a key element in African American spirituals and gospel songs, with the preacher or an elder playing the role of the song leader. Oliver speculates that the decline of the plantation system after the Civil War (1861–1865) led to an increase of solo work songs, in which the singer replies to his own call with either an answering line or meandering calls or hollers, which led to the development of blues.

Work songs—many of which may have been performed during slavery—continued to be a powerful form of black expression well into the twentieth century,

SLAVE WORK SONGS

Narrative of the Life of Frederick Douglass, an American Slave (1845) provides one of the most famous accounts of slave work songs in American literature. In the following extract, Douglass described the nature and function of work songs and challenged the assumption, held by many of his contemporaries, that they signified the happiness of enslaved people:

> While on their way, they would make the dense old woods, for miles around, reverberate with their wild songs, revealing at once the highest joy and the deepest sadness. They would compose and sing as they went along, consulting neither time nor tune. The thought that came up, came out—if not in the word, in the sound;—and as frequently in the one as in the other. They would sometimes sing the most pathetic sentiment in the most rapturous tone, and the most rapturous sentiment in the most pathetic tone.... I have sometimes thought that the mere hearing of those songs would do more to impress some minds with the horrible character of slavery, than the reading of whole volumes of philosophy on the subject could do...
>
> I have often been utterly astonished, since I came to the north, to find persons who could speak of the singing, among slaves, as evidence of their contentment and happiness. It is impossible to conceive of a greater mistake. Slaves sing most when they are most unhappy. The songs of the slave represent the sorrows of his heart; and he is relieved by them, only as an aching heart is relieved by its tears. (2001, pp. 20–21)

SOURCE: Douglass, Frederick. *Narrative of the Life of Frederick Douglass, An American Slave,* ed. John W. Blassingame, John R. McKivigan, and Peter P. Hinks. New Haven, CT: Yale University Press, 2001.

performed by gangs of (mostly, if not all, black) prisoners. As H. Bruce Franklin pointed out, "black slavery in the United States did not end with Emancipation; it merely changed its forms somewhat" (Franklin 1979, p. 6). This continued bondage, especially in the guise of the convict-lease system, kept traditional slave work songs alive until recent memory ("How can I pick a bale of cotton?" a well-known song asks. "How can I pick a bale a day?" The response: "You big enough and black enough to pick a bale of cotton, you big enough and black enough to pick a bale a day").

Lazarus Ekwueme described the work song' place in African American history in 1974:

> Perhaps it is in the area of worksongs that the black man's universal identity through the world manifests itself most vividly. He has had to work very hard throughout history, either toiling labo-

riously to eke out a living with primitive tools on over-worked pieces of land or sweating his life away in the mines, railroads, cotton fields, or sugar cane plantations for the enrichment of the white man, both in Africa and in the New World ... a lot of his sustaining capacity comes from the power of his song. Music becomes particularly helpful when a group of people work together and team-work is needed. Not only does music act as a diversion—nay, a distraction—from the burden of the work, but also it contributes to the coordination of energy ... tied up with the rhythm of the song, be it paddling a canoe, tugging at ropes, laying a rail, or slashing cane. (Ekwueme 1974, p. 129)

Or, as an abolitionist pointed out more succinctly in 1839, one could safely say that slaves—like prisoners—did not sing because they were happy. They sang because they wanted to be.

BIBLIOGRAPHY

Ekwueme, Lazarus. "African-Music Retentions in the New World." *The Black Perspective in Music* 2, no. 2 (1974): 128–144.

Epstein, Dena J. "Slave Music in the United States Before 1860." *Music Library Association Notes* 20 (1965): 195–212, 377–390.

Franklin, H. Bruce. "Songs of an Imprisoned People." *MELUS* 6, no. 1 (1979): 6–22.

Oliver, Paul. "Twixt Midnight and Day: Binarism, Blues, and Black Culture." *Popular Music* 2 (1982): 179–200.

Troy D. Smith

ANTISLAVERY SONGS

In the June 24, 1842, issue of *The Liberator*, a seminary student suggested taking August 1—the anniversary of emancipation in Britain—as a date for abolitionists to celebrate annually. The celebration should be in the form of picnics, which would begin with "declamations, dialogues, songs, and hymns in meetinghouse or hall." A pastor seconded the idea in the same issue, calling for "songs and anthems and shouts of gladness. It does the heart of man good to huzza for freedom ... We must have music—joyful noises, shouts, and long and loud huzzas" (Studley 1943, p. 567).

The August 1 picnics were to be a special affair, but the idea of opening up antislavery gatherings with song was by no means new. This was already an established practice by the 1840s, in both formal and informal gatherings. While traditional hymns may have been used in the beginning, eventually special topical songs were composed for the occasion. Pamphlets such as *Antislavery Hymns* (1834), *The Antislavery Harp* (1848), and others were popular among antislavery activists. In almost all cases, such hymns were written by white authors—sometimes assuming a black narrative voice,

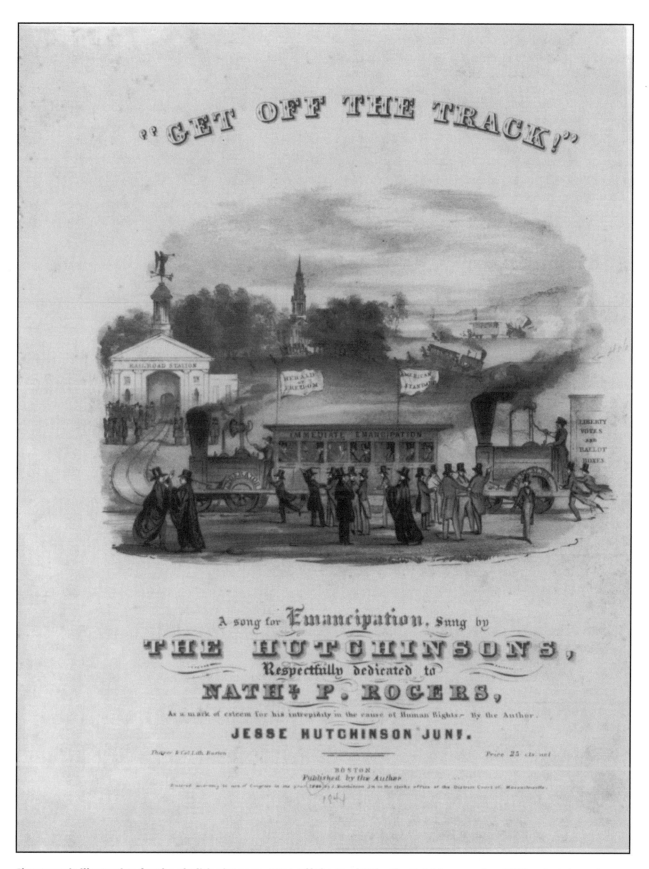

Sheet music illustration for the abolitionist song, "Get Off the Track!" by the Hutchinsons, circa 1843. Anti-slavery hymns were often written by white composers, sometimes assuming a black narrative voice. *The Library of Congress.*

thus producing a vision of slavery as envisioned by (often elite) northern whites. Sheet music was very popular at that time, much of it in the same vein of white writers assuming a black persona, although usually to romanticize slavery; sometimes, though, it condemned slavery and romanticized the slave. At any rate, as historian Caroline Moseley notes, "No genteel home was complete without music." She points out, however, that the average antislavery hymn, "being rhetorical and didactic, is simply not very singable" (Moseley 1984, p. 4). She argues that such songs were meant more for the public meeting than the private parlor. Whether that assertion is true or not, there is no denying that the pathos invoked in many of the songs were designed to tug mightily at the heartstrings—those of the mostly white believers in the cause, as well as potential white converts to it. One song, for example—found in *The Antislavery Harp* collection—tells the story of a blind slave boy. "Come back to me, Mother!" the little boy plaintively wails, for his cruel master, not wanting to be burdened with an unprofitable piece of property, has sold the child away for one dollar. Other examples, these from William Lloyd Garrison's (1805–1879) 1834 collection, include the following excerpts:

Hymn 2

Hark to the clank! What means that sound?
'Tis slavery shakes its chains!
Man driving man in fetters bound,—
And this where freedom reigns!

Hymn 7

Christians—boast not the name you bear,
While you that sacred name deprave;
Oh! Hear a suppliant brother's prayer—
In mercy spare the kneeling slave!—
Dare not to mock your Saviour's name,
By actions with which misery blends;
What you profess by works proclaim,
And be the Negro's guiding friends;
Nor them from home and kindred tear,
And with a lawless curse pursue;
In pity hear, in mercy spare,
Lest heaven its mercy turn from you.

Garrison himself admitted in his preface to the *Antislavery Hymns* collection that some of the songs were lengthy, wordy, and difficult to sing. He recommended, in such cases, to read them aloud instead. Their message was the important thing. Garrison (1834) presented them as "a judicious selection of Hymns, descriptive of the wrongs and sufferings of our slave population, and calculated to impress upon the minds of those who read them, or commit them to memory, or hear them sung, a deep sense of their obligations to assist in undoing every burden, breaking every yoke, and setting every captive free."

BIBLIOGRAPHY

Brown, William Wells, ed. *The Antislavery Harp: A Collection of Songs for Antislavery Meetings.* Boston: B. Marsh, 1848.

Garrison, William Lloyd, ed. *Antislavery Hymns, for the Use of Friends of Emancipation.* Boston: Garrison and Knapp, 1834.

Moseley, Caroline. "'When Will Dis Cruel War be Ober?': Attitudes toward Blacks in Popular Songs of the Civil War." *American Music* 2, no. 3 (Autumn 1984): 1–26.

Studley, Marian H. "An 'August First' in 1844." *The New England Quarterly* 16, no. 4 (December 1943): 567–577.

Troy D. Smith

THE RING SHOUT

The Ring Shout has its origins in a dance form indigenous to much of Central and West Africa, in which the dancers move in a counterclockwise circle. "Wherever in Africa the counterclockwise dance ceremony was performed," Sterling Stuckey wrote, "the dancing and singing were directed to the ancestors and gods, the tempo and revolution of the circle quickening during the course of the movement" (Stuckey 1987, p. 12). In some cases leaping was associated with the dance, and this was sometimes true of the North American variant as well.

The ring shout as practiced by slaves was a religious activity, with Christianity augmenting the African elements. Participants moved in a circle, providing rhythm by clapping hands and patting feet. One individual would set the tempo by singing, and his lines are answered in call-and-response fashion. In some cases, another individual rhythmically beat the (usually wooden) floor with a broomstick or other piece of wood. The dancers achieved a sense of euphoria.

One white witness to a Civil War-era ring shout described it thus:

> The "shout" is a peculiar service in which a dozen or twenty jog slowly round a circle behind each other with a peculiar shuffle of the feet and shake of arms, keeping time to a droning chant and hand-clapping maintained by bystanders. As the exercise continues, the excitement increases, occasionally becomes hysterical. Some religious meaning is attributed to it (Stuckey 1987, p. 85).

The fact that white observers would call the ring shout hysterical and vaguely note that some religious meaning is attributed to it may help explain why the shout was rarely performed in front of outsiders. In fact, ring shouts were often performed, semi-secretly, after regular religious services had been conducted (especially in denominations where dancing was frowned on).

Another white Civil War witness to a ring shout, Colonel Thomas Wentworth Higginson (1823–1911), described it in his memoirs:

> All over the camp the lights glimmer in the tents, and as I sit at my desk in the open doorway, there come mingled sounds of stir and glee. Boys laugh and shout,—a feeble flute stirs somewhere in some tent, not an officer's,—drums throb far away in another ... and from a neighboring cook-fire comes the monotonous sound of that strange festival, half pow-wow, half prayer-meeting, which they know only as "shout." These huts are usually enclosed in a little booth, made neatly of palm-leaves and covered in at top, a regular African hut ... This hut is now crammed with men, singing at the top of their voices, in one of their quaint, monotonous, endless, negro-Methodist chants, with obscure syllables recurring constantly, and slight variations interwoven, all accompanied with a regular drumming of the feet and clapping of the hands, like castanets... Then the excitement spreads: inside and outside the enclosure men begin to quiver and dance, others join, a circle forms... some "heel and toe" tumultuously... others whirl, others caper sideways... and still the ceaseless drumming and clapping, in perfect cadence, goes steadily on (Higginson 1870, pp. 17–18).

Calling it "an essential ritual of enslaved Africans," historian Jonathan David notes the ring shout's role in "validating a group solidarity in the face of enormous oppression" (David 1999, p. 565). Samuel A. Floyd Jr. asserts that all forms of African American music and performance, and culture in general, are present in the ring shout—especially in call-response, "this master trope, this musical trope of tropes" that makes essential the conversational and performative elements of black culture (Floyd 1991, pp. 53 and 61).

BIBLIOGRAPHY

David, Jonathan. "Shout Because You're Free (review)." *The Journal of American Folklore* 112, no. 446 (1999): 565–567.

Floyd, Samuel A., Jr. "Ring Shout! Literary Studies, Historical Studies, and Black Music Inquiry." *Black Music Research Journal* 11, no. 2 (1991): 49–70.

Higginson, Thomas Wentworth. *Army Life in a Black Regiment.* Boston: Osgood & Co., 1870.

Rosenbaum, Art. *Shout Because You're Free: The African American Ring Shout Tradition in Coastal Georgia.* Athens: University of Georgia Press, 1998.

Stuckey, Sterling. *Slave Culture: Nationalist Theory and the Foundations of Black America.* New York: Oxford University Press, 1987.

Troy D. Smith

MUSICAL INSTRUMENTS

In 1833, English visitor John Finch remarked on slaves' love of creating music. "A black boy will make an excellent fiddle of a gourd and some string. In autumn they play tunes on the dried stalks of Indian corn, when it is still standing in the field. By striking it near the ground or at the top, they make it discourse most excellent music." Finch concluded that "an instrument of music seems necessary to their existence" (Epstein 1965, p. 381).

Solomon Northup, who eventually escaped slavery, seemed to agree with Finch's observation about the importance of musical instruments:

> My master often received letters, sometimes from a distance of ten miles, requesting him to send me to play at a ball or festival of the whites. He received his compensation, and usually I also returned with many picayunes jingling in my pockets ... Alas! Had it not been for my beloved violin, I scarcely can conceive how I could have endured the long years of bondage. (Northup 1853, pp. 216–217)

Talented black musicians were in demand for whites' parties, and—as in Northup's case—were able to gain a measure of mobility, economic remuneration, prestige, and self-satisfaction. They were also in demand for social events in the slave quarters, a service they usually did not charge for. Former slave Gus Smith recounted that "in times of our holidays, we always had our own musicians. Sometimes we sent ten or twelve miles for a fiddler. He'd stay a week or so in one place and den he would go on to de next farm, maybe four or five miles away, and dey had a good time for a week" (*Born in Slavery*, Missouri Narratives, vol. 10, p. 323). Another slave, Fanny Randolph, recalled how in her childhood bands would play "one wid er fiddle an' one ter beat straws, an' one wid er banjo, an' one ter beat bones" (*Born in Slavery*, Georgia Narratives, vol. 4, pt. 3, p. 196).

The instruments themselves varied. Some masters provided instruments for talented slaves, in order to benefit both personally and (as Northup's master did) financially from the use of the pianos and brass horns they provided. Most slave musicians, however, made their own instruments, as demonstrated in the following testimonies:

> Betty Curtlett: The only musical instrument we had was a banjo. Some made their banjos. Take a bucket or pan a long strip of wood. 5 horse hairs twisted made the base string. 2 horsehairs twisted made the second string. 1 horse hair twisted made the fourth and the fifth string was a fine one, it was not twisted at all but drawn tight. They were all bees waxed (*Born in Slavery*, Arkansas Narratives, vol. 2, pt. 2, p. 81).
>
> Hammett Dell: I made some music instruments. We had music. Folks danced more than they do now. Most darkies blowed quills and Jew's harps. I took cane cut four or six made whistles then tuned em together and knit them together in a row like a

Fiddler playing at a barn dance.   An engraving of a fiddler playing at a barn dance in Kentucky, 1865. Ex-slave Solomon Northrup wrote of the importance of music to slaves, "Had it not been for my beloved violin, I can scarcely conceive how I could have endured the long years of bondage." *Peter Newark American Pictures/Bridgeman Art Library.*

mouth harp you see. Another way get a big long cane cut out holes long down to the joint, hold your fingers over different holes and blow. I never had a better time since freedom (p. 141).

Isaac D. Williams: We generally made our own banjos and fiddles, and I had a fiddle that was manufactured out of a gourd, with horse hair strings and a bow made out of the same material. If you put plenty of rosin on the strings, it would compare very favorably with an ordinary violin and made excellent music. When we made a banjo we would first of all catch what we called a ground hog, known in the north as a woodchuck. After tanning his hide, it would be stretched over a piece of timber fashioned like a cheese box, and you couldn't tell the difference between that homely affair and a handsome store bought one (Epstein 1965, p. 384).

Jeff Davis demonstrated the relationship that slave performers had with their instruments: "I'm a musician—played the fife. Played it to a T. Had two kinds

of drums. Had different kinds of brass horns, too. I 'member one time they was a fellow thought he could beat the drum till I took it"(*Born in Slavery*, Arkansas Narratives, vol. 2, pt 2, p. 116). Davis was especially proud that he had two drumsets—drums were usually not permitted at all, as whites feared they might be used to send signals in an uprising. Producing music with their own instruments enabled slaves such as Davis and Curtlett to feel a sense of humanity and pride which still came easily to mind in their old age, and which, as with Northup, sustained them during their bondage.

BIBLIOGRAPHY

Cimbala, Paul A. "Fortunate Bondsmen: Black 'Musicianers' and Their Role as an Antebellum Southern Plantation Slave Elite." *Southern Studies* 18 (1979): 291–303.

Epstein, Dena J. "Slave Music in the United States Before 1860." *Music Library Association Notes* 20 (1965): 195–212, 377–390.

Northup, Solomon. *Twelve Years a Slave.* Auburn:
Derby and Miller, 1853.

*Born in Slavery: Slave Narratives from the Federal
Writers' Project, 1936–1938.* Online collection of
the Manuscript and Prints and Photographs
Divisions of the Library of Congress. Available from
http://memory.loc.gov/ammem/snhtml/
snhome.html.

Troy D. Smith

■ Crafts and Slave Handicrafts

CRAFTS AND SLAVE HANDICRAFTS: AN OVERVIEW

There is ample evidence regarding the production of crafts by slaves in the American colonies and during the antebellum period in the Untied States. Manifests of slave ships identify some of their captives as artisans, such as weavers, woodcarvers, and metalworkers, and records of sale indicate a higher monetary value for these skilled individuals. The value of the skilled slave—those who arrived with skills in traditional African crafts as well as those who were trained during captivity—is documented in both slave narratives and in advertisements for the return of runaways. An advertisement in the *National Intelligencer and Washington Advertiser* on September 19, 1806, posts a reward of $100 each for the return of Bassil, a "house carpenter and wheelwright" and Gerard, a "blacksmith by profession."

Items for Personal Use

Though Alain Locke suggested in 1933 that slavery had destroyed the cultural traditions of displaced Africans taken in the slave trade, other scholars have since argued that many traditions survived the trauma of displacement as well as the severe burden of slavery. The late-nineteenth- and early-twentieth-century dis-

covery of some crafted objects (e.g., small ceramic "face vessels" found in South Carolina, dated to the 1860s) suggests that some cultural practices, such as funerary traditions, were preserved in some measure.

Many of the crafted objects made by slaves for personal use during the colonial period reflect African tradition. Prominent among these are drums, though they were banned by many slaveholders (and prohibited by South Carolina in 1739) for fear of their potential use to foment rebellion. A richly carved wooden drum from Virginia, thought to date to 1645, has been identified as a replica of an Akan chief's drum. Other drums were fashioned from gourds, as were rattles and stringed instruments.

African and African American slaves made baskets using an African coiling technique, and they created wrought iron objects for decorative (perhaps ritual) and practical use. It is speculated that some enslaved blacksmiths may have originated in the Mande and Wolof peoples of West Africa, who used ritual objects made from iron. Slaves were also potters, creating hand-built pottery using African methods. Bowls and jugs made by slaves (later called "colonoware" by twentieth-century scholars) demonstrate similarity to Kongo ceramics as well as to Native American pottery. The so-called face vessels of the late 1800s, found mostly in burial grounds in South Carolina and Georgia, depict a human face in relief on one side. Usually found either cracked or perforated with holes, the small ceramic vessels (about 4–9 inches high) bear some similarity to Kongo pottery and are thought to be mortuary ritual items that served a protective role. Other artifacts, including shell beads and dolls, have been recovered as well, but the details of their use and the history of their design remain unknown.

As was typical of the time, slaves crafted a large variety of utilitarian goods for household use, including soap, candles, and textiles. Female slaves spun thread and wool and wove fabrics, and they sewed clothes and quilts for their family's use and for the use of the slaveholder's family. The best-known of the slave textiles are pieced quilts, created using an appliqué technique, often with embroidered detail. Though influenced by European quilting techniques, the geometric designs of some of the quilts are similar in pattern to West and Central African textiles. These varied craft practices among slaves continued from the colonial period into the nineteenth century, and on the plantations expanded into larger operations.

The Sale of Crafted Goods

Most plantations had facilities for weaving and spinning, as well as blacksmithing and coopering. Often these ventures became additional sources of income for the slaveholder, who sold the products made by slave artisans. Female slaves, following their day's work in the fields or in the slaveholder's household, were often

Artifacts found around the slave quarters at George Washington's Mount Vernon estate. Among them are pipes, buttons and ornate jewelry. Most plantations had facilities for weaving and spinning, as well as blacksmithing and coopering. Often slaveholders sold the crafts made by slave artisans as an additional source of income. *Victor R Boswell/National Geographic/Getty Images.*

required to spin, weave, or sew at night, and quotas were imposed on their production. The textiles produced by the slaves, which included cotton, linen, and wool fabrics, became significant sources of income for some slaveholders.

In the Edgefield District of South Carolina (modern-day Edgefield, Greenwood, McCormick, Saluda, and Aiken counties) several planters established pottery mills, staffed by skilled slaves and white potters. The mills produced an alkaline-glazed stoneware, typically utilitarian pots and storage jars. Prominent among the Edgefield potters was a slave known as Dave, who took the last name of Drake after emancipation, and who produced hundreds, if not thousands, of pots from at least the 1830s through the 1860s. Remarkably, many of his pots are signed and dated, and many are decorated with inscriptions of verse written by the artist.

Professional Artisans

During the colonial period in the South—as well as in the Northern and Middle colonies—a system of apprenticeship emerged that further developed the skills of enslaved craftspeople while enriching slaveholders. Slaves were apprenticed to cabinetmakers, silversmiths, goldsmiths, printers, and engravers. In some cases these skills created benefit for the slaves; some were able to purchase their own freedom, and others fled, assured of their ability to earn a living. Such apprenticeships, to white artisans as well as free blacks, continued into the nineteenth century. In the early 1800s free black artisans and slave apprentices figured prominently in the production of fine craft items, such as furniture, in New Orleans and elsewhere in the United States, until legislation in some states restricted both the number of slave apprentices as well as the number of businesses owned by free blacks.

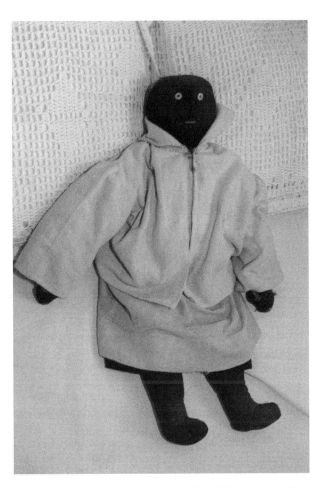

A slave child's doll, circa 1832, from the Belle Mont Mansion, a plantation house in Tuscumbia, Alabama. Female slaves spun wool, wove fabrics, and made clothes and quilts for their own families as well as the slaveholder's family. *© Jeff Greenberg. The Image Works.*

By 1850 these restrictions, coupled with further restrictions on manumission and an increase in industrial development, led to a decline in the numbers of black artisans, both enslaved and free.

BIBLIOGRAPHY

Ball, Charles. *Fifty Years in Chains; Or, The Life of an American Slave.* New York: H. Dayton, 1859. Available from http://web6/infotrack.galegroup.com.

Lewis, Samella, ed. *African American Art and Artists.* Berkeley: University of California Press, 1990.

The National Intelligencer and Washington Advertiser. Washington, DC, September 19, 1806. Available from http://web6/infotrack.galegroup.com.

Patton, Sharon F. *African American Art.* New York: Oxford University Press, 1998.

Dorothy Bauhoff

ARTWORK

Any discussion of the artwork of slaves in the Americas must acknowledge the difficulty of finding evidence for the artistic practices of displaced peoples who lived under the severe hardship of slavery. The traumas of slavery and displacement necessarily prevented many connections with the arts of the slaves' ancestral homes and certainly prohibited most slaves from any knowledge of the fine art practices of the Americas and Europe. It is indeed remarkable that there is any evidence of artistic practice; yet it is known today that some slaves were able to preserve some African artistic and cultural practices. Though in 1933 Alain Locke (1886–1954) contended, in his work *Negro Art: Past and Present*, that slavery had cut the cultural roots of transplanted Africans, other scholars have since argued that many traditions did survive in some measure.

Much of the African artistic practice that slaves brought to the Americas will be categorized as *craft* by some definitions of fine art. Yet the broader postmodern definitions of artistic practice would suggest that these craft practices be considered on an equal footing with European artistic traditions. The discovery of ceramic and other crafted objects, particularly at burial grounds in the South, reveals that some slaves in the Americas continued, probably with difficulty and perhaps in secret, to maintain some of their artistic and ritual practices. Small ceramic face vessels, some dated as late as 1860, found at burial grounds in South Carolina and Georgia, bear a resemblance to Kongo pottery. The vessels, which range in size from 4 to 9 inches high, depict a human face in relief on one side and are usually formed from two different clays, depicting, for example, brown skin and white teeth. According to records from the nineteenth century, the practice of placing pierced or cracked ceramic vessels was observed at slave burial sites, particularly in South Carolina. It is speculated that the face vessels were protective artifacts that reflect an African spiritual practice.

Some traditional African artistic practices were preserved openly because of their value to slaveholders. For example, slaves from the Windward Coast of West Africa continued to create coiled fanning baskets that were used for the winnowing of rice, and they carved wooden mortars and pestles that were used to process the grains. In the case of the fanning basket, it may be suggested that its usefulness in the rice-growing economy of the Low Country of South Carolina and Georgia helped to preserve an African basket-weaving tradition. Indeed, present-day African American basket weavers of Mount Pleasant, South Carolina, weave a traditional fanning basket that is similar to the baskets of West Africa.

A shortage of skilled artisans, particularly during the colonial period, encouraged the acquisition of other artistic skills among American slaves. Slaves were apprenticed to various craftspeople to learn trades that included printing, engraving, and jewelry-making, and slaveholders profited from the work of skilled enslaved craftspeople. Edward Peterson's *History of Rhode Island*, published in 1853, suggested that the prominent portraitist Gilbert Stuart (1755–1828) received his first drawing lesson from a slave named Neptune Thurston, who worked in a Boston engraving shop. Much of the work of slave apprentices and artisans, including engravings, is undocumented, and their influence is unknown. Nevertheless, though most enslaved artists remain anonymous, a few individuals were able to make a transition from their work as artisans to become successful practicing fine artists, despite obvious obstacles.

Scipio Moorhead, an enslaved artist who was active in the late 1700s, is known primarily from his mention by poet Phillis Wheatley (1753–1784), herself a slave in the household of John Wheatley of Boston. Moorhead, a slave of Reverend John Moorhead, was apparently trained by Sarah Moorhead, John's wife, who taught art. Wheatley mentions two paintings by Moorhead: one titled *Aurora* and another that depicts the legend of Damon and Pythias. When her book of poetry, *Poems on Various Subjects*, was to be published in London in 1773—financed by Selina Hastings (1707–1791), the Countess of Huntingdon—Wheatley was asked to provide a portrait of herself to appear on the frontispiece. It is widely assumed that the portrait that appears in the book was engraved after a drawing by Scipio Moorhead, though he is not credited. The skillfully rendered portrait depicts the poet in a contemplative pose at her desk. Wheatley's poem "To S.M., a Young African Painter, on Seeing His Works" is a tribute to Moorhead:

> How did those prespects [*sic*] give my soul
>   delight,
> A new creation rushing on my sight?
> Still, wond'rous youth! each noble path pursue,
> On deathless glories fix thine ardent view:
> Still may the painter's and the poet's fire
> To aid thy pencil, and thy verse conspire!
>   (Wheatley, p. 119)

Joshua Johnston (1763–1832), also known as Johnson, a successful portrait painter of his time who worked in Baltimore, Maryland, is listed in the Baltimore city record of 1817 as a "Free Householder of Colour," but scholars suggest that Johnston was born a slave; he arrived from the West Indies before 1790 and had been freed by 1796, when he advertised his services as a portrait painter. He is thus considered the earliest documented African American professional painter. Scholar J. Hall Pleasants (1942) noted that Johnston might have been the slave of either Charles Willson Peale or Peale's nephew Charles Peale Polk, observing the similarity of Johnston's work to that of Polk; though other historians disagree, it is known that several of Johnston's subjects were also painted by Polk. Johnston painted portraits of white families, including many depictions of children, as

well as numerous portraits of prominent free blacks of Baltimore. Several of Johnston's portraits survive, including: *Sarah Ogden Gustin* (c. 1798–1802), now in the National Gallery of Art; *Portrait of a Cleric* (c. 1805), now in the Bowdoin College Museum of Art; *Portrait of a Gentleman* (c. 1810)—identified as Reverend Daniel Coker, a founder of the African Methodist Episcopal church—in the American Museum in Bath, England; and *James McCormick Family* (c. 1805), in the collection of the Maryland Historical Society.

Sculptor Eugene Warburg was born in New Orleans in 1826, the son of a German Jewish father, Daniel Warburg, and a Cuban mulatto slave, Marie Rose Blondeau. His father freed him (along with his mother) when he was a child. Eugene, who began his career as a marble cutter, opened a shop in 1849, producing mostly tomb sculptures. He studied in the 1840s with Philippe Garbeille, a French sculptor in New Orleans, who may have encouraged Warburg to pursue further study in Paris. Warburg left in 1853 to study at the École Nationale des Beaux-Arts, leaving his brother Daniel, whom he had trained, in charge of the New Orleans shop. Most of Eugene Warburg's works were sculptural portraits of political and military figures. In 1855 four of his works were accepted by the Salon de Paris, including *Portrait de son excellence, le ministre des États-Unis à Paris*, a marble bust of John Young Mason, the U.S. minister to France. Warburg remained in Europe for the rest of his short life (he died in 1859), becoming the first African American expatriate artist.

The antislavery movement was closely connected to the work of black artists, though most of the known artists associated with the movement were free blacks. Abolitionists promoted the work of some artists, and patrons paid for the training of others, such as Patrick Reason, a printmaker and engraver, born in 1816, who produced engravings for the New York Anti-Slavery Society. Sculptor Edmonia Lewis (1845–1911), with a letter of introduction from William Lloyd Garrison (1805–1879), studied under Edmund Brackett and later achieved international acclaim in Europe. Photographer James Presley Ball, a free black, operated a successful daguerreotype studio and gallery in Cincinnati; in 1855 he published an antislavery pamphlet and mounted daguerreotype exhibitions on the subject. By the mid-nineteenth century, some free black artists, such as Robert Scott Duncanson (1822–1872), Robert Douglass, Jr., and Edward Bannister (1828–1901), were gaining acclaim.

In the mid- and late-nineteenth-century United States, it is certain that former slaves were among the many practicing black artists and artisans. Even during the years of slavery, enslaved artisans had sometimes been able to purchase their freedom by extra labor, beyond that which profited the slaveholder. Others fled possessing a marketable skill, as revealed by newspaper advertisements for the return of runaway slaves who were described as silversmiths, carpenters, and seamstresses, among other trades. Regrettably, most of the names of these artists will remain unknown.

BIBLIOGRAPHY

Lewis, Samella, ed. *African American Arts and Artists.* Berkeley: University of California Press, 1990.

Patton, Sharon F. *African American Art.* Oxford; New York: Oxford University Press, 1998.

Pleasants, J. Hall. *Joshua Johnston, the First American Negro Portrait Painter.* Baltimore: Maryland Historical Society, 1942.

Wheatley, Phillis. *Poems on Various Subjects, Religious and Moral.* Philadelphia: Reprinted and sold by Joseph Crukshank, 1886.

Dorothy Bauhoff

WOODCRAFT

Though there are few remaining artifacts of their work, many African and African American slaves were woodcarvers. They were among the numerous craftspeople—including weavers, seamstresses, metalworkers, carpenters, and silversmiths—who worked as enslaved skilled laborers. These skilled slaves worked in plantation enterprises, or their labor was hired out as a source of income for the slaveholder. George Washington's list of his slaves in 1799, for example, relates that approximately one-quarter were skilled workers such as carpenters, blacksmiths, coopers, and bricklayers. The woodwork created by slaves in the Americas may be considered in two categories: work that was directly connected to slaveholders' enterprise, and work that was intended for personal use.

On plantations, enslaved carpenters and woodcarvers constructed buildings for slaveholders' use, often embellishing their exteriors and interiors with architectural ornamentation, and they built utilitarian structures for plantation enterprises. Slaves were commonly apprenticed or hired out to cabinetmakers and carpenters; in the early 1800s slave apprentices in New Orleans figured prominently in the production of furniture.

In the Low Country of coastal South Carolina and Georgia, woodworking skills were directly related to rice production. Planters there paid higher prices for slaves from the Windward Coast of West Africa (from present-day Senegal to the Ivory Coast), who brought skills that were essential to rice cultivation and processing. Skilled slaves created traditional tools for processing the grains, including winnowing baskets and mortars. The rice mortar was created from a hollowed-out section of a tree trunk, in a distinctly West African style; it was used, along with a carved wooden pestle, to remove the outer husk of the grains of rice. The carved wooden mortar and pestle were used throughout the eighteenth and nineteenth centuries in the Low Country. Similar tools were still in use in the early twentieth century on Georgia's Sea Islands.

The carved wooden objects created by slaves for their own use are linked to African woodworking traditions and may illustrate, as John Michael Vlach suggests, "the delicate cultural balance between the African past and the American present" (1990, p. 5). Among the oldest carved artifacts is a wooden drum from colonial Virginia that was acquired by Hans Sloane of London in 1645. A richly carved replica of a West African chief's drum, it is thought to be the work of a highly skilled enslaved woodcarver. The significance of the drum in West African culture, as an instrument for ritual, dance, and communication, suggests the cultural importance of the woodcarver, both in West Africa and in the transplanted slave cultures in America. Many slaveholders prohibited the making and use of drums (and South Carolina prohibited them by law in 1739), apparently fearing their potential use for rebellion, so the scarcity of such artifacts is hardly surprising, despite their cultural importance.

Another carved wooden artifact that survives (primarily in the later work of African American folk artists) is the walking stick, which is connected to West African ritual and to the figure of the tribal chief. The sticks were carved in low relief, often with motifs featuring reptiles, reptile and human figures together, or human figures alone. An ornately carved walking stick, now in the Yale University Art Gallery, is attributed to Henry Gudgell, who was born a slave in 1826 in Kentucky. Though made for sale in 1867, the stick, decorated with a lizard, a tortoise, and a human figure, is considered a superb example of an African woodcarving tradition that survived slavery in the Americas.

BIBLIOGRAPHY

Morgan, Philip. *Slave Counterpoint: Black Culture in Eighteenth-Century Chesapeake and Low Country.* Chapel Hill: University of North Carolina Press, 1998.

Patton, Sharon F. *African American Art.* Oxford and New York: Oxford University Press, 1998.

Vlach, John Michael. *The Afro-American Tradition in Decorative Arts.* Athens: University of Georgia Press, 1990.

Dorothy Bauhoff

POTTERY

Though a fragile medium, practiced largely by anonymous artisans, pottery is nevertheless an art form for which there is ample and definitive attribution to enslaved Africans and African Americans. It thus forms part of a larger picture of skilled labor performed by slaves for the benefit and profit of slaveholders and at the same time provides eloquent evidence of the skill and creative vision of enslaved artists.

The manifests of slave ships identify some of their captured Africans as artisans, suggesting a greater monetary value for these individuals. These slaves arrived in the Americas with skills in traditional African weaving, metalworking, woodcarving, and pottery making. Others were trained during their bondage. The demand for skilled craftsmen in the colonies created a strong market for the labor of these individuals; slaveholders not only used their services on the plantation and in their own households but also rented out their labor and sold their wares, which included furniture, decorative ironwork, and ceramic pots. Advertisements for the return of runaway slaves describe a range of craftspeople and artisans, including carpenters, blacksmiths, and musicians; for example, Abram Hook of Howe's Ferry, Virginia, advertised a twenty-dollar reward for a runaway named Jack, who "since becoming my property was put to the carpenter's trade" (*National Intelligencer and Washington Advertiser*, August 18, 1806).

Edgefield Pottery

Pottery was produced in several areas, including Alabama, northern Florida, Georgia, Mississippi, and the western Carolinas. A thriving pottery-making enterprise, based in part on skilled slave labor, emerged in the Edgefield district of South Carolina (present-day Edgefield, Greenwood, McCormick, Saluda, and Aiken counties) in the early 1800s, using the rich clay deposits of the area to produce a distinctive stoneware with an alkaline glaze made from wood ash or lime. The glazes were typically yellow-green, olive green, or brown, and the pots were mostly utilitarian storage vessels of varying size. The pottery mills and shops, operated by white planters, relied on the labor of both white potters and skilled slaves.

In addition to utilitarian storage jars, an art form known as the "face vessel" is also attributed to the slave potters of Edgefield. Ranging in size from four to nine inches high, these vessels depict a human face in relief on one side. Commonly called "voodoo jugs" in the nineteenth century, they are often referred to as Afro-Carolinian by present-day historians. Their purpose is unknown, but it is conjectured that they had a ritual significance, in part because of their small size. Fragments have been found at burial sites, either cracked or perforated with holes, and historians speculate that the vessels were mortuary artifacts that served a protective role. The vessels are distinguished by the use of two different clays to depict, for example, white teeth and brown skin. They bear a similarity to African Kongo pottery, a relation that is supported by evidence that Kongo slaves were among the Edgefield potters.

Dave the Potter

The most significant examples of Edgefield pottery are the works created by a slave known as Dave (who later, following Emancipation, took the last name of Drake); his pots are distinguished by their aesthetic qualities as well as their impressive size. Perhaps even more remarkable, many are signed, and several are decorated with inscriptions of verse by the artist.

Current research dates Dave's birth at around 1800, to one of eight slaves brought from North Carolina by Samuel Landrum. During his early years Dave worked for one of Samuel's sons, Abner Landrum, who is described as a physician, "scientific" farmer, newspaper publisher, and pottery manufacturer. It is speculated that Dave acquired his literacy during his service as a typesetter for Abner's two newspapers, *The South Carolina Republican* and *The Edgefield Hive*, and it is likely that he learned the potter's craft from him as well. Abner Landrum moved from Edgefield around 1831; Dave remained in Edgefield, perhaps because of his value as a skilled potter, and was eventually passed to Lewis Miles, owner of Miles Mill Factory. Many of Dave's surviving pots are inscribed "LM" and are assumed to be among the hundreds (if not thousands) he produced for Miles.

Most of Dave's pots are dated from 1834 through 1864. Earlier unsigned works from the Landrum Pottery may be his as well, as they demonstrate a similarity of form. His pots, mostly storage vessels, are wider at the shoulders than are other Edgefield pots, tapering to a more typical base. They are distinguished by their bold aesthetic, their rich brown or green glaze, and their remarkable scale. The vessels were made by turning the base on a potter's wheel, then adding coils to create the upper parts, smoothing the clay so that the attachment was seamless. Before firing, the alkaline drip glaze was applied. At the Miles Mill, Dave made larger jars, some of which exceed a capacity of twenty gallons. One of his largest works is a forty-gallon storage jar that bears the inscriptions "Great and Noble jar / Hold sheep, goat, or bear" and "LM [for Lewis Miles] May 13, 1859 / Dave & Baddler [another slave potter]." In this case, the size of the vessel is thought to have required collaboration, simply by the weight of the clay.

Many of Dave's inscriptions refer to the size or purpose of the vessel, and many are rhymed couplets. For example, a jar dated April 12, 1858, is inscribed "A very large jar which has four handles / pack it full of fresh meat—then light candles." Other inscriptions address a variety of subjects, including references to relations with women: "Another trick is worst than this / Dearest Miss, spare me a kiss" (on a pot dated August 26, 1840). A pot dated April 14, 1859, is apparently a dedication to Abner Landrum, who died that year: "When Noble Dr. Landrum is dead / May Guardian Angels visit his bed."

Dave's inscriptions have aroused much speculation among historians. At a time when literacy was forbidden to slaves (an 1837 South Carolina law made it illegal to teach slaves to read and write), Dave not only boldly marked his name, he inscribed verses that offered commentary on a range of subjects, including his own bondage: "Dave belongs to Mr. Miles / wher the oven bakes & the pot biles" (July 31, 1840). Some scholars interpret his inscriptions as not only rare examples of self-expression but as a thinly veiled protest of his bondage. A pot dated July 4, 1859, declares "The fourth of July is surely come / to blow the fife and beat the drum"; though the verse appears to celebrate "Independence Day," it may also suggest African drumming (forbidden by slaveholders as a possible tool of revolt), thus making a poignant reference to freedom.

Dave probably lived until at least 1870; the U.S. Census of that year lists a Dave Drake, a seventy-year-old "turner," as skilled potters of the time were called, born in South Carolina. His works survive in fair number, considering their age and utilitarian nature; more than one hundred exist in various collections, including those of the American Folk Art Museum, the Museum of Fine Arts in Boston, and the Philadelphia Museum of Art.

BIBLIOGRAPHY

Baldwin, Cinda K. *Great and Noble Jar: Traditional Stoneware of South Carolina*. Athens: University of Georgia Press, 1993.

De Groft, Aaron. "Eloquent Vessels, Poetics of Power: The Heroic Stoneware of 'Dave the Potter.'" *Winterthur Portfolio* 33, no. 4 (winter 1998): 249–260.

Koverman, Jill Beaute, ed. *I Made This Jar: The Life and Works of the Enslaved African American Potter, Dave*. Columbia: University of South Carolina Press, 1998.

The National Intelligencer and Washington Advertiser, Washington, DC, August 18, 1806. Available from http://web6.infotrack.galegroup.com.

Patton, Sharon F. *African American Art*. Oxford and New York: Oxford University Press, 1998.

Dorothy Bauhoff

BASKET WEAVING

African slaves arrived in the Americas with knowledge of a diverse range of traditional African skills, which included the cultivation of crops as well as various forms of skilled craft production. Some of the cultural knowledge brought from Africa figured prominently in the plantation economy as well as in the daily life of slaves in the American South; in the low country of South Carolina and Georgia, West African agricultural and cultural practices intersected to form the heart of rice production.

The coastal lowlands of South Carolina and Georgia were well suited to rice cultivation, and planters in the coastal low country paid premium prices for slaves from the windward coast of West Africa, from present-day Senegal to the Ivory Coast, who were familiar with rice cultivation. An important element of the traditional method of cultivation was the winnowing of rice (separating the grain from the chaff) in "fanning" baskets, which were made by slaves in the low country in the manner of West African basket makers.

There was undoubtedly a diverse range of baskets made by slaves in the Americas—probably reflecting, at least during the early years of the slave trade, the diversity of basket weaving among the African peoples who were captured. Baskets were used for various utilitarian purposes well into the nineteenth century, and basket weaving was one of the occupations of slaves on plantations and farms. For example, on Thomas Jefferson's plantation in Poplar Forest, Virginia, there is a record of basket making as a plantation enterprise. Advertisements in nineteenth-century newspapers for the return of runaway slaves mention basket making as an occupation, along with carpentry, blacksmithing, and other skills. For example, an advertisement in the *Raleigh Register and North-Carolina Weekly Advertiser* on November 12, 1807, offers a twenty-dollar reward for the return of Joe, an "excellent basket maker."

The basket that remains the best known of those made by slaves, however, is the fanning basket of the low country rice growers; its prominence may be attributed not only to its widespread use, but also to the preservation of this distinct craft tradition by African American basket weavers of South Carolina. Also called a winnowing basket or a rice fanner, the fanning basket is a coiled, tray-like basket. It is constructed by first creating a coil of either long-leaf pine needles or sweetgrass, a native grass that grows in the coastal dunes, or both. During slavery, it is thought that various rush plants, such as black rush (also called bulrush or needlegrass), were added to the coils for durability. In present-day versions of the fanning basket, sweetgrass is the preferred material. The coils are sewn together in a concentric design using strips of palm leaf; holes for the strips are made using a bone, nail, or needle. Both the methods of construction and the design of the fanning basket closely resemble those of West African fanning baskets, and it is certain that the traditional basket-weaving skills that West African slaves brought to the low country formed an important part of rice production there.

Low country slaves also made a "head tote" basket for carrying wood and other objects on the head. This basket as well had a distinctly West African form and purpose. And in addition to the utilitarian fanning basket, which was often made by men, lighter-weight baskets were made, often by women and children, for other purposes. These lighter baskets evolved into decorative baskets of various forms, including round baskets with shallow sides as well as taller storage baskets. This tradition of basket weaving has been preserved among African American basket weavers of South Carolina, whose practice has centered in Mount Pleasant since the early twentieth century. Though these practitioners weave a wide range of baskets, some still continue to weave a traditional fanning basket, similar in form and material to the baskets of West Africa.

BIBLIOGRAPHY

Morgan, Philip. *Slave Counterpoint: Black Culture in Eighteenth-Century Chesapeake and Lowcountry.* Chapel Hill: University of North Carolina Press, 1998.

Quimby, Ian, and Scott Swank, eds. *Perspectives on American Folk Art.* New York: W. W. Norton, 1980.

Raleigh Register and North-Carolina Weekly Advertiser, November 12, 1807.

Rosengarten, Dale. *Row upon Row: Seagrass Baskets of the South Carolina Lowcountry.* Columbia: McKissick Museum, University of South Carolina, 1986.

Dorothy Bauhoff

SEWING

The production of textiles featured prominently among the duties of female slaves in the Americas. In addition to their work in the fields or the house of the slaveholder, most female slaves were also assigned tasks such as spinning, weaving, and sewing. The textiles created by African and African American slaves, despite the conditions under which they were produced, provide evidence of a continuation of African textile traditions as well as the creation of new forms closely linked to the social traditions of the slave community.

Types of labor

The sewing, spinning, and weaving performed by slaves may be grouped in three categories. First, slaves worked to clothe their own families. A narrative of 1856, described as the personal recollections of a former slave named Peter Still and his wife, Vina, recounts her many tasks related to the family's needs: "She made all their clothes herself, and washed and mended them by night. Their stockings, too, she knit, though she was obliged first to card the wool and spin it" (Pickard 1856, p. 177).

A second category of textiles produced by slaves comprises clothing and other items made for the slaveholder's family; these included woven fabric, bed coverlets, and quilts, often made under the supervision of the mistress. Slave women who had labored in the fields all day were required to spin, weave, or sew at night, usually to fulfill an imposed quota. From these enterprises

emerged a third category of textile production: those made for sale. Often the textiles made by female slaves were sold by the slaveholder as an additional source of income; in some cases the textile enterprises were quite successful.

In addition, female slaves were often trained as seamstresses and dressmakers; their services were hired out as yet another source of income for the slaveholder. Eighteenth- and nineteenth-century ads for runaways reveal that many of these women, who had highly marketable skills, fled. Others were able to purchase their own freedom by sewing. For example, Elizabeth Hobbs Keckley (1818–1907), born in Virginia, became a skilled dressmaker while still enslaved. The slaveholding family hired out her services to such an extent that Keckley developed a loyal clientele, some of whom loaned her the funds to buy her freedom; she easily repaid the loan, as she was finally able to keep her own wages. She eventually moved to Washington, D.C., became dressmaker and companion to First Lady Mary Lincoln (1818–1882), and in 1868 published her book *Behind the Scenes; or, Thirty Years a Slave, and Four Years in the White House.*

Quilts

By far the most well-known textiles produced by slaves are pieced quilts, which were created using pieces (often scraps) of printed fabrics or handwoven cloth, stitched together using an appliqué technique, usually in a geometric design, sometimes further embellished with embroidery. Though some scholars have pointed to the influence of the European pieced-quilt tradition on African American slave quilts, others note the similarity of pattern to the woven and painted textiles of West and Central Africa.

It is certain that quilt-making became an important part of the slave community, particularly on the plantations. According to the account of Peter Still and Vina:

> All the fragments of their worn-out clothes the careful mother saved, and pieced them into bedquilts. She managed to get help to quilt these, by inviting in the other women on Saturday nights. They were not allowed to leave their cabins after the blowing of the horn for them to go to bed; but they were welcome to sit up and work till morning, if they could furnish themselves with lights. (Pickard 1856, p. 177)

Such quilting *bees* or *frolics* were opportunities for unsupervised socializing, and the events often included storytelling, singing, dancing, and the sharing of food. Slave narratives reveal the prevalence of this practice, which must be recognized as a significant element in maintaining cultural tradition.

A somewhat controversial theory has suggested that the quilts made by African American slaves contained secret codes related to the Underground Railroad. In *Hidden in Plain View: The Secret Story of Quilts and the*

Underground Railroad, authors Jacqueline Tobin and Raymond Dobard (1999) present a system of codes, revealed to Tobin by Ozella Williams (d. 1998), an African American quilt vendor in South Carolina. According to Williams, quilt motifs such as *flying geese* and *bear's paw* were used by quilt-makers to suggest escape routes. Slaves hung the quilts outdoors, as if to air, to alert others of plans to escape; the quilt's motif conveyed a message, such as the planned route or the location of a safe house.

Other scholars have refuted this theory, citing lack of evidence in slave narratives, which often discuss escape routes but make no mention of a quilt code. Many of the quilt patterns discussed were not named until the early 1900s; the monkey wrench, cited by Tobin and Dobard (1999) as a signal to prepare for escape, was not invented until 1858, so it seems unlikely that it could have been used as a code.

There is consensus, nevertheless, on the importance of sewing and quilting in the maintenance of tradition and community among enslaved African Americans. Two quilts by Harriet Powers (1837–1910), a former slave, reveal the powerful use of narrative textiles among a largely illiterate group to convey and preserve belief and tradition. Her Bible quilt, dated 1886, is composed of narrative panels that relate the biblical stories of Moses, Noah, Jonah, and Job. Though they originate in a Judeo-Christian tradition, these stories, which frequently appear in African American musical tradition as well, are widely thought to have represented liberation and redemption among the slave community.

BIBLIOGRAPHY

Fry, Gladys-Marie. *Stitched from the Soul: Slave Quilts from the Ante-bellum South*. New York: Dutton Studio Books, 1990.

Keckley, Elizabeth. *Behind the Scenes; or, Thirty Years a Slave, and Four Years in the White House* [1868]. New York: Oxford University Press, [1988].

Pickard, Kate E. R. *The Kidnapped and the Ransomed: Being the Personal Recollections of Peter Still and His Wife "Vina," after Forty Years of Slavery*. Syracuse, NY: W.T. Hamilton, 1856.

Tobin, Jacqueline, and Raymond Dobard. *Hidden in Plain View: The Secret Story of Quilts and the Underground Railroad*. New York: Doubleday, 1999.

Dorothy Bauhoff

QUILTING

Quilts made by African slaves have long been a part of American folk art, but perhaps in different ways than many people have come to believe. In the early years of U.S. history, quilts in general were rare because weaving sheets and blankets as a single piece was the most effi- cient way to make bedding. On the other hand, a quilt required that there be a top layer of fabric (either a single piece or one made with pieces of fabric sewn together), a bottom layer of fabric, and some kind of filling (fabric pieces, cotton, or the like) in the middle. The quilter would bind together the edges of the quilt and sew through all of the layers to secure them.

When quilts were made during the 1750–1825 period, they were of several kinds: whole cloth quilts (made with a single piece of fabric on the top), a central medallion appliqué quilt (in which the quilter sewed a design from another fabric onto the top layer of fabric), or a mosaic piece work (in which the quilter sewed together random pieces of fabric to make the top). When one thinks of quilts in the twenty-first century, one envisions blocks of various sizes and shapes arranged in exact designs. Yet block quilts of this type were not commonly made until sometime in the 1800s.

In plantation households, a great deal of textile work took place. Depending on how self-sufficient the plantation owners wanted to be, it might include grow- ing the cotton or flax, or raising sheep. Sheering sheep, carding wool or cleaning cotton or flax, spinning thread, and weaving fabric all had to be done before any sewing could take place. In Africa textile production had been a man's job, but in America it fell to the women for the most part. Slaves were taught trades, and textile work was one of them. Larger plantations had small buildings used as sewing houses and loom rooms. The diaries of plantation mistresses reveal that making clothing and bedding for everyone on a plantation occupied an enor- mous amount of time each year. Yet both necessity and social pressure stressed that the domestic pursuits were the woman's paramount responsibility.

It has been difficult for historians to locate quilts that can be proven to have been made solely by slaves because quilting is often a group activity, and there is little information about the manner in which mistresses and slaves worked together on quilts. Also, regardless of the situation of their creators, few early quilts were signed (had information sewn onto them) to indicate their origin. Nor in contrast to the making of clothing for the slaves have historians found much evidence in the diaries of plantation women of quilting by slaves. Despite the ravages of use and washing in hot water and lye soap, theft during the Civil War, and use as bandages, some slave-made quilts have survived to testify to their creators' industriousness and creativity.

Although many female slaves worked in the fields during the day, some of them also sewed in the evenings to provide necessities for their families. Even the men and children helped with these household tasks, often with the men threading needles or weaving chair bot- toms of cane and the children holding up candles for light. "Mr. House did not give blankets, the slaves were required to make the necessary cover by piecing together

SEWING FOR FREEDOM

While the role of quilts as signals for slaves' gaining freedom is shrouded in mystery, historians know that sewing was used to support the abolitionist cause. Groups of abolitionist women quilted, sewed, crocheted, and knitted a variety of items that were sold at antislavery fairs. At such a fair in Boston was a cradle quilt made by one of the fair's organizers, Lydia Maria Child. It was a patchwork of small stars with a larger star in the center. On that star Child had written in permanent ink:

Mother! When around your child
You clasp your arms in love,
And when with grateful joy you raise
Your eyes to God above—
Think of the negro mother,
When her child is torn away—
Sold for a little slave—Oh, then,
For that poor mother pray
(Brackman 2006, p. 85).

Slaves also used their sewing skills to buy their freedom. For example, Elizabeth Keckley, the daughter of a slave and a white master who learned to sew from her mother, supported a family of seventeen blacks and whites with her talent. By 1855 she had raised enough money to buy her freedom and that of her son. Five years later Keckley opened a dressmaking shop in Washington, D.C., where she became the seamstress and confidante of Mary Todd Lincoln. Keckley wrote an autobiography *Behind the Scenes, or Thirty Years a Slave, and Four Years in the White House* (1868).

SOURCE: Brackman, Barbara. *Facts and Fabrications: Unraveling the History of Quilts and Slavery.* Lafayette, CA: C&T Publishing, 2006.

---

left over goods. After this process was completed, it was padded with cotton and then dyed in much the same way as homespun. After the dyeing was completed the slave was the owner of a new quilt" (Rawick 1972, vol. 3, p. 180). After fulfilling the plantation owner's requirements for textile production, the slaves might make products, such as quilts, to earn "side money." Many slave men could, and did, many textile tasks, including sewing, quilting, knitting, crocheting, and embroidering (decorative sewing), and many slave women were also apt at carpentry and ironwork.

As far as quilts are concerned, the women used cloth left over from the annual clothing allowance, old clothes, and sacks in which animal feed, sugar, and flour were sold. They also used extra income to buy such fabrics as calico, flannel, broadcloth, and gingham. For the bat between the top and bottom layers of the quilt, they used old clothes, raw cotton, end threads left over from weaving, and bits of wool. Though powdered cloth dyes could be bought in the general store (including indigo, turkey red, and madder), the slaves often made natural

dies from berries, tree bark, and plant parts as well. Plantation mistresses might copy patterns from copybooks and change them to their liking and the slaves did too. When sewing for their white masters, the slaves would make quilts that looked like other quilts made by whites, but when they sewed quilts for themselves, the slave women exercised their own creativity. They might incorporate designs that had significance in their African cultures, and the color red was a favorite, though the reason is unclear.

During Saturday afternoons, Sundays, holidays such as Christmas and Easter, and days when the weather was too bad to allow working the fields, the slave owners—but more likely the slaves themselves—might arrange a "quilting." This is the term the slaves used for what later became known as a quilting bee. Often several (3–12) quilts would be made in the same day because four people could sew simultaneously on the same quilt that was stretched across a wooden frame. "Quiltin's wuz a heap of fun," recalled a Georgia slave. "Sometimes two or three families had a quiltin' together. Folkses would quilt some un' den dey passed 'round de toddy. Some would be cookin' while de others wuz a quiltin' an' den when supper was ready dey all stopped to eat" (Rawick, vol. 13, p. 6). As members of a community, the slaves helped each other by working together to make sure everyone would have enough bedding.

Over the years, a myth has grown up that quilts were somehow used as signals on the Underground Railroad. While this idea sparks people's imaginations, historians have found no evidence to support it. Quilts did, however, support the eradication of slavery in another way: As early as 1834 abolitionist women raised money to support antislavery efforts through craft bazaars. So too, sewing provided escape for some women. For example, one-time slave Elizabeth Keckly sewed and sold her creations to earn the money to buy her freedom. Later she became the seamstress for Mary Todd Lincoln for whom she made a masterful quilt that still survives.

BIBLIOGRAPHY

Beardsley, John, et al. *The Quilts of Gee's Bend.* Atlanta, GA: Tinwood Books, 2002.

Berlin, Ira. *Slaves Without Masters: The Free Negro in the Antebellum South.* New York: Pantheon Books, 1974.

Brackman, Barbara. *Facts and Fabrications: Unraveling the History of Quilts and Slavery.* Concord, CA: C&T Publishing, 2006.

Coppin, L. J. *Unwritten History.* New York: Negro Universities Press, 1968.

Dimond, E. Grey, and Herman Hattaway, eds. *Letters from Forest Place: A Plantation Family's Correspondence, 1846–1881.* Jackson: University Press of Mississippi, 1993.

Fox-Genovese, Elizabeth. *Within the Plantation Household: Black and White Women of the Old South.* Chapel Hill: University of North Carolina Press, 1988.

Fry, Gladys-Marie. *Stitched from the Soul: Slave Quilts from the Antebellum South.* Chapel Hill: University of North Carolina Press, 1990.

Kiracofe, Roderick. *The American Quilt: A History of Cloth and Comfort, 1750–1950.* New York: Clarkson Potter, 1993.

Meltzer, Milton, and Patricia G. Holland. *Lydia Maria Child: Selected Letters, 1817–1880.* Amherst: University of Massachusetts Press, 1982.

Moore, John Hammon, ed. *A Plantation Mistress on the Eve of the Civil War.* Columbia: University of South Carolina Press, 1993.

Rawick, George P., ed. *The American Slave: A Composite Autobiography.* 19 vols. Westport, CT: Greenwood Press, 1972.

Schlissel, Lillian. *Women's Diaries of the Westward Journey.* New York: Schocken Books, 1982.

Smedes, Susan Dabney. *Memorials of a Southern Planter.* Baltimore: Cushings & Baily, 1887.

Yetman, Norman. *Voices from Slavery.* New York: Holt, Rinehart & Winston, 1970.

Jeanne M. Lesinski

■ African Heritage

AFRICAN HERITAGE: AN OVERVIEW
Troy D. Smith

FOLKLORE AND FOLK TALES
Troy D. Smith

SUPERSTITION
Troy D. Smith

TRICKSTER TALES
Troy D. Smith

DREAMS
Troy D. Smith

AFRICAN HERITAGE: AN OVERVIEW

Throughout the entire history of slavery in North America, individuals who spoke African languages and could personally remember another life on that distant continent mingled with others who were at least a generation or two—and sometimes several generations—removed from that experience. The number of actual Africans varied in different eras, of course, and there were proportionately very few by the time the peculiar institution ended. It is also important to ask about what is meant by the term *African* to begin with. The word does not and never has indicated a nationality; Africa is and was a land of many different peoples, tongues, and cultures.

Usually before those Africans who experienced slavery interacted with other slaves who were Creoles in the sense that they had been born in the New World, they interacted with other Africans. Men, women, and children from different social classes, nations, languages, and religions were cast together in crowded holds and on auction blocks, now sharing a new life even if they could not all communicate with one another. Could this have served to strengthen traits that, as West Africans, their cultures may have had in common? As they learned to navigate their new reality, and to communicate in a new language, did they in turn reinforce Africanisms among those slaves born in the Americas?

These are simple questions. Historians' answers, however, have at times been murky and contradictory. Late nineteenth- and early twentieth-century U.S. historians—like most Americans of their time—took it as a matter of course that so-called uncivilized people had no culture to retain to begin with. Serious scholars have not made similar type claims in several decades; rather, they have tended to disagree about the extent to which African culture was retained. Was the slave community a mélange, a mixture of various African, European, and to a certain extent even Native American elements, which coalesced into something distinctly and uniquely African American? Or did it retain strong ties to its African roots throughout, in resistance to the dominant culture—in fact, even influencing white southerners without their knowledge? Or is the truth somewhere in-between?

There is no denying that a distinct African American culture did take shape. It took form over the course of long days toiling with comrades in the fields, or in the masters' kitchens, of nights spent with family in the slave quarters, telling stories and singing songs, and of Sundays spent seeking the Lord together. While scholars can argue about the extent of African cultural retention, it is clear that the slaves' worldview and aesthetics always bore the imprint of Africa. See individual entries under this heading to examine various elements of the slave community, from folklore to toys, and see the ways in which African heritage continued through in African American heritage.

BIBLIOGRAPHY

Gomez, Michael A. *Exchanging Our Country Marks: The Transformation of African Identities in the Colonial and Antebellum South.* Chapel Hill: University of North Carolina Press, 1998.

Stuckey, Sterling. *Slave Culture: Nationalist Theory and the Foundations of Black America.* New York: Oxford University Press, 1998.

Thornton, John. *Africa and Africans in the Making of the Atlantic World, 1400–1800,* 2nd ed. Cambridge, U.K.; New York: Cambridge University Press, 1998.

Troy D. Smith

FOLKLORE AND FOLK TALES

Generations of African Americans toiled their days away in the bonds of slavery. Relatively few of them had the benefit of education, which would have enabled them, perhaps, to leave a more complete written record of their experiences. In fact, few of them would likely have had the time to do so. Of those who were literate, some have indeed bequeathed their readers in the present with their stories; others have transmitted those stories through third parties, who set them on paper. Still, the record is thin. There are inevitable questions, too, about the recorders—their intentions, biases, and foibles. A thin written record, however, does not indicate a lack of history. As Americans, a house full of ghosts has been inherited; the voices are there, if one listens.

SETTING JOHN FREE

Zora Neale Hurston returned to her native Florida in the 1930s to gather folklore, which was collected in her 1935 book *Mules and Men*. One of the tales she collected centered on a slave named John, who rescued his master's children from drowning. The master was so grateful that he promised to set John free after the next crop came in, which resulted in the following exchange:

So Friday come, and Massa said, "Well, de day done come that I said I'd set you free. I hate to do it, but I don't like to make myself out a lie. I hate to git rid of a good nigger lak you."

So he went in de house and give John one of his old suits of clothes to put on. So John put it on and come in to shake hands and tell 'em goodbye. De children they cry, go. So John took his bundle and put it on his stick and hung it crost his shoulder.

Well, Ole John started on down de road. Well, Ole Massa said, "John, de children love yuh."

"Yassuh."

"John, I love yuh."

"Yassuh."

"And Missy like yuh!"

"Yassuh."

"But 'member, John, youse a nigger."

"Yassuh."

Fur as John could hear '"im down de road he wuz hollerin', "John, Oh John! De children loves you. And I love you. De Missy like you."

John would holler back, "Yassuh."

"But 'member youse a nigger, tho!"

Ole Massa kept callin' 'im and his voice was pitiful. But John kept right on steppin' to Canada. He answered Ole Massa every time he called 'im, but he consumed on wid his bag (Hurston 1990, p. 89).

SOURCE: Hurston, Zora Neale. *Mules and Men*. New York: Perennial Library, 1990.

Folklore is, in a sense, the collective voice of past generations. It is not a detailed written report of events, the way history is, but is rather a synthesis of the aspirations and experiences of a group of people, transmitted orally from one generation to the next. Historian Tolagbe Ogunleye describes it thus:

Folklore, also called folk tales, includes myths, storytelling, recollections, ballads, songs, rap, and other orally transmitted lore... Folklore represents a line to a vast, interconnected network of meanings, values, and cognitions. Folklore contains seeds of wisdom, problem solving, and prophecy through tales of rebellion, triumph, reasoning, moralizing and satire. All that African American people value, including the agony enslaved and freed Africans were forced to endure, as well as strategies they used to resist servitude and flee their captors, is discernible in this folk literature. African American folklore is also an historical thread that ties the cultural heritage of Africans in the diaspora and those living on the continent of Africa. (1997, pp. 435–436)

Historian Charles Joyner notes that folk culture "may be regarded as what human beings remember not because it is reinforced by the church, the state, the school, or the press, but simply because it is unforgettable" (1999, p. 3). Author Zora Neale Hurston describes it more concisely as "the boiled down juice of human living" (1995, p. 875).

Human living, in the slaves' world, denoted a unique set of perspectives. When living in a master-slave relationship, it was necessary to be circumspect; hopes, dreams, and fears by necessity were often disguised. This disguise was woven by language. Trickster tales featuring Br'er Rabbit or Old John reflected not only how the world was—hence a reflection of the slave worldview—but how the storytellers and their audience wished it to be, a reflection of the slave ethos. For example, the slave character Old John uses wit and intelligence as tools of resistance and survival, but sometimes the master outwits him. In order for a story to become part of a body of folklore, it must be repeated; in order to be repeated, it must resonate somehow, and connect the storyteller to his or her audience. By thus reflecting both the common values and experiences of a group, using symbols that are universally (within the group) understood, the story not only gives the listeners a sense of the subject being discussed, but in binding them together into a commonly understood experience, gives them a clearer sense of who they are as a group.

African American folktales involved more than just trickster tales and animal stories. They also included tales to illuminate blacks' relationships with one another. One such story later recorded in several sources (including one by Hurston) explained why women were really in control of the household. In the beginning, the Lord made Adam and Eve and set them up in a house together, with both partners being equal. Neither was content with equality, though, and each tried to dominate the other—with Eve getting the upper hand. Whenever it seemed that Adam was about to come out on top, she would employ her secret weapon; she would start crying, and her tears would make her husband feel "low down and dirty." The man went to the Lord for help. Because Eve had the advantage, he wanted one that would trump it, and requested that they no longer be equal physically but that he be made stronger. That way he could beat her, and if she knew that a whipping was nigh she would give in. The Lord granted his wish, and Adam returned home to find Eve surly as ever. When he confronted her she reached into the woodbox and retrieved a piece of kindling with which to beat him in the head. He was unfazed, and took away her weapon and whipped her.

The next morning she consulted with a serpent who lived in an apple tree, who gave her a plan of attack. Then she, also, went to the Lord to ask for help—she asked for two rusty keys, which had hung nearby for so long that the Lord had forgotten what they went to, and he gave them to her. That evening Adam came home and demanded his supper, but Eve informed him the kitchen was locked tight. None of his strength enabled him to open the door. She volunteered to try her conjuring magic on it, and recommended he go cut some wood in the meantime—a task he had intended for her. Naturally, the door opened right up with the old key.

After supper, Adam suggested they "hit de frog-hair"—but was informed that the bedroom door, too, was locked tight. He asked his wife if she would try her magic there, too. She was happy to comply—if only he would patch the roof in the meantime. Once again, she used the secret key.

"So dat de reason," the tale concludes, "de very reason, why de mens thinks dey is boss and de wimmens knows dey is boss, cause dey gots dem two little keys to use in dat slippery sly wimmen's way. Yas, fawever mo and den some!

"An' if you don't know dat already, den you ain't no married man" (Garner, pp. 52–53).

BIBLIOGRAPHY

Dickson, Bruce, Jr. "The 'John and Old Master' Stories and the World of Slavery: A Study in Folktales and History." *Phylon* 35, no. 4 (1974): 418–429.

Hurston, Zora Neale. *Folklore, Memoirs, and Other Writings.* New York: Penguin, 1995.

Joyner, Charles. *Shared Traditions: Southern History and Folk Culture.* Urbana: University of Illinois Press, 1999.

Ogunleye, Tolagbe. "African American Folklore: Its Role in Reconstructing African American History." *Journal of Black Studies* 27, no. 4 (March 1997): 435–455.

Thurman Garner. "Black Ethos in Folk Tales." *Journal of Black Studies*, 1984; 15: 53-66.

Troy D. Smith

SUPERSTITION

In 1875, a frustrated Charles Waddell Chesnutt (1858–1932) noted that "these [black servants] downstairs believe in ghosts, luck, horse shoes, cloud-signs, witches, and all other kinds of nonsense, and all the argument in the world couldn't get it out of them" (Oden 1978, p. 38). Indeed, the superstitions of many blacks often seemed silly, quaint, and backward to white observers. Mark Twain's (1835–1910) youthful protagonist, Huckleberry Finn, is willing to believe, but the narrator himself offers descriptions that are clearly tongue-in-cheek: "Miss Watson's nigger, Jim, had a hair-ball as big as your fist, which had been took out of the fourth stomach of an ox, and he used to do magic with it. He said there was a spirit inside of it, and it knowed everything" (Twain 2003, p. 30).

Such beliefs were hardly silly to slaves, however; they were quite serious. Gloria Oden wrote that conjure, for example, "filled a deep need in the slave's life for a weapon to invoke against the arbitrary and often violent circumstances that made up his existence. It compensated for the powerlessness he felt, and, consciously or unconsciously, it gave him the vitality of his African heritage" (Oden 1978, p. 39). What Europeans interpreted as superstitions were usually reflections of an African worldview. It was a worldview centered on connections and harmony, as described by Mambo Ama Mazama:

> The major articulation of African metaphysics is the energy of cosmic origins that permeates and lives within all that is—human beings, animals, plants, minerals and objects, as well as events. This common energy shared by all confers a common essence to everything in the world, and thus ensures the fundamental unity of all that exists (Mazama 2002, pp.219–220).

Lawrence Levine described African spirituality thus:

> Man was part of, not alien to, the Natural Order of things, attached to the Oneness that bound together all matter, animate and inanimate, all spirits, visible or not ... Survival and happiness and health depended on being able to read the signs that existed everywhere, to understand the visions that recurrently visited one, to commune with the spirits that filled the world (Levine 1977, p. 58).

Therefore, slaves who were alert for omens or other interactions from the spirit world made manifest in the physical were—rather than being backward, fearful, and childlike—respectful toward and cognizant of the relations that bind the universe together. Past and present were bound together as well, and a traditional awareness

SUPERSTITIONS

For some slaves, signs and omens were everywhere. Here are some examples:

> I've heard if a turkle dove, when de season first starts, comes to your house and starts moanin', it's a sign you is goin' to move out and somebody else goin' move in.
>
> If a squinch owl starts howlin' 'round your house and if you turn your shoe upside down at the door, they sure will hush. Now I know that's so.
>
> I used to run myself nearly to death tryin' to get to the end of the rainbow to get the pot of gold.
>
> And I've heard the old folks say if you start any place and have to go back, you make a circle in the ground and spit in it or you'll have bad luck.
>
> *Clark Hill, a former slave (part 3, p. 251)*
>
> I was born with a caul over my face. Old miss said it hung from the top of my head half way to my waist.
>
> She kept it and when I got bog enough she said, 'now that's your veil, you play with it.'
>
> But I lost it out in the orchard one day.
>
> They said it would keep you from seein' h'ants.
>
> *Annie Page, a former slave (part 5, p. 238)*
>
> In slavery times you used to carry a rabbit foot in your pocket to keep old massa from whippin' you.
>
> *Eda Harper, a former slave (part 3, p. 166)*

SOURCE: Works Progress Administration. *Born in Slavery:* Arkansas Narratives, vol. 2, parts 3 and 5.

of one's ancestors' spirits often translated into a belief in ghosts or haunts, as well as the necessary means to avoid angering them.

Ex-slave Cora Torian was a fount of information about the role of superstition in slaves' lives:

> I has dreamed of fish and dat is a sure sign I would get a piece of money, an I always did. Dreamed of buggy and horse an it was a sign of death in family and I no's hits tru. Dream of de ded hit always rains ... I hang horse shoes oer my door to keep the Evil Spirits away ... I sho no dar is ghosts, I seed one once hit was a man wid no head on standin in my house and pullin the crammin out of de house and puttin hit on de table. Oooh I no's dat is so cause I seed hit wid my own eyes... My Mammy had a woman dat lived wid us and she died, and sometimes afterwards ... she slowly ris up and went thru a crack about two inches wide. Now dat's a fak! ... You can find things by spitting in yer han and de way the spit goes if youse will go dar you will be sho to find hit ... When de

moon changes if youse see hit thru de bresh you sho will have bad luck ... if youse sneeze wen you eats you will shorely die (Kentucky Narratives, pp. 103–110).

Another ex-slave, "Mad" Griffin of South Carolina, told a Works Progress Administration (WPA) writer about his experiences with spirits. He and his friends would occasionally steal one of the master's pigs and hold a secret barbecue on Saturday nights in a wooded gulley. The trip to the gulley, though, was often "screechy"—eerie shadows in the moonlight, strange animals calling, and occasionally a spirit showing itself with a weird light "jes like dese 'lectric lights out dar in dat street." Sometimes only one or two of the slaves would see it, and sometimes the whole group would. "Dats zactly how it is wid de spirits," Griffin said. "De[y] acts real queer all de way round." He had little patience for younger, "eddicated" blacks who claimed there was no such thing as spirits. "I rolls my old eyes at dem an' axes dem how comes dey runs so fas' through de woods at night. Yes sirree, dem fool niggers sees dem jes as I does. Realy de white folks doesn't have eyes fer sech as we darkies does; but dey bees dare jes de same" (South Carolina Narratives, pp. 1–4).

Elliott Gorn has noted that, like other forms of oral tradition, "ghostlore offered a way of stepping back, a way of observing one's situation and, through symbols and metaphors, a way of commenting on life ... ghostlore helped Afro-Americans cope with oppression, retain their self-esteem, and survive as a people" (Gorn 1984, p. 565).

Omens and ghostlore reinforced the knowledge that past, present, and future were intimately connected, as were all beings and objects (living, dead, or inanimate) and that there were definite causes and effects in the world slaves inhabited. Or, as Mississippi ex-slave Howard Divinity—who was known to carry on conversations with Jesus, St. Peter, and trees—put it: "Men ain't all" (Gorn 1984, p. 553).

BIBLIOGRAPHY

Gorn, Elliot J. "Black Spirits: The Ghostlore of Afro-American Slaves." *American Quarterly* 36 (1984): 549–565.

Levine, Lawrence. *Black Culture and Black Consciousness: Afro-American Folk Thought from Slavery to Freedom.* New York: Oxford University Press, 1977.

Mazama, Mambo Ama. "Afrocentricity and African Spirituality." *Journal of Black Studies* 33, no.2 (2002): 218–234.

Oden, Gloria C. "Chesnutt's Conjure as African Survival." *Critical Approaches to Ethnic Literature* 5, no. 1 (1978): 38–48.

Stuckey, Sterling. *Slave Culture: Nationalist Theory and the Foundations of Black America.* New York: Oxford University Press, 1987.

Twain, Mark. *The Adventures of Huckleberry Finn*. New York: Penguin Books, 2003.

Works Progress Administration Slave Narrative Project. "Cora Torian." *Kentucky Narratives*: 103–110.

Works Progress Administration Slave Narrative Project. "'Mad' Griffin." *South Carolina Narratives* 14, part 1: 1–4.

Troy D. Smith

TRICKSTER TALES

The folklore of many cultures around the world includes trickster characters. These characters sometimes appear as the protagonist of a single story, but more often they are at the center of a cycle of tales, such as the African American folktales adapted by Joel Chandler Harris (1848–1908) in his *Uncle Remus* (1881) stories. The trickster's incarnation might be human or an anthropomorphized animal; among indigenous peoples in North America, the trickster is often portrayed as a coyote, whereas the African American trickster often took the form of Br'er Rabbit or the slave Old John, as in the Harris stories. For slaves the trickster, who used his or her wit to elude the devices of a more powerful enemy (Br'er Fox, or the white master), was far more than a source of entertainment. For the "trick" to work, it was necessary not only for the trickster to have a superior intellect to their adversary, but for the adversary to act on a presumed mental inferiority in the trickster. The result was, as historian Charles Joyner puts it, "the triumph of the weak over the powerful through the sheer agency of wits" (1989, p. 236).

Origins of the North American Trickster

In the introduction to his collection, Harris notes that trickster tales have appeared in such diverse places as Brazil, India, and Siam (Thailand). The Br'er Rabbit stories he recorded were virtually identical to several American Indian stories. J. W. Powell, a Smithsonian Institution scholar, believed that African slaves borrowed the tales from Native Americans, but Harris found this claim extremely doubtful. That was hardly the last word on the subject. In a 2000 essay Jay Hansford C. Vest proposed a Native American genesis for the Br'er Rabbit stories, surmising that Africans could hardly have originated stories about rabbits, bears, and wolves, animals not native to Africa, and that they must have learned them from southeastern Indians either during the period blacks and Indians were enslaved together or in the nineteenth century, when blacks were in bondage to some Native Americans.

Ultimately, the question of who told the stories in North America first is both unanswerable and moot. There is abundant evidence that a trickster tradition had existed in Africa, and even if slaves transplanted across the Atlantic made some adaptations in their sto-

ries to match their new environment—or blended some elements with those of the Native Americans or Europeans they met—that does not make the motif any less intrinsic to their folklore, or to their own identities. Indeed, Marcia Gaudet has demonstrated that the Louisiana versions of the Br'er Rabbit tales—featuring Lapin (French for *rabbit*) and Bouki (or hyena)—have definite ties to Africa, *bouki* being the Wolof word for hyena. (The word *bouki* also made appearances in Haiti.)

The Trickster as a Model of Defiance

Themes of pride and the value of a quick wit are universal, but trickster tales among African Americans ultimately served as far more than simple morality plays. The trickster served, as Rhonda Jeffries and Susan Schramm noted in their 2000 article, as a "defiant representative for the oppressed group" whose primary goal was "social noncomformity by redefinition of norms for life and existence ... serving the evolving needs of African American communities" (pp. 19–20). Characters such as Br'er Rabbit demonstrated the need for slaves to resist, not physically, but mentally. The rabbit stood little chance one-on-one against the various foxes,

---

OLD JOHN

While Br'er Rabbit tales might be shared with a white audience, stories about the slave trickster Old John (or Père Jean) were for the slave community only. John and his master engaged in an endless tug of war, each trying to gain the upper hand over the other in small ways. John was thus a slave everyman, embodying the aspirations and the very identity of all slaves, using his wiles for whatever personal empowerment he could get. In this struggle it was clear that, although honesty was the best policy when dealing with one's own community, a little guile can go a long way when dealing with the enemy. Whether it was by innocently causing an argument between the master and his dinner guest so no one would notice that John himself had already eaten the main course, or by convincing the master—when caught red-handed stealing a pig—that he was there to deliver said pig to the master's kitchen, Old John was always thinking. Even though the master got the upper hand in some stories, such as when he donned blackface or impersonated God to foil one of John's plans, it was always a contest. "In this way," Bruce Dickson Jr. wrote, "John, whether in success or failure, did indeed get the best of Old Master all the time" (Dickson 1974, p. 429).

BIBLIOGRAPHY
Dickson, Bruce D., Jr. "The 'John and Old Master' Stories and the World of Slavery: A Study in Folktales and History." *Phylon* 35, no. 4 (1974): 418–429.

Joyner, Charles. "The Trickster and the Fool: Folktales and Identity among Southern Plantation Slaves." In *The Culture and Community of Slavery*, ed. Paul Finkelman. New York: Garland, 1989.

wolves, bears, and buzzards that he encountered; he survived by tricking them, thus protecting not only himself but his community, who would suffer along with him if he pursued direct acts of violence. The stories thus also capture the fears of the powerful figures. The natural order of things—at least to a Br'er Bear's way of thinking—would be for the strong to win out. Yet in these stories a weaker character upsets the social order, as in "Mr. Rabbit Grossly Deceives Mr. Fox" (in the sixth chapter of *Uncle Remus*). Rabbit fools the fox into allowing himself to be saddled and ridden like a horse, then proceeds to ride him past the ladies they both wish to impress, much to the humiliation of Mr. Fox. "Ladies, ain't I done tell you Br'er Fox was de ridin' hoss fer our fambly?" Rabbit asks. "He sorter losin' his gait now, but I 'speck I can fetch 'im all right in a mont' er so." The narrator goes on: "En den Br'er Rabbit sorter grin, he did, en' de gals giggle, en' Miss Meadows, she praise up de pony, en' dar wuz Br'er Fox hitch fas' to der rack, en' couldn't he'p hisse'f" (Harris 1974 [1881], pp. 7–9).

Br'er Rabbit seems, within the context of the story, to be acting solely for his own aggrandizement. But sometimes the trickster falls prey to his own conceit. In the famous Tar Baby tale, as told in Harris's book, Br'er Fox temporarily gets the upper hand over Br'er Rabbit. The fox fashions a "baby" out of tar; when the "baby" is rudely unresponsive to Br'er Rabbit, the trickster lashes out violently against it—and is stuck fast, himself a victim of a clever trick. Despite this setback, Br'er Rabbit survives to confound his enemies repeatedly. Br'er Rabbit's occasional episodes of comeuppance may not seem to fit the role of a character who exists to uplift the oppressed. But, as Jeffries points out, the African American trickster is "a free spirit whose behavior is complex and contradictory" (Jeffries and Schramm 2000, p. 20). Ultimately, he is pursuing power for himself—at the expense of those who would dominate him, and solely by the force of his own intellect. The popularity of Bugs Bunny during the Depression and World War II shows that the trickster could strike a chord in later audiences as well. The trickster was more than just wish fulfillment; it was a model of defiance.

The trickster motif was indeed not mere escapism but a matter of practical daily application. In the *Narrative of William W. Brown, a Fugitive Slave*, Brown recounts that he had been told he was to be sold soon and was charged to look out for a suitable new master. Instead he had tried to run away:

> After being in jail about one week, master sent a man to take me out of jail, and send me home. I was taken out and carried home, and the old man was well enough to sit up. He had me brought into the room where he was, and as I entered, he asked me where I had been? I told I had acted according to his orders. He told me to look for a master, and I had been to look for one. He

answered that he did not tell me to go to Canada to look for a master. (Brown 1991 [1847], p. 54)

Brown was sent out to work in the fields under close scrutiny and was sold soon after. Eventually, however, he made his escape for good. Brown's interaction with his master is just one example of the diversionary and subversive mental and verbal tactics he and other slaves used to defend themselves—not unlike Br'er Rabbit.

BIBLIOGRAPHY

Bascom, William. *African Folktales in the New World*. Bloomington: Indiana University Press, 1992.

Brown, William Wells. *The Travels of William Wells Brown* [1847], ed. Paul Jefferson. New York: Markus Wiener, 1991.

Gaudet, Marcia. "Bouki, the Hyena, in Louisiana and African Tales." *Journal of American Folklore* 105, no. 415 (1992): 66–72.

Harris, Joel Chandler. *Uncle Remus, His Songs and His Sayings* [1881]. Savannah, GA: Beehive Press, 1974.

Jeffries, Rhonda B. "The Trickster Figure in African American Teaching: Pre- and Postdesegregation." *Urban Review* 26, no. 4 (1994): 289–304.

Jeffries, Rhonda B. *Performance Traditions among African American Teachers*. Bethesda, MD: Austin and Winfield, 1997.

Jeffries, Rhonda B., and Susan L. Schramm. "African American Trickster Representations in the Work of Romare Bearden." *Art Education* 53, no. 5 (2000): 19–24.

Johnson, Alonzo, and Paul T. Jersild, eds. *Ain't Gonna Lay My 'Ligion Down: African American Religion in the South*. Columbia: University of South Carolina Press, 1996.

Joyner, Charles. *Down by the Riverside: A South Carolina Slave Community*. Urbana: University of Illinois Press, 1984.

Joyner, Charles. "The Trickster and the Fool: Folktales and Identity among Southern Plantation Slaves." In *The Culture and Community of Slavery*, ed. Paul Finkelman. New York: Garland, 1989.

Joyner, Charles. *Shared Traditions: Southern History and Folk Culture*. Urbana: University of Illinois Press, 1999.

Vest, Jay Hansford C. "From Bobtail to Br'er Rabbit: Native American Influences on Uncle Remus." *American Indian Quarterly* 24, no. 1 (2000): 19–43.

Troy D. Smith

DREAMS

"Once I had a dream," ex-slave Easter Sudie Campbell of Kentucky recalled. In her dream a woman glided by her bed and stood beside the fire. She looked so real, and the dream was so vibrant, that at first Campbell thought it was her daughter arisen from bed in the night to eat from the bean pot—but she realized it was not so, for her daughter was no longer living at home. When she awoke she was certain that she had received a sign of impending death, and was frantic with worry for her daughter. Campbell asked her son to take her to the daughter's home to check on her; the son insisted on going alone, no doubt to save his mother from traveling in the night. He returned after a short while, to report that all was well—but that he had a terrible headache. Before morning, he was dead.

"So you see," Campbell said, years later, "dat war de sign of de dream. I war jes warned in de dream an didn't have sense nuff ter know hit" (Works Progress Administration, Kentucky Narratives, Vol. VII, p. 94).

Many African slaves came from cultures that believed in continual revelation from the spirit world—whether the source of the revelation was a god or an ancestor. These revelations would come either through an entranced medium or, more directly, in the form of a dream. "The other world," historian John Thornton once said, "seems to have found it easiest to communicate with people in an unconscious state or in an altered state of consciousness" (1992, p. 243). These beliefs were not eradicated by their descendents' conversion to Christianity; after all, the Bible is full of such visions, and the two worldviews both seemed quite compatible with the idea of information coming to someone from beyond in the form of dreams (Fairley 2003). In fact, members of the slave community often had very specific interpretations for the images brought to them in their sleep. A few are listed below, taken from a list compiled in the 1930s by Works Progress Administration (WPA) writer Louise Oliphant:

> To dream of muddy water, maggots, or fresh meat is a sign of death. To dream of caskets is also a sign of death. You may expect to hear of as many deaths as there are caskets in the dream.
>
> To dream of blood is a sign of trouble.
>
> To dream of fish is a sign of motherhood.
>
> To dream of eggs is a sign of trouble unless the eggs are broken. If the eggs are broken, your troubles are ended.
>
> To dream of snakes is a sign of enemies. If you kill the snakes, you have conquered your enemies.
>
> To dream of fire is a sign of danger.
>
> To dream of a funeral is a sign of a wedding.
>
> To dream of a wedding is a sign of a funeral.
>
> To dream of silver money is a sign of bad luck; cash [is] good luck.
>
> To dream of dead folk is a sign of rain. (Oliphant 1936–1938, Georgia Narratives, vol. 4, part 4, pp. 282–289)

BIBLIOGRAPHY

Fairley, Nancy J. "Dreaming Ancestors in Eastern Carolina." *Journal of Black Studies* 33, no. 5 (May 2003): 545–561.

Oliphant, Louise. Works Progress Administration (WPA) Slave Narratives, 1936–1938, Georgia Narratives, vol. 4, part 4, pp. 282–289.

Thornton, John. *Africa and Africans in the Making of the Atlantic World, 1400–1680.* New York: Cambridge University Press, 1992.

Works Progress Administration (WPA) Slave Narratives, 1936–1938: Easter Sudie Campbell, Kentucky Narratives, vol. 7, pp. 92–94.

Troy D. Smith

■ Games

Most of slave life was taken up with long hours of unpaid labor. But slaves were given time for leisure and recreation. Almost all masters observed Sunday as a day of rest, and slaves were left to themselves. Saturday was usually a partial work day, with Saturday evening a time for gathering and dancing. The Christmas holidays, from December 25 to January 1, were usually observed as a period of no work, for field workers at least. Other holidays, such as Thanksgiving, Easter Monday, and the Fourth of July, might also be observed, depending on the master's practice. Work was usually suspended on rainy days, when fieldwork was impossible. Impromptu holidays might also be declared by masters after planting was done, during slow periods of the agricultural cycle, and in association with weddings, birthdays, and funerals of the master's family.

Slaves created other opportunities for recreation on their own initiative. Illicit nighttime gatherings, for worship and for parties, were a regular part of slave life. Though they might be broken up by slave patrols, they usually went undetected. Or a rest from fieldwork might be accomplished more openly: If a master (or a member of his family) just retuned from a journey, part of the day might be taken up with polite welcomes and spontaneous performance of song and dance—in master's honor. More risky options were pretending to be sick, or simple truancy, leaving the plantation without permission.

During periods of leisure, slaves spent most of their time in parties with music and dancing, in worship services, hunting and fishing, lounging, storytelling, drinking, and courting. However, a variety of games were also enjoyed. Slave codes in the South usually outlawed certain activities, such as cards or dice, gambling, or playing any game of chance for money—indicating that such games were popular pastimes among slaves. Dominos have been unearthed in archeological excavations of Thomas Jefferson's slave quarters at Monticello. Some scholars have suggested that competitive games of physical exertion and prowess reflect societies in which hard work and individual effort are rewarded. Slaves may have favored games of chance in their peculiar situation, where work did not bring personal reward—and success, even survival, was often contingent on a variety of uncontrollable factors.

Slaves engaged in verbal games of wit and humor. Some scholars suggest that the game of joking insults known as "the dozens" or "signifying" reaches back to slavery times, and may even have African roots. Slaves also enjoyed challenging one another with riddles:

Slick as a mole, black as coal,
Got a great long tale like a thunder hole.
[A skillet.]

Crooked as a rainbow, teeth like a cat.
Guess all of your life but you can't guess dat.
[A blackberry bush.] (Webber 1978, p. 182)

Male slaves engaged in various athletic games, including foot races, wrestling, boxing, and other sports. Such athletic competitions were sometimes performed for the amusement of masters, but they were not without roots in slave culture. Some African traditions of wrestling and fighting may have been secretly preserved among male slaves in South Carolina, for example, as *capoiera* survived in Brazil. Other forms of sport were played by slave men. A report on the recreations of a black regiment during the Civil War, on Thanksgiving Day 1864, lists pole climbing, foot racing, sack racing, wheelbarrow racing, jig dancing, turkey shooting, and pig chasing. As baseball became a popular sport among whites in the nineteenth century, slaves also played the game, though without equipment and without knowledge of official rules. A stick might serve as a bat, and a ball of yarn covered by a sock could become a ball. Simply hitting the ball as far as possible was one version of the game.

Slave children on many plantations were not required to work much until they were at least eleven or twelve (there were exceptions: for example, some slave children were rented out to perform household tasks for small landowners and urbanites). During their childhood years, though, many remained relatively free to roam and play. Frederick Douglass remembered his early years in slavery in almost idyllic terms: "The first seven or eight years of the slave-boy's life are about as full of sweet content as those of the most favored and petted *white* children of the slaveholder" (Douglass 1855, p. 40).

The most enjoyable amusement of slave children was roaming the fields and woods of their home plantation and surrounding areas while their parents worked. They could wade in streams, swim, chase rabbits, explore, fish, and gather nuts, roots, and berries. They also played games. Slave children had limited access to toys and balls, but marbles were popular. "De best game us had was marbles," Tom Hawkins, a former slave from South Carolina recalled, "and us played wid homemade clay marbles most of the time" (Webber 1978, pp. 180–181). Charlie Davenport also remembered improvising equipment to play traditional games, as a slave child on a Mississippi plantation: "Us tho'owed horse shoes, jumped poles, walked on stilts, an' played marbles" (Wiggins 1980, p. 24).

Slave children usually played games that required only their bodies or a minimum of equipment: hide and seek, tag, I spy, hop skotch, goose and gander, house, skeeting (sliding over a frozen lake), jump rope, hen and hawk, blind man's bluff, and so forth. Children played a wide variety of cooperative "ring games" that often included joining hands in a circle, chanting rhymes, dancing, performing, or spinning around. One popular ring game was Little Sally Walker, which imitated adult courting behavior. With a designated "Sally" in the middle of a circle, acting out the words, the children chanted:

Little Sally Walker,
Sitting in a saucer,
Crying for the old man
To come for a dollar.
Ride, Sally, Ride.
Put your hands on your hips,
And let your backbone slip.
Oh, shake it to the East.
Oh, shake it to the West.
Shake it to the one that you love the best.
(Holland 2002, p. 99)

If they could obtain a ball, or improvise one, slave children enjoyed playing simple ball games. Some children played a version of dodge ball called Sheep Meat. A yarn ball was thrown, and whoever was hit was out until the next game. Anti-Over or Once Over was another ball game children played. In one form, a group of children would throw the ball over a cabin to children on the other side. Whoever caught the ball would then run around the cabin and try to hit someone from the other team with it.

Slave children engaged in elaborate imitative play, staging church services, baptisms, funerals, weddings, and grand meetings—even slave auctions. Through these games, they could imitate the activities of adult slaves, and occasionally even masters. Benny Dillard, who had lived as a child on a Georgia plantation, remembered, "The best game of all was to play like it was big meeting time . . . We would have make-believe preachin' and baptizin'. When we started playing like we were baptizing them we throwed all we could catch right in the creek, clothes and all, and dunked them" (Wiggins 1980, pp. 25–26). Anna Woods from Arkansas recalled:

Yes, ma'am, we children played. I remember that the grown folks used to have church—out behind the old shed. They'd shout and they'd sing. We children didn't know what it all meant. But every

Monday morning we'd get up and make a play house in an old wagon bed—and we'd shout and sing too. We didn't know what it meant, or what we was suppose to be doing. We just aped our elders (Holland, p. 103).

Any serious analysis of slave children's games can reveal a great deal about the realities of daily life in slavery. But this requires some decoding by contemporary historians.

The award-winning television series on the history of the English language, *The Story of English* (MacNeil-Lehrer Productions/BBC, 1986), includes a segment on the contributions of black people to American speech. The camera recorded a performance of Shoot Turkey, a slave children's game, as an illustration of the influence of plantation dialects. The recording has appeared many times on television and in classrooms on videotape.

Janey Hunter, a Gullah woman who, according to the narrator could boast of 100 grandchildren and 20 great-grandchildren, led some of these youngsters in a round of Shoot Turkey. She chanted the lyrics to the song and kept time by clapping her hands. Several of her grandchildren formed a line and crouched down in a squat, each child putting both hands on the shoulders of the child in front. The song took the form of a call and response, with Hunter starting off:

Hunter: Get ready. Let's go!
Children: Shoot, Turkey! Shoot! Shoot!
(Repeated four times in unison)

Hunter: Hon-ey!
Children: Ma'am!

Hunter: D'you went to the weddin'?
Children: Yes, ma'am.

Hunter: D'you get any wine?
Children: Yes, ma'am.

Hunter: How good that wine?
Children: Good, good!

Hunter: You ras-cal!
Children: Shoot, Turkey! Shoot! Shoot!
(Repeated four times in unison)

During the singing of the chorus Shoot Turkey, the children hopped along, frog-like, in a circle, in time to the music. During the rest of the song, they remained still. The narrator made no comment on the game, except to say that Hunter was passing on the traditions of the plantation to the next generations. But there is more.

This music and rhymes of Shoot Turkey (sometimes called Shoo Turkey) had been recorded earlier in variant forms in audio recordings made in the mid-1960s on John's Island, South Carolina (part of the Southern Folklife Collection at the University of North Carolina, Chapel Hill). The television documentary segment may have been the first video recording of the game, however. In the earlier recordings, the song could have several verses, including one beginning with "D'you

HIDE THE SWITCH: A SLAVE CHILDREN'S GAME

The games played by children in the slave quarters naturally reflected the realities of daily life. Children acted out in play not only the happy experiences of church gatherings and parties, but also more frightening events that they may have seen or heard about. Such play may have helped slave children to conceptualize their world, to cope emotionally with unpleasant realities, and to prepare themselves for their future lives as slaves.

One game played by slave children was some form of bogeyman. In one form, a child would assume the role of an evil spirit and attempt to frighten other children at night. In another form, a child would become the bogeyman and attempt to catch other children as they screamed, ran, and attempted to hide. Whomever got caught would be the bogeyman, until he or she caught someone else.

Hide the Switch was another game that slave children played repeatedly. One child would hide a switch made from a tree branch. When someone found the switch, the other children would yell and scatter, while the finder tried to hit them with it. Such games were as popular among the girls as they were among the boys. They acted out one of the primary fears associated with slave daily life—beatings—and perhaps prepared slave children for future realities. Julia Banks, who had been enslaved in Texas, recalled that the slave children would "get switches and whip one another. You know after you was hit several times it didn't hurt much" (Rawick 1972–1979, Vol. 4, part 1, p. 97).

BIBLIOGRAPHY
Rawick, George P., ed., *The American Slave: A Composite Autobiography*, 19 vols. Westport, CT: Greenwood Press, 1972–1979.

get any cake?" as well as verses for turkey, rabbit, and wine.

At first glance, this would appear to be a simple ring game, with nonsense verse and random movement, which could have no other purpose than the amusement of children. However, placed in the context of slavery and slave daily life—a context in which cake, wine, and turkey would normally be unavailable to slaves—the game takes on new meanings.

As the exclamation "You rascal!" suggests, the game is transgressive. One might decode it in the early twenty-first century as a game that celebrates stealing food—a normal part of slave life, and an activity in which slaves are known to have taken great pleasure. "The wedding" seems to be an ironic reference to the master's house and/or his meals. The children crouch and creep, as if hiding from view. And the exchange of call and response is quite humorous when understood to be a sarcastic reference to stealing the luxury foods usually reserved for whites.

The game Shoot Turkey provides a window into slave life, demonstrating that (with a little coding) slave children's games could take on multiple meanings and be used to serious purpose—among other things, expressing solidarity among slaves, satirizing masters, and flaunting their transgressions in full view of uncomprehending whites. The game could be used to socialize children into the realities of slave life, and perhaps to even teach them the skills that they would need as adults to avoid detections when finding a little cake or wine in the kitchen.

BIBLIOGRAPHY

Douglass, Frederick. *My Bondage My Freedom.* New York: Dover Publications, 1855.

Holland, Jearold Winston. *Black Recreation: A Historical Perspective.* Chicago: Burnham Publishers, 2002.

Southern Folklife Collection. Guy and Candie Carawan Collection. Field Recordings from Johns Island, South Carolina. University of North Carolina, Chapel Hill.

The Story of English. "Black on White." MacNeil-Lehrer Productions/BBC, 1986.

Webber, Thomas L. *Deep Like the Rivers: Education in the Slave Quarter Community, 1831–1865.* New York: W. W. Norton, 1978.

Wiggins, David K. "The Play of Slave Children in the Plantation Communities of the Old South, 1820–1960." *Journal of Sport History* 7, no. 2 (Summer 1980): 21–39.

Anthony A. Lee

■ Holiday and Celebration

HOLIDAY AND CELEBRATION: AN OVERVIEW

The bleakness and brutality of slave life was alleviated, in small measure, by the celebration of holidays. Most slaves in the eighteenth and nineteenth centuries looked forward to several holidays during the year: Those residing in the South were allowed three major holidays, usually Easter, Christmas, and New Year's Day; in the North, slaves and freedpeople also observed Black Election Day and Pinkster.

Although the majority of slaves welcomed such respites from their grueling existence, former slave and African American leader and journalist Frederick Douglass (1817–1895) believed holiday festivities were primarily a means to control and manipulate slaves rather than a gesture of appreciation or affection. In *My Bondage and My Freedom*, he wrote: "I believe these holidays to be among the most effective means, in the hands of slaveholders, of keeping down the spirit of insurrection among the slaves.... These holidays serve the purpose of keeping the minds of the slaves occupied with prospective pleasure, within the limits of slavery" (2003 [1855], p. 253).

Many scholars echo this interpretation. Shauna Bigham and Robert May (1998) note that many slave owners cared genuinely about at least some of their slaves, especially household servants, but caution that "unless historians relate slave Christmases to the peculiar institution's exploitative context, they run the risk of leaving their readers with inappropriately benign imagery." They write that granting material concessions to slaves allowed slaveholders "to maintain [slaves'] health and thus value in the domestic slave trade, as well as to avert the possibility of slave resistance and to encourage slaves to work harder." Gift-giving at Christmas "confirmed the slaveowners' power even as it seemed to substantiate their pretensions to paternalism" (pp. 263–288).

Holidays in the South: Customs and Constraints

Holidays, especially Christmas, took hold in the South earlier than in the North. Christmas became a legal holiday as early as the 1830s in some southern states. Orville Burton, in his 1985 study, attributes its mandatory celebration to slaves' manipulation of owners and not vice versa. Owners continually exhorted their slaves to accept the doctrines of Christianity and desired their conversion; thus, Burton argues, slaves may have used their conversions to persuade slaveholders to allow them to celebrate the holiest of Christian holidays, Christmas and Easter.

Of course, profit making took precedence over the observance of holidays. On cotton plantations, where slave life was often harshest, celebrating Christmas was ancillary to getting the cotton picked and stored. Charles Ball, who was born circa 1781 in Calvert County, Maryland, was separated from his mother and siblings as a child. He later married and was separated again from his family when sold and sent to a cotton plantation in Georgia. In his narrative of his own life, he recalls one Christmas:

As Christmas of the year 1805, approached, we were all big with hope of obtaining three or four days, at least, if not a week of holiday; but when the day at length arrived, we were sorely disappointed, for on Christmas eve, when we had come from the field, with our cotton, the overseer fell into a furious passion, and swore at us all for our laziness; and many other bad qualities. He then told us, that he had intended to give us three days, if we had worked well, but that we had been so idle, and had left so much cotton yet to be picked in the filed [*sic*], that he found it impossible to give us more than one day. (1970 [1836], p. 231)

Economics, not a slave owner's good nature, determined the celebration of holidays. If slaves were behind schedule in gathering, planting, or storing crops, only the most liberal and munificent slaveholders granted more than a few hours or a day of holiday celebration. When not given time off, slaves might receive some paternalistic token, including gifts of clothing, special food items, household items, or cash.

The more lenient and generous slaveholders gave their slaves the entire week from Christmas to New Year's, a stretch of time long enough to travel, visit with relatives, marry, engage in games and sports, work for extra wages, or work for themselves cultivating crops, sewing clothes, or repairing household objects. During this period, most slaveholders took down the color barrier and attempted—with motives either sincere or self-serving—to treat their charges like family rather than property. Christmas was, for some slaves and their owners, the only color-blind holiday.

Christmas was a day for singing, dancing, performing, drinking, dining, and the exchange of gifts, with even the harshest of owners allowing celebrations and providing feasts and gifts, such as toys or candy for children and blankets or clothing for adults. Solomon Northup, who was born free in 1808 in Minerva, New York, was kidnapped at the age of thirty-three and forced into servitude. He was taken to Louisiana where he worked on a cotton plantation. In his book about his twelve years as a slave, Northup describes Christmas as a time of respite and festive celebration:

It was Christmas morning—the happiest day in the whole year for the slave. That morning he need not hurry to the field, with his gourd and cotton-bag. Happiness sparkled in the eyes and overspread the countenances of all. The time of feasting and dancing had come. The cane and cotton field were deserted. That day the clean dress was to be donned—the red ribbon displayed; there were to be re-unions, and joy and laughter, and hurrying to and fro. It was to be a day of liberty among the children of Slavery. Wherefore they were happy, and rejoiced. (2000 [1853], p. 282)

After Christmas came New Year's, a time when slaves were generally given fresh provisions such as meat, vegetables, sugar, salt, remnants of cloth, and other household needs, but which initiated another year of slavery. Once the year was under way, Easter was the next day to look forward to, when slaves could dress in their finest to attend religious services and often had the following day off. Some slaves were given an hour or two every Sunday for religious observance; for the many who were not, Easter was an important ritual and celebration. Easter observance among slaves also fulfilled slaveholders' demands that slaves practice Christianity.

Holidays in the North

In the North and along the East Coast, slaves and freedpeople celebrated Christmas, New Year's, and Easter, as well as Black Election Day and the Pinkster festival. Black Election Day began in the early eighteenth century in New England's major cities as a parallel to white elections, with blacks choosing their own symbolic kings and governors. Celebrations of this day included a mixture of African American and European American activities, such as singing, dancing, racing, wrestling, and other sports and games. The postelection party featured a parade ending at the home of the winner's master, who provided food and drink for the revelers. The elected black leaders enjoyed no actual power other than social status. Whites found the holiday observances harmless and perhaps beneficial, as they could enlist the help of the elected black leaders to help keep up standards of behavior. Shane White, in his article on black holidays, notes that, "initially, slaves had merely participated in holiday activities organized by their masters, but gradually they took the festivals over, infusing them with new life and meanings, so that what had begun as white practices, relics of a European past, had by the end of the century become recognized as African American events" (1994, pp. 13–50).

Pinkster began as a Dutch holiday, particularly in New York, celebrating springtime renewal (the word is derived from *Pentecost*, a Christian feast day seven Sundays after Easter). The holiday came to be closely associated with blacks, who infused it with their own African traditions. The Pinkster festival was celebrated over several days, with blacks allowed to take time off from work to travel to visit relatives. Celebrations featured large gatherings in public squares, with sports, dancing, music (particularly drumming), eating, drinking, and revels that poked fun at white masters. According to White, African American festivals displayed "a striking dynamism and cultural fluidity. . . . There was a lightness of touch, a quality simultaneously threatening and tongue-in-cheek, an unpredictability, in the ways in which northern slaves used what they found around them to reinvent these holidays" (ibid.). Election-day festivities gradually lost steam in the latter part of the nineteenth century, following emancipation.

BIBLIOGRAPHY

Ball, Charles. *Slavery in the United States: A Narrative of the Life and Adventures of Charles Ball, A Black Man* [1836]. Detroit, MI: Negro History Press, 1970.

Ball, Charles. *Fifty Years in Chains; or, the Life of an American Slave* [1859]. Mineola, NY: Dover, 2003.

Bigham, Shauna, and Robert E. May. "The Time o' All Times? Masters, Slaves, and Christmas in the Old South." *Journal of the Early Republic* 18, no. 2 (1998): 263–288.

Bruce, Henry Clay. *The New Man: Twenty-nine Years a Slave, Twenty-nine Years a Free Man* [1895]. Lincoln: University of Nebraska Press, 1996.

Burton, Orville Vernon. *In My Father's House Are Many Mansions: Family and Community in Edgefield, South Carolina.* Chapel Hill: University of North Carolina Press, 1985.

Douglass, Frederick. *My Bondage and My Freedom* [1855]. New York: Modern Library, 2003.

Northup, Solomon. *Twelve Years a Slave: Narrative of Solomon Northup* [1853]. Mineola, NY: Dover, 2000.

White, Shane. "'It Was a Proud Day': African Americans, Festivals, and Parades in the North, 1741–1834." *Journal of American History* 81, no. 1 (June 1994): 13–50.

Nelson Rhodes

FESTIVALS

Festivals are generally public events that celebrate religious or cultural traditions. Nonetheless, they can also be construed as public performance spaces in which conventional assumptions of power can be challenged or renegotiated. According to the theorist Mikhail Bakhtin (1984), at a festival the powerless can subvert the role of the powerful—albeit often humorously—and reconfigure the public square. Samuel Kinser argues that they can also function as a liminal, in-between space where new cultural forms and identities may emerge (1990, p. 31). For enslaved African Americans during the colonial and antebellum periods, public festivals represented both kinds of spaces. Although slaves ostensibly mimicked the actions and rituals of the ruling class during their parades, they often engaged in ironic, subtle jabs at their slaveholding masters. This undoubtedly provided some respite from the harsh and dreadful conditions that they were forced to endure. But they did not merely exaggerate or humorously reference white customs.

Whereas most of the slave festivals centered around the public or ritual events to which white society subscribed, the descendents of slaves also developed distinctly African American performances and rituals that were an amalgamation of traditional African cultural practices and the European, Native American, and Caribbean forms they encountered in the New World. Both the Christmas masking festival of Jonkonnu in the Carolinas and Virginia and Negro Election Day in New England are examples of distinctive African American public celebrations. Like most slave festivals they included energetic dancing formations, singing, sporting-like competitions, and parades led by an outlandishly garbed king who was accompanied by fantastically dressed musicians and by militiamen who fired muskets in the air. William Pierson notes that festivals that included parades such as the Negro Election Day "typically featured boisterous, improvised music and back-and-forth interaction between male and female spectators and parade performers," that were common to cultural rituals in the Caribbean and West Africa (2002, p. 256).

Author Robert Farris Thompson concludes that Yoruba and Bakonga performance aesthetics were particularly influential in the development of American slave festivals and parades. Thompson states that the Yoruba verb *pagbo*, to parade, combines concepts of joining things together (*pa* bring things in contact with one another) and circularity, *agbo* stands for circle (Thompson 1988, p. 19). The Bakonga (people from the Congo) as Thompson suggests, "believed that processioneering around a village can mystically heal its hidden problems, [and] can 'cool' the entire settlement with circularing gestures of felicity and good faith" (Thompson 1988, p. 20). Slaves continued this parading tradition and also adapted the percussive rhythms, the "call-and-response" between groups of performers, and the "battles of aesthetic virtuosity" between dancers in their own festivals (Thompson 1988, p. 19).

One of the most important West African features that slaves maintained were the circular dance patterns. The circling, which involves negotiation between the groups and between the performers and the audience, also suggests a negotiation of power spaces. In discussing the Jonkonnu festival, Pierson suggests that this "exchange was purposely subversive to artificial distinctions of power and prestige"—specifically to the distinctions set in place by the white slave owners (2002, p. 264). In other words, the communal, ecstatic bond between dancers as they ritually reenacted age-old African dance patterns, allowed them to deny their subservient enslaved position. That slaves were allowed to hold such gatherings may seem surprising. Undoubtedly, such festivals were "more palatable for white society to swallow than serious, solemn gatherings" (Kinser 1990, p. 57).

Though there were a variety of other popular slave festivals, especially the corn shucking contests that occurred throughout the country, the remainder of this essay will focus on the Pinkster in New York and the contribution of African American dance traditions to the Mardi Gras festival in New Orleans. The Pinkster, the most famous of which occurred in Albany, New

York, was originally a Dutch festival that celebrated the Christian feast of Pentecost. By the eighteenth century however, it had been reconfigured as a slave celebration. Like the Negro election days and coronation festivals in New England, the Pinkster involved a parade, dancing, singing, competitions, satire, and other forms of merriment. During the festival, which lasted anywhere from three to five days, the slaves constructed tents or built twig-like shelters reminiscent of those in Africa. They voted for a ruler who, while dressed in Harlequin-like attire and mounted on a horse, led them down from the hill where the New York capitol now stands, and then through the Albany streets. As Kathlyn Gay notes, this "ironic display'" represents the Bahktinian "reverse of power" (2007, p.182). Here, the African ruler is overlooking the white street below. Nevertheless, to his white observers, he was a figure of ridicule who unsuccessfully copied white dress and used the "most lewd and indecent gesticulation" (White, 1989, p. 61).

Unlike a white monarch, the Pinkster King did not merely rule over his subjects. He was expected to participate in the traditional asking for gifts and in the drumming and dancing that accompanied the parading. In fact, the well-known Angolan King Charley was renowned for his dance ability, which he derived from the Congo circular patterns that had been around for centuries (Stuckey 1994, p. 60). This suggests that his knowledge of traditional and sacred African dance belies the notion that he was imitating white movements or that his dance was lewd. Indeed, the dance and performance, which included exaggerated gestures and heel and toe movements that later evolved into tap, was clearly mystifying to whites (Stuckey 1994, p. 69). For slaves, the festival engendered communal spirit and allowed them to establish a sense of identity and belonging. Not surprisingly then, the Pinkster festival was a favorite among northern slaves. It allowed them to both subvert the dominant white culture and to remember their African identities.

Though some of the slave festivals in the South paralleled those in the North (such as the corn shucking), there were also some marked differences between them. Nowhere is this more evident than in New Orleans with its unique political history and blend of French, Spanish, Caribbean, Native American, and African American cultures. It was from this cultural mélange that the well-known and spectacular Mardi Gras festival emerged. The slave dancing at Congo Square in New Orleans and the free black carnival groups and balls played an important role in this development.

Before the 1830s, when slaves were forbidden from participating in public celebrations, assemblies of slaves would gather and engage in dancing and singing at Congo square. Though little information is available about what occurred, some white writers have recorded their impressions about these performances. In 1826, Timothy Flint, a minister from New England recorded the following:

> The great Congo-dance is performed. Every thing is license and revelry ... By [the dancer's] thousand mountebank tricks, and contortions of countenance and form, he produces an irresistible effect upon the multitude. All the characters that follow him, of leading estimation, have their own peculiar dress, and their own contortions. They dance, and their streamers fly, and the bells that they have hung about them tinkle. (Kinser 1990, p. 35)

For dancers, though they may have mimicked white traditions, it was important that they win the attention and support of the audience; otherwise they might be cut from the circle. Hence, they employed humor and exaggerated gestures to solicit an audience response. As noted above, white observers generally did not have any knowledge as to what the dances represented—or to the traditions they recollected. According to historian Sterling Stuckey, "slave dance was the most difficult for slaveholders to suppress ... and could constitute an act of resistance" (1994, pp. 52–53).

Although the Congo square gathering was banned in the early nineteenth century, slaves participated in balls and other festive events that were supposedly closed to them. In New Orleans, which had been governed by the French and then the Spanish before being acquired by the United States in 1803 as part of the Louisiana Purchase, there was a long-established tradition of throwing balls for almost any occasion. Generally private events, they were distinctly segregated affairs. Public balls for free blacks (an established class before the Louisiana Purchase) and whites were licensed in the early nineteenth century. Though slaves were not allowed to participate, they went to the free black balls and injected their dancing and performance aesthetics into the celebrations. Like the many whites who also attended, slaves could assume different identities when they wore the masques that were common at these events.

Well-to-do free blacks and those of lesser means also formed their own carnival groups prior to the Civil War (1861–1865) in order to participate in what had been a French Catholic traditional holiday that occurred before the beginning of Lent. As Kinser contends, the anomalies of New Orleans three-tiered caste system were thus disregarded because Mardi Gras "allowed for kinds of contact between blacks and whites, male and female, which were unthinkable in the streets" (1990, p. 24). Thus slaves, though nominally excluded from carnival groups, undoubtedly wore the costumes of colorful feathers that reflected both Native American and African traditions—costumes that are still donned at Mardi Gras today. According to Thompson (1988), "feathers on masks or headdresses in Congo are medicines, referring to confidence and strength built into the vaunting of the power to fly" (p. 25). They allow the individual to get outside oneself, so to speak. Like the Pinkster parade, during the carnival slaves could subvert the position in which whites had thrust them. At these festivals, they could reenact the traditions of their African past, hold a "distorting mirror" up to white society, and construct or imagine a new way of life (Kinser 1990, p. 318). Festivals, in other words, were more than carnivalesque.

BIBLIOGRAPHY

Bakhtin, Mikhail. *Rabelais and His World.* Bloomington: Indiana University Press, 1984.

Gay, Kathlyn. *African American Holidays, Festivals, and Celebrations: The History, Customs, and Symbols Associated with Both Traditional and Contemporary Religious and Secular Events Observed by Americans of African Descent.* Detroit: Omnigraphics, 2007.

Kinser, Samuel. *Carnival, American Style: Mardi Gras at New Orleans and Mobile.* Chicago: University of Chicago Press, 1990.

Pierson, William D. "African American Festive Style and the Creation of American Culture." In *Riot and Revelry in Early America*, eds. William Pencak, Matthew Dennis, and Simon P. Newman. University Park: The Pennsylvania State University Press, 2002.

Stuckey, Sterling. *Going Through the Storm: The Influence of African American Art in History.* New York: Oxford University Press, 1994.

Thompson, Robert Farris. "Recapturing Heaven's Glamour: Afro-Caribbean Festivalizing Arts." In *Caribbean Festival Arts: Each and Every Bit of Difference*, eds. John W. Nunley and Judith Bettelheim. Seattle, WA: Saint Louis Art Museum and the University of Washington Press, 1988.

White, Shane. "Pinkster: Afro-Dutch Syncretization in New York City and the Hudson Valley." *Journal of American Folklore* 102, no. 403 (January–March 1989): 68–75.

Anna M. Dempsey

HARVEST TIME

The principle reason for slavery in the United States was the need for labor. Africans were first brought to America for the purposes of clearing the wilderness and establishing farms. As American slavery developed into an institution, the southern economy rested on the production levels of black slaves to provide their commercial strengths and give them a competitive edge against the heavy industrial market of the North. Although the labor cycle depended upon the crop, the harvest for any agricultural product was the most taxing time of the year for slaves. The plantations of the South produced three staple crops—cotton, sugar, and tobacco—each with distinct harvests. Southern plantations cultivated other crops, such as indigo, rice and wheat (espe-

cially during the colonial era), but not to a widespread extent overall.

The most widely cultivated crop in the antebellum South was cotton. From eastern Texas to the shores of North Carolina, cotton was commercially grown and shipped worldwide. The burdensome duty of harvesting cotton, however, was left to plantation slaves. The harvest for cotton typically began in late summer, depending on the bloom of the cotton "bulbs." At that time, planters sent all hands (slaves) to their fields to pick cotton from dawn until dusk. Even children worked, carrying buckets of water. Organized into gangs, the slaves were given a sack and put on a "row" of cotton plants. The slave driver, usually on horseback, followed the slaves as they picked, whipping any slave who lagged behind. Indeed, as one ex-slave notes, "the lash [was] flying from morning until night" (Blassingame 1977, p. 522).

Historians agree that a seasoned plantation slave picked around 125 to 150 pounds of cotton per day. The length of the harvest season depended on the size of the plantation, with some large plantations having seasons that stretched from late summer to the early spring. On a daily basis, the sacks of picked cotton were taken to the gin house and weighed. As one ex-slave stated, "No matter how fatigued and weary he may be—no matter how much he longs for sleep and rest—a slave never approaches the gin house with his basket of cotton but with fear. If it falls short in weight—if he has not performed the full task appointed him, he knows that he must suffer" (Blassingame 1977, p. 522). Indeed, as one planter noted, "I think my hands have Picked cotton worse this year than in several years . . . intend Whipping them straght [sic]" (Davis 1967, p. 219).

On some plantations in the Louisiana, slave owners cultivated sugarcane. During the nineteenth century, sugarcane became an important cash crop for the southern economy. Cane planting was popular in Louisiana because of its warm, humid climate and easily arable soil. Slaves planted sugarcane in early spring and it grew for approximately nine months. The larger the cane grew, the more sucrose juice it contained (the chief ingredient in making sugar). The harvest or "grinding" season began in October, when the cane reached its maximum maturity, and lasted until December. The short harvest season forced slaves to work intensively, with sugar mill shifts running twenty-four hours per day.

During the harvest, cane was cut from the fields and transported by cart to the sugar house. There, the cane was crushed in giant rollers, or "grinders," which extracted the juice before it was sent to a series of large kettles for boiling. Once the juice was boiled down to thick syrup, it was set in pans to crystallize. The crystallized sugar was then packed in large barrels, called hogsheads, for shipping. All the slaves who labored in the highly organized process of grinding had specific jobs,

SOUTHERN COTTON PLANTATION.
"Knowing thy master also is in heaven."

An illustration showing African American life in the South in 1807. During the late summer harvest time for cotton, planters sent all their slaves into the fields to pick cotton from dusk to dawn. Even children were put to work carrying buckets of water. *MPI/Hulton Archive/Getty Images.*

such as fire tenders, cart loaders, grinders, and packers. Orchestrated with efficiency, the sugar houses produced a lucrative product for the planters, which in turn, bought more slaves.

Male slaves were usually preferred over females on sugar plantations, due to the brutal nature of the work. Injuries, such as being burned or receiving a slash from a cane knife, were common during the harvest season. All hands labored seven days per week until the harvesting ended. As an ex-slave noted, "On the cane plantations in sugar time, there is no distinction as to the days of the week" (Osofsky 1969, p. 331). When the harvesting finally ended, slave owners occasionally had a party for their slaves, before the next planting cycle began.

As of 1854, tobacco was the third most cultivated crop on the plantations of the South. Grown in most southern states, tobacco's main concentration was in Virginia and the Carolinas. Beginning in the mid-seventeenth century, newly imported African slaves began working tobacco farms and small plantations, creating an economic legacy that would last until emancipation. Slaves typically planted

tobacco in the early spring after the cold weather abated. Harvest time varied due to climactic conditions, but usually fell in the late summer when the tobacco leaves were at their fullest. During the harvest, gangs of slaves delicately cut the tobacco plants from the ground and loaded them onto carts. The tobacco leaves were then dried or cured by the air or by a process called flue-curing. After the tobacco cured, it was put in bushels and shipped to a refinery.

Unlike sugar production, the harvest season for tobacco lasted only during the daylight hours. One ex-slave wrote that on her tobacco plantation "we commenced work as soon as we could see in the morning, and worked from that time until 12 o'clock before breakfast, and then until dark, when we had our dinner, then hastened to our [personal] night work for ourselves." Nonetheless, slave drivers used their whips to insure that that the field hands worked to their full potential. Looking upon his former tobacco field, one slave stated, "I have never seen blood flow anywhere as I've seen it flow on that field" (Blassingame 1977, p. 134).

Slaves bringing in the cotton harvest. A seasoned plantation slave picked around 125 to 150 pounds of cotton per day. © *North Wind Picture Archives.*

Effective sugar, cotton, and tobacco harvesting were crucial to the labor cycle on antebellum plantations. Slaves worked their hardest during these time periods, laboring in schemes characterized by monotony, injury, and toil. The South became an economic powerhouse because of its plantation labor, owing its strength to systems of seasonal crop cultivation.

BIBLIOGRAPHY

Blassingame, John W. *Slave Testimony*. Baton Rouge: Louisiana State University Press, 1977.

Davis, Edwin Adams. *Plantation Life in the Florida Parishes, 1836–1846, as Reflected in the Diary of Bennet H. Barrow*. New York: AMS Press, 1967.

Follett, Richard. *The Sugar Masters*. Baton Rouge: Louisiana State University Press, 2005.

Kulikoff, Alan. "The Origins of Afro-American Society in Tidewater Maryland and Virginia, 1700 to 1790." *The William and Mary Quarterly* 35 (1978): 226–259.

Landon, Charles E. "Tobacco Manufacturing in the South." *Annals of the American Academy of Political and Social Science* 153 (1931): 43–53.

Osofsky, Gilbert, ed. *Puttin' On Ole Massa: The Slave Narratives of Henry Bibb, William Wells Brown, and Solomon Northrup*. New York: Harper and Row, 1969.

Rothman, Adam. *Slave Country*. Cambridge, MA: Harvard University Press, 2005.

Taylor, Joe Gray. "Louisiana Slaves at Work." In *The Louisiana Purchase Bicentennial Series in Louisiana History*, Vol. 4: *Antebellum Louisiana, 1830–1860*, ed. Carolyn E. DeLatte. Lafayette: University of Louisiana at Lafayette, 2004.

Matthew Mitchell

SHUCKINGS

The term *shuckings* was used in slave-populated plantation communities to describe the process by which the outer shells or husks were separated from ears of corn to expose the grains. Corn shucking took place after harvesting when the ears were removed from stalks in the field. Solomon Northrup, who had been a free black man in Washington, D.C., when he was forced into slavery on a Louisiana plantation in 1841, gave a detailed description of the entire process of corn production. Corn, more particularly, white corn, was planted in February but harvesting of the corn was delayed until after the harvesting of cotton because the corn crop was of much less importance than the cotton crop. At least on his plantation, corn was grown mainly to "fatten hogs and feed slaves" (Bracey and Sinha 2004, p. 138). Northrup explained further that, beginning in August, during the period when there was a delay in harvesting the corn, it was preserved in the fields by a process of stripping the leaves from the stalks, and turning down the ears to prevent rains from "penetrating" to the grains. When the ears of corn were removed from the stalks, which could have grown as high as eight to ten feet, the ears, with husks still attached were stored in "corncribs" until the appointed time for shucking. Northrup explained that the reason for keeping the husks attached to the ears while they were stored in the cribs was to prevent destruction of the grains by weevils (Bracey, and Sinha 2004, p.138).

On plantations across the slave-holding South, owners allowed enslaved people to engage in celebrations at certain times of the year including Christmas, New Year's, and the Fourth of July, sometimes referred to as "lay-by time." But decidedly the largest and most elaborate celebration was permitted at the time when corn was to be shucked by the slaves. Many owners of corn-producing plantations allowed communal, ceremonial affairs, whereby slaves from neighboring plantations, including children, would assemble on one plantation to shuck corn. Primarily at night, with outdoor torches lit, slaves motioned and maneuvered ritualistically, to the rhythms of their own spontaneously composed songs as they shucked the corn. They were fed liquor, mostly whiskey and corn liquor, as they shucked. And after all the corn had been shucked, a general party ensued. There would be music sometimes provided by a fiddler, singing, dancing, eating and playing sports of various kinds. A supper, certainly more elaborate than they were accustomed to having, was made available for the slaves at corn-shucking time.

Corn-shucking time provided an opportunity for the enslaved people to undergo some psychological and emotional releases from the drudgery and hardships of everyday slavery. They basked in moments of joy and celebration as can be gleaned from their own accounts. Henry James Trentham, an ex-slave from a Camden, North Carolina, plantation stated in an interview, "The cornshuckings was a great time. Marster give good liquor to everybody then. When anybody shucked a red ear, he got a extra drink of whiskey. We had big suppers then, and a good time at cornshuckings. After the shucking, at

CORN GATHERING

The process of reaping corn was sometimes done by hauling up the corn with a yoke of oxen. Interviewed on December 11, 1888, by the *Atchison Daily Champion*, ex-slave Plankett declared that it was not an easy job: "You have to jerk and haw and gee to keep 'em from pulling their necks oll stretching out for eating on each side, and the man that can drive 'em under such circumstances and not cuss is a deserving man for sure" (p. 7).

SOURCE: *Atchison Daily Champion*, December 11, 1888, p. 7.

night, there would be a wrestling match to see who was best on the plantation" (Hurmence 1993, p. 7).

Dan Bogie had been enslaved in Kentucky. He stated when interviewed, "We used to have big times at the corn shuckings. The neighbors would come and help. We would have camp fires and sing songs, and usually a big dance at the barn when the corn was shucked. Some of the slaves from other plantations would pick the Banjo, then the dance" (*Born in Slavery*, Kentucky Narratives).

But the cathartic results of corn-shucking celebrations sometimes reflected the pain and sorrow of slave life that the enslaved people endured. An unnamed, ex-slave interviewed in Arkansas lamented that during corn shucking some of the songs were "pitiful and sad." He repeated the words of one of the songs he remembered singing: "The speculator bought my wife and child and carried her clear away" (Rawick 1972–1979, vol. 11, pt. 7, p. 52). Some of the songs had nostalgic tones, contained curious quirks of mixed emotions, but at the same time expressed hope for, or the reality of, freedom.

In a December 11, 1888, article from the *Atchison Daily Champion*, an ex-slave named Plankett, highlighted the fact that white people also took part in corn-shucking celebrations on plantations. He stated, "Corn gathering then was a frolic, for we knowed that a good time was coming. The corn wasn't thrown in the cribs in them days, but a big pile was made in the lot, and then the night was set for shucking and the settlement gathered in—white and black—and the corn was shucked... ." It is reasonable to assume that the white people to whom Plankett referred were "poor whites" who lived in areas adjoining plantations, and were sometimes hired for small wages on many plantations. Elias Thomas, another ex-slave from North Carolina, explained that during "harvest time" on his plantation the slaves worked and sang together with poor whites (Hurmence 1993, p. 11).

Allowing the enslaved people to work in ritual fashion to the pace of their own rhythms and songs resulted, no doubt, in faster completion of the corn-shucking process and consequently higher production rates for plantation owners. Some plantation owners rewarded timeliness with monetary incentives and prizes. James Boyd was interviewed in Texas but had actually been enslaved in Oklahoma. He said that sometimes, "there would be a dollar for the one that could shuck the most corn in a certain time" (Waters 2003, p. 7). Another ex-slave interviewed in Texas recalled that, "De prize would usually be a suit of clothes or something to wear and which would be given at some later date" (Baker and Baker 1997, p. 36). Plankett explained that he saw as many as three thousand bushels of corn shucked and put into cribs in one night. The shucks were also "penned" during the same night. It is very likely that "penning" was the process of storing the shucks in pens to be used as food for mules and oxen. Every part of the corn plant was made use of on the plantation. Northrup noted that the leaves, also, when stripped from stalks in the field were "dried in the sun, bundled and stored as fodder for mules and oxen" (Bracey and Sinha 2004, p. 138).

Interviews with ex-slaves from Arkansas point to much more subdued celebrations during corn shucking, but still a strong sense of appreciation for the camaraderie and fellowship that the occasion allowed. Louis Davis remembered, "We had corn shucking, but it wasn't made to be a party. We done the shucking in the daytime, and everybody was sent to the crib together. They would sing and have a good time, but they didn't have no prizes" (Memories of Slavery: Recollections). Lizzie Norfleet indicated that there were no celebrations for Christmas or corn shucking on the plantation where she had been enslaved. She stated, "On rainy days we had corn shuckings, but that wasn't no party. Course we liked it cause we was all together, laughing, singing and having a good time. At that the corn had to be shucked all the same" (Memories of Slavery: Recollections, Mississippi Narratives).

Corn shucking seems to illustrate that it is possible that gender specifications or role distinctions were practiced in job categories in some plantation societies, based maybe on the discretion of some plantation owners to exempt women from the rigors of certain jobs. An unnamed, ex-slave woman, born in South Carolina and interviewed in 1938, stated, "Den dem kind of task was left to de men folks de most of de time cause it been so hot, dey was force to strip to do dat sort of a job." The woman claimed that while corn shucking was going on she, "must been somewhe' huntin something to eat" (Rawick 1972–1979, vol. 2, pt. 1, p. 23). And Amanda Oliver who had been enslaved in northern Texas said that it was men who would shuck corn all night while women pieced quilts together (Baker and Baker 1997, p. 64).

The opportunity for communal gathering, grouping and working that corn shucking offered, no doubt, allowed the enslaved people to reconnect with the extended family traditions of their African heritage. African ancestral, ritual techniques such as "call-and

response" were evidenced in their singing. White and White relate that the slaves would organize themselves in competing song teams and respond to their "captain's or song leader's calls" (2005, p. 10). But even as the connections with Africa were manifested in their social selves, the seeds of the formation of the African American self defined by the new environment, and the impact of the juxtapositioning of European culture were being sown. While White and White say the "sounds" or the "sonic realm" belonged to Africa, the dancing seemed to have belonged to Europe. An unnamed ex-slave from Arkansas declaring her preference for the kinds of dancing she did during slavery times as compared to post slavery, stated, "In them days they danced what you call square dances....There was eight in a set" (Rawick 1972–1979, vol. 11, pt. 7, p. 52). And Lucy Lewis, born in Texas declared, "... a used to cut all kind of steps, de cotillion and de waltz and de shotty [schottische] (Rawick 1972–1979, vol. 5, pt. 3, p. 15).

In his autobiography *Narrative of the Life of Frederick Douglass: An American Slave* (1846), Frederick Douglass expressed great abhorrence at the drunkenness and debauchery in which slaves were allowed to engage during, particularly, the Christmas holidays. Slaves were exempt from any work at all for the entire week between Christmas and New Year's, and were allowed to wallow in alcohol. He contended that the objective of the plantation owners was to make the slaves, "disgust themselves with freedom" (1968 [1846], p. 85), and therefore, appreciate the time for returning to slave work and industry. Douglass saw these drunken celebrations as diversionary tactics on the parts of plantations owners, aimed at, "keeping down the spirit of insurrection (p. 84). While, contrary to the celebration during the Christmas holidays, the corn-shucking celebration did involve work; certainly the drunkenness allowed at corn shucking time can be viewed in the same light in which Douglass conceived the drunkenness allowed at Christmas. Drunkenness as one aspect of the overall ritual celebration, must have contributed to those moments of psychological release, but it must also have served to distract the enslaved people from their real plight in slavery.

Some very strange activities that saw plantation owners actually participating in the celebratory phase of corn-shucking festivals, point to other complex motivations, on the part of the owners, for permitting the festivals. It appears as though some plantation owners carried out a kind of cat-and-mouse or hide-and-seek game with their slaves, ostensibly to bond with the slaves, but embedded with the subtle purpose of reinforcing their supremacy in the "master/slave" relationship. The game would end with a ritual exaltation of the plantation owner. The unnamed ex-slave from Arkansas, previously mentioned, related the following that had been told to her by her mother. "When they got through shucking, they would

Slaves at a corn-husking.   Slaves having a social gathering at a plantation corn-husking, or shucking. Shuckings were communal, ceremonial affairs in which slaves from neighboring plantations would assemble on one plantation to shuck corn. Shuckings usually happened at night and included ritualistic movements and spontaneously composed songs.   © *North Wind Picture Archives.*

hunt up the boss. He would run away and hide just before. If they found him, two big men would take him up on their shoulders and carry him all around the grounds while they sang (Rawick 1972–1979, vol. 11, pt. 7, p. 52).

White and White provided more supporting details about this unusual happening. They told that after the shucking was done, "the slaves would seize their master, carry him around the Big House, occasionally toss him in the air, and take him inside." Then, quoting the experience of a former slave, George Woods, they continued to explain that, the slaves would, "place him [the owner] in a chair; comb his head; cross his knees for him and leave him alone" (2005, p. 10).

Excluding those bizarre moments when plantation owners were actually injected in the corn-shucking celebrations, in those celebrations and others on the plantation were planted the seeds of an American culture that saw white people as spectators of the bourgeoning manifestations of African American culture. Tinie Force and Elvira Lewis, two ex-slaves from Kentucky, commented that singing and dancing by black people, with white people in the audience was "one of the most favorite classes of entertainment" (*Born in Slavery*, Kentucky Narratives). Later, when white people began to enact

caricatured imitations of black performances in minstrel shows, those shows also saw their genesis in plantation celebrations such as corn shuckings.

BIBLIOGRAPHY

Atchison Daily Champion. " Old Time Corn." December 11, 1888. Available from http://infotrac.galegroup.com/itw/infomark/279/779/776/104060687.

Baker, Lindsay T., and Julie P. Baker, eds. *Till Freedom Cried Out: Memories of Texas Slave Life.* College Station: Texas A&M University Press, 1997.

Born in Slavery: Slave Narratives from the Federal Writers' Project, 1936–1938, Kentucky Narratives. Manuscript and Prints and Photographs Divisions, Library of Congress. Available from http://memory.loc.gov/ammem/snhtml/snhome.html.

Bracey, John H., Jr., and Manisha Sinha, eds. *African American Mosaic: A Documentary History from the Slave Trade to the Twenty-First Century*, vol 1: *To 1877.* Upper Saddle River, NJ: Prentice Hall, 2004.

Douglass, Frederick. *Narrative of the Life of Frederick Douglass: An American Slave* [1846]. New York: Penguin, 1968.

Hurmence, Belinda, ed. *My Folks Don't Want Me to Talk About Slavery.* Winston-Salem, NC: John F. Blair Publisher, 1993.

McBride, Dina C., ed. "Memories of Slavery: Recollections of Lives of Slavery and Emancipation." Familytreemaker,genealogy.com. Available from http://familytreemaker.geneaology.com/users/m/c/b/Dina-C-McBride/FILE/000.

Rawick, George P., ed. *The American Slave: A Composite Autobiography.* 19 vols. Westport, CT: Greenwood Press, 1972–1979.

Waters, Andrew, ed. *I Was Born in Slavery.* Winston-Salem, NC: John F. Blair Publisher, 2003.

White, Shane, and Graham White. *The Sounds of Slavery: Discovering African American History through Songs, Sermons and Speech.* Boston: Beacon Press, 2005.

Marguerite P. Garvey

SOCIALS

Social life and social activity played a vital role in the lives of enslaved African Americans in the United States. Not only were social activities critical to the process of socializing enslaved children to navigate the institution of slavery and the religious practices of the enslaved community, social activities importantly provided slaves the opportunity to find relief from the harsh day-to-day

SOCIALS

While social life and activities for enslaved Africans and African Americans provided a critical source of catharsis from the brutality of enslavement, slave owners also worked to employ the dynamics of social life to maintain their tight grip on those they held in captivity. Many planters holding blacks in captivity believed that by allowing their enslaved population time and space for social engagement, the likelihood of slaves resisting and rebelling against their authority would be mitigated. Beyond simply allowing enslaved Africans and African Americans to hold social activities, slave owners also forced slaves to participate in social festivities for their own benefit. Scholars such as Saidiya Hartman argued that slave owners forced the enslaved to participate in social activities to help conceal the harsh reality of life under enslavement. Other scholars, including George Rawick, argued that slave owners forced their slaves to participate in socials for their personal entertainment as they joined the enslaved in the activities.

BIBLIOGRAPHY

Hartman, Saidiya. *Scenes of Subjection: Terror, Slavery, and Self-Making in Nineteenth-Century America.* New York: Oxford University Press, 1997.

Rawick, George P. *From Sundown to Sunup: The Making of the Black Community.* Westport, CT: Greenwood Publishing, 1972.

existence of enslavement and life on the plantation. As the political economy of slavery shifted from small-scale agricultural and artisan production, where slave owners had few slaves, who resided in their homes, to large-scale agricultural production of tobacco, and later cotton, where owners had many slaves who resided separately in slave quarters, the enslaved population's opportunity to engage in social activities greatly increased. "African American cultural activities blurred the distinction between work and leisure, by the late antebellum years enslaved blacks claimed a slightly wider margin of off-time activities than before" (Trotter 2001, p. 149). The slave quarter, one of the few areas on the plantation where slaves were not under the immediate control of their owners, became the center of everyday social life.

The slave quarter provided a space for slaves to gather in the evenings. Shane and Graham White (2005), in *Sounds of Slavery*, have discussed the informal gatherings that took place within the slave quarter after the day's grueling work had concluded and before the enslaved retired to sleep. In the words of the formally enslaved Clara Young, "We'd set 'round and sin' an talk." In former slave Green Cumby's Works Progress Administration (WPA) interview, he conveyed that "at night the slaves would gather roun' the cabins in little bunches and talk til' bed time" (White and White 2005, p. xiv). Social activities that took place after hours within the slave quarter usually combined singing, dancing, eating, telling folktales, and gossiping about local affairs.

In addition to less formal social activities that took place when enslaved African Americans were able to scrape time out of their days and nights, slave owners reserved specific times for leisure activities for their slaves. Much of this owner-designated leisure time took place on Saturdays, Sundays, and holidays. John Hope Franklin and Loren Schweninger (2006) report that during the Christmas holiday in and around Nashville, Tennessee, the black population moved about freely, gathered for social occasions, and stayed out past curfew. On Andrew Jackson's (1767–1845) Nashville plantation enslaved African Americans gathered to dance, play cards, and stage cockfights. Others would take advantage of the increased mobility afforded by the holiday to visit friends on neighboring plantations and socialize within the slave quarters.

Outside of the major holiday seasons, the ability of the enslaved population to participate in collective social activities was more challenging. On Sundays, however, the enslaved Nashville population did create the space to stage horse races and barbecues where they cooked pigs, chickens, consumed alcohol, and sang. Friday and Saturday evenings were typically reserved for social activities centered on singing, dancing, and drinking. Slave owners often provided the alcohol for their slaves to consume during these events. Slave owners, in the absence of musically inclined slaves on their plantation, often hired quasi-professional bands of enslaved and free musicians to perform during these. Franklin and Schweninger reported that in Nashville

> McGowan, a free black, established a music school, gave private lessons, conducted a dance band, and booked engagements on nearby plantations. Rachael Gaines, ... recalled how her owner sent for McGowan every two weeks. The Band would arrive early Friday evening, and the plantation hands would dance ... late into the evening. (Franklin and Schweninger 2006, p. 90)

Shane and Graham White have described the nature of the dancing and singing at Friday and Saturday night frolics. They have offered that, "many of these dances performed at slave frolics took place within a circle, on the perimeter of which other slaves sang, patted, played musical instruments, and called out encouragement to the participants" (White and White 2005, p. 50). Perhaps the most famous and well-known of these circular shaped frolics are the ring shouts that took place at the Congo Square in New Orleans beginning in the early 1800s and lasting until the eve of the Civil War (1861–1865).

In addition to holiday celebrations and weekend frolics, social activities also took form in festival celebrations. In the decades preceding emancipation one of the most important of these festivals was the corn shucking festival that took place at the close of the season's corn harvest. After the corn was harvested slaves from several area plantations would gather and form teams and compete to see which team could shuck the fastest. At the conclusion of the competition slaves would sing, eat, dance, and drink. Social activities were a key aspect in the lives of enslaved African Americans. Though the ability of slaves to engage in collective social activity fluctuated, the opportunity to create a dynamic social life increased in the final decades of the institution's existence. Ultimately, social activity provided the enslaved momentary tastes of freedom as they attempted to cope with an institution that controlled nearly every aspect of their lives.

BIBLIOGRAPHY

Donaldson, Gary. "A Window on Slave Culture: Dances at Congo Square in New Orleans, 1800–1862" *Journal of Negro History* 69, no. 2 (1984): 63–72.

Franklin, John Hope, and Loren Schweninger. *In Search of the Promised Land: A Black Family and the Old South.* New York: Oxford University Press, 2006.

Trotter, Joe. *The African American Experience.* New York: Houghton Mifflin, 2001.

White, Shane, and Graham White. *The Sounds of Slavery: Discovering African American History through Songs, Sermons, and Speech.* Boston: Beacon Press, 2005.

Nicholas Gaffney

LANGUAGE AND DIALECTS

It can be argued that an understanding of the role of language is absolutely critical to an understanding of the transformation of the African into the African American. Slaves born in America—as opposed to those who were born in West Africa—were only conversant in an English that was expanded to include a minimum of African words and/or phrases that had been passed down to them by the older members of their own slave community. Those slaves who had been captured in West Africa, ones who had suffered through the Middle Passage, obviously labored—for both practical and sentimental reasons—to retain and promote their African language. During the early days of slavery in the American South, from the seventeenth through the mid-eighteenth centuries, bondmen were required to function both in their own black/African world and in their masters' white world. Thus, for those in bondage, the creation of a world exclusive to them was supremely important. The retention of African language and the formation of new black dialects were ways by which slaves expressed separateness from their masters and reflected their human desire and ability to preserve important aspects of their pasts while, at the same time, adjusting to the new realities of life in a new world. Slaves were challenged not only to learn the languages of their slave owners but to also create a form of speech uniquely their own. Thus, early in their North American experience, newly arrived slaves began to lay the foundation of a linguistic combination that would eventually be classified as black English. Black English, in the manner of all living languages, is organic and is thus continuously in a state of transformation.

Typically, African languages were successfully preserved for a few generations. This was made possible, in part, by the frequency by which newly captured slaves from any given region or tribe in West Africa were transported to an American colony where their tribal or ethnic members already resided. For example, in the early years of American slavery, Igbos were often shipped to Virginia, whereas those of the Bambara tribe were relocated to lower Mississippi, and in both cases the new arrivals ensured perpetuation for a while longer of the native African languages. Unfortunately, as time passed, fewer and fewer slaves on farms and plantations had any direct link to Africa, and as a result the African languages eventually became extinct. Obliteration of the African languages was also the result of mobility within the slave population. For example, if an Igbo were sold off his Virginia plantation to a slaveholder in Georgia, both reason and opportunity to retain his or her native language would be greatly reduced.

Many slaves—particularly ones who had been born in Africa or were only one or two generations removed from that continent—resisted the language of their owners. Although most slaves for practical reasons picked up rudimentary English or French during their first years in the New World, many chose in their personal interactions in their own community to communicate solely in their African tongues. However, slaves' need to communicate with Africans and African Americans of dissimilar ethno-linguistic backgrounds, combined with their challenge to effectively communicate with their American-born progeny, forced them to eventually find a non-African language means of verbal communication. In Anglophone North America, some form of English was the obvious solution. Obviously, white English was not acceptable; an African could not allow himself to parrot those words, tones, and inflections that he heard from the very fount of oppression. With pride and in resistance, he altered the language transmitted to him from the white's world and created a syntax that gave his form of English an African character.

Still other slaves felt little desire to resist the languages of their owners. Some even became fluent in several European languages, among which were English, French, Spanish, and Dutch. These unusual individuals may have developed such facility either in coastal areas of West Africa or in the Americas; in both locales, tribal African could have been exposed to multiple European tongues.

Ethnographic studies reveal that Africans enslaved in North America, despite many difficulties, were successful for varying lengths of time to retain their native languages, rich with their own grammatical structures and words. However, such success greatly depended upon geographical and cultural considerations. For example, in those cases in which a critical mass of individuals sharing a common linguistic background either resided together or in close proximity to one another, languages had a reasonable likelihood of survivability, albeit not necessarily in a pure form. Those languages and dialects were thus sheltered from the process of "decreolization," a process by which Creole speech is gradually changed by the influences imposed by the prevailing language of a given place or people. For example, by 1730, Africans and African Americans of similar ethnic background were sufficiently numerous in coastal South Carolina and Georgia to successfully maintain enough African linguistic interaction to eventually produce a distinctive linguistic tongue that came to be called Gullah. The term *Gullah* may have come from the word *Gola*, the name of a people indigenous to Liberia and Sierra Leone. Concentrated primarily in coastal South Carolina and lowland Georgia, speakers of this dialect perpetuate a genuine "Creole" language, the only Creole English in use in the United States in the twenty-first century.

In the early twenty-first century, the speaking of Gullah is limited to some inhabitants of the coastal islands—the so-called rice islands—that stretch for approximately 160 miles along the seaboard of South Carolina and Georgia; to a very

limited degree, it is also used by blacks residing in very limited areas on the adjacent mainland. The Charleston colony, founded in 1670, was originally the geographical hearth of Gullah. This language form had roots in the Caribbean, where slaves who claimed Gold Coast ancestry spent time in bondage before being relocated to the Sea Islands of South Carolina and Georgia. It was later influenced by others who interjected elements of languages and dialects common to the coastal area of West Africa, stretching from Senegal to Angola, an expanse of 3,000 miles. For many decades, those island settlements where Gullah was spoken were relatively isolated, producing a population of rice farmers who had little need to learn white or even black English. They survived using a language very much different from that spoken by the vast majority of their fellow countrymen, both black and white. Gullah is interesting to ethno-linguists as a curiosity and as an exception. It is, however, a cousin of some of the Creoles still in use in the Caribbean: Jamaican, Guyanese, Trinidadian, Barbadian, and others.

Many Americans, although they do not know it, incorporate Gullah words in their everyday speech. These include such food terms as *okra, yam, benne, cush,* and *goober,* as well as other words such as *buckra* ("white man"), *hoodoo* ("sorcery"), and *cooter* ("tortoise or turtle").

BIBLIOGRAPHY

Gomez, Michael A. *Exchanging Our Country Marks: The Transformation of African Identities in the Colonial and Antebellum South.* Chapel Hill: University of North Carolina Press, 1998.

Palmer, Colin A. *Passageways: An Interpretive History of Black America*, Vol. 1: *1619-1863.* Fort Worth, TX: Harcourt Brace College Publishers, 1998.

Webber, Thomas L. *Deep Like the Rivers: Education in the Slave Quarter Community, 1831–1865.* New York: W. W. Norton, 1978.

Wilson, Charles Reagan, and William Ferris, eds. *Encyclopedia of Southern Culture.* Chapel Hill: University of North Carolina Press, 1989.

Katherine E. Rohrer

■ Customs and Practices

CUSTOMS AND PRACTICES: AN OVERVIEW
Josh J. Hem Lee

NAMES AND NAMING
Tanya M. Mears

RITES OF PASSAGE
Gwendolyn N. Hale

DEATH AND FUNERAL CUSTOMS
Nelson Rhodes

WEST AFRICAN INFLUENCES
Nicholas Gaffney

CUSTOMS AND PRACTICES: AN OVERVIEW

Many customs encompassed the entire life cycle of a slave; some customs and practices varied from region to region but shared many common tenets. Slave owners often encouraged slaves to get married in the hope that the union would produce offspring. Wedding ceremonies differed from region to region and among plantations; in his memoir, ex-slave James Williams said: "The field hands are seldom married by a clergyman. They simply invite their friends together, and have a wedding party" (1838, p. 33). Sometimes the simple act of jumping a broom together was enough to bind a couple together. Slaves usually had to obtain permission from their masters to marry and in many places slave marriages were not recognized by law.

The broom played an important role in slave life as it had in African cultures such as the Asante. A broom was believed to have a spiritual value and symbolized sweeping away evil or bad luck. When couples married, brooms were waved over their heads to ward off evil spirits. When couples jumped a broom, the person who jumped highest was said to be the one who would rule the marriage. Brooms were not always positive symbols; if a broom touched one's body accidentally it was believed to shorten one's life. Also, it was believed that sweeping near a woman's feet prevented her from marrying.

When a slave died, his or her fellow slaves would sacrifice white chickens over the grave in order to release the deities from the world of the spirits. In the world of the living lights guided people at night but for the dead they were used to guide deceased people into the world of the afterlife; hence the placing of lamps and bonfires on graves. Whenever a death occurred, a typical slave custom was to stay up all night guarding the body from prowling animals. Funerals were held at night because slaves worked during the day. Bodies were buried east-west with the head pointed west so that their eyes would face Africa. It was not uncommon to see the corpse with the head tied so that the mouth would not open and allow the soul to wander. It was believed that a dead person would not be at rest for some forty days. At funerals, participants would dance, sing, and pray around the grave before smashing bottles and dishes in order to "break the chain," that is, ensure that no other family members would die.

Songs and dances were a way both to preserve the African culture as well as to ease the burden of the

African Americans singing and dancing the Bamboula in New Orleans. A woodcut, circa 1800, showing people in New Orleans singing and dancing the Bamboula, a rhythmic dance from Africa. Songs and dances were a way to preserve African culture as well as to ease the burden of suffering. © *North Wind Picture Archives.*

suffering endured. The ex-slave Frederick Douglass observed, "They would sometimes sing the most pathetic sentiment in the most rapturous tone, and the most rapturous sentiment in the most pathetic tone. This they would sing, as a chorus, to words which to many would seem unmeaning jargon, but which, nevertheless, were full of meaning to themselves ... Slaves sing most when they are most unhappy" (1846, p. 15).

Slaves believed that spirits roamed the earth and many customs involved either seeking their help or trying to ward them off. To protect a home from evil spirits bottles would be tied to trees outside a home in order to lure and trap evil spirits; these bottles were sometimes filled with dirt from a grave. In *Memoir of Phillis Wheatley: A Native African and a Slave,* Benjamin Thatcher recalled of Wheatley, "One circumstance alone, it might have been said, she remembered; and that was, her mother's custom of pouring out water before the sun at his rising. This no doubt was a custom of the tribe to which she belonged, and was one of their religious rites" (1834, p. 13).

BIBLIOGRAPHY

Douglass, Frederick. *Narrative of the Life of Frederick Douglass: An American Slave.* Boston: 1846.

Northup, Solomon. *Twelve Years a Slave.* Auburn: Darby and Miller, 1853.

Opala, Joseph A. "The Gullah: Rice, Slavery and the Sierra Leone-American Connection." Available from http://www.yale.edu/glc/gullah/05.htm.

Thatcher, Benjamin Bussey. *Memoir of Phillis Wheatley: A Native African and a Slave,* 2nd edition. Boston: 1834.

Williams, James. *Narrative of James Williams: An American Slave: Who Was for Several Years a Driver on a Cotton Plantation in Alabama.* New York: 1838.

Josh J. Hem Lee

NAMES AND NAMING

Historians have written of enslaved men and women and their descendants that they are unable to trace an unbroken thread back to their African ancestors. However, this thread is found in many aspects of the lives of enslaved people, one of which is the process they used to identify themselves by name. Names and naming reflect many cultural values of enslaved African Americans and their family members: the desire to maintain one's African identity, the importance of both symbolic and blood kinship networks, and the desire to maintain these networks, cultural patterns, and social aspirations, as well as simple preference. In all, the process of naming was not a trivial one.

The first generation of enslaved people brought from Africa to America was the first to be named. After they were purchased, masters gave these men and women simple English names, classical names, names of English cities, or American city names. This happened for two reasons. Pragmatically, it was easier for white people to remember and pronounce. Symbolically, this naming process marked the beginning of a new life for the African in America. The original name and identity of the enslaved was at that moment unimportant and a fact of the past. The newly enslaved must now learn to be a slave, to act like a slave, under the total control of the master. A name is at the same time basic and important. One's name gives voice to one's identity and, in the case of the enslaved, slave owners thought original African names must be obliterated in order for masters to impose their will.

Naming Practices

A bit of ethnic identity was sometimes preserved in the naming process. Some men and women, although given English names, were still referred to by the ethnic group from which they originated. For instance, Gullah Jack, Jack Gambia, John Gola, Igbo Beckey, Angola Peter, and African Ned are names that reflect Europeans' awareness of the variety of ethnic groups in the area. Additionally, they reflect ethnic pride on the part of African men and women. Although it was more convenient for masters to give enslaved people English names, the enslaved made masters aware they were unwilling to give up the names they had been given by their parents back home. "Country names," the names that were given to enslaved Africans before they arrived in America, are recorded early in the history of enslavement. These were the names that tied men and women to home and to the family members from whom they were taken. As a result, men and women clung fiercely to these names.

New arrivals were more prone to respond to names their parents had given them than to the name their masters had given them. West African names were preserved by whites who approximated what these names sounded like given the accents and ways of interpretation and pronunciation of both groups. Ketu became Cato, Yanie became Jenny. The name Sukai, a woman's name found commonly in the Gambia, appears in historical records as Sukey, Sucky, or Sukie. This name became synonymous with enslaved black women; there are no records of white women with this name.

Masters searching for runaway African slaves printed the country name of the enslaved in the advertisement alongside names such as John and Chloe. Masters looking for enslaved men and women who ran away realized the enslaved were more likely to respond to their "country names," names given to them by their community of origin, however difficult it was for whites to pronounce them properly.

In recording the names of enslaved Africans, observers of first-generation African arrivals have recorded several trends in West African naming practice. One is the use of "day names," names given to a child that correspond to the day of the week the child was born. The more popular names for men were Cuffee, Coffee, and Cuff (Friday) and Cudjoe and Cudjo (Monday). For women, Abba (Thursday), Juba (Monday), and Phibba (Friday) were common. These names were often Anglicized: Abba to Abby, Juba to Judy, Phibba to Phebe, Cudjoe to Cooper Joe, Cuffee to Coffee. Other West African naming practices include naming a child based on the season or month of the year or something significant in the parents' life when the child was born. These naming practices continued through the generations. Naming children after their day names meant there were many Mondays, Tuesdays, Januaries, Decembers, and East(h)ers. In addition, there are names that recall the past: An enslaved person named Africa was purchased by John Cohoon.

Distinct from the European renaming process is the naming practice unique to people of African descent of having two names. One name is a formal name, a person's "real" or "right" name. In slave-holding America, this is the name a man or woman would be called by people who were outside a person's immediate community: someone with whom he or she was not intimately familiar, a person to whom one had recently been introduced, such as a master or mistress. On the other hand, a person was given a "basket name," a nickname that made reference to an idiosyncrasy, a physical trait, or other unique characteristic. Some basket names originate from the African American tradition of signifying, a tradition that, among other things, uses language to gently poke fun at someone's appearance or another unique characteristic. These names, which often follow a person from childhood to old age, may have originated from an embarrassing or private moment and are therefore not for public ears. For example, a person with inward-turning feet might be called "Parrot," a person with large eyes might be called "Hoot," a person with a quick temper might be called "Mad Dog," a person with a pleasant disposition might be called "Laffy." Because these names were private names that were transmitted orally by family members and close friends who were illiterate, it is doubtful that plantation records accurately record the basket names of men and women enslaved on these plantations and many may be lost.

Recorded basket names include Yellow Clara and Yellow Mary, indicating a woman of light complexion. John Frog, Duck, Kitty, Lad, and Tom T. are potentially basket names overheard by plantation masters and mistaken for real names. Additionally there were several Georges: Little George, House George, Fortune's George, and Long George. Each man's name indicated a personal characteristic about him: Little George was

SLAVE NAMES

The naming of slaves contained many more complexities than historians previously assumed. Many believed that masters often chose the names of their slaves' children for them, often giving the children names that seemed to be whimsical and amusing to the master, such as Caesar or Cato. While some masters did indeed name their slaves' children, the majority of slave parents named their own children. They chose from traditional African names, chose names that related to some trait pertaining to the child, and adapted Western names to their own culture and unique circumstances. Many slaves did indeed take the surname of their owners, but many slaves went through life with only first names.

SOURCE: Genovese, Eugene. *Roll, Jordan, Roll: The World the Slaves Made.* New York: Vintage, 1976.

the descendant of an elder George; House George had some affiliation with the plantation household; Fortune's George was the son of a woman named Fortune; and Long George was perhaps a tall, thin man.

Generational Patterns

Throughout the generations children, male and female, were frequently named for their fathers and grandfathers. Yellow Joe had descendants named Little Joe and Josephine. Nat Little's son was named Little Nat. Only rarely were children named for their mothers. More likely they were named for their grandmothers in the case of Big Nan, Nanny, and Nannette. An unusual example is the case of Ananiac, of the Carlisle Plantation. Her name is a combination of the names of her mother, Lavinia, and her maternal grandparents, Mary Ann and Isaac. In the cases of women being referred to as Big and Little, like Big Esther and Little Esther of the Bennehan-Cameron Plantation of Orange County, North Carolina, evidence shows that they were not related. Instead the designations were used to differentiate between women with the same name. Likely, the names Big and Little referred to personal characteristics: Big might indicate a woman who was full-figured, older, or taller. Little might be used for a woman with a slight build, a younger or shorter woman, or a combination of all three characteristics. In other cases, the terms *Big* and *Little* were designations used for cousins.

Perhaps a clue to this trend can be found in the folk saying, "Mama's baby, Papa's maybe." Maternity is much more easily proven than paternity. Given the fact that mothers passed along their condition to their children, and these children were readily identified as the children of an enslaved woman, to have the name of one's father created a paternal legacy of sorts. Having his name created a bond between him and his children. If the family had broken up, a child would have inherited his or her father's name.

Newborn children were named for deceased members of their immediate family. It was not an uncommon practice for parents to give one child the same name as a recently deceased child. In the Yoruba cultural tradition (among many West African traditions) it was common to name children born after the death of a father or grandfather Babatunde, meaning "father has returned," or to name a girl born after the death of a mother or grandmother Yewande, meaning "mother has returned."

In addition to selecting first names for themselves, enslaved people also selected their own last names. Historian Herbert Gutman wrote, "[A] social fact that remained hidden from most nineteenth-century slave owners and other whites ... [was] ... many slaves had surnames; and they often differed from the surnames of those who owned them" (1977, p. 230). Whites assumed that "a name is no name unless the bearer has a legal right to it. No slave *could* have a surname because he could not have a *legal* sire" (Ibid., p. 231). Enslaved people were expected only to have one name and if they did have a surname, it was to be the name of the master. This was not always the case. "Uncle" Alfred Jackson, the personal slave to President Andrew Jackson, was the only one of his family to keep the Jackson surname. The rest of his family used the name Bradley. Frequently, enslaved people selected their own last names for personal reasons. George Washington's former slave Daniel Payne did not adopt Washington's name after leaving his plantation; Payne saw no need to identify himself with his former master. In the case of Paul Cuffe, a ship captain and merchant, he refused to take his West African father's adopted surname, Slocom. Instead, he took his father's first name, Cuffe, and made it his last name. In the case of Michael One, he gave himself the last name One because he was proud of the work he did in his occupation. He was "[n]umber one carpenter" and his name reflected the fact of that accolade.

The naming process of African Americans is a topic that deserves a great deal more exploration. Day names are identifiable because the Akan use the same pattern for naming today. Names like Cuffee, Yaa, and Cudjo are easily recognized because the same names are used in modern Ghana and other places. But what of other names and naming practices that fell out of favor in Africa in the 350 years since people of African descent began to arrive in the New World? Naming practices could not have remained static for generations. Might African names still exist in the records of enslaved people's names that are simply not recognized because sufficient research has not been done on the topic? Additionally, what are the effects of "translating" West African names from various tonal languages to English? How many other names could have been lost in translation? Although a great deal of scholarship has addressed the naming process of enslaved men and women, there is much more to learn.

BIBLIOGRAPHY

Douglass, Frederick. *Narrative of the Life of Frederick Douglass, an American Slave, Written by Himself: With Related Documents,* ed. David W. Blight. Boston: Bedford/St. Martin's Press, 2003.

Franklin, John Hope. *From Slavery to Freedom: A History of African Americans.* New York: Knopf, 2000.

Gutman, Herbert George. *The Black Family in Slavery and Freedom, 1750–1925.* New York: Vintage, 1977.

Joyner, Charles W. *Down by the Riverside: A South Carolina Slave Community.* Urbana: University of Illinois Press, 1984.

Morgan, Philip D. *Slave Counterpoint: Black Culture in the Eighteenth-Century Chesapeake and Lowcountry.* Chapel Hill: University of North Carolina Press, 1998.

Tanya M. Mears

RITES OF PASSAGE

Life changes and transitions are normally marked by ceremonies and rituals, or rites of passage. Dennis O'Neil referred to these transitions as "life crises," and listed among them "birth, the onset of puberty, marriage, life-threatening illness or injury, and finally death" (O'Neil 2007). Modern cultures often also mark passage for events such as graduation from school, divorce, and career retirement. Although O'Neil's definition fits many cultures and peoples, it does not accurately describe the rites of passage experienced by slaves in America from the onset of slavery to emancipation in the nineteenth century.

The Belgian anthropologist Arnold van Gennep (1873–1857) remarked that rites of passage are "intentionally ritualized ceremonies [that] help individuals making the transition, as well as their relatives and friends, pass through an emotionally charged, tense time" (O'Neil 2007). For slaves during the early stages of U.S. slavery, this definition applied only partially. Their rites of passage were certainly emotionally charged and traumatic, but there was no celebration. One rite of passage for early slaves was their introduction to the West African slave trade. The initial capturing, selling, and forced voyage of these slaves across the ocean in cramped, inhumane conditions was a nightmarish initiation into a life of slavery; it was the "birth" into their new lives of bondage. For many, this Middle Passage was too much to bear, and many slaves chose not to make this horrifying passage into a life of servitude.

As for those who survived the Middle Passage, perhaps reasoning that conditions would improve once land was reached, their rites of passage were not typical either. Moreover, once enough slaves were brought to America to sustain the ugly business of slavery, and as more slaves were encouraged to have children in order to strengthen the labor force on plantations, the Middle Passage became less frequent. The birth of children into slavery brought about new and numerous rites of passage.

Although childhood is often considered a special time, if it was special for a slave child, it was because the mother made it so. The parents—particularly the mother, because the father was often the plantation's master or a slave who was sold off to another plantation—were responsible for looking out for the child's well-being and for providing any happiness that might be achieved under such circumstances. Nevertheless, children's bonds with their parents were often severed at an early age by slave owners, who sought to maintain psychological control over their chattel. Frederick Douglass remarked of his passage from infancy to child slave:

> My mother and I were separated when I was but an infant—before I knew her as my mother. It is a common custom ... to part children from their mothers at a very early age. Frequently, before the child has reached its twelfth month, its mother is taken from it, and hired out on some farm a considerable distance off, and the child is placed under the care of an old woman, too old for field labor. (Douglass [1845] 1997, p. 310)

Such separation hindered the child's bond with his or her mother. In cases where children were born to a slave who had been impregnated by her master, the slave was often sold off at the request of the plantation's mistress.

A slave child's life was never easy, and his or her formative years were colored by dread and fear and weighed down by the ever-present knowledge of being a slave. Although some slave children were cared for by infirm slaves while the child's parent(s) were out in the field or working in the master's house, many children were not afforded such an opportunity. Many were strapped to their mothers' backs while the mothers worked in the fields; others were placed on pallets at the end of crop rows, kept in view of their mothers. Others, as soon as they were physically capable, were given chores and had to assume the duties of a slave, just like the adults. For slaves, youth was lost once they were physically mature enough for labor. If a child survived early age, he or she was set to work on the plantation, for no child was spared labor, whether it was in the fields or in the house.

Both males and females suffered physical brutality at the hands of the masters, but often the females suffered sexual abuse as well. This was a dreaded passage into womanhood. Harriet Jacobs describes the fear in *Incidents in the Life of a Slave Girl* (1861). When confronted with the choice of securing her freedom or succumbing to the sexual advances of a man who would buy her freedom, Linda, shackled by guilt and shame, expresses the dilemma female slaves often faced:

> You never knew what it is to be a slave; to be entirely unprotected by law or customs; to have the laws reduce you to the condition of chattel, entirely subject to the will of another. You never exhausted your ingenuity in avoiding the snares, and eluding the power of a hated tyrant; you never shuddered at the sound of his footsteps, and trembled within hearing of his voice. I know I did wrong. No one can feel it more sensibly than I do. The painful and humiliating memory will haunt me to my dying day. Still, in looking back, calmly, on the events of my life, I feel that the slave woman ought not to be judged by the same standard as others. (Jacobs [1861] 1997, p. 220)

Female slaves, no matter how virtuous they attempted to remain, always knew they were considered property and stood a chance of being raped and perhaps impregnated; their bodies simply were not theirs to govern. Such were the rites of passage into womanhood for many female slaves.

Beyond the milestones of abuse that marked a slave's indoctrination into adulthood, small milestones that are often taken for granted were neglected in a slave's life. For example, because records either were not kept or were carelessly tended to, birthdays were not celebrated as many slaves did not know their actual date of birth. Although birthdays are occasions for celebration for most people, slaves usually did not celebrate being brought into a life of bondage. Frederick Douglass remarked on this phenomenon:

> By far the larger part of the slaves know as little of their ages as horses know of theirs, and it is the wish of most masters within my knowledge to keep their slaves thus ignorant. I do not remember to have ever met a slave who could tell of his birthday. They seldom come nearer to it than planting-time, harvest-time, cherry-time, spring-time, or fall-time. (Douglass [1845] 1997, p. 310)

Although many slave owners did not recognize marriages between two slaves, many slaves formed familial units. These relationships created a small amount of stability and contentment for slaves, and for many slaves, the establishment of a family became another milestone in their lives. Nevertheless, the comfort found in these relationships was fleeting because slaves lived in fear that one or more members of the family would be sold to another plantation.

With these relationships and the bearing of children came one of the ultimate rites of passage. If a slave had a decent master, she was indeed lucky; she was even luckier if that master allowed her to pursue extra, money-making jobs outside of her regular duties. For example, some slaves completed all their labor during the day, then baked when night came and sold their products the next morning, only to go to work again. Many times, children helped their mothers or fathers with such duties. Masters often made it a condition that if slaves

A wedding ceremony tradition. A woodcut showing slaves jumping the broom in a Virginia wedding ceremony. Many slave owners did not recognize marriage between slaves. *© Northwind Picture Archives.*

earned money, they would clothe their own children. As the slaves worked for money, they bought extra food and the clothes they needed in order to survive. Still, they often put aside money in order to buy their freedom or the freedom of their children. This goal kept the slaves motivated, and it also allowed them to feel hope in the face of oppression—someday they could be free if they worked hard enough. This freedom became the ultimate goal of many slaves. The act of saving money to buy one's freedom became a rite of passage, just as the eventual purchase of one's freedom did. Extra, money-making work became a symbol of hope, and slave children came to understand extra tasks as part of admittance into adulthood.

Rites of passage for slaves simply cannot be described with complete accuracy because few records were kept. Often, from birth to death, a slave's life was monotonous, and few days varied——though this depended on the slave's master and region. Beyond the physical work, there was the learning of field songs, traditions, and oral histories. Although most slaves' lives are not well documented, their life transitions are certainly apparent; these were not, however, the joyous celebrations that marked others' passages from one stage of life to the next.

BIBLIOGRAPHY

Douglass, Frederick. *Narrative of the Life of Frederick Douglass, Written by Himself,* [1845]. Reprinted in *The Norton Anthology of African American Literature,* ed. Henry Louis Gates Jr. and Nellie Y. McKay. New York: W. W. Norton, 1997.

Jacobs, Harriet. "Incidents in the Life of a Slave Girl." [1861]. In *The Norton Anthology of African American Literature,* ed. Henry Louis Gates Jr. and Nellie Y. McKay. New York: W. W. Norton, 1997.

A NEGRO FUNERAL.

A funeral on a rice plantation, 1859. On some homesteads, funerals were considered a waste of time and when slaves died, they were buried with little or no fanfare. More beneficent owners gave their slaves small funeral services and proper burials. Slaves who were considered part of the family were often given lavish funeral services and buried on plantation property. *The Granger Collection, New York. Reproduced by permission.*

O'Neil, Dennis. "Rites of Passage." Process of Socialization. 2007. Available from http://anthro.palomar.edu/social/soc_4.htm.

Gwendolyn N. Hale

DEATH AND FUNERAL CUSTOMS

Life for slaves was never easy, but for those living and working on large cotton plantations, conditions were harsh and unusually brutal. While some slaveholders treated their charges fairly and with a modicum of respect, they were the exception and not the rule. On other homesteads, despotic owners and overseers relished in their dominion over dozens and sometimes even hundreds of slaves, and threatened their existence on a daily basis. Death was not uncommon, and like any so-called property that became worn out or damaged, slaves were either sold or left to die when they outlived their usefulness. They were expendable, a fact few were ever allowed to forget.

Death: Violent or Otherwise

In the best of circumstances, slaves were considered valuable property and treated accordingly. Their value was tied to their productivity, and healthy slaves were productive slaves. Slave owners who believed it was their Christian duty to teach their slaves about religion often took better care of their charges than others. They saw that they had ample food, clothing, housing, and medical care. Medical care was usually based on a slave's stature

DEATH AND FUNERAL CUSTOMS

In May 1991, plans to erect a thirty-four-story office tower in New York City were disrupted by a compelling archaeological finding. An excavation of the site located at Broadway and Duane Streets in lower Manhattan unearthed more than 400 human skeletal remains and a vast array of burial artifacts that indicated their owner's African heritage. This site, now known as the African Burial Ground, provides critical insights into the funeral customs of enslaved people of African descent in eighteenth-century New York and demonstrates the tremendous resilience of enslaved people to preserve African traditions and rituals.

Artifacts discovered at the African Burial Ground indicate the persistence of African cosmologies and customs in both life and death. Among the artifacts is a coffin featuring an Ashanti-influenced heart-shaped design known as a *Sankofa* rendered on the lid with nails. Filing patterns on the front teeth of many were identified as consistent with a rite of passage among adolescent children in many parts of West and Central Africa. Moreover, a string of blue, green, and white glass beads was discovered on the remains of a young woman. Worn around the waist, these beads represented a passage over water in the afterlife, possibly back home to Africa. Others, consistent with African burial practices, were wrapped in cloth and adorned with cowrie shells. Taken together, these archaeological findings demonstrate the ongoing importance of African practices in the funeral customs of enslaved people of African descent.

BIBLIOGRAPHY

Blakey, Michael L. "The New African Burial Ground Project: An Examination of Enslaved Lives, a Construction of Ancestral Ties." *Transforming Anthropology* 7, no. 1 (1998).

Laroche, Cheryl J., and Michael L. Blakey. "Seizing Intellectual Power: The Dialogue at the New York African Burial Ground." *Historical Archaeology* 31, no. 3 (Fall 1997).

within the household; personal servants, breeders, wet nurses, and cooks were given far better care—medical and otherwise—than field hands. For privileged slaves, illnesses and injuries were treated by white doctors who would either visit slave quarters or have ailing slaves brought to the porch of their owner's house.

Field hands, who lived under the most severe conditions and were the backbone of most plantations, were mostly cared for by other slaves. Actual medical training was generally nil; remedies were homemade from plants and herbs, tinged with superstition and folklore, sometimes even voodoo. Unfortunately for female slaves, many died during and after childbirth, usually in two extremes—the young (those barely into their teens) and the middle-aged, who had given birth to many children, often as many as fifteen or more.

Far more slaves died from injuries suffered during punishment than from illness. They were punished for many infractions, large and small—including talking back, being late, not working fast enough, taking time off (without permission or a pass), drinking too much (whether water or alcohol), stealing, or running away. Punishment ranged from beatings, whippings, being bound and dragged over logs, hanging by the thumbs or wrists for lesser crimes, to death for crimes considered more serious. Death could be by hanging, burning at the stake, being torn apart by hounds, beating, or simply disappearing.

In addition to injury, illness, and the whims of their slaveholders, slaves also faced the wrath of roaming gangs—aimless bushwhackers with no affiliation of any kind, neighboring whites with a grudge, or in the later years, the Ku Klux Klan. As Stephen McCray, a slave born in Huntsville County, Alabama, who worked on the McCray plantation near Scottsboro, commented: "Bushwhackers, nothin' but po' white trash, come thoo' and killed all the little nigger chillums they could lay hands on. I was hid under the house with a big rag in my mouf many a time" (*Born in Slavery*, Oklahoma Narratives, vol. 13, p. 209).

Funerals and Burial

On some homesteads, funerals were considered a waste of time, time when slaves could be harvesting crops, milking cows, or performing any number of daily chores. When slaves died—whether of illness, injury, or old age—many were buried with little or no fanfare. As Octavia George, a slave who lived most of her life in Tennessee and relocated to Oklahoma after the war, commented, "Funerals were very simple for slaves, they could not carry the body to the church so they would carry it to the graveyard and bury it. They were not allowed to sing a song at the cemetery" (*Born in Slavery*, Oklahoma Narratives, vol. 13, p. 113).

More beneficent owners gave their slaves small funeral services and proper burials. Mintie Wood, who was born in Tennessee and worked most of her life in Arkansas for the Gilbert family, talked of her owner's practices: "...[H]e had so many of his family and darkies, too, he has his own graveyard where every one of us, black or white dat ever been in de Gilbert family can be buried without costing us a penny" (*Born in Slavery*, Missouri Narratives, vol. 10, p. 375).

Some funerals were massive affairs in the same custom of the slaveholders themselves and their families. Slaves who were considered part of the family (and many were, being the sons and daughters of their so-called masters), were often given lavish funerals and buried on plantation property. As Cordelia Thomas, a slave born and raised in Georgia, related:

> When somebody did die, folkses come from miles
> and miles around for de buryin.' Dey give de

slaves de same sort of funeral de white folkses had. De corpses was washed good all over in hot water and home-made soap, den dey was dressed and laid out on de coolin' boards til the carpenter man had time to make up de coffins. (*Born in Slavery*, Georgia Narratives, vol. 4, part 4, p. 20)

Such celebrations were not the norm, but allowed slaves to be buried with dignity. For these lucky souls the funeral process was respectful, often followed by a specially prepared dinner, drinking, and sometimes dancing. Most all of the homestead's slaves were able to attend, and the slave-holding family ate and drank alongside them for this particular day or evening.

BIBLIOGRAPHY

Born in Slavery: Slave Narratives from the Federal Writers' Project, 1936–1938. Manuscript and Prints and Photographs Divisions, Library of Congress. Georgia Narratives, volume 4, part 4. Available from http://memory.loc.gov/ammem/snhtml/snhome.html.

Born in Slavery: Slave Narratives from the Federal Writers' Project, 1936–1938. Manuscript and Prints and Photographs Divisions, Library of Congress. Missouri Narratives, volume 10. Available from http://memory.loc.gov/ammem/snhtml/snhome.html.

Born in Slavery: Slave Narratives from the Federal Writers' Project, 1936–1938. Manuscript and Prints and Photographs Divisions, Library of Congress. Oklahoma Narratives, volume 13. Available from http://memory.loc.gov/ammem/snhtml/snhome.html.

Nelson Rhodes

WEST AFRICAN INFLUENCES

Before the 1940s historical interpretations of slavery suggested that the experience of the long and brutal voyage across the Atlantic Ocean and the humiliating and dehumanizing effect of enslavement destroyed the enslaved Africans' identity and severed them from their culture. The anthropologist Melville J. Herskovits challenged this interpretation in his 1941 book, *The Myth of the Negro Past*. Based on the structural similarities between West African cultural practices and the cultural traditions of African Americans, Herskovits's research revealed that enslaved Africans in the new world, and the United States, had indeed not been divorced from their culture and that West African cultural influences were present in African American culture during slavery, through emancipation, and beyond.

Focusing on West African influences present in the cultural practices of enslaved African Americans, historians have offered new interpretations of the institution of slavery and its effects on the enslaved. As George Rawick (1972) argues, "if we are to understand the develop-

A book cover, circa 1820–1830, showing a wedding ceremony for slaves in West Africa. The strongest examples of West African influences on African American cultural practices are found in the folklore, music, religion, rituals, and language that slaves used. *Image © Stapleton Collection/Corbis Photographer Philip Spruyt.*

ment of African American culture and community, then we must have some understanding of the role African experience played in the making of the American black people" (1972, p. 14).

It is important to remember that enslaved blacks' African ancestors did come from diverse areas and ethnic groups along the western coast of Africa. Despite the geographic and ethnic variation among Africans transported to the United States, the historian Lawrence Levine suggests that, "though [enslaved Africans] varied widely in language, institutions, gods, and familial patterns, they shared a fundamental outlook towards the past, present, and future and a common means of cultural expression which could well have constituted the basis of a sense of common identity and world view capable of withstanding the impact of slavery" (1977, p. 4). The shared cultural practices of the diverse West African ethnic groups brought to the United States through the middle passage had a powerful impact on

MUSICAL INFLUENCES

African American musical styles have been and continue to be the strongest vehicles for the preservation and evolution of West African cultural characteristics arriving in the United States, by way of the Middle Passage, some four centuries ago. Not only has African American music carried traces of West Africa, but importantly West African cultural characteristics have helped to connect several different styles of African American music over time. While the blues, jazz, rhythm and blues, and hip-hop are unique styles of black musical production with different social meanings and uses, they all share elements that can be traced back to the ring shout and plantation gang-labor work song. One of the most prominent of these shared characteristics is the A-B-A-B-C-C lyric pattern that originated in the work songs of enslaved Africans. Initially this lyric pattern helped to coordinate and synchronize movements of enslaved Africans while collectively working. This lyric pattern persisted in the post-emancipation moment as the emerging blues musical style adopted it. This same lyrical structure can often be found in the hooks of many jazz, rhythm and blues, and hip-hop songs being produced in the early twenty-first century.

SOURCE: Baraka, Amiri. *Blues People: Negro Music in White America.* New York: William Morrow, 1963.

the culture of enslaved African Americans, most evident in slaves' folklore, music, religion, rituals, and language.

Folklore

As John Blassingame notes, "African scholars have traced many slaves' folktales directly to Ghana, Senegal, and Mauritius and the lore of such African peoples as the Ewe, Wolof, Hausa, Temne, Ashanti, and Ibo" (1972, p. 32). One of the common threads among these folktales is the trickster figure—commonly in the form of an animal such as a tortoise, rabbit, or spider—who uses intellect and cunning to outwit a physically stronger foe. In the 1920s Zora Neal Hurston, the novelist and anthropologist, researched and documented the folklore traditions of southern African American communities along the Gulf Coast. Based on her interviews with African Americans either who had experienced slavery as a young child or who were a part of the first generations born after emancipation, she showed that the West African trickster continued to be an important element of black folklore. In the folktales of these Gulf Coast communities, the trickster figure often took the form of the rabbit, who time after time outsmarted his physically stronger foe, the fox. Some suggest that enslaved African Americans saw the relationship between the rabbit and the fox as a metaphor for the relationship between the enslaved and the slave owner.

Music and Performance

Structural elements of West African music and performance, including call and response, group participation, bodily expression through dance, polyrhythmic complexity, improvisation, harmony, and tonal quality, became the foundations of the music created by enslaved African Americans. Lawrence Levine (1977) observes that the song style of African Americans, during the slavery era and following emancipation, retained and reflected West African styles of music and performance. By relying on the West African tradition of call and response in "work songs," enslaved African Americans were able to adjust to gang labor systems. Work songs helped the enslaved coordinate their collective energy and effort to work more efficiently. As they simultaneously worked and sang, their individual parts in the call and response pattern of the song told them when to execute their specific work function.

The "ring shout," an essential part of West African ritual performance, was another important influence on the cultural practices of enslaved African Americans. According to Sterling Stuckey, "an integral part of religion and culture was moving in a ring during ceremonies honoring the ancestors. . . . Wherever in Africa the counter clockwise dance ceremony was performed, . . . the dancing and singing were directed to the ancestors and gods, the tempo and revolution of the circle quickening during the course of movement" (1987, pp. 11–12). Perhaps the most celebrated instances of this West African tradition in the United States were the ring shouts performed on Sundays in New Orleans' Congo Square until federal troops put a stop to the practice during the Civil War. Enslaved Africans congregated to sing, dance, worship, and pay homage to their ancestors. Like the work song, call and response and collective participation governed the structure of singing while a layered multitude of rhythmic beat patterns produced by many drummers kept time for the dancers. Gary Donaldson notes that "these rings represented various African tribes and nationalities as they danced, sang, and played the various instruments of their homeland" (1984). Each West African ethnic group represented in the circle usually had a specific part in the call and response pattern and a distinct drum cadence. As the various voices and cadences formed one collective song, an ethnically diverse group of Africans were transformed into African Americans. The roots of jazz, argued to be the most uniquely American musical form, have been traced back to the ring shouts of Congo Square.

West African culture had its most pronounced influence on the culture of enslaved African Americans in areas—namely the Gulf Coast, New Orleans, the Gullah Coast, and the islands off the coast of Georgia and South Carolina—where slaves had less interaction with white Americans and the desire to assimilate into white culture was minimal. With the closing of the trans-Atlantic slave trade in 1808, ending the importation of individuals who experienced West African culture first-hand, the growth of the free black population, and their assimilation into white society and culture, the prominence of West African influences began to fade. Yet these influences did leave their mark on African American and American culture. West African words like "goober," "yam," "cola," and "tote," introduced into the United States by enslaved Africans, have become common usage in American English.

BIBLIOGRAPHY

Blassingame, John. *The Slave Community: Plantation Life in the Antebellum South.* New York: Oxford University Press, 1972.

Donaldson, Gary A. "A Window on Slave Culture: Dances at Congo Square in New Orleans, 1800–1862." *Journal of Negro History* 69, no. 2 (1984): 63–72.

Herskovits, Melville J. *The Myth of the Negro Past.* New York: Harper, 1941.

Hurston, Zora Neale. *Mules and Men* [1935]. New York: Perennial Library, 1990.

Hurston, Zora Neale. *Every Tongue Got to Confess: Negro Folk-tales from the Gulf States.* New York: HarperCollins, 2001.

Levine, Lawrence W. *Black Culture and Black Consciousness: Afro-American Folk Thought from Slavery to Freedom.* New York: Oxford University Press, 1977.

Rawick, George P. *From Sundown to Sunup: The Making of the Black Community.* Westport, CT: Greenwood Publishing, 1972.

Stuckey, Sterling. *Slave Culture: Nationalist Theory and the Foundations of Black America.* New York: Oxford University Press, 1987.

Nicholas Gaffney

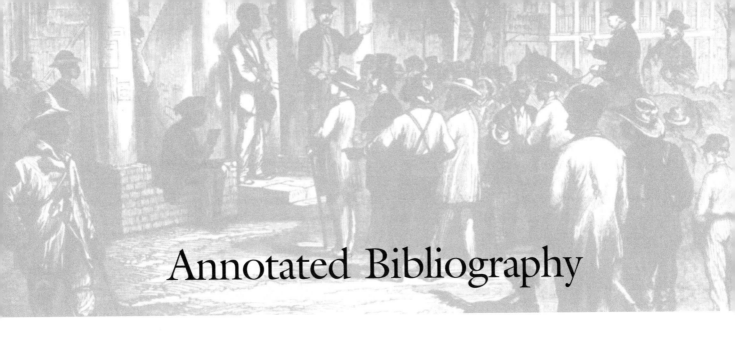

Annotated Bibliography

The following resources, which provide overviews of slavery in America, are recommended for their broad scope and availability.

GENERAL READING

Aptheker, Herbert, ed. *Documentary History of the Negro People in the United States.* New York: Citadel Press, 1951. An early anthology of depictions of slavery and its aftermath.

Berlin, Ira. *Generations of Captivity: A History of African-American Slaves.* Cambridge, MA: Belknap Press, 2003. Profiles successive generations of slaves, from "Charter Generations" to "Plantation Generations" to "Freedom Generations."

Berlin, Ira. *Many Thousands Gone: The First Two Centuries of Slavery in America.* Cambridge, MA: Belknap Press, 1998. Emphasizes the broad diversity of the experience of slavery.

Berlin, Ira, Marc Favreau, and Steven F. Miller, eds. *Remembering Slavery: African Americans Talk about Their Personal Experiences of Slavery and Emancipation.* New York and Washington, DC: The New Press and Smithsonian Institution, 1998.

Blassingame, John W., ed. *Slave Testimony: Two Centuries of Letters, Speeches, Interviews, and Autobiographies.* Baton Rouge: Louisiana State University Press, 1977.

Botkin, B. A., ed. *Lay My Burden Down.* Chicago: University of Chicago Press, 1945. A short compilation of various slave family narratives collected by the Federal Writers' Project in the 1930s. [For the complete FWP narratives, see Rawick.]

Davis, David Brion. *Inhuman Bondage: The Rise and Fall of Slavery in the New World.* New York: Oxford University Press, 2006. Considers American slavery as part of the first system of production aimed at serving mass markets.

Davis, David Brion. *The Slave Power Conspiracy and the Paranoid Style.* Baton Rouge: Louisiana State University Press, 1969. Three groundbreaking essays about slavery's pernicious psychological impact on white Southern society.

"Documenting the American South." University of North Carolina. Available from http://docsouth.unc.edu/.

Douglass, Frederick. *Narrative of the Life of Frederick Douglass, an American Slave* [1845]. New York: Chelsea House, 1988. The most renowned autobiographical account of slavery by the abolition movement's greatest orator.

Drake, St. Clair, and Horace R. Clayton. *Black Metropolis: A Study of Negro Life in a Northern City* [1945]. 2 vols. New York: Harcourt, Brace, and World, 1970.

"Federal Writers' Project Interviews." Available from http://xroads.virginia.edu/~hyper/wpa/wpahome.html.

Franklin, John Hope. *From Slavery to Freedom, A History of the Negro in America* [1947]. 2 vols. New York: Knopf, 2000. Covers the rise of slavery, the interaction of European and African cultures in the

New World, and the emergence of a distinct culture and way of life among slaves and free blacks.

"The Geography of Slavery." University of Virginia. Available from http://www.vcdh.virginia.edu/gos/documents.html. A collection of official records, newspaper advertisements, slaveholders' records, and slave narratives.

Genovese, Eugene D. *Roll, Jordan, Roll: The World the Slaves Made.* New York: Pantheon, 1972. A broad examination of the world of African Americans living under Euro-American hegemony.

Horton, James Oliver, and Lois E. Horton. *Slavery and the Making of America.* New York: Oxford University Press, 2005. Considers slavery as a primary shaper of American culture, from colonial politics to Southern cuisine.

Jordan, Winthrop D. *White over Black: American Attitudes toward the Negro, 1550–1812* [1968]. New York: Norton, 1977. Makes the argument that while racism did not produce the enslavement of blacks, it was there from the start and developed progressively, especially with independence.

Lerner, Gerda, ed. *Black Women in White America: A Documentary History.* New York: Random House, 1972. An early work in women's studies, beginning in the era of slavery.

Myrdal, Gunnar. *An American Dilemma: The Negro Problem and Modern Democracy.* 2 vols. New York: Harper & Row, 1944. A bell-weather, internationalist perspective on slavery's legacy that was influential on the civil rights movement.

Patterson, Orlando. *The Sociology of Slavery.* Rutherford, NJ: Fairleigh Dickinson University Press, 1969. A powerful indictment of previous interpretations of slavery.

Phillips, Ulrich Bonnell. *Life and Labor in the Old South.* Boston: Little, Brown, 1929. An early, benign depiction of slavery.

Rawick, George P., ed. *The American Slave: A Composite Autobiography.* 41 vols. Series 1, Supplement Series 1 and 2. Westport, CT: Greenwood Press, 1972, 1978, 1979. Contains thousands of verbatim interviews with family members of former slaves, conducted by the Federal Writers' Project in the 1930s.

Rose, Willie Lee, ed. *A Documentary History of Slavery in North America.* New York: Oxford University Press, 1976. An extensive single-volume collection of documents.

Stampp, Kenneth. *The Peculiar Institution: Slavery in the Ante-Bellum South.* New York: Knopf, 1956.

A landmark portrayal of slavery as a method of controlling labor under the guise of beneficent paternalism.

THE MIDDLE PASSAGE AND AFRICA

Appiah, Kwame Anthony, and Henry Louis Gates Jr. *Africana: The Encyclopedia of the African and African American Experience.* New York: Oxford University Press, 2005. A comprehensive, five-volume compendium.

Azurara, G. E., *The Chronicle of the Discovery and Conquest of Guinea.* London: Hakluyt Society, 1896–1899.

Boxer, C. R. *The Dutch Seaborne Empire, 1600–1800.* New York: Knopf, 1965. Examines the beginning of Northern European participation in the slave trade.

Bridenbaugh, Carl, and Roberta Bridenbaugh. *No Peace beyond the Line: The English in the Caribbean, 1624–1690.* New York: Oxford University Press, 1972. Discusses Britain's entry into the markets for sugar, tobacco, and slaves.

"A Chronology of Slavery." Available from http://henryburke1010.tripod.com/id2.html. A timeline of the earliest slave trade along the African coast.

Curtin, Philip D., ed. *Africa Remembered: Narratives by West Africans from the Era of the Slave Trade.* Madison: University of Wisconsin Press, 1968.

Curtin, Philip D. *The Atlantic Slave Trade: A Census.* Madison: University of Wisconsin Press, 1969. Thorough preliminary estimates of the number and size of forced migrations from different African countries.

Equiano, Olaudah. *The Interesting Narrative of the Life of Olaudah Equiano, or Gustavus Vassa, the African* [1789]. New York: Penguin Classics, 2003. Equiano's autobiographical account of his kidnapping in Africa at the age of ten, his enslavement in the British Navy, and ten years of labor on slave ships before he was able to purchase his freedom in 1766.

Foner, Philip S. *History of Black Americans: From Africa to the Emergence of the Cotton Kingdom.* Westport, CT: Greenwood Press, 1975.

George, Claude. *The Rise of British West Africa.* London: Cass, 1968.

Goveia, Elsa V. *Slave Society in the British Leeward Islands at the End of the Eighteenth Century.* New Haven, CT: Yale University Press, 1965.

Kingsbury, Susan Myra, ed. *The Records of the Virginia Company of London.* 4 vols. Washington, DC: Government Printing Office, 1906–1935. The complete extant official documentation concerning early Virginia.

Smith, John. *Captain John Smith's History of Virginia* [1624]. Indianapolis: Bobbs-Merrill, 1970.

Smith, Venture. *A Narrative of the Life and Adventures of Venture, a Native of Africa* [1798]. New York: Kessinger Publishing, 2004. Smith's autobiography, from his birth in Guinea in about 1729 to his time in Rhode Island.

Vaughan, Alden T. "Blacks in Virginia: A Note on the First Decade." *William and Mary Quarterly,* 3rd Ser., 29, no. 3 (1972): 469–478. A close look at the first Africans to arrive in the British colonies. [Available through JSTOR.com.]

THE BUSINESS OF SLAVERY

Aitken, Hugh G. J., ed. *Did Slavery Pay? Readings in the Economics of Black Slavery in the United States.* Boston: Houghton Mifflin, 1971. Collected essays evaluating the profitability of slavery.

Bancroft, Frederic. *Slave Trading in the Old South.* Baltimore, MD: J. H. Furst, 1931. Discusses the transport and auctioning of slaves.

Conrad, Alfred H., and John R. Meyer. *The Economics of Slavery and Other Studies in Econometric History.* Chicago: Aldine, 1964.

Craven, Wesley Frank. *White, Red, and Black: The Seventeenth-Century Virginian.* Charlottesville: University Press of Virginia, 1971. Focuses on the early development of the enslavement of Native Americans and Africans in the British Colonies.

Curtin, Philip D. *The Rise and Fall of the Plantation Complex.* New York: Cambridge University Press, 1990. Examines the success and perils of cotton production, in terms of land, labor, and fertilization use.

Fogel, Robert W., and Stanley Engerman. *Time on the Cross: The Economics of Slavery in the Antebellum South* [1974]. 2 vols. New York: Norton, 1995. A controversial, statistical study denying the view that ultimately slavery would have collapsed from its own economic failure, and arguing instead that investment in slaves was more profitable than investments in free labor.

Fox-Genovese, Elizabeth, Eugene D. Genovese, and Harold D. Woodman. *Fruits of Merchant Capital: Slavery and Bourgeois Property in the Rise and Expansion of Capitalism.* New York: Oxford University Press, 1983. Considers slave property as a basis of capital and collateral.

Galenson, David W. *Traders, Planters, and Slaves: Market Behavior in Early English America.* New York: Cambridge University Press, 1986.

Genovese, Eugene D. *The Political Economy of Slavery: Studies in the Economy and Society of the Slave South.* New York: Knopf, 1967. Examines the economics of slavery in light of its central place in the social structure of the South.

Genovese, Eugene D., ed. *The Slave Economy of the Old South: Selected Essays in Economic and Social History.* Baton Rouge: Louisiana State University Press, 1968.

Morgan, Edmund S. *American Slavery, American Freedom: The Ordeal of Colonial Virginia.* New York: Norton, 1975. An examination of various forms of labor and their exploitation.

Parker, William N., ed. *The Structure of the Cotton Economy of the Antebellum South.* Berkeley: University of California Press, 1970.

Shugg, Roger W. *Origins of Class Struggle in Louisiana.* Baton Rouge: Louisiana State University Press, 1968. A Marxian analysis of free and unfree labor.

Sutch, Richard. "The Breeding of Slaves for Sale and the Westward Expansion of Slavery, 1850–1860." In *Race and Slavery in the Western Hemisphere.* Ed. Stanley L. Engerman and Eugene D. Genovese. Princeton, NJ: Princeton University Press, 1975.

Tadman, Michael. "Slave Trading in the Ante-Bellum South: An Estimate of the Extent of the Inter-Regional Slave Trade" [1974]. In *Slave Trade and Migration, Domestic and Foreign,* Ed. Paul Finkelman. New York: Garland, 1989.

"Tobacco and Slavery." Available from http://www. slaveryinamerica.org/history/hs_es_tobacco_slavery. htm.

Vaughan, Alden T. *American Genesis: Captain John Smith and the Founding of Virginia.* Boston: Little, Brown, 1975. A broad view of the first American settlement to incorporate African slaves.

WORK

Allen, Ruth Alice. *The Labor of Women in the Production of Cotton* [1931]. New York: Arno Press, 1975.

Berlin, Ira, and Philip D. Morgan, eds. *Cultivation and Culture: Labor and the Shaping of Slave Life in the Americas*. Charlottesville: University Press of Virginia, 1993. Essays reassessing life and labor on plantations.

Breen, T. H. *Tobacco Culture: The Mentality of the Great Tidewater Plantations on the Eve of the Revolution*. Princeton, NJ: Princeton University Press, 1985.

Jones, Jacqueline. *Labor of Love, Labor of Sorrow: Black Women, Work, and the Family, from Slavery to the Present*. New York: Basic Books, 1986. A discussion of the complex interconnection of work, sex, race, and class.

Scarborough, William Kauffman. *The Overseer: Plantation Management in the Old South*. Baton Rouge: Louisiana State University Press, 1966.

Starobin, Robert S. *Industrial Slavery in the Old South*. New York: Oxford University Press. Examines the transposition of slavery from field to factory.

Yetman, Norman R. *Life under the "Peculiar Institution."* New York: Brown, 1970.

FAMILY AND COMMUNITY

Beatty, Richmond Croom. *William Byrd of Westover*. Boston: Houghton Mifflin, 1932. A biography based on this eccentric plantation owner's very personal diaries.

Billington, R. A., ed. *The Journal of Charlotte Forten: A Free Negro in the Slave Era*. New York: Collier Books, 1967.

Blassingame, John W. *The Slave Community: Plantation Life in the Antebellum South*. New York: Oxford University Press, 1979. A classic depiction of the institution of slavery based on the eyewitness accounts of slaves, planters, and visitors.

Boles, John B. *Black Southerners, 1619–1869*. Lexington: University Press of Kentucky, 1983.

Elkins, Stanley. *Slavery*. Chicago: University of Chicago Press, 1959. Examines the psychological effects of American bondage through the prism of the Nazi Holocaust.

Fox-Genovese, Elizabeth. *Within the Plantation Household: Black and White Women of the Old South*. Chapel Hill: University of North Carolina Press, 1988.

Franklin, John Hope. *In Search of the Promised Land: A Slave Family in the Old South*. New York: Oxford University Press, 2006. A distinguished historian traces a Tennessee mulatto family through three generations, from 1800 to 1865.

Gutman, Herbert G. *The Black Family in Slavery and Freedom, 1750–1925*. New York: Pantheon, 1976. A multigenerational study of African American families, both dynasties of slaves and free blacks.

Jacobs, Harriet. *Incidents in the Life of a Slave Girl, Written by Herself* [1861]. Ed. Jean Fagan Yellin. Cambridge, MA: Harvard University Press, 1987. A moving and eloquent account by a North Carolina woman who suffered most of slavery's horrors.

Johnson, Charles S. *Shadow of the Plantation*. Chicago: University of Chicago Press, 1966.

Kemble, Frances Anne. *Journals of Residence on a Georgian Plantation* [1863]. Atlanta: University of Georgia Press, 1984. An Englishwoman's critical diary of plantation life.

Rawick, George P. *From Sundown to Sunup: The Making of the Black Community*. Westport, CT: Greenwood Press, 1972. An anthology of the slave narratives collected by the Federal Writers' Project in the 1930s.

Schoolcraft, Mrs. Henry Rowe. *Black Gauntlet: Plantation Life: The Narratives of Mrs. Henry Rowe Schoolcraft* [1852–1869]. New York: Negro Universities Press, 1969.

CULTURE AND LEISURE

Abrahams, Roger D. *Singing the Master: The Emergence of African-American Culture in the Plantation South*. New York: Penguin, 1993. A folklorist's descriptive analysis of Southern plantations' corn-shucking contests, which were typified by singing, dancing, and feasting.

Allen, William Francis, et al., eds. *Slave Songs of the United States*. New York: A. Simpson, 1867. Available from http://docsouth.unc.edu/church/allen/menu.html.

Armstrong, M. F. et al., eds. *Hampton and Its Students; by Two of Its Teachers, Mrs. M. F. Armstrong and Helen W. Ludlow. With Fifty Cabin and Plantation Songs*. New York: G. P. Putnam's Sons, 1874.

Hughes, Langston, and Arna Bontemps, eds. *Book of Negro Folklore*. New York: Dodd, Mead, 1958.

Jones, LeRoi [Amiri Baraka]. *Blues People: Negro Music in White America*. New York: Morrow, 1963.

Joyner, Charles. *Down by the Riverside: A South Carolina Slave Community*. Urbana: University of Illinois Press, 1985.

Joyner, Charles. *Shared Traditions: Southern History and Folk Culture.* Urbana: University of Illinois Press, 1999.

Levine, Lawrence W. *Black Culture, Black Consciousness: Afro-American Folk Thought from Slavery to Freedom.* New York: Oxford University Press, 1978.

Southern, Eileen. *The Music of Black Americans: A History.* New York: Norton, 1997. Traces the development of African American music from 1619 to the present, through a consideration of instrumention, minstrelsy, dance, and gospel.

Stuckey, Sterling. *Slave Culture: Nationalist Theory and the Foundations of Black America.* New York: Oxford University Press, 1987.

White, Deborah Gray. *Ar'n't I a Woman? Female Slaves in the Plantation South.* New York: Norton, 1985.

RELIGION

Boles, John, ed. *Masters and Slaves in the House of the Lord: Race and Religion in the American South, 1740–1870.* Lexington: University Press of Kentucky, 1988.

Carwardine, Richard J. *Evangelicals and Politics in Antebellum America.* Knoxville: University of Tennessee Press, 1997.

"The Church in the Southern Black Community." Available from http://docsouth.unc.edu/church/texts.html.

Cornelius, Janet D. *Slave Missions and the Black Church in the Antebellum South.* Columbia: University of South Carolina Press, 1999.

Creel, Margaret W. *"A Peculiar People": Slave Religion and Community-Culture among the Gullahs.* New York: New York University Press, 1988.

Davis, David Brion. *In the Image of God: Religion, Moral Values, and Our Heritage of Slavery.* New Haven, CT: Yale University Press, 2001. Essays on both the spiritual and the capitalist aspects of slavery.

DuBois, W. E. B. *The Souls of Black Folk* [1903]. Ed. Henry Louis Gates Jr. and Terri Hume Oliver. New York: Norton, 1999. An influential early work by this sociologist, historian, novelist, and activist, whose career stretched from Reconstruction to the civil rights movement.

Herskovits, Melville J. *The Myth of the Negro Past* [1941]. Boston: Beacon Press, 1990.

Johnson, Curtis D. *Redeeming America: Evangelicals and the Road to Civil War.* Chicago: I. R. Dee, 1993.

Jones, Charles Colcock. *Suggestions on the Religious Instruction of the Negroes in the Southern States.* Philadelphia: Presbyterian Board of Publication, 1847. Provides evidence of Southern white attitudes toward "Christianizing" slaves in the context of a biblical defense of slavery.

Loveland, Anne C. *Southern Evangelicals and the Social Order, 1800–1860.* Baton Rouge: Louisiana State University Press, 1980.

Raboteau, Albert J. *Slave Religion: The "Invisible Institution" in the Antebellum South.* New York: Oxford University Press, 1980.

HEALTH, MEDICINE, AND NUTRITION

Fett, Sharla M. *Working Cures: Healing, Health, and Power on Southern Slave Plantations.* Chapel Hill: University of North Carolina Press, 2002. Focuses on the slaves' use of their own cures, in contrast to their owners' medical practices.

Genovese, Eugene D. "Medical and Insurance Costs of Slaveholding in the Cotton Belt." *Journal of Negro History* 45, no. 3 (1960): 141–155.

Hilliard, Sam. "Hog Meat and Cornpone: Food Habits in the Ante-Bellum South." *Proceedings of the American Philosophical Society* 113, no. 1 (1969): 1–13.

Postell, William Dosite. *The Health of Slaves on the Southern Plantations.* Baton Rouge: Louisiana State University Press, 1951.

Savitt, Todd L. *Medicine and Slavery: The Diseases and Health Care of Blacks in Antebellum Virginia* [1978]. Urbana: University of Illinois Press, 2002. A classic in its field by a medical doctor.

Savitt, Todd L. *Race and Medicine in Nineteenth- and Early-Twentieth-Century America.* Kent, OH: Kent State University Press, 2006.

Savitt, Todd L., and Ronald L. Numbers, eds. *Science and Medicine in the Old South.* Baton Rouge: Louisiana State University Press, 1989.

REGULATING SLAVERY

Campbell, Stanley W. *The Slave Catchers: Enforcement of the Fugitive Slave Law, 1850–1860* Chapel Hill: University of North Carolina Press, 1968.

Davis, David Brion. *Antebellum American Culture: An Interpretive Anthology.* University Park: Pennsylvania State University Press, 1997.

Doyle, Bertram Wilbur. *The Etiquette of Race Relations in the South: A Study in Social Control.* Chicago: University of Chicago Press, 1937.

DuBois, W. E. B. *The Suppression of the African Slave Trade* [1896]. New York: Schocken Books, 1969.

Filler, Louis. *The Crusade against Slavery, 1830–1860.* New York: Harper, 1960.

Flanigan, Daniel J. *The Criminal Law of Slavery and Freedom, 1800–1868.* New York: Taylor and Francis, 1987.

Fogel, Robert William. *Without Consent or Contract: The Rise and Fall of American Slavery.* New York: Norton, 1989.

Fox-Genovese, Elizabeth, and Eugene D. Genovese. *The Mind of the Master Class: History and Faith in the Southern Slaveholders' Worldview.* New York: Cambridge University Press, 2005.

Gross, Ariela J. *Double Character: Slavery and Mastery in the Antebellum Southern Courtroom.* Princeton, NJ: Princeton University Press, 2000.

Kolchin, Peter. *American Slavery, 1619–1877.* New York: Hill and Wang, 2003.

Kolchin, Peter. *First Freedom: The Responses of Alabama's Blacks to Emancipation and Reconstruction.* Westport, CT: Greenwood Press, 1972.

Northup, Solomon. *Twelve Years a Slave* [1853]. Baton Rouge: Louisiana State University Press, 1967.

Outwin, Charles P. M. "Securing the Leg Irons: Restriction of Legal Rights for Slaves in Virginia and Maryland, 1625–1791." Available from http://www.earlyamerica.com/review/winter96/slavery.html.

Richards, Leonard. *Slave Power: The Free North and Southern Domination, 1780–1860.* Baton Rouge: Louisiana State University Press, 2000. Examines the way in which slaveholder interests dominated the Federal government from the birth of the country to the Civil War.

Schwarz, Philip. *Twice Condemned: Slaves and the Criminal Laws of Virginia, 1705–1865.* Baton Rouge: Louisiana State University Press, 1988.

Van Deusen, Glyndon G. *William Henry Seward.* New York: Oxford University Press, 1967. A biography of the Senate's leading abolitionist.

RESISTANCE AND REBELLION

Addington, Wendell G. "Slave Insurrections in Texas." *Journal of Negro History* 35, no. 4 (1950): 408–434.

Aptheker, Herbert. *Nat Turner's Slave Rebellion.* New York: Citadel, 1951.

Aptheker, Herbert. *American Negro Slave Revolts.* New York: International Publishers, 1966.

Bentley, Judith. *Harriet Tubman.* New York: Franklin Watts, 1990.

Berry, Mary Frances. *Black Resistance/White Law: A History of Constitutional Racism in America.* New York: Penguin, 1994.

Blockson, Charles L. *Underground Railroad.* New York: Prentice Hall, 1987.

Bontemps Arna. *Free at Last: The Life of Frederick Douglass.* New York: Dodd, Mead, 1971.

Buckmaster, Henrietta. *Let My People Go: The Story of the Underground Railroad and the Growth of the Abolition Movement.* Boston: Beacon Press, 1959.

Franklin, John Hope. *The Militant South, 1800–1861.* Cambridge, MA: Belknap Press, 1956. Explains how slavery contributed to the violence of American culture.

Franklin, John Hope, and Loren Schweninger. *Runaway Slaves: Rebels on the Plantation, 1790–1860.* New York: Oxford University Press, 1999.

Mullin, Gerald W. *Flight and Rebellion: Slave Resistance in Eighteenth-Century Virginia.* New York: Oxford University Press, 1972.

Painter, Nell Irvin. *Sojourner Truth: A Life, A Symbol.* New York: Norton, 1996.

Sterling, Dorothy. *Ahead of Her Time: Abby Kelley and the Politics of Antislavery.* New York: Norton, 1991. A biography of an abolitionist.

Styron, William. *The Confessions of Nat Turner.* New York: Random House, 1967. A novel about Nat Turner's rebellion.

Villard, Oswald Garrison. *John Brown, 1800–1859* [1910]. New York: Knopf, 1945.

Wax, Donald D. "Negro Resistance to the Early American Slave Trade." *Journal of Negro History* 51, no. 1 (1966): 1–15.

REACTIONS TO SLAVERY

Calhoun, John C. *Basic Documents.* ed. John M. Anderson. State College, PA: Bald Eagle Press, 1952. Writings expressing Calhoun's pro-slavery beliefs.

Calhoun, John C. *Disquisition on Government* [1854]. Union, NJ: Lawbook Exchange, 2002. A "reasoned" defense of slavery.

Degler, Carl N. "Slavery and the Genesis of American Race Prejudice." *Comparative Studies in Society and History* 2, no. 1 (1959): 49–66. In response to the thesis of Oscar and Mary Handlin [see below], Degler argues here that American slavery is a product of preexisting racist attitudes embedded in English culture.

Dillon, Merton L. *Slavery Attacked: Southern Slave States and Their Allies, 1619–1865*. Baton Rouge: Louisiana State University Press, 1990.

Dumond, Dwight Lowell. *Antislavery: The Crusade for Freedom in America*. Ann Arbor: University of Michigan Press, 1961.

Elliott, E. N., ed. *Cotton Is King and Pro-slavery Arguments*. Augusta, GA: Pritchard, Abbott, and Loomis, 1860. Summarizes the various arguments that made up the ideology of the slave-owning community.

Filler, Louis. *The Crusade against Slavery, 1830–1860*. New York: Harper, 1960.

Fitzhugh, George. *Cannibals All! or, Slaves without Masters* [1857]. Cambridge, MA: Belknap Press, 1960. Among the most inflammatory of pro-slavery arguments.

Fitzhugh, George. *Sociology for the South; or, The Failure of Free Society* [1854]. Chapel Hill: University of North Carolina Press, 1998.

Foner, Eric. *Free Soil, Free Labor, Free Men: The Ideology of the Republican Party before the Civil War*. New York: Oxford University Press, 1970. Examines the connections between slavery and the founding of the Republican Party.

Fox-Genovese, Elizabeth. *To Be Worthy of God's Favor: Southern Women's Defense and Critique of Slavery*. Gettysburg, PA: Gettysburg College Press, 1993.

Handlin, Oscar, and Mary Handlin. "Origins of the Southern Labor System." *William and Mary Quarterly*, 3rd Ser., 7, no. 2 (1950): 192–222. Makes the argument that racism toward Africans in the American colonies was a by-product of the debased status of blacks under slavery; Degler and Jordan later demurred, arguing that racist perceptions predated slavery. [Available through JSTOR.com].

Holt, Michael F. *The Political Crisis of the 1850s*. New York: Norton, 1978. Traces the last decade of the long road toward civil war.

Martineau, Harriet. *Retrospect of Western Travel* [1838]. Westport, CT: Greenwood Press, 1969. A British visitor's perspective on American slavery.

McKitrick, Eric, ed. *Slavery Defended: The Views of the Old South*. Englewood Cliffs, NJ: Prentice-Hall, 1963.

Miller, John Chester. *The Wolf by the Ears: Thomas Jefferson and Slavery*. New York: Free Press, 1977. Considers the dilemma posed by Jefferson, a slave-owner who penned the words, "All men are created equal."

Priest, Josiah. *Bible Defence of Slavery and the Origins, Fortunes, and History of the Negro Race*. Glasgow, KY: W. S. Brown, 1852.

Smedley, R. C. *History of the Underground Railroad*. New York: Arno, 1969.

Sterling, Dorothy. *Ahead of Her Time: Abby Kelley and the Politics of Antislavery*. New York: Norton, 1991.

Weld, Theodore, ed. *American Slavery As It Is: Testimony of a Thousand Witnesses*. New York: American Anti-Slavery Society, 1839.

Wish, Harvey. *George Fitzhugh, Propagandist of the Old South* [1943]. Gloucester, MA: P. Smith, 1962.

THE GEOGRAPHY OF SLAVERY

Abdy, E. S. *Journal of a Residence and Tour in the United States of North America* [1835]. New York: Negro Universities Press, 1969.

Bassett, John Spencer. *Slavery in the State of North Carolina*. Baltimore, MD: Johns Hopkins University Press, 1899.

Berlin, Ira, and Leslie Harris, eds. *Slavery in New York*. New York: New Press, 2005.

Berlin, Ira, and Ronald Hoffmann, eds. *Slavery and Freedom in the Age of the American Revolution*. Urbana: University of Illinois Press, 1986. Considers the role and significance of African American civilians and soldiers in the War of Independence.

Berwanger, Eugene H. *The Frontier against Slavery: Western Anti-Negro Prejudice and the Slavery Extension Controversy*. Urbana: University of Illinois Press, 1967.

Boyd, Minnie C. *Alabama in the Fifties: A Social Study*. New York: Columbia University Press, 1931.

Brackett, Jeffrey R. *The Negro in Maryland*. Baltimore, MD: Johns Hopkins University Press, 1889.

Brown, Letitia Woods. *Free Negroes in the District of Columbia*. New York: Oxford University Press, 1972.

Craven, Wesley Frank. *The Southern Colonies in the Seventeenth Century: 1607–1689*. Baton Rouge: Louisiana State University Press, 1949.

Davis, Charles S. *Cotton Kingdom in Alabama.* Montgomery: Alabama State Department, 1939.

Davis, David Brion. *Slavery in the Colonial Chesapeake.* Williamsburg, VA: Colonial Williamsburg Foundation, 1986.

Featherstonhaugh, George W. *Excursion through the Slave States, from Washington on the Potomac to the Frontier of Mexico: With Sketches of Popular Manners and Geological Notices.* New York: Harper, 1844.

Fields, Barbara Jeanne. *Slavery and Freedom on the Middle Ground: Maryland during the Nineteenth Century.* New Haven, CT: Yale University Press, 1985.

Johnson, James Hugo. *Race Relations in Virginia and Miscegenation in the South, 1776–1860.* Amherst: University of Massachusetts Press, 1970.

Jordan, Weymouth T. *Ante-Bellum Alabama: Town and Country.* Tallahassee: Florida State University Press, 1957.

Kulikoff, Allan. *Tobacco and Slaves: The Development of Southern Cultures in the Chesapeake, 1680–1800.* Chapel Hill: University of North Carolina Press, 1986.

McColley, Robert. *Slavery and Jeffersonian Virginia.* Urbana: University of Illinois Press, 1964. Examines the culture that produced four of the first five presidents.

Myers, Robert M., ed. *The Children of Pride: A True Story of Georgia and the Civil War.* New Haven, CT: Yale University Press, 1972.

Olmstead, Frederick Law. *A Journey in the Seaboard Slave States* [1856]. New York: Negro Universities Press, 1968.

Ottey, Roi, and William T. Weatherby. *The Negro in New York: An Informal Social History.* New York: Oceana Publications, 1967.

Perdue, Charles L., Jr., Thomas E. Barden, and Robert K. Phillips, eds. *Weevils in the Wheat: Interviews with Virginia Ex-Slaves.* Charlottesville: University Press of Virginia, 1976.

Sellers, J. B. *Slavery in Alabama.* Tuscaloosa: University of Alabama Press, 1950.

Slotkin, Richard. *Regeneration through Violence: The Mythology of the American Frontier, 1600–1860.* Middletown, CT: Wesleyan University Press, 1973. Discusses the ways in which the demands of survival on the frontier and the institution of slavery both perpetuated violence.

Sydnor, Charles S. *Slavery in Mississippi.* New York: D. Appleton-Century, 1933.

Tate, Thad W. Jr. *The Negro in Eighteenth-Century Williamsburg.* Charlottesville: University Press of Virginia, 1965.

Taylor, Joe Gray. *Negro Slavery in Louisiana.* New York: Negro Universities Press, 1969.

Towne, Laura M. *Letters and Diary of Laura M. Towne, Written from the Sea Islands of South Carolina, 1862–1884.* Holland, Rupert Sargent, ed. Cambridge: Riverside Press, 1912.

Turner, E. R. *The Negro in Pennsylvania.* Washington, DC: American Historical Association, 1911.

WAR

Abels, Jules. *Man on Fire: John Brown and the Cause of Liberty.* New York: Macmillan, 1971. A biography of the violent abolitionist.

Andrews, E. F. *War-Time Journal of a Georgia Girl.* Macon, GA: Ardivan Press, 1960.

Berlin, Ira, Joseph P. Reidy, and Leslie S. Rowland, eds. *A Documentary History of Emancipation, 1861–1867.* New York: Cambridge University Press, 1982.

Berlin, Ira, and Leslie S. Rowland, eds. *Families and Freedom: A Documentary History of African-American Kinship in the Civil War Era.* New York: New Press, 1997.

Chestnut, Mary Boykin. *A Diary from Dixie.* Ed. B. A. Williams. Cambridge, MA: Harvard University Press, 1980. The most well-known Civil War plantation journal.

Dumond, Dwight Lowell. *Antislavery Origins of the Civil War in the United States.* Ann Arbor: University of Michigan Press, 1959.

Faust, Drew Gilpin. *Mothers of Invention: Women of the Slaveholding South in the American Civil War.* Chapel Hill: University of North Carolina Press, 2004. Considers the impact of secession, invasion, and conquest on Southern white women, who assumed greater social and economic responsibilities as the prewar gender contract of dependence-for-protection collapsed.

Fehrenbacher, Don E. *Prelude to Greatness: Lincoln in the 1850's.* Stanford, CA: Stanford University Press, 1962. A concise study of Lincoln's preparation for the presidency.

Foner, Eric. *Nothing but Freedom: Emancipation and Its Legacy.* Baton Rouge: Louisiana State University Press, 1984. A brief overview of emancipation.

Foner, Eric. *Reconstruction: America's Unfinished Revolution, 1863–1877.* New York: Harper & Row, 1988. The definitive study of the era.

Franklin, John Hope. *The Emancipation Proclamation.* Garden City, NY: Anchor Books, 1965. A realistic appraisal of the Proclamation's intentions and effects.

Gooding, James Henry. *On the Altar of Freedom: A Black Soldier's Civil War Letters from the Front.* Ed. Virginia Matzke Adams. Amherst: University of Massachusetts Press, 1991.

Higginson, Thomas Wentworth. *Army Life in a Black Regiment.* Boston: Fields, Osgood, 1870.

McPherson, James M. *The Negro's Civil War: How American Negroes Felt and Acted during the War for the Union.* New York: Pantheon Books, 1965.

Oakes, James. *The Radical and the Republican: Frederick Douglass, Abraham Lincoln, and the Triumph of Antislavery Politics.* New York: Norton, 2007. Examines the contrasting views of the orator and the president.

Potter, David M. *The Impending Crisis, 1848–1861.* New York: Harper & Row, 1976. A thorough examination of the long build-up toward the war.

Ross, Fitzgerald. *Cities and Camps of the Confederate States.* Urbana: University of Illinois, 1958.

Taylor, Susie King. *A Black Woman's Civil War Memoirs.* Ed. Patricia W. Romero and Willie Lee Rose, eds. Princeton, NJ: Markus Wiener, 1988.

Thomas, Emory M. *The Confederate Nation, 1861–1865.* New York: Harper & Row, 1979. A useful history of the rise and fall of the Confederate government.

Wiley, Bell Irvin. *Southern Negroes, 1861–1865.* New Haven, CT: Yale University Press, 1938.

Wiley, Bell Irvin. "The Movement to Humanize the Institution of Slavery during the Confederacy." *Emory University Quarterly* 5, December (1949): 207–220.

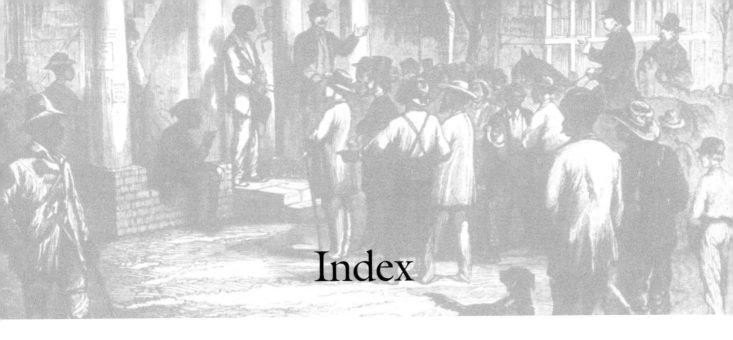

Index

Note: **Bold** page numbers indicate main discussions. *Italic* page numbers indicate images. Colons separate volume numbers from page numbers.

A

Abbott, James Monroe (slave), 1:99

Abel, Annie Heloise (scholar), 1:137

Abercrombie, Lt. Col. James, killed by African American soldier, 2:264

Abolition of slavery
  Bible as backbone of debate on, 2:162
  broadsides and posters for, *2:158, 159*
  celebrations after banning of slave trade, 2:85–86
  Lincoln, Abraham, early thoughts about, 2:82
  in Middle States, 2:240, 241
  moral debates on slavery and, 2:215–218
  Native American slave owners and, 1:137
  in northern states, 2:99
  Northwest Ordinance and, 2:103
  ratification of U.S. Constitution and, 2:75–76
  sewing and quilting for fund raising for, 1:176
  visual images of slavery and, 2:204, 205–206
  See also Antislavery arguments; Antislavery literature; Antislavery societies; Emancipation Proclamation

Abolitionist newspapers, **2:225–226**, *226*
  The North Star, 2:226–227
  The Provincial Freeman, 2:227–228

women's role in, 2:226
  See also Freedom's Journal (newspaper)

Abolitionists
  achievements of, 2:218
  antislavery songs and, 1:162, *1:163*, 1:164
  British, 2:84–85, 204
  broadsides produced by, 2:167–168
  dispersal of organizations after 15th Amendment, 2:159
  dissatisfaction with Emancipation Proclamation, 2:90–91
  poems as tool of, in antebellum period, 2:195
  splits within the movement and, 2:157
  support for artwork by slaves, 1:170
  voluntary disunion advocated by, 2:157
  See also Quakers

Abrams, Joseph (African American preacher), 2:34

Abuse. *See* Discipline and punishment; Female slaves; Sexual abuse of slaves

Adam and Eve, folk tale about, 1:178–179

Adams, James (governor of South Carolina), 1:13

Adams, John Quincy (U.S. president), 2:143, 152

Adams, Nehemiah
  on cheerful disposition of slaves, 2:68

on internal economy of slaves, 1:154
  rejection of abolitionism, 2:206
  The Sable Cloud : A Southern Tale, with Northern Comments, 2:214
  A South-Side View of Slavery, 2:206, 214–219, *2:216, 218*

Adams, Will (slave), 1:92

Adams, William (conjure doctor), 2:26

Adams-Onis Treaty, 2:251

Adger, Rev. John (author), 1:127

Adkins, Ida (slave), 2:271

Adolescence, 1:100
  See also Children of slaves

Africa, **1:2–6**
  capture and sale of slaves in, 1:4–6, *1:5*
  economic effects of slave trade, 1:9
  enslavement of women in, 1:5–6
  Gambia River, 1:53
  kinship system of, 1:2–4
  Phillips, Ulrich, negative view of, 1:1
  post-Atlantic slave trade period, 1:4
  pre-Atlantic slave trade period, 1:2–4, *1:3*
  retention of culture by slave descendants, 1:7
  rice growing in, 1:54, 61, 74
  social systems in, 1:2–4
  trade relations with Europeans, 1:6
  women's role and value in, 1:3, 4
  See also African heritage; West African influences

number of slaves on farms and plantations, 1:59

overview, 1:43, 50–52, *1:51*

overworking of, 1:50

rice cultivation by, 1:61–63

seasonal rhythms of life and, 1:54–56, *1:55*

seasoning of, 1:42–43

sugar cultivation by, *1:63,* 1:63–65

tobacco cultivation by, 1:52–53, 59–61, *1:60*

tools and technology and, 1:70–72

See also Cotton cultivation and plantations; Gang system of work; Rice cultivation and plantations; Sugar cane cultivation and plantations; Task system of work; Tobacco cultivation and plantations

Fighting between slaves
  causes of, 1:124–125
  punishment for, 1:125

Fillmore, Millard (U.S. president), 2:77, 78–79

Finch, John, on slave music, 1:165

Finkelman, Paul (scholar), 2:77

Finley, Robert, and founding of American Colonization Society, 2:229

Finney, Charles (abolitionist), 2:181

Firearms

Fire-eaters, 2:80–82, *2:81*
  gun control laws, and slave codes, 2:72
  guns hidden by slaves, 1:78–79
  hunting by slaves, 1:72, 73
  Muhammad, Bilali and, 2:30
  Virginia law forbidding slaves to own, 2:60

First African Church of Savannah, GA, 2:21

First Great Awakening. *See* Great Awakening

Fishing, 1:73

Fitzhugh, George (proslavery author), 1:24, 2:42, 67, 217

Flanders, G. M. (proslavery author), 2:177

Fleming, George (slave), 1:129, 133–134

Fletcher, Thomas C. (governor of Missouri), 2:245

Florida
  acquisition by U.S. as territory, 2:251
  Maroon communities in, 2:131–132
  slave owners in, 2:253, 254
  slavery in, 2:249–254

Floyd, Samuel A., Jr. (scholar), 1:165

Fogel, Robert (historian), 1:28, 74, 86, 149, 2:44

Foley, Brendan (historian), 1:76

Folk religion, 1:107, **2:23–26**, *25*

Folk remedies, **2:50–51**

Folkes, Minnie (slave), 2:137

Folklore and folk tales, **1:178–179**
  definition, 1:178
  Old John tales, 1:181
  storytelling by elders, 1:110
  trickster tales, 1:178, 181–182, 2:219
  West African influences on, 1:208

"Follow the Drinking Gourd" (song), 2:151

Food and nutrition, **2:52–62**
  alcoholic beverages, 2:57–59
  amount of food supplied by masters, 2:54
  basic foods, 2:53, 54, 55, *2:55*
  children's food, 1:98
  cornmeal and pork as staples, 2:53, 54
  Emancipation Proclamation breakfast cake, 2:56
  food eaten on slave ships, 2:36, 53, 55
  hogs as source of plantation food, 1:66
  hunting, trapping, and fishing as source of food, 1:67, 72–73, 2:54
  mealtimes, 1:104–105
  New England slaves, 2:236
  overview, 2:52–54, *2:53*
  slave accounts of, 2:55–57
  slave gardens for supplemental food, 1:55, 151–152, 2:55
  on slave-breeding plantations, 2:56–57
  sugar and industrialization, 1:64
  theft of food by slaves, 1:125, 185, 2:133
  troughs for feeding slaves, 1:98, 105, 2:36, 55

Force, Tinie (slave), 1:195

Forrest, Nathan Bedford (Confederate general), 2:268

Fort Mose, fugitive slaves and, 2:131

Fort Pillow, TN, execution of African American soldiers at, 2:268

Fort Wagner, SC, Union Army assault on, 2:267–268

Foy, Thomas D. (poor white), 1:146

Francis, Sam, Turner rebellion and, 2:140

Frank Freeman's Barber Shop: A Tale (Hall), 2:183

Frank Leslie's Illustrated Newspaper, 2:226

Franklin, Benjamin (publisher), 2:221

Franklin, H. Bruce (scholar), 1:162

Franklin, John Hope (historian), 1:196, 2:91, 92, 121

Franks, Dora (slave), 2:270

Frazier, Franklin E. (scholar), 2:22–23

Frederick Douglass's Paper, 2:225, 227

Free African Americans. *See* African Americans

Free Soil Party (United States), *2:100,* 2:157, 161, 205

Free vs. slave states, **2:99–108**
  balance between, overview, 2:99–102, *2:100, 101*
  exclusion laws and, 2:106–108
  list of states by 1860, 2:100–101
  map of 1850 division, *2:75*
  Missouri Compromise and, 2:99–100, 104–106, *2:105*
  Northwest Ordinance and, 2:102–104, *2:103*
  voluntary disunion advocated by abolitionists, 2:157
  See also Geography of slavery

Freedmen's Inquiry Commission (Freedman's Bureau), 1:100, 101, 103, *2:177*

Freedom
  abolitionist view of, as basis for society, 2:217
  baptism of slaves and, 2:15
  buying of freedom by slaves, 1:18, 25–26, 77–78, 204
  requirements for freedom suits, 2:87–88
  sermons and slaves' idea of, 2:19–20
  slavery as threat to free American society, 2:217–218
  suing for freedom (Dred Scott case), 2:86–88
  as tenet of Christianity, 2:12
  See also Emancipation; Manumission

Freedom of activity
  of rice plantations slaves, 1:62
  of skilled slaves, 1:62, 81
  task system of work and, 1:85

Freedom's Journal (newspaper), **2:223–225**
  colonization debate and, 2:223, 225
  Cornish, Samuel, as publisher of, 2:222, 223
  northern African Americans as audience for, 2:223–224
  Russwurm, John Brown as publisher of, 2:222, 223

Freehold property, 2:107

French and Indian War, 2:249

French colonies. *See* Caribbean islands; Haiti

French Revolution
  Gabriel's rebellion and, 2:142
  Haitian revolution and, 2:256

"Get Off the Track" (abolitionist song), *1:163*

"Get on the Gospel Train" (song), 2:151

"Gettysburg Address" (Lincoln), 2:262

"Ghostlore," 1:180

Giddings, Joshua Reed (historian), 2:131

Gienapp, William (scholar), 2:245

Gift exchange, **1:120–122,** 1:187

Gill, Frank (slave), 1:69

Glory (film), 2:268

"Go Down Moses" (song), 2:150

Gomez, Michael A. (historian), 2:29, 31, 32

Gone With the Wind (film), 2:208

Goodell, William (scholar), 2:53, 54, 107

Gordon, Nathaniel (slave trader), 1:14

Gorn, Elliott (scholar), 1:180

Grandy, Moses (slave)
    on abuse of slave wives, 2:112
    on his master's family, 1:132–133
    self-purchase of his freedom, 1:25
    on separation from his family, 1:57

Gray, Lewis (historian), 1:149

Gray, Thomas R., and *The Confessions of Nat Turner*, *2:201,* 2:201–203, *2:203*

Grayson, William John (author), 2:54

Great Awakening, **2:21–23**
    conversion experience and, 2:8, 34
    emotionalism in, 2:22
    expansion of outreach to slaves, 2:7, 11
    leaders of, 2:21
    revivalism and, 2:22
    Second Great Awakening, 2:22, 181
    slave participation in, 2:21, 22

Great Britain. *See* United Kingdom

Great Depression, 2:189

Great Dismal Swamp, as fugitive slave destination, 2:125

Greeley, Horace
    Lincoln, Abraham, letter to, 2:82
    Missouri Compromise and, 2:104, 105
    publisher of *New York Tribune,* 2:221
    on the South's dependence on slavery, 2:70

Green, Beriah (abolitionist), 2:215

Green, Thomas Jefferson, and California gold rush, 2:234

Gregoire, Abbé, and Haitian revolution, 2:257, 260

Grenada, 1:151

Griffin, "Mad" (slave), 1:180

Griffith, D. W. (film maker), 2:184

Griffiths, Mattie (author), 1:129, 131

Grimes, William (slave), 2:16

Grimké, Angelina Emily (abolitionist and author), 2:161, 163, 226

Grimké, Sarah (abolitionist and author), 2:161, 163, 226

Gross, Seymour, criticism of Phillis Wheatley by, 2:195

Guadeloupe island, revolution on, 2:259

Gudgell, Henry (slave), 1:80, 171

Gudger, Sarah (slave), 1:103

Gullah culture and language, 1:85, 198

Guns. *See* Firearms

Gurney, Joseph John, on slave construction, 1:64

Gutman, Herbert (historian), 1:89, 92–93, 111, 149, 202

H

Habeas corpus, for slaves, 2:70

Hahn, Steven (historian), 2:82, 88, 271

Haiti, **2:256–261,** *257, 258*
    effects of revolution on U.S., 2:260
    free blacks *(gens de couleur)* in, 2:256–257
    Hassal, Mary, letter about, 2:260
    independence of, 2:259–260
    request to French government for equal rights, 2:256–257
    revolution in, 1:127, 2:257–260
    sugar production in, 2:255
    voudou in, 2:27

Half-slaves, 1:146

Hall, Baynard (proslavery author), 2:183

Hall, Douglas (scholar), 1:149

Ham (son of Noah), and biblical justification for slavery, 2:66, 181–182, 217

Hamilton, Alexander, economic plan of, 1:35

Hamilton, James, Jr. (fire-eater), 2:80

Hammond, James Henry (U.S. senator)
    his rules for governing slaves, 1:89, 90
    on importance of cotton industry, 1:32, 2:65

on quality of slave masters, 2:55

on slavery as historical institution, 2:68

theft of alcohol by his slaves, 2:58

white control of slave religion and, 2:34

Handicrafts. *See* Crafts and handicrafts

Hansberry, Lorraine (African American playwright), 2:189

Harkins, George (Choctaw leader), 1:137

Harlem Renaissance, 2:189

Harmon, Jane Smith Hall (slave), 1:160

Harper, Eda (slave), 1:180

Harper, Frances E. W. (African American author), 2:189

Harper, Pierce (slave), 2:271

Harpers Ferry, John Brown's raid on, **2:145–147,** *146,* 2:159

Harris, Anna (slave), 1:16

Harris, Joel Chandler, and Uncle Remus stories, 1:181, **2:219–221,** *220*

Harvest time, **1:190–192,** *191, 192*

Harvie, Daniel (kidnapper), 2:129

Hassal, Mary, letter about Haitian revolution, 2:260

Hastings, Selina. *See* Huntingdon, Countess of (Selina Hastings)

Hawkins, Tom (slave), 1:184

Haynes, Henry (slave owner), 1:124

Health and medicine, **2:36–62**
    alcoholic beverages, 2:57–59
    antebellum medical practices and, 2:38
    childbirth and midwifery, 2:42
    conjure magic and, 2:38
    elder care, 2:43–44
    hygiene, 2:45–47, *2:46*
    life expectancy and mortality rates, 2:39–41
    older women as healers, 1:110
    overview, 2:36–38
    physicians' attitudes toward slaves and, 2:37
    rice cultivation and, 1:61–62
    sale of slaves and, 1:16
    southern myths about slaves' health, 2:38
    tobacco and smoking, 2:59–62
    See also Disease and treatment; Food and nutrition

Hedin, Raymond (scholar), 2:220

Hemings, Sally, and Thomas Jefferson, 1:131, 2:192–193

Henderson, George (slave), 1:66

Henderson, John (U.S. senator), 2:97

I

Olwell, Robert (historian), 2:11, 33

One, Michael (slave), 1:202

O'Neil, Dennis (scholar), 1:202

Oregon/Oregon Territory
    as free territory, 2:233
    joint occupancy by England and
        U.S., 2:233
    outlawing of slavery in, 2:234

Oregon Treaty, 2:233

Osteen, Mark (scholar), 1:120

Outsiders' views of slavery,
    2:204–213
    British view of American slavery,
        2:204, *2:205*
    Democracy in America (Tocque-
        ville), 2:208–210, *2:209*
    *Journal of a Residence on a
        Georgian Plantation in
        1838–1839* (Kemble),
        2:212–213, *2:213*
    overview, 2:204–208, *2:205*
    Society in America (Martineau),
        2:210–212, *2:211*
    A South-Side View of Slavery
        (Adams), 2:214–219, *2:216, 218*
    visual images of slavery and,
        2:204–207
    See also Reactions to slavery

"Over the River and Through the
    Woods" (Child), 2:172

Overseers, **1:141–143**, *142*
    duties, 1:141
    health care of slaves and, 2:49
    poor whites as, 1:144, 145
    relationship with slave owners,
        1:141
    right to use violence, 2:180
    role of, 1:50

Owens, Leslie (historian), 1:16

P

Page, Annie (slave), 1:180

Paine, Thomas (patriot), 2:221

Painters and painting, 1:170

Pamphlets, 2:81, **2:168–172**, *170, 171*

Parades, 1:188, 189

Parasitic disease, 2:47

Paravisini-Gebert, Lizabeth (scholar),
    2:27, 28, 29

Parker, Allen (slave), 1:144

Paternalism, **1:128–129**
    archetypes of slaves and,
        2:175–176
    economic justification of, 2:67
    ideology of planters and, 2:68
    interstate slave trade and, 1:21
    legal codes and, 1:94
    philosophy of, 1:128
    proslavery arguments and,
        2:175–176

slave living conditions and, 1:128
    slaveholder as father of slave
        families, 1:90, 94

Patriarchy, 1:92–93, 94

Patrols. *See* Slave patrols (patter-rollers)

Patterson, John (slave), 1:103, 2:50

Patterson, Orlando (African Ameri-
    can sociologist), 1:89

Paul, William, Vesey conspiracy and,
    2:147, 148

Payne, Daniel (slave), 1:202

Payne, Harriet McFarlin (slave), 1:109

Peale, Charles Wilson (painter and
    slave owner), 1:170, 2:30

Peculiar institution, definition of, 1:9

The Peculiar Institution (Stampp),
    1:1

Penningroth, Dylan (scholar), 1:150

Pennington, James William Charles
    (slave), 1:23, 110

Pennsylvania
    abolition of slavery in, 2:241
    origins of slavery in, 2:231

Peppinger, Abraham (slave owner),
    1:145

Perdue, Theda (scholar), 1:135

Personal servants, 1:45–47, *1:46*

Peter, King of Liberia, 2:229

Peters, John (husband of Phillis
    Wheatley), 2:195

Petersburg, VA, Siege of, 2:268

Peterson, Charles Jacobs (proslavery
    author), 2:183

Peterson, Edward (historian), 1:170

Petite, Phyllis (slave), 1:45

Petitions against slavery, 2:178

Pettiford, Martha (slave), 1:26

Peyton, John Lewis, on *Uncle Tom's
    Cabin*, 2:166

Philadelphia, PA
    death rate of slaves in, 2:39
    slave population in, 2:40

Philadelphia Female Anti-Slavery
    Society, 2:161

Phillips, Ulrich B.
    on branding of slaves, 2:115
    on culture and leisure of slaves,
        1:157
    on internal economy, 1:149
    negative views of Africa of, 1:1
    on paternalism, 1:128, 2:67
    on rebellions, 2:117

Phillips, Wendell (abolitionist),
    2:157, 200

Phrenology, and justification of slav-
    ery, 2:66, 175

Physical characteristics
    bodies of slaves, 1:114–117, *1:115*
    skin color, 1:113–114

Physician-slave relationships,
    2:48–49, 52

Physiognomy, theory of, 2:175

Pickaninny character, in minstrelsy,
    2:45

Pickard, Kate E. R. (author), 1:97, 123

Picquet, Louisa (slave), 1:139

Pieh, Sengbe (Joseph Cinqué), and
    Amistad rebellion, 2:143

Pierce, Abijah (slave), 2:236

Pierce, Lucy, as first African American
    poet, 2:236

Pierson, George Wilson (scholar),
    2:210

Pierson, William (scholar), 1:188

Pilmoor, Joseph (Methodist minister),
    2:23

Pinckney, Charles (1757–1824, U.S.
    senator), 1:12, 19

Pinckney, Charles Cotesworth
    (1746–1825), 2:6, 7

Pinckney Treaty, with Spain, 2:249

Pinkster festival, 1:187–188

Pitcairn, Maj. John, killed by African
    American soldier, 2:264

Plankett (ex-slave), 1:193, 194

Plantation literature, 2:185

Plantation owners
    absolute authority of, 2:179–180
    as aristocrats, 2:180, 209
    Native Americans as, 1:136–137
    rumor of land distribution after
        Civil War, 2:153

Plantation workers. *See* Field slaves;
    House slaves; Work of slaves

Plantations
    construction and clearing of land
        for, 1:67–70, *1:68*
    cotton plantations, 1:56–59, *1:57,
        58*
    rice plantations, 1:53–54, 61–63, 68
    running of, by slaves, during Civil
        War, 2:270–271
    skilled labor for, 1:74–75
    sugar plantations, *1:63*, 1:63–65
    tobacco plantations, 1:52–53,
        59–61, *1:60*, 2:60
    tools and technology and,
        1:70–72

The Planter's Northern Bride
    (Hentz), 2:183, **2:186–187**

Pleasants, J. Hall (scholar), 1:170

Plummer, Jonathan, Jr. (publisher),
    2:169, 170

Pneumonia, 2:40, 47

Poe, Edgar Allen (poet), 2:185

Poems and Poetry
    African American authors of,
        2:189
    courtship verses, 1:122